Room to Manoeuvre? Globalization and Policy Convergence

Proceedings of a conference held at
Queen's University 5-6 November 1998

Thomas J. Courchene
Editor

PUBLISHED FOR THE SCHOOL OF POLICY STUDIES, QUEEN'S UNIVERSITY
BY MCGILL-QUEEN'S UNIVERSITY PRESS
MONTREAL & KINGSTON • LONDON • ITHACA

ISBN: 0-88911-810-8 (bound)   ISBN: 0-88911-812-4 (pbk.)
© 1999   John Deutsch Institute for the Study of Economic Policy
Queen's University, Kingston, Ontario K7L 3N6
Telephone: (613) 533-2294   FAX: (613) 533-6025
Printed and bound in Canada

Canadian Cataloguing in Publication Data

Main entry under title:

Room to manoeuvre? : globalization and policy convergence

(The Bell Canada papers on economic and public policy ; 6)
Proceedings of a conference held at Queen's University, Nov. 5-6, 1998.
Includes bibliographical references.
ISBN   0-88911-810-8 (bound)   ISBN   0-88911-812-4 (pbk.)

1. Canada - Economic policy - 1991 -   - Congresses. 2. International
economic integration - Congresses. I. Courchene, Thomas J., 1940-
II. John Deutsch Institute for the Study of Economic Policy. III. Series.

HC115.R617 1999   338.971   C99-931629-X

Acknowledgements

On behalf of the John Deutsch Institute it is a pleasure to recognize the tremendous contribution of JDI Administrative Assistant, Sharon Sullivan. Not only did Sharon serve as the conference and participant coordinator but, as well, orchestrated the challenging process of converting the manuscripts into publishable form.

Others also made valuable contributions — Marilyn Banting for her editing skills, the School of Policy Studies desktop publishing unit (Mark Howes and Valerie Jarus) for assisting in producing camera-ready copy.

Above all, I wish to express my thanks to the authors, the discussants and the session chairs for fulfilling their side of this venture so effectively. I would also like to thank Adil Sayeed for editing the floor discussion.

Finally, I am stepping down, at least during my sabbatical, from the Directorship of the John Deutsch Institute. It is a pleasure to acknowledge the full support and cooperation I have received over the past six years from all quarters and especially from the Department of Economics. However, the JDI is fortunate indeed in having David C. Smith as the interim Director. David was instrumental in creating the John Deutsch Memorial (the forerunner of the JDI) and was its Director until 1983 when he became Principal of Queen's University.

Thomas J. Courchene
Director
John Deutsch Institute
July 1999

Contents

Contributors

Table of Contents:

Bell Canada Papers, Volume 1, *Productivity, Growth and Canada's
International Competitiveness,*T.J. Courchene and D.D. Purvis, editors

Bell Canada Papers, Volume 2, *Stabilization, Growth and
Distribution: Linkages in the Knowledge Era,* **T.J. Courchene, editor**

Bell Canada Papers, Volume 3, *Technology, Information
and Public Policy,* **T.J. Courchene, editor**

Bell Canada Papers, Volume 4, *Policy Frameworks for a Knowledge Economy*, **T.J. Courchene, editor**

Bell Canada Papers, Volume 5, *The Nation State in a Global/ Information Era: Policy Challenges*, **T.J. Courchene, editor**

Recent Publications from Queen's Policy Studies

Introduction

Thomas J. Courchene

The Bell Canada Papers: A Retrospective

Room to Manoeuvre? Globalization and Policy Convergence is the sixth and the last volume in the series, *The Bell Canada Papers on Economic and Public Policy*. On behalf of the John Deutsch Institute for the Study of Economic Policy, and on behalf of the Canadian policy community, it is a pleasure to express thanks and gratitude to Bell Canada for the generous support for the Bell Canada Papers.

With the opening of the Queen's Policy Studies building in 1989 and the bringing together of many of the teaching and research activities in the policy area under a single roof, the opportunity for capitalizing on the resulting synergies became very evident. The Bell Canada Papers represented one of the first tangible benefits of this interdisciplinary cooperation. The project was initiated when Thomas J. Courchene, then Director of the School of Policy Studies, Richard G. Harris, then Acting Director of the John Deutsch Institute for the Study of Economic Policy and the late Douglas D. Purvis, Head of the Economics Department, jointly designed a proposal for a conference and volume series that would attempt to provide for Canada something comparable in status and influence to what the *Brookings Papers on Economic Activity* provided for the United States. Our perception was that there is an important niche for a continuing source of information and analysis on the medium-term empirical/policy challenges facing Canada.

The timing could not have been better in the sense that, with ongoing developments such as the Canada-U.S. Free Trade Agreement and Europe 1992, the mindset of the country was attuned to restructuring and to globalization. In effect, our proposal amounted to the analytical or intellectual equivalent of a restructuring or a rethinking on the policy front. Bell Canada thought so too when we presented the proposal to them, the result of which is that we entered into a partnership that guaranteed the series for an initial five years, later extended to a sixth year. In this regard, we again acknowledge the role of various Bell executives, including Dale Orr, Chief Economist; West Scott, Executive Vice-President, Ontario Region and Jean Monty; then President and CEO. On the Queen's side, we acknowledge the support and encouragement of Principal David C. Smith and the Development Office. In recognition of this support, the series was entitled *The Bell Canada Papers on Economic and Public Policy*.

The agreed-upon mandate of the Bell Canada Papers was to provide an accessible source of information, analysis and evaluation with respect to the medium-term policy challenges facing Canada. Within the overarching theme, which related to the public policy implications of globalization and technology, there were to be four sub-themes. The first of these four core areas we labelled "political economy issues" and it included, among other items, regulatory issues, the financial-industrial interface and the approach to governance in an information economy. The second area dealt with economic growth concerns, such as the constellation of issues in the related areas of R&D, innovation, diffusion, technical change and productivity. Included also was the general area of competitiveness in a knowledge/ information world. Social policy issues constituted the third area. Part of this was motivated by the fact that in a knowledge-intensive environment, aspects of social policy become progressively indistinguishable from economic policy. The final area fell under the rubric of "international issues". This provided a convenient framework for assessing the national-global interface in terms of such areas as the environment, macro-policy harmonization, international competitiveness, the tendency towards international regulation and, more generally, for assessing the implications of increasing globalization in terms of the challenges and choices facing our policy authorities.

The Bell Canada Papers series has, we believe, delivered on this mandate.

Bell 1, the inaugural volume, was entitled *Productivity, Growth and Canada's International Competitiveness*. Beyond the papers on productivity and growth and on assessing alternative visions and versions of competitiveness, the volume also included surveys on the cost of capital, competition policy, worker cooperation/productivity and technical change, entrepreneurship and the competitiveness implications of the environmental movement.

Bell 2, *Stabilization, Growth and Distribution: Linkages in the Knowledge Era*, began with two comprehensive macroeconomic surveys, one domestic and one international. This was followed by an analysis of the emerging endogenous growth literature, where knowledge and increasing returns play a critical role, as well as a paper on innovation and technology policy. The volume then switched to human-capital issues, with papers on income polarization, training and industrial relations.

Bell 3, *Technology, Information and Public Policy* opened with a rethinking of the theory of economic growth and a companion empirical piece on the degree to which Canadian firms are incorporating technology/information in their operations. Two other papers focus on the international and domestic institutional changes triggered by the new techno-economic paradigm. The remainder of the volume focused on the implications of the information revolution — on services, on interest group behaviour and policy making and on the economics of the information superhighway.

Bell 4, *Policy Frameworks for a Knowledge Economy* addressed a range of policy areas in terms of where we have been and where and how we are likely to evolve. Focus was directed, in turn, to the Bank of Canada, to the government sector, to universities, to the environment, to social policy and in particular to the imperative of early childhood development, to intellectual property and, finally, to labour markets.

Bell 5, *The Nation State in a Global/Information Era: Policy Challenges* looked forward in terms of the likely future of nation states. After the keynote paper, which looked at states, markets and citizens in the twenty-first century, attention turned to harmonization of national regulatory regimes, the internationalization of the social contract, the evolving nature of national and international democracy and, appropriately, the evolution of the nation state. The remainder of the contributions related to intergovernmental fiscal relations — market-preserving federalism on the analytical side and alternative decentralization strategies on the empirical front — and the emergence of subnational region states.

Copies of the detailed Table of Contents for these five volumes are appended to this volume.

I turn now to a brief descriptive overview of the issues and themes that comprise Bell 6, *Room to Manoeuvre? Globalization and Policy Convergence*. Readers wishing a more analytical overview and assessment may wish to go directly to Jack Mintz's excellent integrative summary in his role as conference rapporteur.

Room to Manoeuvre: An Overview

Constitutionalizing Neo-Conservatism and Regional Economic Integration: TINA x 2 (H.W. Arthurs)

Magesterial in its sweep and passionate in its analysis, Harry Arthurs has articulately penned a lament for a more activist, interventionist state. His one-word assessment on whether Canada has room to manoeuvre over the foreseeable future is "no". Underpinning this conclusion is a three-pronged set of rationales, two of which fall under the TINA acronym. The first is "there is no alternative", reflecting the pervasiveness of ongoing neo-conservatism. While this TINA is specific to our time, as it were, the second is specific to our place — trapped in North America or continentalism. These are related in the sense that one reason why there is no alternative for Canada is precisely because we are trapped in North America. The third rationale relates to the set of forces — decentralization, juridification and populism — all of which tend to undermine the policy ability of the federal government: decentralization because the centre becomes less relevant; juridification because Canadians are increasingly turning to the courts as policy arbiters; and populism because, in its current variant (balanced budgets, referenda, and in Ontario reducing the number of politicians) it views the state as alien, even hostile. In effect, the sum of these influences is more than the component parts, for example, populism speaks to the means while neo-conservatism speaks to the ends.

Arthurs' view is that, in tandem, these forces are influencing our belief systems and constraining our options to such an extent that this belief system is effectively becoming institutionalized, and in a broader sense, constitution-alized. In short, they dramatically constrain our room to manoeuvre.

Daniel Schwanen rises to Arthurs' challenge. Among his many observations and critiques, he notes that it is difficult to argue that we are unduly constrained in pursuing our objectives as a country when we have often imposed such constraints on ourselves (e.g., indebtedness), when we do not even use the policy flexibility we do have, and when so many of the new so-called "time and space" constraints such as free trade and the elimination of deficits can actually enhance our room to manoeuvre in the face of more severe "generic" constraints imposed by technology, by a more integrated world and by the demographic challenge. For example, while Arthurs views halting the accumulation of public debt as falling under the rubric of the TINAs or of right-wing populism, it can also be seen as liberating in the important sense that it provides new fiscal room to manoeuvre in terms of the unprecedented challenges related to the aging of the population.

All in all, an ideal opening session for a volume on globalization and policy convergence.

The "Culture" of Multinational Corporations and the Implications for Canada (Louis W. Pauly)

Louis Pauly addresses the issue of just how global are the global corporations. His answer is as clear as it is striking:

> ... the phenomenon of corporate multinationalization across the leading industrial states essentially remains a process through which still-national corporations, and the innovation and investment systems within which they remain rooted, are inserted into the home markets of their competitors. Those corporations then adapt themselves at the margin, but not at the core. Ultimately, leading multinational corporations continue to reflect that concatenation of variables commonly depicted as their dominant national cultures.... indeed, a commitment to defending distinctive national cultures was hard-wired into many of the world's leading MNCs.

This conclusion flows from research into the "cultures" of American, Japanese and European (largely German) multinationals. Important differences continue to exist in areas such as corporate governance, financing, innovation and investment systems, R&D, technology trade, intercorporate trade and the degree of local production, among others. Thus these leading multinational corporations (MNCs) are not, or at least not yet, embodying a cosmopolitan culture, but rather, they remain reflections of their deeper national histories and identities with distinctively different social purposes.

Pauly then attempts to draw some implications of this analysis for smaller national economies and their own multinationals. He notes that Austria has learned to accommodate the challenge of getting the most out of deepening economic interdependence with a powerful neighbour (Germany) while maintaining a high degree of political independence, by focusing its policies around subsidies, explicit negotiation of the internal distribution of adjustment costs and a fixed exchange rate with Germany. But Canada has moved in the opposite direction in all three areas. While there are presumably alternative avenues for reconciling regionalism, distribution and international competitiveness, Pauly's message here is similar to that of Arthurs' — our policies are such that we appear to be losing our room to manoeuvre. Part of this may be that we are operating under the illusion that global markets, rather than the MNCs that are embedded within them, rule supreme.

Maureen Appel Molot's comments are surely an editor's dream. Not only does she situate Pauly's analysis within the context of the larger body of research on the culture of multinationals, but she then attempts to distile the available Canadian literature in a manner that is consistent with Pauly's methodology. In particular, she compares Canadian and U.S. multinational behaviour in terms of the various criteria Pauly employed for his own comparative analysis (e.g., governance, financing, innovation, investment, technology transfers, etc.). The result is not only a valuable distillation in terms of Canadian MNC behaviour but, as well, a comprehensive agenda for future research in this area.

Canadian Information/Culture Policy in the Information Age: Mediums are the Message (Leonard Waverman)

Leonard Waverman focuses on the implication of technology and technology convergence for the regulation of broadcasting, telecommunications and multimedia, or what he refers to as Canadian Information and Cultural Policy (CICP). Phrased differently, what is the role for national policy in an increasingly global or universal "information age"? The answer is that technology is dramatically altering the erstwhile separate markets and, therefore, policy convergence must follow technological convergence across CICP. Waverman's backdrop for the policy component of the paper is a series of comprehensive cross-classifications with respect to base technologies (land lines, wireless, air broadcast, satellite), multimedia services (telephony, video, Internet, data transmission) and policy areas (communications, entertainment). In a word, the story is "technological bypass" and, therefore, the effective blurring of the line between local and long distance, between cable and telephone, between broadcasting and programming, and between communications and entertainment.

What is the future for CICP policy? Waverman's view is that the existing attempts to regulate the various components of the market differently are futile and inefficient. Technology convergence means that market entry for any given service is now ubiquitous. Thus, maintaining differential restrictions on different delivery platforms tilts the playing field and encourages substitution between systems which may be neither efficient nor equitable. Rather, the Canadian Radio-Television and Telecommunications Commission (CRTC) needs to utilize market-based policy instruments that rely on increased consumer choice, not CRTC-organized "beauty contests" and quantitative restrictions. In particular, his policy prescription includes: a reliance on end-user taxes (e.g., TV licences), a revaluation of administrative constraints on program providers; temporary subsidies to Canadian programing, auctioning of licences, and leaving the Internet unregulated. By thus liberalizing conventional media rules under a temporarily enhanced subsidy/tax scheme, the way would be paved for a fully liberalized CICP market.

Dale Orr is generally sympathetic with the Waverman paper and, in particular, with the emphasis on competition and consumer sovereignty. In designing his own set of recommendations, he begins by recognizing four challenges to Canadian information and cultural policy: (i) increasing technological bypass (*à la* Waverman); (ii) potential retaliation from the Americans; (iii) competition for the fiscal dividend from other policy areas; and (iv) societal, and especially business, distrust of the detailed intervention in CICP. Not surprisingly, his recommendations would eliminate all forms of "protection" in broadcasting, especially content regulations. On the promotion side, he would opt for a subsidy for program production. Orr would prefer that this be financed out of general revenues and not from a UK-type TV tax, as suggested by Waverman.

Regulatory Diplomacy: Why Rhythm Beats Harmony in the Trade Regime (Robert Wolfe)

How does the international trading system, centred on the World Trade Organization (WTO), accommodate increasing openness on the one hand and national policy priorities on the other? In Robert Wolfe's creative phraseology, the answer lies in *regulatory diplomacy*. Regulatory diplomacy is, Wolfe argues, at the same time a normative framework and a set of techniques. By way of comparison, he notes that the manner in which the postwar international community accommodated the twin goals of free trade and the evolution of the welfare state is best referred to as the diplomacy of embedded liberalism. End-point solutions (i.e., transferring power to international organizations, leaving everything to markets, having all countries adapt uniform standards, etc.) are inconsistent with national autonomy. Enter regulatory diplomacy which, among other things, is a process for discovering new rules that recognize the legitimacy of behaviour and outcomes in the context of what is collectively possible. And what is collectively possible in what everyone can accept without the system collapsing. Among the norms that underpin regulatory diplomacy are transparency, non-discrimination, due process, proportionality and the like, all of which are fundamental WTO principles.

The techniques that drive regulatory diplomacy will vary across policy areas. Some areas will allow only "negative integration" while others may permit "positive integration". When only implicit norms are possible, then the solution may run in terms of best-practice standards or perhaps multilateral standard-setting bodies. When norms or rules can be formalized, regulatory diplomacy can take the form of national treatment, mutual recognition and, in the limit, harmonization (i.e., deeper integration).

In the second half of his paper, Wolfe focuses on a concrete example, the "reference paper" for telecommunication services. The challenge here is not to develop a uniform body of law. Rather it is to understand and reconcile national differences in a way that structures trade in a fair and predictable way. In his view, policy convergence requires that states regulate to the same beat (or rhythm), not to the same tune (or harmony). Regulatory diplomacy defined as rhythm rather than harmony will leave national governments with some room to manoeuvre.

Klaus Stegemann in his *Diplomacy and the Discovery of New Rules for the Trading System* assesses and extends Wolfe's analysis. For example, while he applauds the insights that come from Wolfe's experience as a former career diplomat, insights that are then filtered through a political science filter, he questions Wolfe's proposition that if an area "does not have an impact on trade, it is not a legitimate focus for WTO action". To buttress this claim, Stegemann discusses the TRIPS agreement (Trade-Related Aspects of Intellectual Property Rights). Towards this end, he presents an informative table that cross-classifies GATT, GATS, TRIPS with national treatment, prohibitory constraints, and the existence of standards, where his conclusion is that TRIPS stands apart from GATT and GATS because it depends on prescribing specific standards for domestic policy which are not trade-related. The point of this is to argue that Wolfe may well be under-playing the "prescriptive potential" of regulatory diplomacy.

Notwithstanding this caveat, the end result of these two papers is to provide new analytical insights into the manner in which multilateral pro-cesses and procedures generate international policy convergence in ways that maintain domestic room to manoeuvre.

Globalization and the Meaning of Canadian Life (William Watson)

We were fortunate indeed to have Bill Watson as the Conference after-dinner speaker and to have him share with us some highlights of his then-just-published book, *Globalization and the Meaning of Canadian Life* (since then, the book was judged runner up for the Donner Prize for the best Canadian public policy book published in 1998). In the first part of his address (and of the book), Watson reminds us that much of the fanfare about globalization is not really that new. Among other things, he notes that international trade grew by a factor of 25 during the last century, far more than twentieth-century growth. Moreover, the nineteenth-century telecom-munications revolution was every bit as dramatic as the one we are now wit-nessing. And, of course, our immigration in the first decade of this century equalled roughly 25% of the population compared with 6% in the last decade. Watson's message here is that this earlier opening up of borders and dramatic cuts in telecommunications costs did *not* restrict our ability to manoeuvre. In particular, this led to the era of big government so he, at least, is holding his breath in terms of the supposed reduction in tax rates that is anticipated from the current resurgence in globalization.

In the second half of his address (which addresses the "Meaning of Canadian Life"), Watson attempts to debunk a few key premises that play a large role in Canadians' value systems. "Not so" is his assessment of (among others) the following premises:

- The United States is an unregulated *laissez-faire* jungle.
- Canadians pioneered statism in North America.
- We have always been the kinder, gentler North Americans.
- It is crucial that Canadian policy be different from American.

Watson concludes his address with an intriguing twist on the ongoing information revolution and on the "room to manoeuvre" theme of this volume: "The danger here is not so much that nation states will be *forced* to become alike, but that they will *want* to be alike because everyone in all countries will have become culturally American, whatever their passports may say." Specifically, if collectively we call upon the public sector to, in effect, *force* us to be distinct (by higher tax rates, by encouraging rent-seeking and by continuing to do too many things through the public sector) then we may well run the risk of sending our ship of state into very rough waters indeed.

Towards a North American Common Currency: An Optimal Currency Area Analysis (Thomas Courchene)

The thrust of Courchene's contribution is that increasing globalization and the demonstration effect of the Euro may well lead to further policy convergence and, in particular, North American currency integration. The analysis addresses three interrelated issues: (i) that the flexible exchange rate is not serving Canada well; (ii) that there is a persuasive case for exchange rate fixity; and (iii) that the longer term objective of exchange-rate fixity should be a North America currency union (NAMU), designed along Euro lines. Among the arguments marshalled against Canada's experience with flexible rates are that the secular fall in the dollar in lowering Canada's living standards vis-à-vis the Americans, that having the dollar track the fall in commodity prices is serving to divert economic activity from the high-tech and human-capital-based sectors, and that the inherent volatility of the Canada-U.S. exchange rate is, over the longer term, inconsistent with the degree of Canada-U.S. trade integration. This latter point serves as a bridge to the positive case for greater exchange-rate fixity, namely that the Canadian economy is more integrated trade-wise with the United States than is the typical European economy with the other members of Euroland. For example, in Ontario's case, nearly 45% of its GDP is now destined for U.S. markets.

The final section is more speculative. Under the assumption that further currency integration within NAFTA is likely if not inevitable, Courchene argues that North American monetary union is preferable to dollarization, that is, to adopting the U.S. dollar as legal tender in Canada. In the conclusion, Courchene suggests that there is a degree of urgency attending this issue because recent developments suggest that, elsewhere in the Americas, dollarization is on the rise. The policy challenge facing Canada is to ensure that the NAMU option is not foreclosed.

In his comments on the Courchene paper, Richard Harris advances the thrust of the general argument. Drawing from the optimal currency area literature, he notes that the increased Canada-U.S. integration increases the benefits to be derived from the elimination of exchange-rate volatility. Moreover, since the within-Canada terms of trade are at least as volatile as the Canada-U.S. terms of trade, fixed rates may be as effective as flexible rates in terms of addressing "asymmetric shocks". Over the medium term, Harris would opt for fixed exchange rates as the "only realistic policy alternative" for Canada, with a preference for NAMU over dollarization over the longer term, if further currency integration is in the cards.

National Tax Policy for an International Economy: Divergence in a Converging World? (Nancy Olewiler)

Nancy Olewiler advances the "room to manoeuvre" theme by focusing, initially, on the empirical evidence relating to the link between globalization and the convergence of national tax regimes and, later, on the challenge facing Canadian tax policy in an integrating North America. Drawing on the received analytical literature with respect to the presumed effects of globalization on national tax policies, Olewiler posits three hypotheses that this literature would support: (i) that taxes on mobile factors across countries will converge; (ii) that national tax mixes will move towards relatively higher taxes on less mobile inputs; and (iii) that tax revenues as a share of GDP will fall. She then presents a wide range of interesting and relevant G7 and OECD empirical evidence on these three issues which, with many caveats, and with oversimplification on my part, suggest that there is, at least as yet, little support for any of these hypotheses (although there is selective evidence that indicates that taxes on immobile factors are rising relative to taxes on mobile factors). This is a surprising result, one that runs against much of the globalization rhetoric. Among her observations here is that "the data presented suggest that countries can have different mixes of taxes, different rates, and still maintain their mobile inputs".

In the second half of the paper, Olewiler focuses on the Canada-U.S. tax comparison and what this might imply for tax reform in Canada. In spite of the earlier findings, her prescription as she surveys the range of Canadian taxes (personal and corporate taxes, consumption taxes, payroll taxes) is for reductions in marginal rates on the most mobile inputs, combined with base broadening on the business side and modest increases in payroll and consumption taxes. While this prescription also obtains in the absence of globalization, the enhanced pressures on the Canadian tax structure as a result of the forces of globalization mean that ignoring these principles may well imply "fewer choices in the future about the type of country we want to have". Any process of reform, however, must also address the perennial challenges posed by federal-provincial interaction on the tax front. She warns that if Canadian governments do not cooperate in setting tax policies, globalization could trigger a destructive internal competition. However, with harmonization across governments, globalization need not imply a race to the bottom: "We can maintain tax rates that are somewhat higher than those in the United States ... if we use those tax dollars to invest in human capital, infrastructure, a healthy environment and other public goods and services that improve the quality of life and our investment climate ... There is scope for divergence in a converging world, just not too much".

Robin Boadway begins his comments on the Olewiler paper by noting that the internal Canadian federal system has been a "mini-global economy" for decades, with little in the way of tax convergence. He offers several reasons why this may be the case. First, some factors are not as mobile as we think they are. In particular, once in place, capital is essentially immobile. Second, migration is presumably triggered by overall net fiscal benefits, which suggest that the focus has to be broadened to include the expenditure side of the fiscal equation and not just the tax side. Beyond this, Boadway notes that the allocation of tax bases between Ottawa and the provinces is "out of whack". Were we to start from scratch, it would be preferable to assign taxes on capital solely to the federal government in exchange for more provincial room in the sales and payroll areas. His conclusion is that there remains significant room to manoeuvre: "Given that the bulk of taxes are borne by residents, and that the international mobility of residents is really quite limited, it is not at all clear to me that ... there is any real need for nations to conform in levels of taxation and hence the public services that they provide to their citizens."

The Canadian Financial Sector in the Information Age (John Chant)

In addressing the financial services industry challenge arising from globalization (and, in particular, the information technology aspect of globalization), John Chant's contribution has two broad objectives. The first is to provide an analytical perspective of the emerging nature of banks in an information era. With this as backdrop, Chant then turns his attention to some of the proposals and policies relating to regulation and reform. He begins by noting that banks are both horizontally and vertically integrated. In terms of the former, on the "distribution side", the banks collect deposits and originate loans while on the "production side" they simultaneously invest funds and extend credit. Vertical integration is less well understood — the banks simultaneously engage in both distribution of services and their production. By interweaving this vertical and horizontal integration framework with the advances in information technology, Chant generates insights with respect to the forces of convergence and divergence in the financial service area. We reiterate only one — the distribution function is converging whereas the production function is diverging in the sense that the way is opening up for a host of new competitors. Prudential regulations must adopt itself to these information-driven trends.

In terms of the policy implications that follow from his analysis, Chant begins with the merger issue. The McKay task force (for which Chant was research director) recommended the jettisoning of the "big-shall-not-buy-big" rule. Rather, mergers should be evaluated on their own merits, that is, on their implications for competitiveness and on the basis of prudential concerns. His overall conclusions with respect to mergers is captured in the last paragraph of his paper:

> Canadian institutions must be given the freedom to adapt to the changes in ways that allow them to serve Canadians and develop their international strengths. It is not clear whether the recent rejection of the mergers of major banks was a delay or a dead-end. Even delay could be costly given the rapid pace of technology. A dead-end would almost certainly be detrimental to both Canadian banks and their customers.

Beyond this, he notes that the undoing of vertical integration means that banks may increasingly be distributing products produced by others (i.e., they will as an agent, not principal) and this has information and monitoring implications that regulators must take into account. As a final challenge he focuses on "entry without a physical presence" — the ultimate information approach to financial services, as reflected in foreign firms doing financial transactions with Canadians on, say, the Internet. Here, about all that the regulatory process can do is provide Canadians with as much information as possible in terms of those foreign institutions operating in Canada without a physical presence.

In his comments, Ted Neave begins by taking aim at the McKay report's focus on protecting consumer interests. He asserts that, in effect, the McKay report views banks as an "instrument of public policy", that is, as a social policy instrument rather than as an industrial sector. This view needs more debate and discussion than it has as yet received. In terms of the general issue of bank and financial-institution regulation, Neave's view is that the answer has to be a substantial increase in the amount and kinds of information made available to the public. He recognizes that there is a view out there that suggests that some banking crises can be handled better and quicker if information is not widely available. However, he believes that, on balance, more information and, in particular, timely information must surely be part of the solution and, therefore, must be the centrepiece of financial institution regulation in an information era.

Rapporteur's Assessment (Jack Mintz)

Jack Mintz does a superb job in integrating and assessing the various policy areas addressed in the conference and how they relate with the conference theme, room to manoeuvre. As noted earlier, readers may prefer to approach this volume by reading first Mintz's integrative overview.

Acknowledgement

By way of a few final introductory comments, let me be the first to admit that there are many important policy areas missing from this volume. A critical area in this regard is Canada's social policy framework. In this case, and in others as well, these policy areas are assessed in earlier volumes of the Bell Canada Papers. For example, in Bell 5, Keith Banting addresses room to manoeuvre on the social policy front. His conclusion is that while the forces of globalization are influencing social policy everywhere, within this general constraint there is nonetheless considerable room for national social policy systems to gear themselves to their domestic priorities.

Second, following each session (except William Watson's dinner speech) is an edited version of the ensuing floor discussion. I would like to express my thanks to Adil Sayeed for handling this difficult task in such an admirable fashion.

Third, I wish to recognize the contribution of the session chairs. In this regard, special thanks are due to Marvin McInnis, James MacKinnon, David Slater, Steve Kaliski, Roger Ware and Peter Kirkham. Also critical to the success of the Bell Canada Papers is an informed and interested audience. Not only do conference attendees provide motivation for authors and discussants alike, but their role in generating the floor discussion contributes an important ingredient to the conference and volume.

Finally, it is a pleasure to thank the people that make the volume possible — the authors and discussants. Indeed, I take this opportunity to thank all the authors and discussants who have contributed to the Bell Canada Paper series.

All that remains for me is to present the sixth and last Bell Canada Papers volume — *Room to Manoeuvre: Globalization and Policy Convergence*. The papers are uniformly excellent, they are provocative, they provide an ideal platform for policy discussion and research and, most of all, by focusing on Canada's room to manoeuvre they provide a fitting conclusion to the Bell Canada Papers' mandate to address the policy implications of globalization and the information revolution.

Constitutionalizing Neo-Conservatism and Regional Economic Integration: TINA x 2

H.W. Arthurs

Introduction

This conference poses a difficult question: Does Canada have room for manoeuvre? Can we make thoughtful choices about the kind of country we want to be? Can we make those choices democratically? Can we make them effectively? Can we then continue to learn from experience, adapt to new circumstances, assimilate new ideas and make new choices? Alas, the answer for the foreseeable future is "no".

For Canada, as for other countries, choices in any given situation are limited. Policy making is inevitably polycentric: known choices pre-empt unknown choices; short-term choices prefigure long-term choices; circumstantial choices shape structural choices; economic choices determine social choices; and, increasingly, international choices become domestic choices. These are generic, one might almost say existential, constraints on policy-making. However, as I will argue, Canada also confronts constraints which

I should like to thank Patrick Monahan, Bob Wolfe and Stephen Clarkson for their helpful insights, Robert Kreklewich for his able research assistance, the SSHRC for its financial support and Tom Courchene, Daniel Schwanen and other Bell Conference participants for their comments, both constructive and critical, which will help to shape future iterations of this essay.

are not generic, which are specific to our time and place. These constraints are analytically distinct, but coincide in time and have ramifying consequences which dramatically narrow our room for manoeuvre. They are embedded in our political culture, social consciousness and institutional structures to the point where they operate as a virtual constitution. Two, as it happens, are both captured by the same acronym: TINA. The third is the crisis of governance being experienced by the Canadian federation.

TINA x 2

The first, the neo-conservative TINA of Margaret Thatcher (Young, 1989, pp. 204-205), is specific to our time and passes for conventional wisdom in most western industrialized democracies: *"there is no alternative"*, Mrs. Thatcher said in repudiating the postwar compromise of embedded liberalism; *"there is no alternative"* to monetarism, to lower taxes, to deregulated and globalized markets, to radically diminished social welfare programs, to significantly lower levels of state regulation of markets. Indeed, in Mrs. Thatcher's neo-conservative world view, the question posed to this conference — "do *we* have room to manoeuvre?" — would be incomprehensible: there is no *we*, no society, no entity capable of collectively seeking and exploiting room to manoeuvre: only self-aggrandizing individuals pursuing their interests in an open market. But what began as a pre-emptive rhetorical strike at opponents and doubters by this determined and combative ideologue has ended up as revealed and incontrovertible truth for most bond traders, financial analysts, treasury officials, academic economists and political parties in the United Kingdom, in most advanced democracies, in many countries which aspire to join their ranks, in the international markets and agencies which constitute and administer the global economy and, of course, in Canada.

Yet even if one concedes that in the particular circumstances which Mrs. Thatcher encountered, hers was indeed the best way to build a prosperous and confident society, that the conventional wisdom has got it right, that similar policies will have salutary effects elsewhere, surely there *are* alternatives. It defies both logic and experience to assert that a ubiquitous and unchanging Thatcherism is the only possible policy for all countries in all circumstances for all time. And if there are alternatives, is it appropriate for Canada to continue to constitutionalize the assumptions and values of Thatcherism, thereby seriously compromising its capacity to respond to new

H.W. Arthurs

analytical insights, a new economic environment, a new political consensus? Yet that is what we are doing, I argue, in part because of the second TINA.

If the first TINA is specific to our time, the second is specific to our place: we are *"trapped in North America"*. Canada's geography joins it at the hip to the United States, a vastly richer and more powerful country which happens also to be our major supplier of foreign capital, the head office of half of our largest corporations, our best customer, our supplier-of-choice, our military and foreign policy ally, the dominant intellectual influence and inspiration for our knowledge-based elites and for grassroots and emancipatory movements, and a veritable cornucopia of pop culture, science and technology, intellectual property and much else. Naturally, we will think carefully — possibly to the point of paralysis — before taking steps which might seriously disturb this complex and, arguably, profitable relationship. But, as in the case of Thatcherism, ought we to be institutionalizing — ultimately constitutionalizing — the specifics and possibly the fundamentals of our relationship with the United States? These are likely to change over time, even if our geography does not, and when they do, it will be difficult for us to respond.

Moreover, our two TINAs are mutually reinforcing. The TINA of our time, neo-conservatism, Thatcher's TINA, is embedded in what is called, after its provenance, "the Washington consensus". The TINA of our place — our many, deep and complex connections with the United States — ensures that Canada will be amongst the last to abandon that consensus. And our tendency to constitutionalize the two TINAs makes it more than likely that long after the Washington consensus dissolves — as it almost surely will, some day — Canadian public policies will continue to be shaped by it.

This last contention, that we are constitutionalizing our two TINAs, is one of the central themes of my argument. The other theme, as noted earlier, is that the deep structures of Canada's institutions of governance are being transformed, not only by the exogenous influences of neo-conservatism and regional economic integration, but also by the endogenous forces of decentralization, juridification and populism. This transformation of deep structures, I will argue, is also constitutional in its character. Because both of these themes are organized around the idea of "constitutionalization", I must digress to say something about what constitutions are and what they do.

The Multiple Meanings and Functions of "Constitutions"

Neither "constitution" nor "constitutionalize" has a precise and authoritative meaning in Canadian legal and political discourse,[1] a convenient circumstance which allows me to stipulate how I intend to use these evocative terms. Constitutions, I will argue, are identifiable as such because they perform certain social, political and juridical functions: they are normative bedrock; they express fundamental principles; they are prior to and constitutive of legislative, judicial and executive institutions; they give legal validity and social meaning to statutes and common law, public policy, political ideology, administrative practice and even national self-interest. Hence, to "constitutionalize", in my lexicon, is to endow texts, institutions and processes with these same properties.[2]

It is in this sense that I contend that we are constitutionalizing the key assumptions and values of neo-conservatism and continentalism: we are incorporating them into our system of fundamental principles, and reconfiguring our public and private institutions, processes and policies to ensure that they are embedded deeply and permanently in our polity, economy and society. In other words, we are treating the two TINAs not just as the parameters of present policies — because they are inescapable, expedient or prudent — but as prime determinants of future action. By doing so, we make it difficult for ourselves to imagine a different future, to work towards it, to adopt new policies, to act on new information, to cope with new circumstances. I will offer evidence to support that argument in the next section of this essay. However, I must first say something more about constitutional law, practice and politics.

---

[1] See e.g., the current controversy over whether the comprehensive Nisga'a land claims settlement in British Columbia constitutes a "constitutional amendment" requiring approval in a referendum under the *Constitutional Amendment Approval Act*, R.S.B.C. 1996, c.67.

[2] I acknowledge that there are other ways of defining "constitutions". See Clarkson (1998).

Constitutional Law

Constitutions, for our purposes, come in two basic models, the organic model of the United Kingdom — all ancient customs, evolutionary modifications and modern grafts — and the more rationalistic and explicit American model. Canada's constitution, as every school child knows, is "somewhere in between". The original British North America Act of 1867, an ordinary act of the United Kingdom Parliament, was sandwiched between one statute respecting the marriage of British subjects in Odessa and another levying a tax on dogs. Nonetheless, in its very first words it recites that Canada should have "a Constitution similar in Principle to that of the United Kingdom"[3] — unwritten, inchoate, yet (as Victorian Englishmen imagined) the envy of the world. However, the Act itself was very precise, fully formed and quite un-British: its 147 carefully worded clauses defined the substantive, institutional and procedural arrangements of the new Canadian federation.

In consequence, there is an important connection, but by no means exact congruence, between the juridical force of the "constitution similar in principle to that of the United Kingdom" and the legal rights, powers and duties conferred on institutions and individuals by the Constitution Act itself. Some important constitutional norms are found neither in the Constitution Act nor in any other "constitutional" document — the conventions of the Westminster parliamentary system (see Heard, 1991), for example, or the invented traditions of the pre-1981 amending process.[4] Others are firmly embedded in crucial language of the Constitution Act — "peace order and good government",[5] for example — but have been "interpreted" to the point where their juridical significance has been virtually transformed. And still others appear to have lost whatever legal significance they once may have had — the federal right to disallow provincial legislation, for example, or the provisions for achieving uniformity of law amongst the original four

---

[3]*British North America Act, 1867* (U.K.) 30 & 31 Vict., c.3, Preamble.

[4]*Re Resolution to Amend the Constitution (Patriation Reference)*, [1981] S.C.R. 753.

[5]*Constitution Act, 1867* (U.K.), 30 & 31 Vict., c.3., s. 91, "reprinted in R.S.C. 1985, App. II, No. 5 (hereafter *Constitution Act, 1867*].

provinces.[6] Despite occasional amendments, despite patriation, despite a grandiose new title — the Constitution Act, despite the grafting-on of an American-style Charter of Rights and an explicit amending formula, we still cannot say, "here, in this text, within the four corners of this document, can be found the law of the Canadian constitution."[7]

Constitutional Practice

Constitutions change and — notwithstanding the existence of a carefully-worded amending formula — they change without constitutional amendment. After all, there is hardly a single significant Canadian public institution or branch or level of government which does not differ radically today from what it was in 1867 or, for that matter, 1937. But exactly *how* change is accomplished — especially purposeful change — is something of a puzzle.

In principle, of course, changes can be effected by formal amendment. The 1867 constitution was amended in this way, and can in principle be amended again, although the 1982 procedure is workable only in limited circumstances.[8] And, of course, unwritten constitutional "conventions" evolve, though how they can be modified is a matter of some controversy and whether and when this has been accomplished is knowable only after the fact (see Heard, 1991; Forsey, 1984; Russell, 1993, 107 ff.). Most changes, however, result neither from formal amendment nor from the aggregation of convention-generating precedents, but by other, inexplicit, means.

Judges are important agents of such inexplicit changes, whether they mean to be or not. As even the most technically-minded lawyer would now

---

[6]*Constitution Act, 1867*, ss. 90 & 94. The federal disallowance power has not been exercised since 1943.

[7]The Constitution Act actually compounds the confusion: under s. 92 "the provincial constitution" can be amended by mere provincial legislation.

[8]Three amendments in 1996-98 disestablished confessional educational systems in Newfoundland and Quebec. (See Fraser, 1997 and 1998.) However, these amendments were unusual in that under s. 43 of the Constitution Act, 1982, they could be effected by a proclamation by the Governor General, following resolutions of the Senate, House of Commons and legislative assembly(ies) of the province(s) to which they applied.

concede, the written constitution is what the courts say it is, and the unwritten constitution ultimately exists, like beauty, only in the eye of some curial beholder. Hence the familiar (though controversial) story of how the highly centralized federation which our founding fathers apparently imagined themselves to be creating was transformed into one of the most decentralized in the world, thanks to the constitutional rulings of the Judicial Committee of the Privy Council (Pierson, 1960; Laskin, 1964; MacDonald, 1957). Hence the fantastical and self-serving inflation by courts of their own independence and reviewing powers and their immunity from Charter standards and the financial tribulations which afflict the rest of us.[9] Hence the ability of the Supreme Court by a process of divination and conjury to "find" standards of legality and legitimacy governing Quebec secession in a constitution which is admittedly silent on the point.[10]

Constitutions are transformed by other agents as well. The decentralized federation wrought by the Privy Council was challenged by the aggressive use of legislative powers during the Great Depression (Scott, 1937), transformed by the use of executive powers during wartime (Marx, 1970) and then, after the war, rewrought — arguably overwrought — by the stratagems of fiscal and cooperative federalism (Smiley, 1970; Bothwell *et al.*, 1984, chap. 5-7; Simeon and Robinson, 1990). And finally, sometimes constitutional change just seems to happen incrementally, over time. Bits of the constitution become rusty and flake off — the federal disallowance power (La Forest, 1969); others — Quebec's right to international representation (Ratelle, 1988) — seem to emerge through autopoeisis, the almost imperceptible reflexive process by which closed systems, social fields or epistemic communities transform themselves (Teubner, 1993; for a critique, see Beck, 1994).

---

[9]Deschênes and Baar (1981); Lederman (1987); Friedland (1995). See *Crevier v. A.G. Quebec*, [1981] 2 S.C.R. 220; *Retail, Wholesale Union v. Dolphin Delivery*, [1986] 2 S.C.R. 573; *Reference Re Remuneration of Judges of the Provincial Court of Prince Edward Island; Reference Re Independence & Impartiality of Judges of the Provincial Court of Prince Edward Island; R. v. Campbell; R. v. Ekmecic; R. v. Wickman; Manitoba Provincial Judges Assn. v. Manitoba (Minister of Justice)*, [1997] 3 S.C.R. 3 [hereinafter *Judicial Salaries Reference*].

[10]*Reference re Secession of Québec*, [1998] S.C.J. No. 61 (QL).

Thus, constitutions, written or unwritten, are by no means immutable. But neither are they infinitely malleable. At any given moment, and for considerable periods of time, we operate within a normative hierarchy, whose original sources, precise contours and future configuration may be obscure and contested, but which is nonetheless understood to mandate the behaviour of both state actors and ordinary citizens, and the terms on which they must relate to each other. Behaviour which departs from this normative hierarchy is regarded as constitutionally illicit.

But how is the normative hierarchy of the constitution actually translated into operational reality? How is constitutionally illicit conduct suppressed and constitutionally licit conduct validated? Positivist jurists and political scientists usually postulate a command model of constitutional implementation: the constitution speaks; public officials and citizens listen and obey. If they do not obey, their conduct is judged by the courts to be illegal; and if so judged, the state uses its coercive power to achieve compliance (see e.g., Whyte and Lederman, 1992, chap. 1).

This command model obviously has some descriptive power, but not much. For one thing, it overstates the clarity and power of commands. The constitution's speech is often slurred and incoherent. For another, it overstates the attentiveness of its audience. Governments and public officials do not usually consult the constitution as the first step in developing new policies and programs; they focus on achieving specific practical outcomes. If reminded of possible constitutional difficulties, they usually find a way to navigate around them or to comply minimally and formally but sufficiently. If they find themselves on the losing end of constitutional litigation, they usually manage to do the same thing in a slightly different way, and to escape constitutional censure a second time.[11] If matters occasionally degenerate to the point where someone refuses to obey the constitution, the state and the offender are both likely to suspend disbelief willingly, in order to reach a

---

[11]The recent Ontario separate schools litigation may be a case in point. A judge struck down a provincial statute which restructured the financing and administration of the education system, on the ground that it derogated from the constitutionally-guaranteed right of Catholic separate school boards to levy taxes. However, according to newspaper reports, the successful litigants have asked the government to negotiate a resolution of the matter rather than pursuing an appeal. *Ontario English Catholic Teachers' Assn.* v. *Ontario (Attorney General)*, [1998] O.J. No. 2939 (QL) [hereinafter *Ontario English Catholic Teachers' Assn.*]. See Mackie (1998a).

practical compromise and avoid the use of force.[12] And if worst comes to worst, if the state's coercive power is actually applied, it is by no means clear that this will produce constitutional compliance in situations involving deep conflicts of politics, culture, language, social values or religion or where compliance involves a challenge to entrenched, low-visibility bureaucratic cultures and practices (Bogart, 1994; Rosenberg, 1991).

Thus, the command model seems to provide at best only a partial account of real-life constitutional behaviour. At a minimum, this account ought to be augmented by taking note of the powerful "shadow" effects of the constitution. Specific language in the constitution and actual judicial pronouncements tend to shape constitutional outcomes rather less than the threat, cost and uncertainty of constitutional litigation. All litigation is unpredictable, and constitutional litigation more so than most. And it is especially risky for governments because — win or lose — unlike their non-governmental opponents, they are likely to be confronted with prolonged uncertainty, the disruption of programs, administrative chaos, spillover effects, gratuitous advice from the bench and, ultimately, political embarrassment. Hence, one "shadow effect" is that governments tend to be somewhat litigation-averse, especially when confronted by credible opponents — other governments, large corporations and organized interest groups — though perhaps less so when confronted by those who lack status, legal resources, economic power or political influence. I do not want to overstate: governments are not traumatized by the mere prospect of con- stitutional litigation. They sometimes initiate constitutional litigation as a diversionary or delaying tactic; and they tend to resist vigorously if sued on constitutional grounds. But by and large, governments prefer to avoid con- stitutional litigation if possible. This tendency, I will argue next, contributes to the detumescence of the Canadian state.

One reason is that the government's legal advisers act as risk managers, mandated to vet proposed legislation and official action to ensure both constitutional legality and legitimacy. This ostensibly technical function gives them what amounts to a virtual power of revision and veto, a power

---

[12]But, as the case of Louis Riel reminds us, not always. More typical is the case of *Re Lewis* (1918), 13 Alta. L.R. 423, 41 D.L.R. 1, some 30 years later, when *habeas corpus* was issued to invalidate the illegal conscription of a soldier. The military refused to release him, but a potential confrontation with the Alberta Supreme Court was averted when Lewis was quietly moved beyond its jurisdiction, to another province. The events are described in Bowker (1954, p. 933).

which from the earliest days of the welfare state lawyers (and judges) have used to discourage state activism (Arthurs, 1985). Nor is this simply a matter of legal ideology; self-interest is involved as well. After all, there is less risk of government being attacked on constitutional grounds for doing nothing than for doing something, and consequently, less risk that the advisers themselves will be the subject of criticism.[13] More recently, as Canada's encounter with the two TINAs has coincided with a period of unusual constitutional volatility, constitutional legitimacy has become even more contestable, the risks associated with litigation have increased considerably and litigation-averseness has grown commensurately (Monahan and Finkelstein, 1992). Indeed, litigation-averseness seems to have increased in certain areas — national unity and trade policy, for example — to the point where risk-management is no longer regarded as solely a technical matter for legal advisers. Increasingly, it has come to involve as well political advisors and senior civil servants with specific responsibilities for sensitive policy areas, which in turn has reduced the influence of Justice ministries in some key areas of policy making. This is but one aspect of the widely-noted trend towards the interpenetration of law and politics following adoption of the Charter (Manfredi, 1992; Bryden et al., 1994; Mandel, 1994; Knopff and Morton, 1992; Schneiderman and Sutherland, 1997). But whoever manages risk, the result is the same: litigation-averseness discourages the use of state powers especially in policy-sensitive areas such as trade, investment and regulation, which are populated by actors with the capacity to make constitutional claims and initiate political and economic reprisals. This is a partial explanation of Canada's relative passivity in the face of the powerful forces of regional economic integration and neo-conservatism.

Even this more complex and dynamic description of how constitutions work does not take into account their social and cultural dimension. Quite apart from the operative provisions of the Constitution Act, the values embodied in the constitution are said to be fundamental to Canadian society. The Charter's preamble, for example, recites that "Canada is founded upon principles that recognize the supremacy of God and the rule of law" while the unwritten constitution, in its more recent formulations, portrays Canada as held together by commerce — "the economic union" — or compassion — "the social union". But whether deity or jurisprudence, mammon or mercy

---

[13]Of course, there are important exceptions. Two recent royal commissions — the Somalia Inquiry and the Krever Inquiry — both castigated government inaction.

H.W. Arthurs

conveys the appropriate message, the intent is the same: to mobilize broad public support for constitutional values supposedly shared by politicians, public officials, judges and ordinary citizens. This, surely, explains the Supreme Court's invocation, in the *Quebec Secession Reference*, of the four fundamental principles of federalism, democracy, constitutionalism and the rule of law, and respect for minorities.[14]

To the extent that this project of mobilization succeeds, it may secure widespread and willing adherence by citizens to constitutional norms and legitimate acts of state perceived to be in accordance with those norms. But it may not succeed. The cultural meaning of constitutions is often hotly contested. Like other cultural artifacts, they are capable of being appropriated for diverse and unanticipated purposes, as the raw material of symbolic behaviours and emotive appeals. For example, equality-seeking groups tend to wrap themselves in the Charter; regional politicians campaign for constitutional change so as to identify themselves as the tribunes of their disaffected constituents; and Quebec nationalists and native peoples attack the constitution as a symbol of the historic injustices and indignities which they have suffered. Or, to take another example, public officials and politicians may cite constitutional reasons as an explanation for their own inability or obligation to act, despite their professed preference for doing the contrary, or to criticize the action or inaction of their opponents.

Constitutional Politics

The indeterminacy, shadow effects, and symbolic and cultural power of constitutions combine to make possible — perhaps make inevitable — the practice of what might be called constitutional politics. What distinguishes constitutional politics from the common or garden variety is that contending views are advanced not on the basis of their superior wisdom, equity or cost-effectiveness, but because of their claimed legitimacy, their supposed congruence with fundamental or transcendant norms, their allegedly unique fit with constitutionally-mandated institutions, structures and practices.

This argument from constitutional legitimacy changes the nature of political discourse by effectively removing certain options from the agenda. Can we any longer talk about revising our patent and copyright laws, for

---

[14]Supra note 10.

example, in an effort to ensure that foreign drug manufacturers and publishers act in accordance with our national interests? Or is not all such discussion likely to be pre-empted by a timely reminder that we live in a global economy, that the markets will punish countries guilty of such atavistic tendencies, and that we will surely find ourselves on the receiving end of a World Trade Organization (WTO) or North American Free Trade Agreement (NAFTA) complaint? Could anyone seriously propose the creation of a national labour market agency or a national securities regulator? Or would this not be viewed as such an egregious affront to provincial sensibilities — especially those of Quebec — as to imperil national unity? Is there any serious prospect of reasoned debate on the issue of whether judges have inappropriately advanced their own institutional prerogatives and ideological preferences? Or will any such debate be brought to premature closure because no government wants to be accused by every editorial writer in the country of unconstitutional meddling with the independence of the judiciary or the rule of law? In short, we have come to tacitly accept the existence of a new set of norms concerning the limits of national law and policy, the federal-provincial distribution of powers, and power relations between the judiciary and the other branches of government. It is in this sense — by defining what is legitimate, thinkable, feasible — that constitutional politics tend to fix the limits of debate and foreclose straight-forward, if controversial, changes in current policies.

In the following section of this paper, I propose to show how the two TINAs have given rise to a series of related regimes[15] — in the world economic order, in the North American regional economic space, in trans-national corporations and in civil society — and how these regimes have begun to function as a virtual constitution, limiting Canada's "room to manoeuvre". Next, I will turn to various constitutional developments within Canada, not directly related to the two TINAs, which are producing similar effects. And finally, I will conclude with some ruminations on the theme of constitutional change, in the hope of escaping from the *cul de sac* to which I have apparently consigned not only Canada but myself. To reiterate: throughout, I will be using the term "constitution" expansively, not only to describe formal, juridical arrangements, but also more broadly, to encompass the shadow effects, social and cultural implications and symbolic

---

[15]The concept of "regime" is used deliberately here to highlight the notion that international and domestic orders are political constructions, embedding political and social choices. See Wolfe (1997, p. 83); and Ruggie (1995).

significance of normative regimes which limit our ability to imagine, construct and execute alternative policies.

The Constitutionalization of the Two TINAs

In this section of the paper, I will briefly describe the formal and informal, transnational and domestic regimes which have begun to entrench the assumptions, values and institutions of neo-conservatism and continental economic integration.

The Constitution of the World Economy

The WTO, like its more-than-embryonic, less-than-viable child, the Multilateral Agreement on Investment (MAI), has been described as "the constitution of the global economy". The description is equally apt to encompass other foundational documents such as the Charter of the World Bank, and the statutes of the Organization for Economic Cooperation and Development (OECD). Nor are all such so-called constitutional documents concerned with economics. The International Labour Organization (ILO) Conventions, the United Nations Declaration of Human Rights and a host of other regimes in the social and cultural spheres also exhibit the characteristics of constitutions, insofar as they are deemed normatively superior to national law. States which adhere to them must amend their domestic law to conform to these international regimes and concede normative priority to them if they conflict with domestic law. This obligation is not merely a moral one. International treaties usually provide for a process of dispute resolution outside any national legal system, often culminating in adjudication. Failure to adhere to the obligations they create may result in sanctions, whether imposed by an international tribunal or by way of self-help by the injured party. Nor is it always possible to escape these consequences by amending the "constitution" or resigning from the regime. Like most constitutions, treaties and conventions are usually difficult to amend or abrogate. The WTO, for example, can only be amended by reinforced majorities, and states which fail to ratify such amendments may resign voluntarily or, in designated circumstances, be required to do so.[16] Some treaties, including those dealing with human rights, simply do not contemplate that countries will declare themselves no longer bound.[17] And finally, in the case of Canada and other peripheral and semi-peripheral countries, the consequences of unilateral resignation — at least in the economic sphere — are likely to be so traumatic as to virtually guarantee that the right to resign will never be exercised.

Of course, the actual text of treaties is not everything. Like most domestic constitutions, the WTO and other international regimes do not simply promulgate the "original intention" of their authors. What is permitted and forbidden, how one institution relates to another, which of several competing values is to be given priority all change over time. And, as in the case of domestic constitutions, change to international regimes comes about not simply through formal amendment and adjudicative interpretation, but as the result of conventional practices, negotiations and agreements, shadow effects and political strategies derived from events of symbolic and cultural significance. What the signatories to the General Agreement on Tariffs and Trade (GATT)/WTO were initially unable to agree upon — free trade in cultural goods, for example (see e.g., Schott, 1994, pp. 99-111) — remained on the agenda for subsequent negotiations. Those negotiations, for the MAI, also failed to achieve a "constitutional amendment" to the world trade system because Canada and several European countries insisted on reserving the right not to extend "national status" to American-owned media conglomerates.[18] Litigation is likely to be the next step. For example, the United States might seek a ruling from a WTO tribunal on the ground that one of those very conglomerates has been denied protection under existing treaty

---

[16]Final Act Embodying the Result of the Uruguay Round of Trade Negotiations, Dec. 15, 1993, 33 I.L.M. 1 (signed at Marrakesh on April 15, 1994, entered into force January 1, 1995).

[17]Keith (1997) argues that it is not possible to resign from certain international regimes.

[18]See McCarthy (1997). It has also been suggested that popular opposition, mobilized through the Internet, was responsible for the failure of the MAI negotiations (Drohan, 1998).

language.[19] If its claim fails, the United States would very likely bring pressure to bear on the "cultural protectionist" countries one by one, whether by asserting its legal rights, flexing its political muscle or using its economic power to their disadvantage in some other strategically-chosen area of trade activity, thereby creating a bargaining chip which can be exchanged for concessions in the form of favourable access to local markets for American cultural products (see Eggertson, 1997; Herman, 1997; *Globe and Mail*, 1998a). Whichever strategy is ultimately chosen, the outcome is likely to be a change in the "constitutional" regime which is as authoritative as any accomplished by formal amendment.

Finally, as with domestic constitutions, not all elements of the new, global constitution are found in formal instruments, such as treaties, which modify or override state law. In the domestic sphere, the boundaries between state and civil society seem to be shifting, and "law" seems more and more often to have a private and informal, rather than public and formal, character (Arthurs, 1997a). So too in the transnational sphere where state and international legal regimes are complemented, modified or displaced, by private processes of negotiation, legislation, regulation, adjudication and administration (Arthurs and Kreklewich, 1996). For example, the fate of economic and social policies, public institutions and even political leadership of many states is determined, in effect, by codicils to loan agreements negotiated with the World Bank and the International Monetary Fund (Williamson, 1983; also Pastor, 1989; Grinspun and Kreklewish, 1994, pp. 37-41; Dow Jones Service, 1998). Large transnational corporations enter into agreements with governments and social movements to regulate themselves through codes of business, employment and environmental practices.[20] Business relations in the global economy are increasingly governed by a new uncodified *lex mercatoria* fashioned by negotiators and draftspersons from private law

---

[19]The argument might resemble that used by domestic courts to "read in" protection for categories of persons whose situation is analogous to those already protected. Cf. *Egan v. Canada*, [1995] 2 S.C.R. 513, *Vriend v. Alberta*, [1998] 1 S.C.R. 493.

[20]Compa and Hinchliffe-Darricarrere (1995). See also Workplace Code of Conduct, drafted by the Apparel Industry Partnership of major clothing retailers and manufacturers, together with labour, consumer and human rights organizations. The Code was signed at the White House and applauded by U.S. President Bill Clinton, *New York Times,* April 14, 1997, A17.

firms and consulting firms (Dezalay, 1990; Dezalay and Sugarman, 1995; Trubek *et al.*, 1994), by international commercial arbitrators (Dezalay and Garth, 1996), and by the internal governance structures of major corporations themselves (Robé, 1997; Muchlinski, 1997). Indeed, similar developments are visible even outside the sphere of business and finance. A new *jus humanitatus* — a common law of humanity — is arguably emerging in the form of generally acknowledged standards of human rights and ecological protection (Santos, 1995, part 4), while non-governmental organizations (NGOs), such as Amnesty International and Transparency International seem to be slowly building a transnational criminal "law" by lobbying, cajoling, embarrassing and ultimately persuading governments to comply with proper penal practices and integrity standards.[21] These developments seem to suggest the emergence of something like constitutional conventions of transnational law, which facilitate or permit the growth of regimes of transnational law that do not depend upon the action of state or transnational agencies.

To sum up: in the globalized economy, the sovereignty of all states remains in principle unimpaired. But in reality, the "constitution" of the global economy — a mélange of treaties, state practices, commercial undertakings, technical standards, consultative processes, conventional behaviours and shared values and assumptions — establishes a normative order to which individual states are subordinated, both juridically and in a practical sense.

The Constitution of the North American Economic Space

North America is a special case of globalization, defined not only by the geographic contiguity of the NAFTA partners and the political and cultural hegemony of the United States, but by a long historical movement towards integration of the three economies. The NAFTA serves as its "constitution".[22] Like many constitutions, it builds upon, formalizes and facilitates a pre-existing reality: a hub-and-spoke economic relationship between Canada and the United States, and Mexico and the United States. This relationship

---

[21]Amnesty International, in particular, has been spearheading efforts to establish an international criminal court. See Amnesty International (1998). See also Transparency International (TI), 1997; Transparency International, 1996; Transparency International, 1995; Pope, 1996; Galtung, 1994).

[22]This notion is carefully elaborated in Clarkson (1998).

— both before and since the commencement of NAFTA — has been generating ever-higher levels of cross-border investment, intra-firm shipments and arm's length trade in goods, services and information between the two "spoke" countries and the "hub".[23] As levels of trade rise, as economic integration of the regional economy broadens and deepens, as it is increasingly accepted as irreversible, as it begins to generate non-economic side-effects in diverse realms from politics to the environment to popular culture to law enforcement, the logic of systematizing and institutionalizing the relationship becomes more and more compelling. This logic is ultimately re-ordering the normative hierarchies of the three NAFTA countries, though not in identical or even commensurate fashion.

As in the case of globalization more generally, normative adjustments are often accomplished by each country exercising its own sovereign powers. For example, the adoption of NAFTA led to the amendment or repeal by Canada of over 30 federal statutes,[24] and many provincial statutes. More importantly, NAFTA also prevents the enactment of future legislation that departs from its fundamental assumptions, contravenes the specific rules it embodies, or seeks to shelter domestic policies from its dispute-resolving procedures. Ongoing sectoral consultations are clearly paving the way for more legislative changes, in the interests of more complete "harmonization" (Wolfe, 1998). And enforcement of these new NAFTA-derived norms is, ultimately, a matter for national courts and tribunals,[25] albeit with a prominent role assigned to special transnational agencies[26] including those established to administer the

---

[23]Ontario is approaching something like complete dependence on American markets: exports to the United States account for 90% of Ontario's international exports, and fully 40% of its GDP (Mackie, 1998b).

[24]*North American Free Trade Agreement Implementation Act*, S.C. 1993, c.44.

[25]*North American Free Trade Agreement between the Government of Canada, the Government of Mexico and the Government of the United States*, 17 December 1992, Can. T.S. 1994 No. 2, 32 I.L.M. 289 (entered into force January 1, 1994) [hereinafter NAFTA], chapters 19 and 20 generally. For more background, see Johnson (1994, chap. 11); Leycegui *et al.* (1995); Abbott (1995, pp. 109-115).

[26]NAFTA, article 2001, establishes a trilateral Free Trade Commission, composed of Cabinet-level representatives of the three partners, mandated to

environmental and labour side accords.[27] That at least is the formal account of how our NAFTA "constitution" operates. But the command model tells us no more about NAFTA than it does about our own constitution. As in all comprehensive constitutional narratives, the informal is at least as important as the formal, the implicit and tacit as the explicit and overt, the cultural and symbolic as the prescriptive and coercive.

Not for nothing has NAFTA been characterized as a "conditioning framework" (Grinspun and Kreklewich, 1994) — a term which might equally apply to any constitution. It is certainly a powerful constraint on public policy formation, both explicit and implicit. Reported examples of its explicit effects include the abandonment by the Ontario New Democratic Party (NDP) government of its plans to institute public auto insurance,[28] and by the federal Liberal government of its plans to ban MMT, a gasoline additive, and to prohibit the cross-boarder movement of PCBs.[29] As to its implicit effects, as the NAFTA economies become more and more fully integrated, virtually all trade issues become linked to each other and to non-trade issues, regardless of whether NAFTA speaks directly to them or not. It is at least conceivable that, for example, Canada's publicly-funded health-care system may be attacked as an illicit subsidy which relieves Canadian

---

administer the NAFTA agreement; adjudicate disputes over interpretation and application of NAFTA rules and supervise the work of the various committees and working groups established under NAFTA. See Johnson (1994, pp. 494-499).

[27]Commission for Environmental Cooperation, established by the *Canada-Mexico-United States: North American Agreement on Environmental Cooperation,* 32 I.L.M. 1480 (concluded September 8-14, 1993; entered into force January 1, 1994); Commission for Labour Cooperation, established by the *Canada-Mexico-United States: North American Agreement on Labour Cooperation,* 32 I.L.M. hereinafter NAALC] (concluded September 8-14, 1993; entered into force January 1, 1994).

[28]Campbell (1993, pp. 92-93). Others suggest that the Rae government's reversal on public auto insurance was precipitated by the prospects of huge unemployment losses in the insurance industry, particularly among women clerical employees, emanating from government restructuring and rationalization. See Walkom (1994); Monahan (1995); and Rae (1996).

[29]McCarthy (1998); and *Globe and Mail* (1997). The federal government has been sued for imposing the ban by a U.S. company. See Scoffield (1998a).

manufacturers of a significant payroll cost, to the prejudice of their American and Mexican competitors. If such a complaint were made, Canada would very likely win — though there is always the possibility that adjudication in a Mexican or American forum might produce an unexpected and bizarre ruling in favour of the complainant. However, even a definitive ruling in Canada's favour might not bring this issue to closure. Similar complaints might well reappear in slightly different contexts, as part of an overall strategy designed to create a bargaining counter to exact concessions from Canada on some other front. In this sense, social policies are linked to economic policies, fisheries are linked to banking, cultural industries are linked to softwood lumber, chicken imports are linked to border controls; whatever happens in any given sector has the capacity to upset the relationships amongst the participants in a regionally-integrated economy.

Indeed, it is not difficult to see how linkages take on a life of their own. The abandonment in the 1970s of any attempt to regulate the transnational flow of capital, and the facilitation of such flows by NAFTA, has reinforced the *de facto* linkage between Canadian and American economic policies. For example, Canadian interest rates cannot be set without regard to their relationship with those in the United States, and a change in U.S. rates is sure to trigger an adjustment in Canada.[30] Now suggestions have surfaced for even closer integration of fiscal and monetary policy, by replacing the declining Canadian dollar with the U.S. dollar, or with a new regional currency based upon it, much as the Euro is effectively based on the deutschmark.[31] Such developments underline how fragile and possibly transient is Canada's capacity to create its own policies in virtually any sphere, foreign or domestic.

And finally, NAFTA's dispute resolution processes — however imperfect — are becoming "domesticated", being made part of the repertoire of strategies available to actors engaged in domestic disputes with governments and private parties. A good example is the North American Agreement on Labour Cooperation (NAALC) which is being used by national trade unions

---

[30]Apparently a delay by the Bank of Canada of one hour in following the downward adjustment of U.S. interest rates — instead of the usual five minutes — led to precipitous selling of the Canadian dollar and the largest drop in its value in over three years (see Stinson, 1998).

[31]Discussed in T. Courchene, "Towards a North American Common Currency: An Optimal Currency Area Analysis" in this volume.

as a forum in which to at least embarrass, if not sanction, employers engaged in unfair practices, and public agencies and tribunals deemed delinquent in protecting labour rights. The experience is still limited, but U.S. and Canadian unions are learning not only to process complaints through the National Administrative Offices (NAOs) — the recourse of first instance under NAALC — but to cooperate with each other in doing so.[32] Similar developments may be under way in the environmental field (Audley, 1997; Johnson and Beaulieu, 1996).

For all of these reasons, the formal processes of norm-creation and dispute-resolution embedded in NAFTA are likely over time to become more and more powerful, pervasive and constitution-like. However, NAFTA — like any constitution — has its informal as well as its formal dimensions. These, in effect, depend on the creation of something which might be characterized as "civil society". Of course, civil society in this context has very specific connotations. It does not embrace all potential participants, and does not extend beyond certain defined limits in terms of subject matter. On the contrary, "civil society" in the NAFTA context is essentially confined to networks and communities of business and professional people, public officials, journalists and other economic and political actors. Sectoral committees are being convened to set North American standards for automobiles, telecommunications and other industries, thereby reinforcing efforts to displace national regulatory regimes;[33] and seminars on labour law and policy are held for employers, unions, academics and regulators from the three partner countries.[34] These initiatives have generated extensive contacts amongst the elites of the three countries which, if not explicitly mandated by

---

[32]A recent complaint against a Canadian-based auto-parts firm (Echlin) involved some 40 human rights, church and labour groups across North America (see Scoffield, 1998b). The Canadian National Administrative Office for NAALC has agreed to investigate the complaint further (Scoffield, 1998c). For an overview of previous complaints under the NAALC, see Adams and Singh (1997).

[33]NAFTA Standards-Related Measures www.infoexport.gc.ca/section 4/mktx4.-e.asp (I am indebted to Bob Wolfe for this reference, among others.)

[34]The Cooperative Work Program of the North American Agreement on Labour Cooperation (NAALC) has sponsored four annual industrial relations conferences.

H.W. Arthurs

NAFTA, are nonetheless inspired by and have the effect of reinforcing it.[35] Moreover, informal processes of consultation, cultivation and coordination are designed to encourage harmonization of domestic laws, policies and practices not only by formal legislation or treaties but also by "globalization of the mind", a process which facilitates the convergence of intellectual structures, of fundamental values and ultimately, of normative systems.[36]

Hence the symbolic and cultural effects of NAFTA. Obviously, NAFTA was not adopted, nor does it survive, in a political vacuum: neo-conservative policies did not begin or end with the adoption of free trade. But to the extent that NAFTA exemplifies, entrenches and institutionalizes these policies — and marginalizes "deviant" views — it impresses itself on public consciousness as being inevitable for Canada — a North American country in a globalized world of disempowered states. Praise for the sound principles and practical achievements of NAFTA by political figures, the media and experts in the policy disciplines contributes to this sense of inevitability, as does the enthusiastic conversion, grudging acquiescence or quiet resignation of most of its mainstream opponents. And repeated direct and vicarious, real and imagined encounters with NAFTA-generated dispute resolution, normative systems and networks by Canadian businesses, workers and governments only reinforce the impression that NAFTA is neither anomalous nor time-limited. NAFTA, in other words, has ceased to be what it once was: the text of a treaty and of an omnibus Act of Parliament, the expression of a transitory policy adopted by a particular government at a particular moment in time. It can no longer be disaggregated from the other great transformations Canada has experienced in the last decades of the century. It is — we now are coming to believe — an ineluctable fact of the Canadian condition, a way of doing things to which there is no alternative: TINA x 2.

The Constitution of Transnational Corporations

The global economy is ultimately driven by transnational corporations and their extended families of suppliers, distributors, customers and investors. Key actors within their internal governance structures take decisions about

---

[35]The American Fulbright scholarship program was extended to Canada for the first time in 1990, shortly after the original Canada-U.S. Free Trade Agreement came into force.

[36]See below, the section on the Constitution of Civil Society.

whether to make or buy, to invest or disinvest, to create jobs or eliminate them, to tolerate local businesses as competitors, engage them as partners and co-venturers, destroy them or fold them into the parent firm. They are often able to persuade governments to enact or repeal legislation, to set the rules of trade through the standard form contracts they force on their suppliers and customers (Belley, 1993), to enhance or degrade local labour, human rights and environmental standards, to support research, the arts or community development projects. Indeed, Teubner and others have recently argued that transnational corporations themselves generate norms which govern not only their own internal affairs, but those of the entire transnational legal order (Teubner, 1997; Robé, 1997; Muchlinski, 1997). If so, the constitutions of transnational corporations are as deserving of attention as those of most states.

In Canada, this is particularly true. As a country highly dependent on foreign capital and international trade, we are particularly vulnerable to the constitutional structures and processes of foreign-based transnationals. After all, they account for some 30% of all corporate assets and 40% of corporate operating revenues (Statistics Canada, 1997), represent 35-50% of our largest corporations[37] and are the source perhaps of 60-70% of all Canada's exports. More to the point, some 50% of all our exports is accounted for by intra-firm transfers between Canadian subsidiaries and their U.S.-based parent firms.[38] In addition to these "hard" statistics, the influence of foreign-owned transnationals can be traced across a number of "soft" dimensions: they are highly influential in debates over economic and social policy, prime users of infrastructure, dominant inventors, developers and purveyors of intellectual property, leading consumers of producer services and major contributors to charities and the arts. And finally, more amorphously, in

---

[37]In 1995, five of the ten largest Canadian companies and 37 of the largest 100 companies were foreign-owned transnationals. Composite of annual surveys of *The Globe and Mail*, Report on Business, "The Top 1000", *The Financial Post*, "The Financial Post 500" and *Canadian Business*, "The Performance 500".

[38]Krajewski (1992) estimates that 60% of all exports to the United States are represented by intra-firm transfers. Weintraub (1994) puts this figure even higher — at 70%; 40% being intra-firm, another 30% resulting from intra-firm licensing and inter-firm understandings. The United States accounts for about 80% of all Canadian exports.

Canada and around the world, these corporations play an important role in the shaping of consumer markets, popular culture, urban architecture and human resource policies. How corporate decisions are made within transnationals, and how these decisions reflect — or fail to reflect — Canadian interests, values and concerns, is an important determinant of our national well-being.

As I have described elsewhere (Arthurs, 1999), the governance structures of transnational corporations operating in Canada seem to have recently changed quite markedly. While there are examples to the contrary, their Canadian corporate structures have been reduced in importance, Canadian shareholders have been bought out as subsidiaries have been "taken private", local boards of directors have been abolished, disempowered or filled with placeholders, and (subject to caveats about the meagreness of available evidence) the autonomy of local management has been diminished.

The causes of these changes are not hard to imagine: the liberalization of trade and the reduction in state regulation of local commodity, product, capital and labour markets; the restructuring and revision of product and service mandates as part of new global manufacturing and marketing strategies; the de-layering of management to improve intra-firm coordination and reduce costs; the globalization of capital markets and accounting, consulting and legal services; and the vast improvements in information and communications technology which make all of these possible by facilitating uninterrupted and rapid flows of data and commands. Nor are the ultimate consequences difficult to foresee: greater concentration of corporate headquarters, decision-making and support functions in a limited number of "global cities" (Sassen, 1994); increased vulnerability of localized corporate functions and community welfare to the stern calculus by headquarters of worldwide profitability; increased homogenization of policies, practices and products within and amongst global corporations; and increased risk of exposure to economic fluctuations, currency speculation and government mismanagement in far-off countries.

Notwithstanding that globalization is experiencing something of a crisis at the moment, trade theorists argue that these developments will produce significant benefits around the world and in Canada in particular. This proposition informs our national policies, and has done so for two generations: it is why we signed the Autopact, the original FTA, NAFTA, and the GATT/WTO, and why we continue to favour trade liberalization and the regional economic integration. While somewhat agnostic, I am prepared to accept — and want to accept — that in particular ways, in given circumstances and in the aggregate, these developments may turn out to be highly advantageous to Canada. But what I cannot accept is that they give Canada room to manoeuvre. Essentially, my concern is this: as a result of changes in the governance structures of transnational corporations, we seem to be experiencing a "hollowing out" of corporate Canada, an attenuated presence within Canada of executives who know much or care much about Canada, of senior business people who have a personal or financial stake in the success of Canadian subsidiaries as opposed to their foreign-based parent firms, and of Canadian providers to these firms of legal, accounting, consulting, research, software and advertising services.[39]

If that is indeed happening, what will we have lost? We will have lost the capacity for meaningful dialogue between Canadian governments and important actors in the private sector, the ability of Canadian directors, managers and investors to influence important decisions made by transnational corporations, the incentive and capacity to adjust transnational corporate policies to local Canadian laws and practices, and the direct and indirect contribution of Canadian corporate headquarters, senior executives and providers of producer services to their local economies, communities and cultural life. In an historical moment when the boundaries of civil society are said to be expanding, and those of the state contracting, these are very significant losses. And, at least on the evidence of recent experience, they are unlikely to be wholly offset by a commensurate rise in the population of our home-grown transnationals and their corporate cadres. Few Canadian-based companies rank with the leading transnationals, their Canadian character is increasingly dilute,[40] and many promising smaller Canadian firms are bought

---

[39]The"brain-drain" of Canadian managers, academics and health-care professionals to the United States accelerated dramatically between 1989 and 1996, from 2,700 to 27,000 per annum (*The Globe and Mail,* Oct. 15, 1998, B5). During this same period most large American transnationals took their Canadian subsidiaries private. And, during the same period, a severe recession and falling tax revenues led to the imposition of significant financial constraints on the health-care and education sectors, especially in Ontario. The relationship amongst these events invites speculation.

[40]Recent studies show that the two largest Canadian-based transnationals rank first and fourth in a "transnationality" index which measures the share of corporate activity which takes place outside a company's home country (McKenna, 1998).

out or forced into subordinate roles. Whether Canada has too little capital, too few consumers, too modest a pool of entrepreneurial and managerial talents[41] or too inhospitable a physical or political climate, it seems unlikely that our branch plant economy will ever become, in global terms, a head office economy.

The Constitution of Civil Society

I earlier suggested that the ambiguity, shadow effects, and symbolic and cultural significance of constitutions enables them to be used politically, to mobilize support for (or opposition to) state action. In this sense, constitutions function as repositories of tacit assumptions and explicit agreements about national values, historical experience and destiny. However, the significance of symbols, the formative influences upon culture, the content of assumptions and the meaning of agreements all change over time, permitting and even requiring the adjustment of constitutional roles and responsibilities, as outlined earlier. If this description of normative change is something like accurate, it is clear that strategically-located, knowledge-based elites — in politics and government, business, the media, popular and high culture, the professions and policy disciplines — are important agents of such change.

I want to emphasize the limits of this argument. Elites seldom conspire or consense; they are usually in competition and often in conflict. They are not disinterested custodians of national values or interests; they are often moved by idiosyncratic world views, personal or collective self-interest and protection of their intellectual capital. And they do not enjoy unlimited powers, even when ensconced in positions of formal authority: their ability to effect lasting change is ultimately a function of their ability to persuade each other and the broader public. But conceding these limits, an important

---

[41]According to recent reports, "more than two dozen major Canadian companies" have recently hired CEOs and other senior executives from the United States, who continue to reside there, commute to Canada weekly or communicate electronically with their Canadian managers, have no contact with the company's local community, but "are setting a gruelling pace and adopting drastic cost-cutting measures to bolster profits". The *Globe and Mail* notes that some observers fear that these U.S.-based executives are "undermining standards and traditions that distinguish Canadian business" (McNish, 1998).

point remains. Strategic knowledge-based elites exercise a formative, arguably crucial, influence on a country's fundamental — "constitutional" — values and therefore on the normative regimes through which these are expressed.[42]

Such elites often owe their strategic location to the fact that they represent the point of connection between national and transnational influences. They may be importers or exporters of goods, capital or services; they may be domestic exemplars of "world-class" artistic, scholarly or sporting achievement; they may be participants in a universalistic discourse of human and environmental rights; they may be politicians, civil servants, journalists or academics who conceptualize, organize, enact and administer the framework of policies and laws within which other elites function. Many of Canada's knowledge-based elites are, therefore, closely identified with the two TINAs. Indeed, it could hardly be otherwise, since American business and investment play a dominant role in our economy, American media shape our views of politics and culture, and American scholarship sets the pace in disciplines such as law, economics, sociology and management.

The consequence is, however, that many of our assumptions and values are coming to resemble those of the United States. And more importantly, these assumptions and values are becoming constitutionalized, in the sense that they are deeply embedded in the institutions of civil society — professions and sports leagues, universities and families, art galleries and workplaces, even counter-hegemonic social movements and political parties. And as this happens, it becomes increasingly unthinkable that we should abandon neo-conservative policies or withdraw from the many public and private processes which are advancing North American integration.

Of course, this is by no means a complete account of how our knowledge-based elites have been shaped by their encounters with the two TINAs. In fact, Canada's elites are in considerable disarray. While the majority may be the agents and effective implementers of neo-conservatism and continentalism, some elite members resist one or both of these forces. While some have their base in national and metropolitan institutions, others draw strength from peripheral and anti-cosmopolitan constituencies. While some claim to represent broad coalitions of economic and social interests, others are concerned about single issues. And finally, while some elite members are closely associated with wealth, power and privilege, others

---

[42]I have developed this argument in Arthurs (1997b).

H.W. Arthurs

speak for marginalized groups defined by race, gender, disability, language or class. In short, dissensus amongst Canada's elites is particularly widespread at the moment. While much of the conflict addresses the two TINAs and their effects, much does not — as the referendum on the Charlottetown Accord famously reminded us. The complex and confusing constitutional politics which result seriously impair our capacity to discuss realistically where our "room for manoeuvre" might be found.

The Constitution of the Canadian State: Decentralization, Juridification and the Populist Reconfiguration of Government

I have tried to show that TINA-related influences on Canada's constitution have resulted in the imposition of constraints on the powers of Canadian governments which are far-reaching and long lasting, if not actually permanent. Without debating the wisdom of these arrangements, and without denying that there may indeed have been "no alternatives" precisely because we are "trapped in North America", I now want to examine how other recent developments in Canadian law and politics have reinforced the effect of the two TINAs. These developments — which I describe as decentralization, juridification and the populist restructuring of government — have vastly complicated, if not essentially foreclosed, any future attempts to revive the activist state. Moreover, while their cumulative effect has made state intervention more difficult for all levels of government of all political stripes with all kinds of programs, it has become especially so for the federal government, for progressive and nationalist governments, and for governments seeking to implement economic policies, and social programs which depend upon them, rather than for governments seeking to impose public morality and social discipline.

I will argue, first, that the constitutional interpretations and strategies which facilitated national action in Canada in the past are no longer available; second, that the development of new constitutional justifications for judicial oversight of state action has reinforced a process of juridification at all levels of government; and third, that the constitutionalization of populist and individualistic — and neo-conservative — values, which is proceeding apace, will ultimately frustrate most forms of activism by Canadian governments.

These arguments require a few introductory observations. If we had somehow successfully resisted the two TINAs instead of embracing them, activist government today would be in difficulty in any event. The causes are various: the increasing complexity and polycentricity of problems referred to earlier; new technologies which can frustrate the implementation of state regulation in key sectors such as transportation and telecommunications; the mounting interest charges on large national and provincial debts; the overhanging costs of situations over which governments have little control, such as an aging population, variable climates and a backlog of equity claims; and the need to rethink strategies of intervention, given the indifferent results of long-term social-democratic initiatives in fields such as low-cost housing, town planning, welfare and public education.

But the decline in government's ability to act does not mean that the need for action has diminished or disappeared. Even the neo-conservative agenda is activist in certain respects. After all, it includes interventionist measures to ensure the honest and orderly operation of markets, the suppression of fraud, money laundering and violent crime, and in some versions, the enforcement of private morality and social discipline. Some of these concerns — a diminishing number, in a globalizing world — may require purely local action. However, most have a national or transnational dimension, and can be addressed, if at all, only by an empowered and energized federal government. Ironically, constitutional politics in Canada have recently tended to operate centrifugally, not centripitally; the central government is losing power and energy, not gaining it.

Decentralization: Centrifugal Forces in the Canadian Federation

In the sphere of economic policy making, small may be beautiful but it is fated to be a languorous rather than a vivacious kind of beauty. Widely-dispersed authority and a high degree of local legislative autonomy is no more practical for states eager to influence their economic fate than for the world's trading blocs or for great transnational corporations.[43] Small,

---

[43]Which is perhaps why 300 TNCs own about 25% of the world's productive assets, and why 47 of the world's 100 largest economies are TNCs. See Brecher and Costello (1994, pp. 18, 19 quoted in Nissen, forthcoming).

localized political units such as provinces are likely to lack technical and financial resources; they have no legal capacity to function internationally; few of the relevant actors are likely to be present in or subject to their jurisdiction and most of those who are can exit with relative ease; they cannot mobilize human and financial capital to support or complement private sector initiatives or spread the costs of infrastructure and investment over time and space; and so long as they act autonomously, they cannot define their field of comparative advantage, diversify, or exploit efficiencies of scale. Moreover, localized provincial action (or inaction) may well create nationwide problems: fiscal instability or improvidence at the provincial level may undermine the credit rating of the country as a whole; pollution generated in the air or water of one province may spread to others; shifts in local welfare policies may provoke intra- and interprovincial migration; failure to regulate financial markets in one province may undercut regulation in the others; and the free trade policies of one level of government may frustrate — or be frustrated by — the protectionist predilections of the other.[44]

By no means do I deny that local units of government may contribute constructively in many ways — as custodians of distinctive cultures and forms of social organization (Putnam, 1993), as sites of a "space economy" based on historical or geographical factors (Storper, 1992; Sassen, 1995), as important catalysts for and contributors to national and transnational economic strategies (Wolfe, 1994a; 1994b), or as executors of "subsidiarity" within broad policy lines laid down by a national or transnational political entity.[45] But I do suggest that coherent and effective economic policies, policies which reinforce the collective interests and social values of all Canadians, policies which give us "room to manoeuvre", must be formulated at the national level through democratic institutions. As my narrative will demonstrate, the possibility of mobilizing such national power, never great, has diminished in recent years.

Like any other constitution, Canada's was and is susceptible to multiple meanings reflecting the divergent historical, judicial, cultural, political and symbolic perspectives of its authors and of all the other actors who, over 130-odd years, have had reason to interpret or change it. However, many

---

[44]A prime example is the National Energy Policy of the early 1980s.

[45]For further commentary on the principle of subsidiarity, see Berman (1993, p. 139).

scholars of comparative federalism consider that — for better or worse — Canada's central government has fewer powers than most. In the context of the present argument, two issues are particularly salient. First, in contrast to the United States, the commerce power in Canada was never given the expansive interpretation which might have allowed the central government to effectively create or regulate national markets in goods, services or capital (Smith, 1963; Soberman, 1988). Even international and interprovincial trade, formally areas of federal legislative competence, have been narrowly defined (Soberman, 1988, pp. 303-309; Vegh, 1996, pp. 359-374). Second, the central government has the power to make treaties but, again in contrast to the United States, this power has been held not to encompass the authority to implement them if their subject matter does not otherwise fall within federal legislative competence.[46]

Consequently, the federal government has had to rely on three alternative strategies to create the modern Canadian state. Unlike the treaty power and the commerce power in the United States, each of these three strategies has proved to be time-limited. The first, the emergency power, was used extensively in wartime to virtually pre-empt provincial power over the economy (and much else).[47] However, it could not long survive the outbreak of peace.[48] While used occasionally to combat other notorious dangers to the body politic such as alcoholism and inflation,[49] it is by definition an exceptional power, not one which will support long-term policies. Second, the federal power to tax and spend seemed more durable for some time. However, it too has proved vulnerable although not so much to legal challenges as to constitutional politics (see Driedger, 1981; La Forest, 1981).

---

[46]*A.G. Canada* v. *A.G. Ontario (Labour Conventions)*, [1937] A.C. 326.

[47]*Fort Francis Pulp and Power Co.* v. *Man. Free Press Co.*, [1923] A.C. 695] (price controls); *Wartime Leasehold Regulations Reference*, [1950] S.C.R. 124 (rent controls) *Co-op. Committee on Japanese Canadians* v. *A.-G. Can.*, [1947] A.C. 87 (deportation of Japanese Canadians).

[48]*In re the Board of Commerce Act, 1919, and the Combines and Fair Prices Act, 1919*, [1922] 1 A.C. 191.

[49]See *Toronto Electric Commissioners v. Snider* [1925] A.C. 396 at 412 (alcoholism as a danger to the body politic); *Reference re Anti-Inflation Act*, [1976] 2 S.C.R. 373.

H.W. Arthurs

The problem is that virtually all Canadian governments have lost the desire to tax and with it the willingness and capacity to spend. This has led to the recent spectacle of the federal government reducing some of its own programs and downloading others to the provinces while simultaneously cutting transfer payments. The provinces, in turn, have cut some programs and passed responsibility for others along to end-users, the private sector and local governments, taking care at the same time to reduce the latter's capacity to raise taxes. What has driven this realignment of financial burdens and responsibilities is by no means the desire to recapture the lost innocence of our original constitutional arrangements. Rather it is a pragmatic political judgement that since TINA demands the reduction of government spending, it would be convenient if blame for the erosion of programs could be assigned elsewhere.

Third, the federal government traditionally used cooperative federalism as a political fig-leaf for its use of its taxing and spending powers and, to a lesser extent of its regulatory and criminal law powers, in spheres of activity which were arguably provincial. However, this strategy too seems to have passed its sell-by date. Quebec, of course, but also Alberta, British Columbia and even Ontario, no longer want to cooperate. Only the "have-not" provinces seemed willing to maintain the pragmatic constitutional arrangements which, over several decades, permitted Canada to establish its particular version of the Keynesian welfare state, and even they have recently expressed a preference for limits on the federal spending power. True, the welfare state always owed much to provincial experimentation:[50] but it was also closely linked to the emergence of a Canadian national identity (Jenson, 1990) and, I would argue, to the expression of that identity in important symbolical and practical national policies involving not only social programs but equalization payments, regional development initiatives (Courchene, 1996; Rowlands, 1994; Gagnon, 1991) and rudimentary attempts at national labour market and immigration strategies.[51] No longer: public attitudes have hardened; public generosity has shrivelled; public policy has been cut adrift from the Keynesian moorings of the postwar period; and regional parties and governments have taken to "fed-bashing" for their own purposes.

---

[50]Saskatchewan's 1962 medicare initiative is an obvious example.

[51]Early attempts at such a policy included the Unemployment Insurance Act, S.C. 1940, C. 44 (with the imprimatur of what is now s. 91 (2A) of the Constitution Act). See generally, Johnson and Smith (1994).

In theory, the federal government has one more card to play in the realm of economic policy making, the exercise of its undoubted constitutional power over the banking system, the money supply, interest rates and exchange rates. But, of course, the Bank of Canada is no longer a mere instrument of government, at least in the short- and medium-term, and global money markets and prospective investors are unlikely to respond well to vigorous use of federal powers. Indeed, even if they were vigorously used, the current crisis of our currency shows that they have relatively little power to affect the course of events.

In sum, the constitutional strategies which previously facilitated national approaches to national problems are no longer available. New strategies are needed. But what might they be? Not constitutional amendment, which on several previous occasions[52] provided the federal government with mandates denied it by the Privy Council: the 1982 amending formula[53] virtually guarantees that no significant constitutional amendment will ever alter the present balance of power between the federal and provincial governments. Not judicial interpretation: the Supreme Court seems to be taking pains to avoid decisions which exacerbate the current crisis of federalism.[54] And not pragmatic political compromises: so long as the spectre of Quebec sovereignty hovers over federal-provincial relations, such compromises are likely to be out of reach.

My conclusions, then, are these, there is a need — now more than ever — for national economic and social policies; that the courts at a formative period in our history denied the federal government constitutional power to pursue such policies; that legal strategies were developed in partnership between the federal and provincial governments to circumvent the courts'

---

[52]Constitution Act 1867, s. 91(2A) [unemployment insurance] and s. 94A [old age pensions].

[53]*Procedure for Amending Constitution of Canada*, Part V of the *Constitution Act*, 1982, being Schedule B to the *Canada Act 1982* (U.K.), 1982, c.11. And see generally Meekison (1983) and Monahan (1997, pp. 171-188).

[54]*Quebec Secession Reference, supra* note 11; *Reference re Constitution of Canada*, [1981] 1 S.C.R. 253, (1981), 125 D.L.R. (3d) 1; *Reference re Language Rights under Manitoba Act, 1870*, [1985] 1 S.C.R. 721, (1985), 19 D.L.R. (4th) 1; *Ford v. Quebec (Attorney General)*, [1988] 2 S.C.R. 712, (1988), 54 D.L.R. (4th) 577; *Quebec Hydro v. A.G. (Canada)*, [1997] 3 S.C.R. 213.

H.W. Arthurs

anti-centralist tendencies and to facilitate the creation of a distinctive, national version of the Canadian welfare state; that such strategies have now pretty much run their course; and that there is neither the political will nor the constitutional way to resuscitate them. In that sense, we are back to where we were 50 or 100 years ago: with constitutional doctrines and politics preventing action by the only level of government realistically capable of action.

Juridification: The Role of the Courts in the Disempowerment of the Canadian State

In another sense, however, we are not merely back where we were; we are even further behind. All levels of government, and both the executive and legislative branches, are now subject to new, far-reaching and intrusive forms of judicial oversight.

The most authoritative form of judicial review is based on the Charter. The Charter is supposed to force government to behave more fairly and respectfully to citizens and to enhance their ability to engage in political and other activities designed to change government policy. But things have not quite worked out that way. There is at least some evidence to suggest that the transformative potential of the Charter has been overrated (Rosenberg, 1991; Bogart, 1994). And even when Charter decisions have taken hold — say those guaranteeing due process for accused persons, prisoners, refugees and immigrants[55] — their effect may well have been to shift the shrinking human and material resources of government departments from the provision of substantive benefits to the construction of more elegant procedures. By contrast, when workers, welfare recipients or ordinary citizens have sought to use the Charter to protect themselves against neo-conservative policies, they have almost always either failed[56] or succeeded on circumstantial

---

[55]*Re Singh and Minister of Employment and Immigration,* [1985] 1 S.C.R. 177 (hereafter *Singh*); *Howard v. Presiding Officer of Inmate Disciplinary Court of Stony Mountain Institution,* [1984] 2 F.C. 642 (C.A.) Affirmed [1987] 2 S.C.R. 687; *R. v. Askov,* [1990] 2 S.C.R. 1199.

[56]For litigation arising out of Ontario's neo-conservative "common sense" revolution, see: *Masse v. Ontario (Ministry of Community and Social Services)* (1996), 134 D.L.R. (4th) 20 (Div. Ct.) (failed attempt to stop a 20% reduction in

grounds not related to Charter values.[57] On the other hand, ironically, privileged actors — corporations, professionals and judges — have been able to use the Charter occasionally to frustrate government interference with their particular economic interests[58] although they have not as yet persuaded the courts to invent explicit constitutional protection for property rights, despite being urged to do so by ingenious advocates (Mandel, 1994, 308 ff) and right-wing ideologues.

A second type of judicial review arises from challenges to government administrative action on non-constitutional grounds. The principle which underlies these challenges is a virtual tautology: government agencies do not

---

welfare benefits); *East York v A.G. Ontario* (1997) 34 O.R. (3d) 789 (failed attempt to stop creation of Toronto "mega-city"); *Falkiner v. Ontario (Ministry of Community and Social Services)*, (1997) 140 D.L.R.(4th) 115 (Ont. Div. Ct.) (failed attempt to prevent introduction of "man in the house rule" for welfare recipients); *Dunmore v. A.G. Ontario* (failed attempt to prevent repeal of Agricultural Labour Relations Act); but see *Ferrell v. Ontario (A.G.)*, (1997) 37 O.R. (3d) 287 (successful attempt to prevent retroactive capping of pay equity entitlements). For an earlier series of cases see: *Reference Re Public Service Employee Relations Act (Alberta)*, [1987] 1 S.C.R. 313; *PSAC v. Canada (A.G.)*, [1987] 1 S.C.R. 424; *RWDSU v. Government of Saskatchewan*, [1987] 1 S.C.R. (unsuccessful attempt to constitutionally ground collective labour rights).

[57]See e.g., *Ontario (Attorney General) v. Ontario Teachers' Federation*, [1998] 36 O.R. (3d) 367 (Gen. Div.) per MacPherson J. (injunction against illegal teachers' strike refused because of failure to exhaust statutory remedies and to show irreparable harm); *Ontario English Catholic Teachers' Assn.*, *supra* note 11 (injunction granted against implementation of school board restructuring because of interference with constitutional rights of Catholic Separate Schools).

[58]See e.g., *Hunter v. Southam Inc.*, [1984] 2 S.C.R. 145 (search and seizure provisions of the Combines Investigation Act held to violate s.8 of the Charter); *Wilson v. British Columbia (Medical Services Commission* (1988), 53 D.L.R. (4th) 171 (B.C.C.A.) and *Waldman v. British Columbia (Medical Services Commission)* (1997), 150 D.L.R. (4th) 405 (B.C.S.C.) (billing restrictions designed to redeploy doctors to under-serviced communities held to violate, respectively, s. 7 and ss. 6(2)(b) and s.15 of Charter); *RJR-Macdonald Inc. v. Canada (A.G.)*, [1995] 3 S.C.R. 31 (ban on tobacco advertising struck down as violation of s. 2(b) of Charter; *Judicial Salaries Reference*, *supra* note 9 (including judges within provincial public sector salary constraint policies held to be violation of "rule of law" preamble to the Constitution Act.)

have the right to act illegally. What defines legality is the statute which authorizes the agency's activities — the Labour Relations Act, the Immigration Act, the Securities Act. Of course, it hardly needs saying that such agencies almost never contravene clear provisions of their governing legislation. Rather they are found in contravention because the courts have "read in" presumptions which ground a variety of procedural and substantive rights — the right to a hearing, say, or the right not to be interfered with in one's business without a clear indication of legislative intent. In this way, much as in the Charter cases, the courts have created protections for privileged actors by forcing regulatory agencies to adopt ineffective and inappropriate court-like modes of operation and to accede to nineteenth-century common law presumptions about property rights. This is an odd outcome for a system which is supposed to be securing compliance with "the rule of law", since it was the notorious inability and unwillingness of courts to enforce regulatory statutes which led to the establishment of administrative boards and tribunals in the first place (Arthurs, 1979).

In various respects, judicial review of administrative action is more egregious than Charter review. Under the Charter, individual rights are defined in fairly explicit terms, and subject to "such reasonable limits prescribed by law as can be demonstrably justified in a free and democratic society". However, the substantive "rights" the courts have chosen to protect in administrative law proceedings — the right to carry on one's business or profession, for example — have no explicit constitutional foundation and exist only in the interstices of legislation; and reviewing judgements in the administrative sphere are often characterized by an intemperate rhetoric, ideological exuberance and doctrinal incoherence which exceeds that in Charter cases. Finally, for some time, the worst effects of judicial review of administrative action were mitigated by the possibility, conceded even by its proponents, that legislators could limit or exclude curial intervention by saying so plainly; but ultimately the Supreme Court held otherwise.[59]

Third, more and more individuals who consider themselves victims of government malfeasance or non-feasance have been claiming compensation in court proceedings. While governments have always made *ex gratia* payments to ease suffering or to placate public opinion, increasingly they are being forced to pay damages awarded by courts in private lawsuits based on breaches of contract or negligence by departments or agencies of government

---

[59]*Crevier v. A.G. Quebec*, [1981] 2 S.C.R. 220.

(Galloway, 1991; Reynolds and Hicks, 1992). In many ways this is a positive development. Citizens ought to receive compensation if they have been injured deliberately or negligently by government. However, some injuries are apparently more compensable than others. Government contractors, for example, can collect for defeated business expectations,[60] but welfare recipients cannot sue for defeated expectations that they will continue to receive social assistance.[61] When the justice system malfunctions, individuals may receive large damage awards,[62] *ex gratia* payments[63] or nothing at all.[64] When regulatory systems fail or government policies miscarry, some categories of victims receive full protection,[65] some are

---

[60]As occurred, for example, following cancellation by the federal Liberal government of the contract for private development of Pearson Airport in 1994. See *T1T2 Ltd. Partnership v. Canada* (1995), 23 O.R. (3d) 81 (Gen. Div.), appeal to the Ontario Court of Appeal dismissed on 23 May 1995; see (1995), 24 O.R. (3d) 546.

[61]See e.g., *Masse v. Ontario (Ministry of Community and Social Services)* (1996), 134 D.L.R. (4th) 20 (Div. Ct.) (failed attempt to stop a 20% reduction in welfare benefits).

[62]See e.g., *Jane Doe v. Toronto (Metropolitan) Commission of Police*, [1998] O.J. No. 2681 (QL).

[63]As in the notorious cases of Donald Marshall, Jr., Guy Paul Morin, David Milgaard and others. See generally, Kaiser (1989).

[64]For example, Nurse Susan Nelles, who was acquitted of murdering children in her care, was initially refused compensation and sued in tort; the case was ultimately settled and substantial damages were paid (Bourque, 1995).

[65]*Public Service Alliance of Canada v. Canada (Treasury Board)*, [1998] C.H.R.D. No. 6 (QL) (compensation for federal employees denied equal pay for work of equal value).

grudgingly given interim adjustment grants,[66] and some are told they must shoulder responsibility for their own plight.[67]

The randomness of these outcomes is hardly surprising, however, for anyone who has studied the inefficacy of private litigation as a way of dealing with issues of compensation for victims of other systemic failures including consumers injured by defective products, workers injured at work, or pedestrians and motorists injured in traffic accidents (see e.g., Garber, 1998). Experience shows that litigation-based compensation systems do not effectively deter misbehaviour and often produce the odd distributional outcome of rewarding lawyers and impoverishing claimants.

What, then, is the effect of these three instances of increased judicial activity on government's general capacity for action?

First, the rising cost of legal proceedings and damage awards must now be factored into the overall costs of government with two possible consequences: either total government expenditures are held constant, in which case some program expenditure must be sacrificed; or program expenditures are held constant, in which case total expenditures must rise, and the increased costs must be passed along to taxpayers. For example, compensation for victims of careless administrative practice in the blood supply system may well come out of already inadequate health-care budgets; if not, it will come from some other government program or from increased taxes. To be fair, a similar problem arises whenever significant compensation is paid to victims of government misconduct — land claims settlements and "healing funds" for Aboriginal peoples, say, or damages awarded by a federal Human Rights Tribunal to female civil servants denied "equal pay for work of equal value". In none of these cases can the budgetary and programmatic consequences be addressed in the course of the litigation itself. Nor in a sense should they be: after all, judicial intervention is intended not to determine the equities as between groups of citizens competing for the same public dollars but to ensure that government acts "lawfully".

But second, does judicial intervention in fact result in government behaving more "lawfully"? As indicated earlier, "lawfulness" is imprecise,

---

[66]For example, the Canadian government's costly ($1.9 billion) Atlantic Groundfish Strategy (TAGS), created after the shutdown of the Atlantic cod fishery in 1994. For a critical overview see Harris (1998).

[67]For example, unemployed workers displaced by NAFTA-related restructuring. See Howse (1992).

inchoate and essentially unknowable (to borrow a phrase) "until the blind lady weighs". Precisely because litigation outcomes are so difficult to predict, governments are likely to focus on strategies for dealing with uncertainty rather than on acting lawfully. One such strategy, in addition to the "shadow effects" mentioned earlier, is "juridification", the proliferation of structures designed to render decision making unimpeachable on procedural grounds. But juridification itself generates significant transaction costs: government action may be made more deliberate and procedurally perfect, but also slower, more expensive, less supple and less effective in advancing the public policies of the legislation (Arthurs, 1983). Thus, juridification ultimately affects outcomes, often to the prejudice of government and of the very clienteles sought to be protected under the legislation, if not the individuals directly regulated by it.[68] However, this and other "shadow effects" are distributed rather randomly. Overall, I would say, lawful and praiseworthy government initiatives are deterred about as often as government misbehaviour and illegality, and government agencies are as likely to spend resources and energy on forestalling judicial review as on fundamental re-examination of their *modus operandi* or policy goals.

However, there is a third consequence of the increase in anti-government litigation, in many ways the most important. Litigation has tutelary effects. The Charter, the other legal doctrines used in these cases, the discourse which they generate and the publicity they attract all shape citizens' views of law, of themselves and of their role in the polity. Here is where, I would argue, we have lost room to manoeuvre.

Citizens are coming to think of the state as something alien and hostile to be resisted by all lawful means, not as the main instrument for collective mobilization in the common interest. They are coming to think of themselves as bearers of rights which they can vindicate through individual or group litigation, rather than as participants in broad-based coalitions pursuing long-term changes in public policy goals through social action or the political process. Obviously, they are not entirely mistaken. The state has not always

---

[68]Immigration and refugee claimants are a case in point. Following the decision in *Re Singh and Minister of Employment and Immigration,* [1985] 1 S.C.R. 177, an elaborate tribunal system was constructed to ensure that they received "due process" ; it was promptly overwhelmed with cases, was attacked for both over- and underresponsiveness to its clientele, and has been in an almost perpetual state of "reform" ever since. The moral: procedural rectitude neither dissolves nor resolves conflict over outcomes.

been wise or benign; it is sometimes the cause of problems rather than the provider of solutions; and in some situations, lawsuits are the only recourse available. But in another sense, they are very wrong indeed. Litigation — even so-called "public interest" litigation — has its own deep logic, a logic which is based on a highly individualistic view of society. Litigation cannot and does not vindicate the rights and interests of most people, and it has very limited potential to bring about fundamental social change.

Litigation, after all, is conducted within a conservative, if not closed, intellectual system, not one that is accessible to new perspectives or disposed to absorb new ideas: judges and lawyers share a fairly narrow intellectual formation (some would say deformation) and professional socialization; their formal training in other disciplines is likely to be limited and obsolete; and in law practice as in politics they are likely to espouse the conventional attitudes and values of their mainstream, often privileged, clients and constituents. Moreover, the logic of litigation is circumstantial, not systemic: wrongs are ascertained, remedies are awarded and rights are declared on the basis of the particular facts and arguments presented on the record, not with a view to comprehensively assessing and reconciling conflicting social needs, institutional possibilities, financial implications and competing public policies. Litigation is definitive, not probabilistic: it speaks as if social facts can be ascertained and social consequences predicted with certainty, rather than with mere degrees of likelihood. Litigation is meant to be dispositive, not tentative and subject to revision: rights once declared are declared for all time, not until the next election, the next phase of Canada's economic or social development, or the appearance of new understandings about law and society. Litigation is expensive, and not easily or equally accessible: only those with considerable resources and fortitude can afford to litigate; privileged actors tend to be the most frequent and successful litigants; and on balance, social movements likely win no more than they lose. Finally, litigation is characterized by rituals of deference and delphic pronouncement: only the initiated can participate, only those at the top of the hierarchy can speak with authority and whatever they pronounce — however ill-considered — must be received respectfully and obeyed to the letter; it is not a process which easily accommodates rapid social change, political controversy or even robust academic critique.[69]

---

[69]In a speech to the Canadian Bar Association, Chief Justice Lamer recently mused that judges may need to begin to defend themselves more vigorously against criticism (*Globe and Mail*, 1998b).

For all of these reasons, litigation is by its very nature an inappropriate way to debate and decide important issues of public policy. It is especially inappropriate in Canada's present situation in which public policy making is already complicated by deepening regional dissensus, frustrated by powerful technologies and market forces, and in some key sectors, consigned to the ultimate arbitration of global or regional regimes. Increasing recourse to litigation has burdened government with transaction costs, distorted public policy and spending priorities and juridified decision making. And above all, litigation has created false prospects for individuals and groups, and diverted energies and resources away from broad-based political and social action. In all these ways, its increasing use has diminished the prospects for more vigorous and effective state action to protect the interests of ordinary citizens.

Populist Restructuring of Government

Effective state action, however, is not high on the agenda for the growing number of Canadians — in the Reform Party and elsewhere — who have espoused some form of populism. Populists classically prefer direct democracy over representative government, a position that leads many to mistrust government action in all of its manifestations and to generalized resentment of the politicians, civil servants, professionals and expert advisors who make government work. This mistrust and resentment, often reinforced by neo-conservatism or fuelled by regional grievances, drives a number of populist proposals for restructuring government.

Some of these proposals, such as freedom of information, are designed to increase the transparency of government, thereby permitting extra-parliamentary (and corporate) opposition to mobilize, often with the assistance — not to say at the instigation — of the media.[70] Referendum and initiative laws and provisions for recall petitions and elections are designed to force government to be more responsive to popular majorities as they may become manifest from time to time, not just during the run-up to periodic elections. With the proliferation of opportunities to mobilize voter

---

[70]Ironically, early U.S. studies showed that FOI legislation was invoked most aggressively by industry, third party intermediaries and law firms against regulatory agencies such as the Food and Drug Administration (86%) and the Environmental Protection Agency (83%), see Longworth (1986, pp. 103-108).

H.W. Arthurs

indignation around specific controversies, and a consequent shift in focus from long-term to short-term issues, voter interest in conventional party politics has waned. The humbling of elites, the discounting of their special policy perspectives and the removal of their privileges is a third populist strategy. Restrictions on the pay, benefits and pensions of members of legislative bodies, the establishment of open procedures for vetting appointments to the bench or to top public service posts, the publication of salaries in the civil service and para-public sector are all designed to reduce the social and attitudinal distance between elected representatives, high officials and experts on the one hand, and those on whose behalf they are meant to function, on the other. And finally, various populist measures seek to make legislative bodies more responsive to what is deemed to be the "real" electorate. Procedures, such as referenda, are to be put in place to ensure that governments do not sacrifice the interests of "ordinary" citizens to those of "special" groups such as women, native peoples or francophones. A Triple-E Senate is to be "elected" on a provincial basis in order to undermine the present national party system, "effective" so as to force government to respond to new regional and populist alignments, and "equal" so that voters in tiny and homogeneous (and therefore deserving) provinces will wield some large multiple of the power of voters in the largest and most diverse (and therefore least worthy) provinces. And at both the provincial and federal levels, constituency boundaries are to be drawn so as to permanently privilege down-to-earth commonsensical rural and suburban voters over cosmopolitan, and insufficiently populist, urban voters.[71]

Some of these proposals, such as the triple-E Senate, the approval of judicial appointments and recall elections, are clearly constitutional in character. Others, such as referenda, transparency legislation and the privileging of rural electorates, are only marginally less so. But in their present versions, these proposals all proceed from one particular version of constitutional politics — a version that seeks to put permanent obstacles in the way of state activism. In principle, there is no reason why populism ought to be aligned with neo-conservatism in this way. Indeed, the early populists in both western Canada and the western American states sought to mobilize passive governments against "the interests" — railroads, banks and

---

[71]On the day I wrote these words, I read the following: "Some people think the rural areas of this country still have too much electoral influence. If common sense and living in the real world mean anything, they don't have enough" (Gibson, 1998).

eastern manufacturers. Today, however, the momentum for populist restructuring of government seems to come almost always from the conservative, anti-state side of the political spectrum.[72] This is hardly surprising. For some 30 years, down to the 1970s, most governments across Canada pursued some variant of a social-democratic agenda. Attempts to curb government expenditure and activity and to humble the state and its cadres were therefore most likely to originate with those who favoured a reversal of this long-term tendency. Moreover, governments that are passive are less likely to arouse popular ire than governments that are active. The mere threat of a recall election or a referendum may be sufficient to encourage any government to take the path of least resistance and abandon action that it is contemplating — which, after all, is what is intended. And finally, even though the two must not be conflated, populism converges with neo-conservatism at a very practical level. Referenda and recall elections can usually be triggered only by a petition with a stipulated number of signatures. To cross the threshold of minimum support for such a petition costs money and requires organization as do subsequent referenda or election campaigns. Corporate interests, editorial writers and political parties which favour a radically reduced state have every reason to lend much-needed assistance to like-minded grassroots populists.

Complementing its passion for measures to enable ordinary citizens to keep government on a short leash, populism has an aversion to elites, to experts and to "special interests" which are perceived to enjoy undue influence over government. In the case of elites and experts, this aversion consists not only in reducing their privileges and immunities, but in many cases eliminating their influence altogether. Hence, populist governments — Ontario's Conservatives, for example — have systematically eliminated large numbers of expert and advisory bodies, including both such obvious targets as the Anti-Racism Secretariat and the Women's Secretariat, and more innocuous bodies such as the Law Reform Commission.[73] By doing so they have

---

[72]For an exception see the *Recall & Initiative Act*, R.S.B.C. 1996, c.398. This statute was enacted by a newly-elected NDP government which had promised to pass a recall statute in order to counter a similar campaign promise by its right-wing populist opponent, Social Credit.

[73]Statement of Hon. David Johnson, Chair of the Management Board, *Ontario Legislative Assembly Official Report of Debates (Hansard)* 36th Parliament, 1st session at 3145-47 (29 May 1996).

simultaneously achieved three objectives that have populist appeal. They have "dumbed down" — even lobotomized — government to the point where it has a diminished capacity to engage in activist strategies; they have eliminated channels of formal and informal consultation through which so-called elites (such as unions, ethnic groups and professions) had privileged access to policymakers; and they have dismantled structures, processes and traditions which to some extent enabled civil servants to resist the ideological impulses of politicians who claimed to be faithful interpreters of the will of the people. Each of these measures helps to ensure that "there is no alternative" to the present neo-conservative vision.

Thus, to the extent that Canada is considering, or has actually adopted, populist-inspired changes in its political processes and institutions, it is in the process of reducing its own room for manoeuvre. This is particularly true in connection with legislative provisions designed to require balanced budgets, to forbid tax increases which are not first approved by a referendum, or otherwise to make it difficult, if not impossible, to return to the presumed depravities of the Keynesian welfare state. As Lisa Philipps points out

> In the present reality ... fiscal limits are likely to be formulated, interpreted, and applied in ways which are economically foolish and socially regressive. The rare government with some political will to resist the neoliberal agenda will find that even a moderate fiscal limitation works to strengthen the ideological premises of restructuring discourse, making the retention of public services more difficult to defend. By constructing government as prone to extravagance and inefficiency, and therefore in need of external discipline and constraint, balanced budget laws affirm the prevailing valorization of market forces as the best mechanism for ordering social and economic affairs. In so doing, they inhibit attempts to address the really serious problems of rising insecurity and inequality and the unaccountability of private accumulations of wealth to the needs and interests of less privileged citizens. (Philipps, 1996, p. 273)

Finally, and oddly for a political tendency that claims to value democracy in its purest form, populism has also somehow managed to persuade "the people" that reducing the number of politicians and making them more remote from their constituents represents progress towards more responsive government. Again Ontario provides an interesting case study. The Conservative government — in its odiously named "Fewer Politicians

Act,"[74] — has reduced the number of provincial legislators by almost one-third, has eliminated an entire level of local government in the country's largest city,[75] and has consolidated all local school boards in the province into larger, more distant bodies while reducing the pay of their members to a pittance, and stripping them of taxing power, curricular control and the means of responding to special local conditions or the educational preferences of local communities.[76]

Such derogations from principles of accountability, such consolidation of central power, such disregard for local government, might be expected of proponents of an all-powerful state (if there were any). However, their imposition by self-professed populists requires a few words about the present-day relation between populism and neo-conservatism. In effect, populism speaks to means, neo-conservatism to ends. In the case of Ontario's Conservation government, there is no perceived tension between the two because the ends happen to be ones which most populists would endorse: the reduction of public expenditures and taxes. This is to be achieved, supposedly, by lowering expenditures on legislators, city councillors, school board members and civil servants, and especially by preventing school boards from spending "inordinate" amounts on teachers' salaries, administration, and curricular "frills". However, this reduction of expenditures, to underline the point, is to be achieved by distinctly non-populist, not to say anti-democratic, strategies. The enforcement of social discipline also seems to justify the sacrifice of means in order to achieve important ends. To combat the social harm wrought by unions, welfare recipients, refugee claimants, unruly youths and criminals requires the enactment and enforcement of stringent legislation, the expenditure of significant sums on workfare, policing and boot camps, and ultimately a high degree of state coercion. None of these means is necessarily congenial to populism, but the particular ends in view are apparently important and popular enough to warrant the sacrifice of woolly ideas about disempowering the state. In the "common sense" revolution, as in the marxist version, it seems that omelettes cannot be made without breaking eggs.

---

[74] *"Fewer Politicians Act, 1996"* S.O. 1996, c. 28.

[75] *City of Toronto Act, 1997*, S.O. 1997, c.2.

[76] *Education Quality Improvement Act,* S.O. 1997, c.31; *Fewer School Boards Act, 1997*, S.O. 1997, c. 3.

The result of Ontario's populist-cum-neo-conservative restructuring can thus be summed up as follows: electoral democracy has been diminished at all levels; the civil service has been demoralized and its professional character and technical capacities have been diluted; public consultative processes have been seriously truncated; important institutions through which the state develops policies and delivers services have been significantly undermined or abolished together. All of these changes have weakened the government's capacity for the kind of interventions that characterized Canada's postwar Keynesian welfare state. Moreover, they represent perm- anent impediments for future governments which might have an electoral mandate to be more interventionist, to initiate a new round of benign experiments in social engineering, to curb abuses of private power or to redistribute wealth. In this sense, to borrow again from the marxist lexicon of clichés, it may be that populism contains the seeds of its own destruction.

Ontario's story is, to some extent, the story of all Canadian governments.

Room to Manoeuvre

My argument, as I am all too aware, has involved me in a series of paradoxes or contradictions. First, because I have argued, in a sense, that everything is constitutional, I have left myself open to the retort that nothing is. Second, I have tried to show that constitutional outcomes are unpredict- able, that constitutional innovation is possible even where formal amendment is not, and that in any event, constitutions have less power to command than is generally understood. Logically, then, I ought to be less concerned about the constitutionalization of the two TINAs than I obviously am. And finally, having made the fatal concession that the two TINAs may have been either unavoidable or the least worst policy options available, and that Canada's present crisis in governance was of its own making, how can I complain that we have lost our room for manoeuvre? In this brief conclusion, I will try to resolve each of these three contradictions.

If Everything Is Constitutional, Nothing Is

I have tried to show, throughout this essay, that constitutions are not just the juridical constructs which organize modern states, but that they exist in the realm of social relations, culture and politics, and operate not just at the level of national polities, but also within transnational regimes, large corporations and civil society. My concerns about "constitutionalization", therefore, are not so much about changing the formal systems which prevail in any one of these sites as about the apparently permanent, simultaneous and mutually reinforcing adoption in all of them of *institutional changes* intended to ensure that Canadian public policy, for the foreseeable future, will be defined by the values of neo-conservatism, continentalism, decentralization, juridification and populism. Even if these are the right values for today, I argue, we ought not to adopt barriers to choosing others in the future. To do so, is to deny ourselves room to manoeuvre.

I am not chastened by the argument that Canada's Keynesian welfare state was similarly constitutionalized — by amendments to permit the introduction of old age pensions and unemployment insurance, by inter-governmental agreements and financial structures designed to support higher education and welfare, by the elevation of programs such as medicare into a defining symbol of our "social union", if not our national character. This earlier example of constitutionalization occurred when we had no Washington consensus, no global money markets, no NAFTA, no Charter, no emerging convention requiring constitutional referenda, no legal or polit-ical requirements for a balanced budget, no governments that deliberately crippled their public services and municipalities, no serious prospect of Quebec secession, and no appetite — or perhaps capacity — for obstruction by other provinces and constitutional constituencies. All of these develop-ments have bound the hands of government at the same time and in similar ways. That is why I believe that the current wave of institutional change is more truly "constitutional" — more deeply embedded — than any of its predecessors.

The Weakness of Constitutions

However, as I have argued at several points, constitutions do not operate as rigid barriers to change, as conventional legal and political analysis so often assumes. Why, then, worry about the present tendency to constitutionalize the two TINAs?

There are two answers to this objection. First, as I have tried to show, we are dealing with an unprecedented situation. The two TINAs have been accomplished not simply by changes in Canada's formal constitution, but also by changes in constitutional symbols and politics, in the constitution of civil society and in the thinking of strategically-located, knowledge-based elites. They have also been embedded in transnational regimes which are both public and private, formal and informal. And they converge with a host of other developments — juridification, technology and populism, amongst others — which like the two TINAs contribute to the disempowerment of the Canadian state. Many of the domestic actors who might otherwise be part of a process of constitutional change are likely to resist it because the new *status quo* is more congenial with their own interests, and many of the non-Canadian actors who have helped to create and perpetuate the new transnational regimes are simply not concerned about the long-term interests of a relatively marginal country like ours. That is the pessimistic answer.

But there are optimistic answers as well. The same transnational regimes in which Canada is so deeply implicated may well change quite dramatically, for reasons that have nothing to do with us.

I will not dwell on Utopian solutions. World government, effective global agencies with powers to protect the environment or human rights, even "social Europe" seems too far out of reach. At best, we might find ourselves enrolled in a working party of states engaged in gradually constructing a series of discrete transnational regimes — specialized, impermanent and imperfect — which would come to serve as proxies for some of the domestic regimes whose loss has characterized our recent experience (Trubek and Rothstein, 1998). This, after all, is the way the social democratic state itself was built: not from a master plan, but through almost accidental experiments, noble failures and pragmatic compromises. Our room for manoeuvre would no longer be ours alone, it is true: but there would be some room, some manoeuvre.

The most likely scenario is otherwise, however. Pendulum swings in American politics, for example, might produce a government that is more interventionist and/or isolationist than its recent predecessors. Destabilization of global financial markets and trade patterns might ultimately produce new transnational institutions that reinforce the notion of an activist Canadian state rather than making it appear anomalous. Social unrest in the leading economies, resulting from domestic economic, social or political crises, or from crises in international relations, may lead to modifications in the Anglo-American neo-conservative model of capitalism in the direction of the model of the European social market. No one wants to see the experience of the 1930s rehearsed on a global scale, but it should not be forgotten that the New Deal was born out of a desire to rescue capitalism from its own excesses, and that it triggered a virtual constitutional revolution (Barenberg, 1995). In any of these scenarios, or others we might imagine, in conditions not of its own making, Canada might find itself no longer quite so constrained by the constitution of the world economy, or the constitution of the North American economic space, or the constitution of our own civil society. Some countries are born with room for manoeuvre, some achieve room for manoeuvre, and some have room for manoeuvre thrust upon them. I suspect that Canada falls into the third category.

The Two TINAs Were Unavoidable, Constitutional Changes Have Been Voluntary, How Can We Complain?

My last observation, about Canada's very limited capacity to define its own future, anticipates my response to the argument that we cannot complain that we lack room to manoeuvre.

I do accept that what cannot be cured must be endured. It is quite possible that if we had resolutely rejected neo-conservatism and regional economic integration we might have experienced adverse consequences even more painful than those that accompanied the recent radical restructuring of our economy. Countries more affluent, powerful and politically sophisticated than ours appear to have accepted similar reasoning. But this does not mean that each episode of Canada's social, economic and fiscal policy making during the past 15 or 20 years could be described as a triumph of the will or the intellect, that social solidarity and social justice have been protected as much as possible in the circumstances, that we gained the greatest possible protection of our national interests when we negotiated NAFTA or that persevering with present policies with no respite or reassessment will be the best way ahead. More to the point, our ability to conduct such a reassessment has been seriously compromised by constitutional forces which we ourselves set in motion.

Amongst those forces none is more dangerous than Quebec secession. The rest of Canada (ROC) buffers Quebec — somewhat — against absorption into a world-wide anglophone culture and anglophone-dominated global and regional economy, both aggressively managed by the United States. Quebec makes the ROC politically, and to a lesser extent culturally, indigestible by the same aggressive regional hegemon. If Quebec and the ROC part company, neither will have even the very modest "room for manoeuvre" they now possess in common. However, the end of Canada — a self-inflicted wound, if ever there was one — is a serious possibility. We

H.W. Arthurs

underestimate Quebec's obsession with sovereignty if we imagine we can measure it in monthly polls or deflect it by appeals from charismatic personalities, advertising campaigns or litigation end-games. In my view, the most optimistic scenario — likely to be played out at one minute to midnight — is one in which we acknowledge that, even if we do not love or understand each other, we need each other. Symmetry of interests will ultimately hold the country together, if anything will. But symmetry of interests is unlikely to translate into symmetries of constitutional structures and powers as between Quebec and the other Canadian provinces. Until this inconvenient fact is taken on board by the ROC, we will continue to drift closer and closer to national disaster or, at the very least, we will be so paralysed by the prospect of it that we will be unable to address other issues. Alas, if it is taken on board at all, this is likely to happen only in the depths of a crisis.

Why can we not approach a constitutional settlement in a more deliberate and considered fashion? Partly, it is true, fundamental change is more likely to be achieved when the alternatives are too horrendous to contemplate and too imminent to ignore. Partly, however, our capacity to achieve a constitutional settlement has been impaired by the other constitutional developments mentioned above. The Canadian state has never performed up to its potential because of early judicial barriers to national policies and institutions, and because of political defection from the strategies designed to circumvent those barriers. Moreover, the current vogue for decentralization is closely associated with a determination to diminish the state's role in the economy, culture and social relations. This determination has increased the alienation of already marginalized constituencies — Charter constituencies and resource-dependent communities, for example — which have increasing difficulty in imagining themselves as potential stake-holders in an activist national state. And finally, the recent tendency to juridification has further disabled the state by narrowing the available modalities and increasing the legal risks and financial costs of state intervention. For all of these reasons, this is hardly the best moment to have to make the case that we need a strong and united Canadian state.

Moreover, the forum in which the case must be made has changed over the past 15 years. After Meech, after Charlottetown, after populism's success in eroding the moral, cultural and political authority of experts and governing elites, the case for Canada must now almost certainly be made in a national referendum. The odds are against approval of any constitutional settlement in such a referendum. If my "one-minute-to-midnight" scenario holds, it will almost certainly be held in the aftermath of a secret gathering of the much-maligned "men in suits" and following a foreign exchange and investment crisis inspired by political uncertainty. If the proposed settlement involves asymmetrical institutions and distributions of power, as I have predicted, it is likely to awaken the wrath of those who are fixated on a Canada of "equal citizens and equal provinces". If the referendum is held while we are still grappling with the dislocating effects of the two TINAs, as we are sure to be, it is very likely to become encumbered — as was the post-Charlottetown referendum — by accumulated grievances, discontents and insecurities which have little to do directly with issues of national unity. And finally, all of these potential difficulties in securing a majority vote in a referendum in favour of a new constitutional settlement will haunt efforts to reach such a settlement at the bargaining table.

To sum up, we have created constitutional norms, processes and institutions which work against the logic of a reinvented Canadian federation and a reinvigorated Canadian state. To that extent, we have reduced our collective capacity to respond to the limited opportunities for new policies which exist within the constraints imposed by the two TINAs and/or in whatever policy environment might prevail if their influence abates.

In all this there is considerable irony. As I have already indicated, we may one day witness the modification, perhaps the considerable revision, of the present global and regional regimes. Indeed, many elements in Canadian society are beginning to think critically about the two TINAs and creatively about what might succeed them. Some of these are members of the very elites that have been so supportive of the two TINAs until now. They include entrepreneurs and senior executives whose companies have been absorbed into larger and more centralized global enterprises; academics, artists, doctors and providers of various producer services who must go abroad if they wish to pursue challenging and rewarding careers; and members of the political class who find that their options have been reduced to the point where they have little to do but explain why they can do so little. And many non-elites: manufacturing workers who have lost their jobs to low wage foreign competition, clerical workers who have lost theirs to regional call centres and computer centres abroad, and small retailers whose customers have disappeared into big box stores with advantages derived from North American advertising and global sourcing. Even populism is losing its allure as its proponents exchange their hair shirts for designer clothes and "common sense" for high-handedness.

This does not mean that Canadian executives and professionals and workers and shopkeepers are suddenly going to link arms and march off into a millennial future which bears a strong resemblance to our social-democratic past. Many of the fundamentals of neo-conservatism will be with us for the foreseeable future — reduced taxes, state expenditures, regulation, public services and egalitarian aspirations. Much of the reality of our North American situation will remain unchanged: dependence on the United States for export markets and imported capital, consumer goods, popular culture and ideas. But that much said, I do feel that within the interstices of globalization and regional integration we can, will and must find a margin for creative choice. It is precisely because the margin will be so small, because our choices will always be so few and so critical, that we must recover the capacity for wise, well-informed, subtle and flexible decisions which we have gradually denied ourselves by constitutionalizing the current version of conventional wisdom.

References

Abbott, F.M. (1995), *Law and Policy of Regional Integration: The NAFTA and Western Hemispheric Integration in the World Trade Organization System* (Dordrecht, Boston and London: Martinus Nijhoff).

Adams, R.J. and R. Singh (1997), "Early Experience With NAFTA's Labour Side Accord", *Comparative Labor Law Journal* 18, 161.

Amnesty International (1998), *The International Criminal Court: 16 Fundamental Principles for a Just, Fair and Effective International Criminal Court*, Report No. IOR 40/12/98 (Geneva), May. Website: www.icc.amnesty.it

Arthurs, H.W. (1979), "Rethinking Administrative Law: A Slightly Dicey Business", *Osgoode Hall Law Journal* 17, 1.

_____ (1983), "Protection against Judicial Review", *Revue du Barreau* 43, 277.

_____ (1985), *Without the Law: Administrative Justice and Legal Pluralism in Nineteenth Century England* (Toronto: University of Toronto Press).

_____ (1997a), "'Mechanical Arts and Merchandise': Canadian Public Administration in the New Economy", *McGill Law Journal* 42, 29.

_____ (1997b), "Globalization of the Mind: Canadian Elites and the Restructuring of Legal Fields", *Canadian Journal of Law and Society* 12, 219.

_____ (1999), "The Hollowing Out of Corporate Canada?" in J. Jenson and B. Santos (eds.), *Navigating through Globalizations* (forthcoming).

Arthurs, H.W. and R. Kreklewich (1996), "Law, Legal Institutions, and the Legal Profession in the New Economy", *Osgoode Hall Law Journal* 34(1), 1.

Audley, J.J. (1997), *Green Politics and Global Trade: NAFTA and the Future of Environmental Politics* (Washington, DC: Georgetown University Press).

Barenberg, M. (1995), "Labor and Law in the New Global Economy: Through the Lens of United States Federalism", *Columbia Journal of Transnational Law* 33, 445.

Beck, A. (1994), "Is Law an Autopoietic System?" *Oxford Journal of Legal Studies* 14, 401.

Belley, J.G. (1993), "Contrat et citoyennetée. La politique d'achat régional d'une entreprise multinationale", *Cahier de Droit* 34, 1063.

Berman, A.G. (1993), "Subsidiarity and the European Community", in P.M. Lutzeler (ed.), *Europe after Maastricht* (Providence: Berghahn).

Bogart, W.A. (1994), *Courts and Country: The Limits of Litigation and the Social and Political Life of Canada* (Don Mills, ON: Oxford University Press).

Bothwell, R., I. Drummond and J. English (1984), *Canada Since 1945: Power, Politics, and Provincialism*, rev. ed. (Toronto: University of Toronto Press).

Bourque, P.C. (1995), "Constitutional Torts and Criminal Prosecutions: Making the Prosecutor Pay", *Criminal Law Quarterly* 37, 428.

Bowker, W.R. (1954), "The Honourable Horace Harvey, Chief Justice of Alberta", *Canadian Bar Review* 32, 933-937.

Brecher, J. and T. Costello (1994), *Global Village or Global Pillage: Economic Reconstruction from the Bottom Up* (Boston: South End Press).

Bryden, P., S. Davis and J. Russell, eds. (1994), *Protecting Rights and Freedoms: Essays on the Charter's Place in Canadian Political, Legal, and Intellectual Life* (Toronto: University of Toronto Press).

Campbell, B. (1993), "Restructuring the Economy: Canada into the Free Trade Era", in R. Grinspun and M. Cameron (eds.), *The Political Economy of North American Free Trade* (New York: St. Martin's Press).

Clarkson, S. (1998), "Somewhat Less than Meets the Eye: NAFTA as Constitution", unpublished paper delivered to the International Sociological Association, Research Committee on the Sociology of Law, Working Group on the Sociology of European Union Law, Montreal, July 27.

Compa, L. and T. Hinchliffe-Darricarrere (1995), "Enforcing International Labor Rights through Corporate Codes of Conduct", *Columbia Journal of Transnational Law* 33, 663.

Courchene, J. (1996), "Equalization Payments in the 1990s", in J. Courchene, D.W. Conklin and C.A. Gail (eds.), *Ottawa and the Distribution of Money and Power* (Toronto: Ontario Economic Council).

Deschênes, J. and C. Baar (1981), *Masters in their own House: A Study on the Independent Judicial Administration of the Courts* (Ottawa: Canadian Judicial Council).

Dezalay, Y. (1990), "The Big Bang and the Law: The Internationalization and Restructuration of the Legal Field", *Theory, Culture and Society* 7, 279.

Dezalay, Y. and B. Garth (1996), *Dealing in Virtue: International Commercial Arbitration and the Construction of a Transnational Legal Order* (Chicago: University of Chicago Press).

Dezalay, Y. and D. Sugarman, eds. (1995), *Professional Competition and Professional Power: Lawyers, Accountants and the Social Construction of Markets* (London: Routledge).

Dow Jones Service (1998), "IMF Delays Disbursements of Funds to Indonesia: Aid to be Held up until Political Situation Becomes Clearer", *The Globe and Mail,* May 21, B10.

Driedger, E. (1981), "The Spending Power", *Queen's Law Journal* 7, 124.

Drohan, M. (1998), "How the Net Killed the MAI", *The Globe and Mail,* April 29, A1.

Eggertson, L. (1997), "Trade Body Sinks Magazine Policy: Panel Turns Down Canadian Excise Tax, Sides with U.S. Against Postal Subsidies", *The Globe and Mail,* July 1, A1.

Forsey, E.A. (1984), "The Courts and the Conventions of the Constitution", *University of New Brunswick Law Journal* 33, 11.

Fraser, G. (1997), "Constitution Amended over Quebec Schools: Rideau Hall Ceremony Marks Official End for Province's Denominational Boards", *The Globe and Mail,* December 20, A16.

_____ (1998), "Newfoundland School Changes Proclaimed: Prime Minister Clearly Relieved by Amendment", *The Globe and Mail,* January 9, A3.

Friedland, M.L. (1995), *A Place Apart: Judicial Independence and Accountability in Canada* (Ottawa: Canadian Judicial Council).

Gagnon, A.G. (1991), "The Dynamics of Federal Inter-Governmental Relations: Delivery of Regional Development Programmes in Canada", *Regional Politics and Policy* 1, 1.

Galloway, D. (1991), "The Liability of Government: Just, or Just and Reasonable?" *Administrative Law Review* 44, 133.

Galtung, F., ed. (1994), *Accountability and Transparency in International Economic Development* (Berlin: Transparency International).

Garber, S. (1998), "Product Liability, Punitive Damages, Business Decisions and Economic Outcomes", *Wisconsin Law Review,* 237.

Gibson, G. (1998), "The Town that Gerry Furney Helped Build", *The Globe and Mail,* August 18, A15.

The Globe and Mail (1997), "PCB Export Ban Lifted", July 7, A4.

_____ (1998a), "Canada Criticized at WTO: U.S. Wants Details on Magazine Tax", March 26, B11.

_____ (1998b), "Antonio Lamer: Should Judges Hold their Tongues? The Chief Justice Worries that, by Keeping Silent, Judges are Helping Misconceptions to Spread", August 25, A13.

Grinspun, R. and R. Kreklewich (1994), "Consolidating Neoliberal Reforms: 'Free Trade' as a Conditioning Framework", *Studies in Political Economy* 43, 33.

Harris, M. (1998), *Lament for an Ocean: the Collapse of the Atlantic Cod Fishery* (Toronto: McClelland & Stewart).

Heard, A. (1991), *Canadian Constitutional Conventions: The Marriage of Law and Politics* (Toronto: Oxford University Press).

Herman, L.L. (1997), "Canada Loses Periodicals Case in WTO Appellate Body", *Legal Alert* 16, 33.

Howse, R. (1992), *The Case for Linking a Right to Adjustment with the NAFTA* (Toronto: Ontario Centre for International Business, University of Toronto).

Jenson, J. (1990), "Representations in Crisis: The Roots of Canada's Permeable Fordism", *Canadian Journal of Political Science* 23, 653.

Johnson, A.F. and P.J. Smith (1994), *Continuities and Discontinuities: The Political Economy of Social Welfare and Labour Market Policy in Canada* (Toronto: University of Toronto Press).

Johnson, J.R. (1994), *The North American Free Trade Agreement: A Comprehensive Guide* (Aurora, ON: Canada Law Book).

Johnson, P.-M. and A. Beaulieu (1996), *The Environment and NAFTA: Understanding and Implementing the New Continental Law* (Washington, DC: Island Press).

Kaiser, H.A. (1989), "Wrongful Conviction and Imprisonment: Towards an End to the Compensatory Obstacle Course", *The Windsor Yearbook of Access to Justice* 9, 96.

Keith, K. (1997), "Sovereignty: A Legal Perspective", in G. Wood and L. Leland (eds.), *State and Sovereignty: Is the State in Retreat?* (Dunedin, NZ: University of Otago Press).

Knopff, R. and F.L. Morton (1992), *Charter Politics* (Scarborough, ON: Nelson).

Krajewski, S. (1992), *Intrafirm Trade and the New North American Business Dynamic* (Ottawa: Conference Board of Canada).

La Forest, G.V. (1969), *Disallowance and Reservation of Provincial Legislation* (Ottawa: Queen's Printer).

_____ (1981), *The Allocation of Taxing Power Under the Canadian Constitution*, 2d ed. (Toronto: Canadian Tax Foundation).

Laskin, B. (1964), "Peace, Order and Good Government Re-Examined", in W.R. Lederman (ed.), *The Courts and the Canadian Constitution* (Toronto: McClelland & Stewart).

Lederman, W.R. (1987), "Judicial Independence and Court Reforms in Canada for the 1990s", *Queen's Law Journal* 11, 1.

Leycegui, B., W.B.P. Robson and S.D. Stein, eds. (1995), *Trading Punches: Trade Remedy Law and Disputes Under NAFTA* (Washington, DC: National Planning Association).

Longworth, E. (1986), "The Access to Information Act", LL.M. Thesis, Osgoode Hall Law School, York University.

MacDonald, V.C. (1957), "The Privy Council and the Canadian Constitution", *Canadian Bar Review* 29, 1021.

Mackie, R. (1998a), "Court Strikes Down School-Tax Reforms: Bill 160 Violates Catholics' Constitutional Rights, Judge Rules", *The Globe and Mail,* July 23, A1.

_____ (1998b), "Ontario Delays its Drive for Balanced Budget", *The Globe and Mail,* November 6, A1, A15.

Mandel, M. (1994), *The Charter of Rights and Legalization of Politics in Canada,* rev. ed. (Toronto: Thompson Educational Publishing).

Manfredi, C.P. (1992), *Judicial Power and the Charter: Canada and the Paradox of Liberal Constitutionalism* (Toronto: McClelland & Stewart).

Marx, H. (1970), "The Emergency Power & Civil Liberties in Canada", *McGill Law Journal* 16, 39.

McCarthy, S. (1997), "Ottawa Pushing for Investment Screening Rights: Document Shows Government Seeking Cultural Protection in New Trade Deal", *The Globe and Mail,* October 27, B1.

_____ (1998), "Threat of NAFTA Case Kills Canada's MMT Ban", *The Globe and Mail,* July 21, A1.

McKenna, B. (1998), "Seagram Tops 'Transnationality Index'", *The Globe and Mail,* November 11, B5.

McNish, J. (1998), "Running Canada Inc. by Remote Control", *The Globe and Mail,* September 14, A1, A8.

Meekison, J.P. (1983), "The Amending Formula", *Queen's Law Journal* 9, 99.

Monahan, P.J. (1995), *Storming the Pink Palace: The NDP in Power* (Toronto: Lester Publishing).

_____ (1997), *Constitutional Law* (Concord, ON: Irwin Law).

Monahan, P. and M. Finkelstein (1992), "The Charter of Rights and Public Policy in Canada", *Osgoode Hall Law Journal* 30, 501.

Muchlinski, P.T. (1997), "Global Bukowina Examined: Viewing the Multinational Enterprise as a Transnational Law-making Community", in G. Teubner (ed.), *Global Law Without a State* (Gateshead: Tyne & Wear).

Nissen, B. (forthcoming), *Alliances Across the Border: The U.S. Labor Movement in the Era of Globalization.*

Pastor, M. (1989), "Latin America, the Debt Crisis, and the International Monetary Fund", *Latin American Perspective* 16, 79.

Philipps, L. (1996), "The Rise of Balanced Budget Laws in Canada: Legislating Fiscal (Ir)responsibility", *Osgoode Hall Law Journal* 34(4), 681-740.

Pierson, C.G. (1960), *Canada and the Privy Council* (London: Stevens).

Pope, J., ed. (1996), *National Integrity Systems: The TI Source Book* (Washington, DC: Transparency International).

Putnam, R. (1993), *Making Democracy Work: Civic Traditions in Modern Italy* (Princeton: Princeton University Press).

Rae, B. (1996), *From Protest to Power* (Toronto: Penguin).

Ratelle, P. (1988), "La capacité de représentation du Québec dans les institutions internationales", *Revue Québecois du Droit International* 5, 169.

Reynolds, L.A. and D.A. Hicks (1992), "New Directions for the Civil Liability of Public Authorities in Canada", *Canadian Bar Review* 71, 1.

Robé, J.P. (1997), "Multinational Enterprises: The Constitution of a Pluralistic Legal Order", in G. Teubner (ed.), *Global Law Without a State* (Gateshead: Tyne & Wear).

Rosenberg, G.N. (1991), *The Hollow Hope: Can Courts Bring about Social Change?* (Chicago: University of Chicago Press).

Rowlands, D. (1994), "The Prospects for Regional Development in Canada", *Canadian Journal of Regional Science* 17, 373.

Ruggie, J. (1995), "International Regimes, Transactions, and Change: Embedded Liberalism in the Postwar Economic Order", in S.D. Krasner (ed.), *International Regimes* (Ithaca: Cornell University Press).

Russell, P. (1993), *Constitutional Odyssey: Can Canadians Become a Sovereign People?* (Toronto: University of Toronto Press).

Santos, B. (1995), *Toward a New Common Sense: Law, Science and Politics in the Paradigmatic Transition* (New York & London: Routledge).

Sassen, S. (1994), *Cities in a World Economy* (Thousand Oaks, CA: Pine Forge Press).

_____ (1995), "When the State Encounters a New Space Economy: The Case of Information Industries", *American University Journal of International Law and Policy* 10(2), 769-790.

Schneiderman, D. and K. Sutherland, eds. (1997), *Charting the Consequences: The Impact of Charter Rights on Canadian Law and Politics* (Toronto: University of Toronto Press).

Schott, J. (1994), *The Uruguay Round: An Assessment* (Washington, DC: Institute for International Economics).

Scoffield, H. (1998a), "PCB Export Ban Breached NAFTA, Firm Says: S.D. Myers Seeks $10-Million (U.S.) in Compensation from Ottawa for Lost Canadian Business", *The Globe and Mail,* September 1, B2.

_____ (1998b), "Labour Groups Challenge Echlin's Practices: Coalition to ask Ottawa to Invoke NAFTA Labour Deal Against Firm", *The Globe and Mail,* June 4, B5.

_____ (1998c), "Ottawa Approves Use of NAFTA Side Deal [for Mexcian Labour Dispute]", *The Globe and Mail,* June 6, B6.

Scott, F.R. (1937), "The Privy Council and Mr. Bennett's 'New Deal'", *Canadian Journal of Economics and Political Science* 3, 234-249.

Simeon, R. and I. Robinson (1990), *State, Society and the Development of Canadian Federalism* (Toronto: University of Toronto Press).

Smiley, D.V. (1970), *Constitutional Adaptation and Canadian Federalism Since 1945* (Ottawa: Information Canada).

Smith, A. (1963), *The Commerce Power in Canada and the United States* (Toronto: Butterworths).

Soberman, D.A. (1988), "Free Movement of Goods in Canada and the United States", *Cahiers de Droit* 29, 291.

Statistics Canada (1997), *Foreign Control in the Canadian Economy, CALURA Pt. 1, Corporations 1995* (Ottawa: Statistics Canada).

Stinson, M. (1998), "Dollar Plunges as Economy Stumbles", *The Globe and Mail*, October 1, A1, A11.

Storper, M. (1992), "The Limits to Globalization: Technology Districts and International Trade", *Economic Geography* 68(1), 60-93.

Teubner, G. (1993), *Law as an Autopoietic System* (Oxford: Blackwell).

_____ (1997), "Global Bukowina: Legal Pluralism in the World Society", in G. Teubner (ed.), *Global Law Without a State* (Gateshead: Tyne & Wear).

Transparency International (TI) (1995), *Annual Report 1995: Building a Global Coalition Against Corruption* (Berlin: TI). Website: www.transparency.de.

_____ (1996), *Annual Report 1996: Sharpening the Responses Against Global Corruption* (Berlin: TI).

_____ (1997), *Annual Report 1997: The Fight Against Corruption* (Berlin: TI).

Trubek, D.M. and J. Rothstein (1998), "Transnational Regimes and Advocacy in Industrial Relations: A Cure for Globalization?" paper presented to the Conference on Conflicts and Rights in Transnational Society, Courmayeur Mont Blanc, Italy.

Trubek, D.M. *et al.* (1994), "Global Restructuring and the Law: Studies of the Internationalization of Legal Fields and the Creation of Transnational Areas", *Case Western Reserve Law Review* 44(2), 407.

Vegh, G. (1996), "The Characterization of Barriers to International Trade under the Canadian Constitution", *Osgoode Hall Law Journal* 34, 355-374.

Walkom, T. (1994), *Rae Days* (Toronto: Key Porter).

Weintraub, S. (1994), "Current State of U.S.-Canada Economic Relations", *American Review of Canadian Studies* 24(4), 473-488.

Whyte, J.D. and W.R. Lederman (1992), *Canadian Constitutional Law* (Toronto: Butterworths).

Williamson, J., ed. (1983), *IMF Conditionality* (Washington, DC: Institute for International Economics).

Wolfe, D. (1994a), "The Wealth of Regions: Rethinking Industrial Policy", Working Paper No. 10 (Toronto: Canadian Institute for Advanced Research).

_____ (1994b), "Institutions of the New Economy: The Emerging Role of the Region State and Interstate Networking", paper presented at the Workshop of the Program in Law and Determinants of Social Ordering, Canadian Institute for Advanced Research, Toronto.

Wolfe, R. (1997), "Embedded Liberalism as a Transformation Curve: Comment", in T.J. Courchene (ed.), *The Nation State in a Global/Information Era: Policy Challenges,* The Bell Canada Papers on Economic and Public Policy, No. 4 (Kingston: John Deutsch Institute, Queen's University).

_____ (1998), "Regulatory Diplomacy and the WTO: Accommodating Domestic Regulation and the Trading System", paper presented to the ADM Network on Regulation and Compliance, Canadian Centre for Management Development, Ottawa.

Young, H. (1989), *The Iron Lady: A Biography of Margaret Thatcher* (New York: Farrar Straus Giroux).

Constitutionalizing Neo-Conservatism and Regional Economic Integration: Comments

Daniel Schwanen

Introduction

> Tout pouvoir vient d'une discipline, et se corrompt dès qu'on en néglige les contraintes. (Caillois)

The sweeping paper by Professor Arthurs seeks to show that a number of recent policy decisions, taking place under the banner of both globalization and "neo-conservative" policies, all serve to wittingly or unwittingly "constitutionalize" a right-wing agenda in Canada. These events are dubbed "TINA", in the sense that, as Margaret Thatcher said, "there is no alternative" to them. When combined with other factors examined in the paper — decentralization, juridification and populism — the TINAs engage Canadians on a path towards disempowerment and, furthermore, do so without any chance of return.

Indeed, constitutionalization is understood in this paper as comprising any development which imposes absolute, or at least severe, constraints on a future government which might seek to implement policies departing from the current agenda.

The paper provides fertile grounds for discussion and research. But as I hope my comments will elucidate, I find myself in disagreement with its main thesis: that we have painted ourselves into a corner offering no alternative. My comments here will focus on the two TINA's, with only occasional references to the other factors mentioned above.

There are three key reasons for my disagreement with the pessimistic view on Canada's room for manoeuvre which pervades much of the paper:

- First, Arthurs does not in my view succeed very well in explaining why he chooses to analyze the two TINAs, and not other types of constraints that are no less binding. Constraints on policy formation in Canada or any country, including self-imposed ones, are not, after all, a new phenomenon: Why would we not be able to deal with them in this case?

- Second, new constraints must be viewed in light of the changing technological, commercial and even demographic environment. Such changes fall under Arthurs' rubric of "generic" constraints, and hence fall outside the scope of "constitutionalizing" events as described in this study, which are defined as "specific" to a time and place. But I argue that new "time and place" constraints such as trade agreements or reduced budgetary deficits, may actually be a way for Canada to manage or reduce the constraining impact of "generic" events, over which we have little control, and hence actually expand rather than reduce our room for manoeuvre.

- Third, I take issue with the description in the paper of how binding the constraints really have been on policy formulation in Canada since the early 1980s, suggesting that while they have had a real impact, they may not have been as "constitutionalizing" as described in the paper.

I will examine these three elements in turn. In conclusion, I argue that complaining about new constraints rings somewhat hollow when we make poor use of our existing room to manoeuvre to begin with, and that the debate should focus less on constraints, self-imposed or otherwise, that attach to certain policy instruments (as a result, for example, of trade agreements), and more on whether or not constraints on specific policies truly hinder us in reaching our overarching policy objectives.

Daniel Schwanen

Focus on some Constraints, but not on Others

For Arthurs, "constitutionalization" means a process by which future policies will be constrained. The process is not only defined by formal agreements, be they actual constitutions or treaties, but also by the less formal interaction of and arrangements between many actors — governments, unions, business interests, political groups — which evolve as a result of the need to manage interdependence, or of commonality of interests, among other factors.

According to the paper, both the North American Free Trade Agreement (NAFTA) and the "neo-conservative" agenda apparently being pursued by Canadian authorities, represent "constitutionalizing" processes in that sense: "we are treating the two TINAs not just as the parameters of present policies ... but as prime determinants of future action".

It seems to me that the main fault of this characterization is that while it may be sensible to include a whole series of constraining choices under the "constitutional" rubric, the analytical power of such a sweeping definition surely must be weak. So many past events in Canada's history and in the policy choices we have made can fall under it, that it could easily encompass many dozens of events and decisions that constrain our choices today. In that context, it is easy (for anyone) to complain about the "constitutionalization" of choices one disagrees with, while remaining silent on similar constraining effects of other policies.

Take an actual constitutional example: the constitutionalization of equalization in Canada in 1982, precisely during the rise of Thatcherism as a global phenomenon (which Arthurs sees as being at the origin of the TINAs). Surely, one does not need to enter a debate about the merit of so entrenching equalization to see that doing it was meant to be of momentous significance, in that it constrains Parliament in deciding future redistributive policies between regions. The point is that every government with a significant tenure leaves its imprint on a country, which does have the impact of closing the door to other choices, or at least making reversals difficult.

Admittedly, some actions may be more constraining than others, but the paper leaves the reader with the (in my view) incorrect impression that only right-wing agendas get entrenched (or "constitutionalized"), for the woe of future generations. Let us look more closely at Arthurs' definition of constitutionalization: "It is in this sense — by defining what is legitimate, thinkable, feasible — that constitutional politics tend to fix the limits of debate and foreclose straightforward, if controversial, changes in current policies." Another fact which would fit this definition is the rapid accumulation of Canada's public debt in the 20 years leading to 1995, a "constitutionalizing" event, in the sense that all future governments are bound under the threat of severe penalty to use a huge portion of their tax revenues on interest payments, thereby limiting what was "legitimate, thinkable, feasible" in terms of policy. Indeed, the author acknowledges that our high public debt is one factor that would have made it difficult to resist the two TINAs. This is surely an admission that rapid peacetime accumulation of public debt has had constitutionalizing effects.

According to the author, the populist "mistrust and resentment" of those who make government work is "reinforced by neo-conservatism or fuelled by regional grievances". But, of course, a persuasive case can be made that such (admittedly debilitating) "mistrust and resentment" has been fuelled instead by the growing gap between taxes paid and services obtained, or regional favouritism in public expenditures. Through choices we have made in our education system, we have also "constitutionalized" ignorance of our history in much of the population, even the well-educated, with measurable consequences on our political choices.

These constraints, hardly of a neo-conservatist facture, will clearly impact many generations of Canadians, and constrain future governments far more, in my view, than the extent to which the reforms of the Harris government in Ontario will prevent a future government to be more "interventionist, to initiate a new round of benign experiments in social engineering, to curb abuses of private power". In short, severe constraints on future policies can hardly be said to be specific to the neo-conservatist agenda.

New Constraints Can Be Liberating

What might seem like a self-contained "constraint" may, viewed in a more global and dynamic setting, not be as binding as first thought and may, indeed, create options rather than foreclose them. New "generic constraints" emerge all the time, and must be dealt with in ways that may seem to impose new "time and place" constraints, but in reality can make the best out of a new situation. Furthermore, a constraint must be viewed in dynamic terms: constraining ourselves in the present may result in a richer menu of options in the future. Constraints therefore must be evaluated in view of the doors which respecting them open up (and which would not be opened if the constraint was not respected).

To provide an obvious example, it is apparent that technology has brought the world together much more surely than trade agreements, which often in fact respond to rather than usher in new technological and commercial realities. Arthurs states, accurately, that

> in the globalized economy, the sovereignty of all states remains in principle unimpaired. But in reality, the "constitution" of the global economy — a mélange of treaties, state practices, commercial undertakings, technical standards, consultative processes, conventional behaviours and shared values and assumptions — establishes a normative order to which individual states are subordinated, both juridically and in a practical sense.

But given the constraints of technology and geography, which are surely "generic", is Canada really closing off its set of options by partaking of this system, indeed by helping to set its rules and to manage it? Or is it not in fact keeping more options open — for example, the option of cooperating with other countries on problems that would be intractable for a single nation, or the option of attracting and keeping talents and technologies in Canada, or even, by embracing the Internet, the option of using it to make Canada better known to Canadians and to others?

A useful, albeit simplistic, exercise would be to think of what Canada would have to do to "regain" a mythical "unimpaired" sovereignty in today's context (and, I suspect, in yesterday's) — we would, of course, become poor and very likely soon beg the United States to absorb us.

I would push the argument further and argue that there are other instances of the "virtual constitution" which Arthur decries which are not in fact "specific to our time and place", that is, something we can do something about, but "generic". Like every natural or social phenomenon, taxes and government programs cannot forever grow faster than the environment that sustains them. In that sense, there was bound to be sooner or later a stop to the relentless rise of the size of governments in Canada since the early 1960s, which is still being paid for through rising personal income taxes. And while halting the accumulation of public debt may seem the same as imposing a constraint on policy, it can also be seen as eventually helping us better afford the challenges posed by the unprecedented aging of our population.

In the same vein, turning again to the area of trade relations, the fact that we are exposed to retaliation by an injured party is surely not a "time and place" constraint, but a "generic" constraint, which has operated throughout history: countries that hurt us expose ourselves to retaliation, and vice versa. The outcome of this universal dynamic depends on factors such as the relative strength of the parties in any given dispute. In that context, trade agreements can loosen up the constraint by providing a more rules-based environment for the settling of disputes.

Likewise, is the "globalization of the mind", also bemoaned in the paper, a constraint or an asset? We travel, exchange, find such exchanges beneficial individually and collectively; and naturally structures emerge to further facilitate these exchanges. What about previous instances of "globalization of the mind": those spurred by the crusades, the age of enlightenment, the spread of scientific method, or the spread of socialism. Did they constrain options, or did they open new ones? And would the paper's description of the attraction of Canada's elites for things American, really have been that far out of place at earlier times in our history, pre-dating the NAFTA and neo-conservatism?

The "Binding" Constraints May not Really Be That

Happily, I think, we are not as constrained as Professor Arthurs' paper suggests. This can be seen by examining what has happened since Margaret Thatcher's "TINA". The author interprets this comment as meaning there is no alternative to lower taxes and to "radically diminished welfare programs". Remarkably, however, since the early 1980s taxes have risen substantially in Canada, and welfare programs have expanded. This empirical observation alone suggests that the constraints are not as binding as implied here — and they certainly do not seem to take the form of a constitution. The "activist state" hardly seems to need to be "revived" after all!

With taxes near an historical high in Canada, to say that "the problem [with using the federal spending power as a means to implement national policy] is that virtually all Canadian governments have lost their desire to tax and with it the willingness and capacity to spend" is surely a mischaracterization of the situation. Perhaps, after all, a closer look at levels of public debt burden and taxation in Canada might explain the "shrivelling" of public generosity, which has brought to a standstill the continued expansion of the welfare state, better than any other factor.

Even the NAFTA, which according to the author "exemplifies, entrenches and institutionalizes" neo-conservative policies and "marginalizes" deviant views, can also be used positively in that unions and environmental groups have learned to make extensive use of the NAFTA complaints mechanisms and are increasingly collaborating across border to that effect. And it is often forgotten that under the NAFTA, trade relations are still by and large governed by the principle of national treatment. Firms of whatever nationality operating in Canada have to comply with a wide range of domestic policies that may considerably differ from those of our neighbours to the south, including competition policy, environmental and labour standards, criminal law, international relations, the health care and pension systems, taxes, local regulations, etc.

Professor Arthurs seems to complain that the "NAFTA is neither anomalous nor time-limited. NAFTA, in other words, has ceased to be what it once was: the text of a treaty and an omnibus Act of Parliament, the expression of a transitory policy adopted by a particular government at a particular moment in time". But I do not remember anything in the treaty, or in myriad other constraining treaties and commitments which Canada has negotiated and signed as a sovereign nation, which said that the treaty was meant to be "transitory". While it is possible to withdraw from a treaty such as the NAFTA, no nation (including aboriginal nations) would wish to sign treaties with Ottawa if somehow Ottawa began to consider treaties as "expressions of transitory policies".

Regarding the actual impact of free trade agreements, it is a great paradox of the era following the Canada-U.S. Free Trade Agreement (FTA) and its successor the NAFTA, that Canadian nationalists, tireless critics of the presence of foreign corporations under a previous regime, now complain that Canadian corporate structures of transnational corporations (TNCs) have been "reduced in importance", or even that some of these firms have closed some of their Canadian operations under free trade. The truth is more complex: we cannot say that Canada is a "branch plant" economy anymore when CN buys Illinois Central Railroad, Teleglobe buys Excel, and Canadian foreign direct investment (FDI) abroad now mirrors that of foreign FDI in Canada. The point is that Canadians have other ambitions than simply "making the case to the head office" located in the United States, and that the past few years have seen some of these ambitions realized.

While it is obvious that the governance of Canadian subsidiaries has been undergoing changes, the evidence presented here that somehow Canada as a whole is being "hollowed out" of services and functions usually associated with a vibrant domestic corporate sector is weak. Indeed, when the author writes of the "attenuated presence" within Canada of "Canadian providers ... of legal, accounting, consulting, research, software and adver-tising services", one wonders from what database the observation is being drawn from. Since the coming into force of the FTA, for example, Canada's trade balance on commercial services has *improved* in absolute terms (the improvements have been particularly noticeable since the NAFTA's entry into force). When scaled for the overall volume of trade, the balance has deteriorated in only 4 of 16 categories of such commercial services: construc-tion, insurance, management services and advertising. It has improved in the 12 others, including architecture and engineering, research and development activities, computer and information services, and personal, cultural and recreational services. Where is the hollowing out?

Conclusion: Constrained Instruments versus Constrained Goals

In conclusion, it seems to me difficult to claim that we are being unduly constrained in pursuing our objectives as a country, when we have often in the past imposed such constraints upon ourselves, when we do not even use the room we have very well, and when so many new "specific" constraints, in the form of policy changes such as free trade and the elimination of the fiscal deficit, can enhance our room for manoeuvre in the face of more severe "generic" constraints posed by technology, a more integrated world, or the demographic challenge.

I wonder, in this context, whether the TINA concept is focusing too much on the "time and place" constraints, which may constrain the use of certain policy instruments, and not enough on whether our ability to reach policy objectives that garner a wide consensus among Canadians, or within Canadian jurisdictions, has been, in fact, seriously compromised. Specula-tions regarding what governments could or could not do under the NAFTA abound, but actual cases in which governments were prevented from imple-menting domestic policy objectives as a result of this or other trade agreements, when the measure could be reasonably linked to the objective pursued, are rare indeed. The evidence so far suggests that governments — legitimately — conserve a wide berth to legislate, regulate, and tax, in spite of apparently having lost their "room for manoeuvre".

Summary of Discussion

Hugh Thorburn shared Professor Arthurs' pessimistic assessment. One of the most serious factors limiting Canada's room to manoeuvre is an adversarial form of federalism, in which federal-provincial quarreling has been institutionalized. Germany and Austria are examples of more integrative federations. The German Länder have an integrated stake in national policy through the Upper House. Canada turned thumbs down on that notion of Senate reform and became seduced by the Triple-E Senate, which thankfully did not go ahead. We have to find a new representative federal-provincial council to resolve conflicts and move away from adversarialism.

Harry Arthurs seconded the call for more integrative machinery. But the populist ascendancy means that there must be a referendum to ratify any institutional change. Everyone loads their own institutional concerns onto any referendum process. So it is extraordinarily difficult to imagine moving in a more integrative direction at the moment. We may not be able to move until a "one minute to midnight" crisis. He also cautioned that we may not be able to transpose German institutions, which arose out of their special historical circumstances.

Tom Kent distinguished between Arthurs' two TINAs. Canada's location in North America is an immutable fact. But the neo-conservative consensus is not immutable. "There is no alternative" has been the cry of ideologues throughout the ages. The neo-conservative consensus is already breaking down. Canada's future problem will be how to deal with the breakdown of neo-conservatism, while we are still next to the United States where neo-conservatism may last longer than in the rest of the world. So we may soon have more room to manoeuvre in terms of ideology, but we will have to deal with an additional complication along the way.

Harry Arthurs agreed. Because our location in North America is immutable, our room for manoeuvre depends on the United States reviewing their attachment to neo-conservative ideology. *Daniel Schwanen* added that North American integration pre-dated the North American Free Trade Agreement (NAFTA) and neo-conservatism. But Canada has been so deeply implicated with the United States for such a long time that a common political culture knits important aspects of Canada and the United States together. Our room to manoeuvre in some of these areas will only expand when the United States begins to re-examine its own policies.

David Slater asked whether current circumstances could be viewed as another episode in a long cycle. In the late 1890s, there was a real concern about the future viability of Canada. This led to the national initiative to settle the west in the following decade. The 1920s were a conservative decade, but the economic crisis of the 1930s led to the Rowell-Sirois Commission and the postwar reconstruction agenda. If there were a serious world economic crisis, might there not be a rallying together for government to do things and to do things differently?

Harry Arthurs accepted that analysis and cited the article by Barenberg, who stressed the fact that until 1935 U.S. labour market policy was under the jurisdiction of U.S. states. Barenberg (1995) suggests that a similar crisis might lead once again to New Deal-style interventions to save capitalism from itself. More effective transnational institutions might be the outcome. Institutional inventiveness is often born out of crisis.

Robert Wolfe asked whether NAFTA and other bilateral regimes might be viewed in a more favourable light as giving Canada some leverage in the U.S. policy debate.

Harry Arthurs replied that it is difficult to influence U.S. policy when the lines of authority within the U.S. government are not clear. Allan Gotlieb has written that the most important job of the Canadian ambassador is to find out who controls policy.

William Watson was disturbed to hear about the end of neo-conservatism since taxes have been rising throughout this period. He questioned Arthurs' contention that NAFTA provisions could be used to sue Canadian governments over medicare. Quebec has introduced universal drug insurance and universal access to day care for children down to the age of three. No one has sued Quebec. Has any government anywhere in the world faced a trade challenge over medicare?

Harry Arthurs agreed that such a case has not been brought yet, but he also pointed to the exponential growth in strategic law suits. This is posing problems that governments have never had to deal with before. A medicare suit is no more fanciful than suing over the administration of the blood supply or suing over cancellation of the Pearson Airport deal. These types of law suits are proliferating everywhere. For example, domestic social policies in the United Kingdom are being challenged before the European Court of Justice and Human Rights Tribunal. The fact that an argument is fanciful and the case is illusory does not prevent a suit from being launched in order to gain leverage and bargaining counters.

Pierre-Paul Proulx had a more positive take on Arthurs' negative conclusions. What Arthurs sees as unnecessary constraints are necessary facts of life. However, necessary facts can be accommodated. Economic integration forces national governments to transfer powers up and down to fit the relevant economic space. Canada shares with Washington policies that we cannot cope with at the national level. Similarly, decentralization can be viewed as a positive, rather than negative, step allowing us to look for synergies and endogenous growth by getting players working together. Consensus on a deregulatory agenda for change would be a more positive outcome than Arthurs envisions.

Daniel Schwanen agreed that a lot of what national governments used to do is being lifted up to the multilateral level and that there is a positive side to this development. NAFTA gives us a voice. In NAFTA, we have one-third of the votes, which is more than we would have if we joined the United States. In some cases, we have imposed some constraints on ourselves. The debt constraint is constitutionalizing in the sense of being long-lasting. But this constraint was of our own making.

Richard Saillant suggested that the causal order may have been reversed. Constitutional political battles may be a symptom, rather than a cause, of the lack of consensus in civil society.

Geoffroy Groleau argued that, while international agreements may impose constraints, they also curb negative externalities generated by activist governments in the international arena. Do Canadians really want an activist state deciding what and with whom we should trade? We have had activist federal governments, but activism has not forged a national identity.

Peter Leslie cautioned against equating "constitutional" with "irreversible". There is also an important distinction between sovereignty and autonomy. Autonomy refers to policy capacity. Legal constraints are truly constitutional because they limit sovereignty. Different policy goals are associated with different constraints. Canadians need to find consensus on what we want to do and then think about where the constraints are.

Tom Courchene distinguished between goals and instruments. Canadians can still attain the goals that we have always had, but there are now constraints on the instruments. For example, Crown corporations were important instruments in the past, but have fallen into disuse. We need to find new instruments to achieve our goals. A fixed exchange rate is one possible new instrument. If we do not find appropriate instruments, we may end up with Canadians having more consumer sovereignty, but feeling that they have less sovereignty as citizens — in other words, a democracy deficit.

Harry Arthurs expressed his admiration of C.D. Howe, the man not the institute. Howe had a vision of Canada and the will to make it happen. He had a collective and national vision, not a local vision. Local visions were incorporated in and energized by his national vision. It was a vision borne out of the Depression and World War II and it was the making of Canada as a modern state. Not all of Howe's instruments are still with us, but some are.

Harry Arthurs closed the session by responding to some of the comments on his paper. He explained his use of the term "constitutional" as a metaphorical device as opposed to a literal or technical construct. He did not accept a neat distinction between legal or constitutional sovereignty and policy autonomy. There is more to the constitution than the actual constitution itself. We have been absorbing values — a process that he has called the globalization of the mind — which are gradually acquiring constitutional force as bedrock assumptions. But these assumptions may not survive forever. The constitutional assumptions of 1867 were transformed by changing values. We now need to focus on the underlying values that are being embedded into institutions. We need institutions that can capture debate and translate debate into effective policies by which we exercise our autonomy. While in theory it makes no difference whether national policies are generated from the periphery inwards or from the centre outwards, we cannot have a country where extreme differences in fundamental values prevent cohesion on national purposes and policies. He called for a true constitution residing in our capacity to come together for national purposes. Alas, this has been rendered more difficult by populism, juridification and decentralization.

Reference

Barenberg, M. (1995), "Labor and Law in the New Global Economy: Through the Lens of United States Federalism", *Columbia Journal of Transnational Law* 33, 445.

The "Culture" of Multinational Corporations and the Implications for Canada

Louis W. Pauly

Introduction

During the last few years of his long and fruitful life, I got to know Louis Rasminsky. In the course of research on a quite separate project from the one implicated in this paper, I met with him in his Ottawa apartment for long talks on his life in the international monetary arena. University of Toronto alumnus, prominent member of the economic and financial staff of the League of Nations, bridge-builder between the Americans and the British at Bretton Woods, Canada's first executive director at the International Monetary Fund (IMF), and exemplary governor of the Bank of Canada, Rasminsky represented for me what many have called the liberal internationalist vision of world order. Rasminsky's own vision was born of the hard and bitter experience of his generation. At the centre of that vision was an international economy, not a "global" one, fully integrated and superseding national and regional aspirations. It was an economy mainly constituted by linkages among distinctive national markets, linkages that would encourage mutual adjustment and political cooperation without compromising national independence. In other words, given overarching aspirations for international security and domestic economic growth, it was an economy that left as much manoeuvring room as possible for the separate states that comprised it.

Experience made Rasminsky a pragmatist, a cast of mind ideally suited for Canadian policy making during the postwar period, when the international economic system looked set to be reshaped completely by the rapid decline of Great Britain and the rapid rise of the United States. The two historic trends had, in fact, already become clearly evident at the time of the Bretton Woods meeting in 1944. Then and thereafter, the specific challenge for Rasminsky's generation of Canadian policymakers was to find the middle ground for Canada between its formerly privileged place as British dominion and its probable future position as satellite of the United States (Plumptre, 1977; Muirhead, 1999). The latter dimension of this dual challenge was the most daunting.

Even if he also enjoyed his winters in Florida after his retirement from public life, Rasminsky remained steadfast in the view that wise policy could win and hold a politically tolerable degree of autonomy for Canada. I remember asking him just last year if monetary union would follow free trade in North America, just as it had in Western Europe. He replied, quite simply, "God forbid. That marks exactly the road we have always sought to avoid." Economic interdependence *and* political independence were central to Rasminsky's liberal internationalist vision. Maintaining room to manoeuvre was not the means to an end, in such a context; it was the end of the international economic game itself. In turn, the peace and prosperity secured by a sound but not overweening international economy was to assist in the advancement of the agendas that nearly always had pride of place in democracies — domestic agendas.

The dynamics of expanding trade, increasingly supplemented and then overtaken by the motor force of foreign direct investment, provided the means for advancing the liberal internationalist vision. A system of pegged exchange rates was also central, but it proved impossible for some to maintain. Canada was one of the first industrial states to see increasingly flexible exchange rates as the handiest tool for accommodating the flows of short-term capital that initially oiled the trade and investment machine but eventually took on a life of their own. Rasminsky's death in September 1998 almost seemed to symbolize the opening of a new era, an era of reaction to where the liberal internationalist vision had apparently led Canada during the previous three decades.

My sense is that much of the reaction in Canada to contemporary economic turmoil, reaction commonly focused on the word "globalization", reflects obfuscation of the complexity of the postwar vision by the generation of Canadian leaders that succeeded Rasminsky's. A truly "global" economy, one characterized by complete specialization and deep integration across discrete political spaces, was only meant to be a metaphor. In more practical terms, it became a far-distant objective, useful for providing a general orientation to policy. It was not actually to be reached. "One-worldism" had been discredited during the interwar years. But the experience of those same years and the years that followed rendered national insularity anathema. The great economic powers of the postwar period certainly understood the nuanced position in between. Sometimes overtly but mainly through the practical interaction of principle, ideology, institutional structure and vested interest, the Americans, the Germans and the Japanese all developed policies that combined external economic engagement with the stout defence of internal social and political values. In advancing those policies, they never lost sight of the importance of maintaining national control at the core of their economies. In all three states, government and business leaders have been able to distinguish rhetoric from interest. "Globalization" in theory has never compromised decisions in practice to build and defend national systems of innovation.

This paper presents evidence on the contemporary organization and behaviour of multinational corporations based in the United States, Germany and Japan, evidence that does not prove but certainly makes plausible just such an argument.[1] In its conclusion, the paper speculates on the implications for countries like Canada. Let me preview that conclusion, and then demonstrate to you how it was reached.

---

[1]This paper draws directly on the findings reported in Doremus *et al.*, 1998; Pauly and Reich, 1997; and Keller and Pauly, 1998. The widest range of empirical support for the analysis is arrayed in the first source. Supplementary research has been facilitated by a grant from the Social Sciences and Humanities Research Council of Canada, the assistance of Jo-Anne Gestrin, and the critical comments of David Wolfe, Stephen Clarkson and Maureen Appel Molot. My collaborators and I have debated the policy issues raised by our findings for many years, both informally and in print, but before this paper none of us has attempted to draw out the implications for so-called "middle powers" like Canada. Agreement among us should therefore not be assumed. Finally, I intentionally pick up on a number of themes raised in the previous volume in the Bell Papers Series, Courchene, 1997.

Multinational Corporate Behaviour in the "Global" Economy

The most basic structures of states — the institutions and ideologies that condition dense networks linking societal actors and political authorities — continue decisively to differentiate American, Japanese and German multinationals (MNCs) from one another. That differentiation remains apparent even when multinationals of different origin operate in the same third markets, even within the same industrial sectors and especially when they encounter crises. We are not in a world where individual citizens, regardless of nationality, must now struggle against overwhelming odds to preserve democracy, social justice and personal prosperity in the face of a global corporate juggernaut. We remain in a world profoundly shaped by the struggle of national states and their societies to preserve crucial degrees of autonomy vis-à-vis one another. In that struggle, corporations are not simple tools of policy, but the world's leading corporations certainly remain reflections of deeper histories and distinctively different social purposes.

Corporate leaders, especially American corporate leaders, routinely proclaim something like the following message: "We are all subject to global market pressures now; capital will not stay where it is not well treated; unbridled foreign investment and burgeoning global financial markets mark the road to prosperity; Japan Inc. is doomed; the German social market economy cannot be sustained; small, more open economies are ahead of the curve. All industrial economies will eventually be as open, as trade-dependent, as foreign-investment dependent as Canada. The great task ahead is to build consensus-based multilateral institutions capable of constructively reinforcing the productive power of markets." But outside corporate boardrooms, few Americans seem to believe this, whether they live in Detroit or Seattle, or serve in Congress. I doubt, frankly, that many American corporate leaders actually believe this kind of rhetoric as they go about their day-to-day business activities. The vast contemporary expansion in corporate lobbying operations in Washington would seem to suggest some gap between image and reality. The same gap seems apparent as we witness American financial leaders rediscovering the importance of official lender-of-last-resort facilities. In other words, the national rootedness of corporations seems still to matter. National dominance in key industries seems still to matter. And international rules compatible with American preferences and traditions seem to matter most of all. Parallel preferences appear to be at work elsewhere.

Framed by theoretical and policy debates concerning the tension between global economic strategies and local political realities, three colleagues and I sought to examine the extent to which multinational corporations were actually moving away from their national moorings. We had the chance to take a series of fine-grained snap-shots of multinational corporate behaviour across the United States, Japan and Europe (mainly Germany) between 1992 and 1996. Our lenses focused on core aspects of the daily life of MNCs — corporate governance, long-term corporate financing, fundamental research and development, and the intimate linkage between direct investment and intra-firm trading activities. We developed and extended our snap-shots, using extensive time-series data from the U.S. Bureau of Economic Analysis and elsewhere. A general orientation to our work and a few highlights from our findings are provided below.

Corporate Governance and Long-Term Financing

Our findings with regard to patterns of corporate control and related mores of long-term financing directly support the kinds of arguments that other prominent students of corporate governance have made in recent years (Kester, 1992; Prowse, 1992; Roe, 1994; Shleifer and Vishny, 1997). Despite all the talk in Japan about the end of traditional systems of corporate governance, and despite all the articles in *The Economist* about an impending revolution in German corporate control, the actual situation is clear. Individual shareholders and their institutional agents remain centrally important in American MNCs, while banks and affiliated firms own Japanese MNCs, and German MNCs own one another. Independent board oversight of management remains limited in the United States, but can be quite extensive in Japan and Germany, especially during crises. Crisis points in the financial lives of corporations often tell us more about the true sources of control in corporations than do, for example, limited share issues in far-off equity markets. Recent crises in Japan, Germany and the United States led us to conclude as follows. Financial institutions retain a strong corporate monitoring role in Japan, a moderate role at the top end of German industry, and a very weak role in the United States.

Despite all the hype concerning cowboys from Goldman Sachs now riding the free range in Europe and East Asia, our research also led us to remain sceptical that hostile takeovers, especially hostile takeovers involving foreign buyers, will soon sweep through Germany or Japan and revolutionize existing norms of corporate control. Similarly, we doubt that the current financial debacle in Japan will inevitably lead to a radical move towards American-style openness, transparency and decartelization. In this regard, we looked very closely at the minimal shifting that has gone on during the past few turbulent years in cross-shareholding ratios among leading Japanese MNCs. The financial crisis of the late 1990s is forcing the Japanese system of corporate control to adapt, but the system itself looks remarkably resilient, at least within the leading *keiretsu*. Specific cross-shareholding mechanisms are under pressure, especially outside the *keiretsu*. It needs to be remembered, however, that cross-shareholding is only one element in a system still accurately labeled "alliance capitalism" (Gerlach, 1992). And even under serious financial constraints, it still remains far from clear that the system is unraveling. This is an important matter for follow-up empirical research, but it is important to remember that contemporary norms were shaped by intense economic, social and political crises in the late nineteenth and mid-twentieth centuries, crises which put the current turbulence in Japan and East Asia into perspective.

Innovation and Investment Systems

Our studies highlight a continuing correlation between patterns of corporate control and national patterns of technological innovation and investment. Innovation systems in the United States, Germany and Japan differ substantively. They differ in the style and focus of underlying national science and technology policies; in the distribution, locations and performance of research and development (R&D) funding; in the technological orientation of the industrial research base; and in the blend of corporate technology development and acquisition strategies. Although there are important interactions and interdependencies across national innovation systems, these systems endure as distinct and powerful institutional environments that shape the overseas investment and technology strategies of MNCs.

The world's leading industrial states have taken distinctly different paths to technological innovation. Direct and indirect government policies filtered through the idiosyncratic state structures that underlie distinctive corporate governance and financing structures explain much of this variation (Figure 1). Compared to Germany and Japan, for example, the United States, United Kingdom and France each devote notably large shares of government R&D

Figure 1: Government R&D Support, by Country and by Socio-Economic Objective

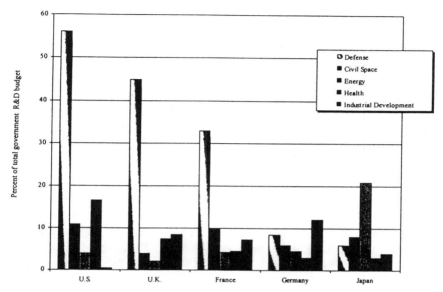

Data Source: NSF, *Science and Engineering Indicators* (1996), Appendix Table 4.32.

expenditures to national defence. The United States and France, moreover, each direct approximately 10% of their official R&D to civilian space applications. The U.S. stands out from all the others, however, in the unusually large share of public R&D resources it devotes to the military and to health, and the unusually small share it devotes to industrial development. German policy, conversely, emphasizes industrial development, while energy applications account for the largest share of public R&D resources in Japan.

Such national variations reflect historically-rooted differences in basic approaches to technological innovation itself, which in turn have influenced the technological orientation of industrial R&D. World War II and the Cold War that followed fundamentally shaped the U.S. orientation towards science and technology, legitimating certain types of governmental intervention in the cause of national security as well as a certain emphasis on big missions and big breakthroughs. In contrast, Germany's style of technology development is more intensely oriented towards diffusion. Government R&D programs and related institutions aim directly to facilitate incremental adaptation to technological change and the dissemination of new knowledge throughout the German economy. This system corresponds to Germany's industrial structure, with its large export-intensive industrial conglomerates and broad and dense supplier subcontracting relationships.

Although similar to Germany in this respect, Japan's producer-oriented innovation system is unique among the advanced industrial nations in its unusual combination of both mission-oriented and diffusion-oriented innovation styles. Grounded in a culture shaped by perceptions of vulnerability and external weakness, the system is characterized by the government's ability to direct national resources towards private sector technology development and diffusion without entirely subordinating market signals to administrative management. In addition, Japan's technological trajectory has depended to a substantial extent on acquiring technology developed abroad.

Certain interesting parallels to these national patterns of technological innovation exist in the policy arena within which corporate investment plans are made. Most direct investment remains concentrated in Organization for Economic Cooperation and Development (OECD) countries. In bilateral terms within that group, direct investment flows vary substantially. Direct investment by Japanese firms in the U.S. economy, for example, has for many decades far exceeded U.S. direct investment in Japan. By contrast, direct investment between the United States and Europe has been much closer in volume over the past two decades.

In part, variation in the direct investment relationship between the United States and both Germany and Japan reflects differences in the size and structure of each nation's economy, differences in the relationship between currencies over time, and a host of additional factors. But these patterns also reflect long-standing distinctions in national styles of direct investment. The United States traditionally has been more accommodating of direct investment inflows than either Japan or Germany, and of these three countries, Japan has clearly been the least accommodating. Our research surveys the structural and policy reasons for such differences, which represent one element of a complex set of factors that condition the behaviour of multinational firms. The bulk of our own empirical analysis, however, demonstrates how MNCs have been responding to this complexity in dissimilar ways. Their actual behaviour exhibits distinct styles of pursuing technology development abroad, investing in foreign markets, trading within or outside affiliated networks, and producing in local markets.

Louis W. Pauly

Corporate Research and Development

Evidence of the continuity of distinctive national styles of investment and innovation may not suggest the emergence of a truly global technology base, but might such an outcome not emerge from the spontaneous convergence of corporate decisions? Are the foundations of a global economy being laid by firms themselves, as competition pushes them towards similar investment and innovation strategies? The evidence suggests not. The recent rapid growth in foreign direct investment has certainly expanded the local presence of foreign corporations, and with that has come growth in overseas research and development and increasingly dense channels for technology transfer across national borders. Yet the magnitude of this trend remains quite small relative to the national innovative activities of the world's leading MNCs. Those firms, moreover, continue to innovate as well as acquire and transfer new knowledge in distinctively different ways. Across the world's leading MNCs, and especially across American, German and Japanese MNCs, unique national patterns can be seen in the three principal mechanisms through which MNCs extend technology across national borders: first, through overseas R&D activities; second, through the direct sale of technology in the form of intellectual property (in exchange for royalties and licence fees); and third, through strategic technology alliances between firms.

The aggregate volume of overseas R&D by corporate affiliates has increased substantially in recent years. It nevertheless continues to account for a relatively small fraction of the total corporate R&D. Even in industries with extensive global production and sourcing networks as well as high R&D intensity levels — such as electronics, computers and pharmaceuticals — R&D across the advanced industrial states remains fairly centralized. The pattern is much the same in less R&D-intensive industries, especially those where basic product technology varies little across national markets. In general, most MNCs centralize core research and product development in the home market, while research oriented towards customization and foreign production support tends over time to be conducted locally as affiliates become more deeply integrated into foreign markets. However, foreign affiliates that do conduct even this kind of R&D abroad do so at different levels and for different purposes.

Over the last decade, for example, R&D spending by foreign affiliates in the United States has increased substantially. Although small relative to total R&D funding by U.S. firms — $93 billion in the mid-1990s — the rate of increase in R&D spending by foreign affiliates has been much more rapid than that of total U.S. business R&D. This rapid increase began in the late 1980s, corresponding to a very active period of merger and acquisition activity by foreign investors. Nevertheless, whether established through acquisition or direct establishment, foreign affiliates based in different countries conduct different levels of R&D per unit of sales. Much of this difference is associated with the sectoral choices MNCs have made in their investments. The R&D intensity of German affiliates, for example, reflects in part the relatively high proportion of their investment directed to R&D-intensive manufacturing sectors, like chemicals and industrial machinery. By comparison, the low R&D intensity of Japanese affiliates in the United States reflects in part the relatively high percentage of Japanese MNC investment directed to wholesale trade.

Like the R&D activity of foreign affiliates in the United States, the overseas R&D by affiliates of U.S. MNCs has increased steadily over time. Moreover, the distribution of R&D expenditures by U.S. affiliates across countries mirrors the relative level of R&D spending by foreign affiliates in the United States. R&D by U.S. affiliates is concentrated in Germany and to a lesser extent the United Kingdom, with comparatively little R&D in France and Japan.

Viewed across countries, the aggregate R&D intensity of U.S. affiliates is relatively similar with one notable exception. U.S. affiliates in Germany consistently display substantially higher aggregate R&D intensity levels. Once again, this pattern conforms in part to differences in the concentration of U.S. MNC investment abroad in R&D-intensive manufacturing industries, such as transportation equipment, chemicals and allied products, electronic and other electric equipment and industrial machinery. But local circumstances in host markets also likely make a difference, for the R&D intensity of U.S. affiliates in a single industry often varies substantially across host countries. Trends in technology trade are consistent with such findings.

Technology Trade

Beyond overt corporate R&D programs, technology can be transferred across national borders in different forms and through various mechanisms, many of which are difficult to measure. For present purposes, a long and complex story boils down to this: except for the United States, the major OECD countries export roughly the same amount of technology as they import. By contrast, during the past two decades U.S. technology exports to its largest trading partners have consistently outweighed imports by a magnitude of between 400 and 600%. Although most of this trade takes place inside MNC networks, disaggregating the share that represents unaffiliated technology trade reveals significant variances across firms based in different countries. Japanese firms, in particular, buy an unusually large percentage of American technology through arm's-length transactions, much of it involving industrial process technologies.

Such findings suggest that corporate R&D behaviour, and the sectoral and strategic choices embedded therein, remain quite variable across home markets. But a global technology base can in theory be developing in other ways. In this context, international strategic alliances and related forms of intercorporate cooperation are often mentioned in the relevant literatures. We found, however, that most alliances remain concentrated in three sectors. Even in these sectors, moreover, we found striking regional and cross-regional differences (Figure 2). Most of the measurable strategic technology alliances undertaken over time and across technologies have involved U.S. firms and other U.S. firms. Of all possible permutations and combinations, the fastest growth in alliance formation has been among U.S. firms in information technology industries. Alliances between American and European firms have become more frequent, particularly in biotechnology and related sectors. By contrast, alliances involving Japanese firms remain relatively infrequent, with the exception of information technology alliances with U.S. firms.

These variations complement the cross-national portrait of MNC behaviour that emerges from R&D and technology trade patterns. In the broadest view, technology development by multinational firms appears concentrated, not diffuse: most of the R&D conducted by MNCs takes place in the home market, and most international technology trade flows from parents to their affiliates. Technology alliances across regions and across a range of sectors may someday break down this pattern, but there exists scant evidence that they are doing so already.

Although our study examines this phenomenon in more sectoral depth, we conclude that MNCs based in different states and operating in different sectors internationalize their technology development functions in different ways and to different degrees. Moreover, the nature and identity of the base itself continues to be mirrored in ultimate corporate behaviour. Such cross-national variations in foreign technology development strategies are similar in nature to cross-national variations in that complex of corporate operations that intimately link investment, intra-firm trade and production.

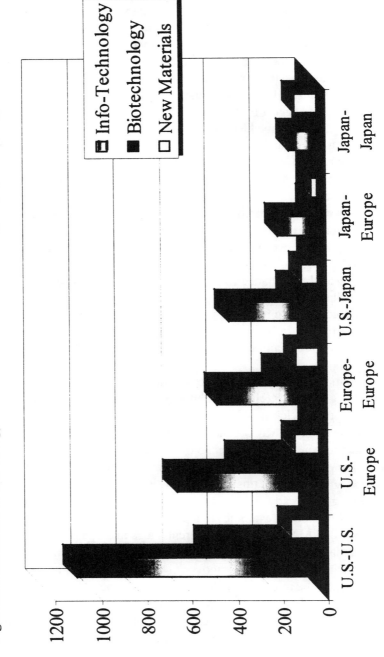

Figure 2: Distribution of Technology Alliances Between Economic Regions, by Technology

Legend:
- Info-Technology
- Biotechnology
- New Materials

Categories: U.S.-U.S., U.S.-Europe, Europe-Europe, U.S.-Japan, Japan-Europe, Japan-Japan

Y-axis: 0, 200, 400, 600, 800, 1000, 1200

Data Source: NSF, *Science and Engineering Indicators* (1996), p. 158.

Louis W. Pauly

Direct Investment and Intra-Firm Trading Strategies

Our research compares the investment and trading operations of MNCs along three closely-related dimensions: the composition of direct investment, the volume and direction of intra-firm trade, and the domestic content of production by foreign affiliates. These indicators measure the types of industries in which multinationals operate outside their home markets, the degree to which they trade within or outside their own internal networks, and the extent to which their foreign operations are integrated with host markets.

The evidence along each of these dimensions suggests that leading MNCs still tend to pursue distinct operational styles in foreign markets and that these styles continue to vary along national lines. American MNCs represent one style, operating largely in foreign manufacturing and financial sectors, using intra-firm trade (IFT) channels relatively moderately, and displaying a comparatively high degree of integration with local economies. Japanese MNCs represent a quite different style, operating largely in foreign wholesale trade sectors, using extensive IFT, and displaying a comparatively low level of integration with local economies. If American and Japanese MNCs are thereby depicted at opposite ends on a spectrum of corporate behaviour, German MNCs may be placed between the midpoint of that spectrum and the Japanese end. In passing, the evidence also suggests that French and British MNCs could be placed between the midpoint and the American end of the spectrum.

Direct investment in the United States by both German and Japanese firms has increased over time, although at different rates and with strikingly different compositions (U.S. Commerce Department, Bureau of Economic Analysis, annual series). Over the 1984-95 period, half of all German direct investment in the United States was in manufacturing industries, slightly higher than the average for all European countries (43%). Twenty-two percent went into the U.S. wholesale trade sector, compared to just 9% for all European countries. The balance went into the petroleum, financial services, real estate and other service sectors.

By comparison, over the same period of time, only 18% of Japanese direct investment in the United States went into manufacturing industries. The wholesale trade sector consistently accounted for the largest share of Japan's direct investment — on average, 41% from 1984 to 1995. Compared to German and other European investors, fairly large shares of Japanese direct investment also went into banking (10%) and services (9%).

The composition of foreign direct investment flowing from the United States to both Germany and Japan also differs, but far less substantially than for foreign investment flowing to the United States from Japan and Germany. The largest share of such flows from the United States has consistently been in the manufacturing sector in both cases, but it overwhelmed flows to all other sectors only in the German case. This sectoral distribution of direct investment is particularly significant across all three cases because of its effects on the operational style of MNCs outside their home bases. By design, MNC affiliates in foreign wholesale trading markets import very large shares of their total output, primarily finished goods for ultimate resale. Affiliates in manufacturing industries may or may not import large shares of their total output, as they can often purchase intermediate inputs (ranging from manufactured components to commodity-type bulk materials) from local suppliers.

In aggregate terms, distinctions in the sectoral distribution of direct investment suggest that affiliates of Japanese MNCs are much less likely than non-German European and U.S.-based MNCs to be deeply integrated in local markets. Foreign affiliates of U.S. firms, in turn, are more likely to be so integrated, and the affiliates of German MNCs would rank in the middle. National variations in trade flows associated with MNCs largely bear out a similar pattern. Time-series data for the mid-1980s to the mid-1990s indicates that IFT within Japanese corporate networks accounted for nearly two-thirds of total merchandise trade between the United States and Japan (U.S. Commerce Department, Bureau of Economic Analysis, annual series). Conversely, less than half of total bilateral merchandise trade between Germany and the United States was accounted for by IFT within German networks. The same data source indicates that IFT within American MNCs represents a small share of bilateral trade with Japan and Germany.

Further detail on the direction of trade within multinational corporations indicates that IFT, in all cases, flows primarily from parents to their foreign affiliates. Outward direct investment, quite simply, consistently creates trade. The relative magnitude and character of such IFT, however, varies considerably across MNCs based in different states. Most of the total IFT between the United States and both Japan and Germany flows from the foreign parent group to affiliates in the United States. Merchandise flows from German MNC parents to their affiliates in the United States are approximately twice the size of flows from U.S. parents to their affiliates in Germany, while merchandise flows from affiliates to parents are similarly low in both directions. In the case of U.S.-Japan trade, merchandise trade

Louis W. Pauly

flows from Japanese parents to their affiliates in the United States far outweigh any other IFT flow. In addition, unlike the U.S.-German trade relationship, IFT from Japanese affiliates in the United States to their foreign parents is over three times the volume of trade flows from U.S. parents to their affiliates in Japan.

Such cross-national variations in the volume and direction of IFT are consistent with variations in the volume and composition of direct investment. In short, cross-national variation in the sectoral composition of direct investment provides some basis for understanding the net tendency of affiliates from individual countries to trade within or outside MNC networks. Overseas investment by American, German and Japanese MNCs creates trade, but U.S. MNCs invest abroad in ways that tend to create less IFT than either German or especially Japanese MNCs.

The fact that MNCs from different countries engage foreign markets in different ways is further suggested when IFT is disaggregated. IFT flows from parents to their foreign affiliates generally fall into two categories: goods for resale without further manufacture (typically finished goods) and goods for further manufacture (typically intermediate goods). The mix of these two types of goods provides an approximate measure of the degree to which affiliates are integrated in local markets: the higher the share of imports for further manufacture, the more likely that the affiliate is adding value through local production. In this regard, our research indicated that U.S. affiliates were more likely to add value in foreign markets than other MNCs, collectively as well as individually. Mindful that such differences could reflect differences in the sectoral composition of investment or in other idiosyncrasies associated with local production, we pushed our analysis more deeply by looking at local content data. We found that even when MNCs from the United States, Germany and Japan were producing and competing in the same sector in the same host market they pursued quite distinctive strategies and achieved different outcomes in terms of local engagement.

The Endurance of National Corporate "Cultures"

Persistent divergence in corporate structure and strategy points directly to the endurance of national systems of innovation and investment. The term "corporate culture" is commonly used to refer to such distinctions, but I have in mind the different underlying ideologies and unique ways institutions are organized to frame the complex relationship between modern states and civil societies. Such domestic structures still appear decisively to shape the internal organization and external strategies of the world's leading multinational firms. The core activities of those firms, in turn, continue to have a vital influence on the creation and maintenance of national technological competencies. In other words, different ways of organizing the dynamic interaction between state and society continue to be mirrored directly in the key relationships that drive fundamental corporate operations. And in a world where the lion's share of actual technological innovation takes place within corporate networks, the nature of those relationships continues to vary along national lines. Not coincidentally, the strategic behaviour of multinational firms continues to vary widely (Table 1).

Three main explanations have been advanced to account for this variance. The first sees firm behaviour as most heavily influenced by the nature of the industrial sector. A second explanation emphasizes the importance of internal influences such as the maturity of main product lines. The third explanation underlines the essential malleability of the MNC and the determinative influence of the specific environment within which it operates. The most significant differences in corporate behaviour we observed in our research do not correlate with industrial sectors, although historical choices regarding the sectoral composition of key industrial competencies do have lagging effects. They are also not associated with industrial maturity. Moreover, they remain observable even within identical host environments. We argue, therefore, that the domestic structures within which firms are most firmly embedded offer the most plausible explanations of the aggregate differences we observe.

If we are right, the phenomenon of corporate multinationalization across the leading industrial states essentially remains a process through which still-national corporations, and the innovation and investment systems within which they remain rooted, are inserted into the home markets of their competitors. Those corporations then adapt themselves at the margin, but not at the core. Ultimately, leading multinational corporations continue to reflect that concatenation of variables commonly depicted as their dominant national cultures. Are their core operations also shaped decisively by a deep commitment to defending those cultures? Our evidence does not permit a definitive answer. We have traced correlations and not proved causation. But in this type of research, it is rarely possible to discover tight causal chains. It is obvious to us that the behaviour of the firm at any discrete point in time occurs at the intersection of a complex array of feedback loops. The weight of our evidence, and more importantly the sense we got from an intensive

Louis W. Pauly

Table 1: National Context and MNC Behaviour

Context	United States	Germany	Japan
Corporate governance	Short-term shareholding managers highly constrained by capital markets; risk-seeking financial-centred strategies	Managerial autonomy except during crises; little takeover risk; conservative and long-term strategies	Stable shareholders; network constrained managers; takeover risk only within network; aggressive market-share-centred strategies
Corporate financing	Diversified global funding; highly price sensitive	Concentrated, regional funding; limited price sensitivity	Concentrated; national funding; low price sensitivity
Innovation system	Mission-oriented policy environment; mixed public and private funding and R&D performance; strong linkages across higher education and industry; high foreign R&D funding; national focus on science sensitive, high-tech industries	Diffusion-oriented policy environment; industry-centred funding and R&D performance with moderate public sector role; strong interindustry linkages; low foreign funding of R&D; national focus on specialized supplier and scale-intensive medium-tech industries	Mixed policy environment (diffusion/mission); industry-centred funding and R&D performance, with low public sector role; strong interindustry linkages; very low foreign funding of R&D; national focus on supplier and scale-sensitive medium-tech industries
Investment system	Liberal; no constraints on inward or outward direct investment	Modified liberal; indirect constraints on inward, no constraints on outward	Resistant; formal and informal constraints on inward; selective constraints on outward
Behaviour			
Research and Development	Centralized; larger overseas presence (especially in Germany and UK); growing slowly; high R&D intensity of foreign affiliates (especially in Germany)	Centralized; moderate overseas presence growing steadily; high R&D intensity of foreign affiliates	Centralized; smaller, quickly growing overseas presence; low R&D intensity of foreign affiliates
Technology trade	Centralized; export-oriented (large trade surplus)	Centralized; exchange-oriented (balanced trade)	Centralized; acquisition-oriented (large unaffiliated imports, low-exports)
Technology alliances	Large number; mostly intra-U.S.	Moderate number, mostly Europe-U.S. and regional	Small number, mostly Japan-U.S.
Outward investment	Manufacturing, finance, services	Manufacturing, wholesale trade	Wholesale trade
Intra-firm trade	Moderate	Moderate to high	High
Local production	High integration	Moderate integration	Low integration

series of interviews with corporate executives in the United States, Japan and Germany, led us to conclude that, indeed, a commitment to defending distinctive national cultures was hard-wired into many of the world's leading MNCs.

Of course, German corporate managers will use the threat of moving jobs to foreign affiliates as a brake on the demands of their workforce back home. Of course, their Japanese counterparts will seek to diversify their sources of funding and to insulate themselves as much as possible from financial turbulence in their home market. Of course, American executives will use sophisticated transfer-pricing mechanisms to reduce taxes payable at home. But none of this necessarily or inevitably transforms the fundamental identities of their firms, their identities rooted in history, in national laws of incorporation, in the citizenship of senior management and directors and in the political and social relationships underpinning their head offices. Exports, the spread and diversification of production, service, and supplemental research operations abroad, and even the geographic diversification of workers and middle managers do not presage the inexorable rise of cosmopolitan corporate cultures. Indeed, the quite distinctive patterns of firm behaviour in external markets traced in our research suggest the opposite.

I must confess that a sense of cognitive dissonance dogged us at every step in our research. As we were doing our fieldwork, contrary views were trumpeted on the business pages of our leading newspapers on a daily basis. The consensus view in the academy was well expressed in a prominent book on corporate governance in Canada.

> In short, government itself has become a competitive business in the new global economy. In the past governments were monopolies. Businesses and people who did not like the government of the day could work to change it, but rarely could they simply take their business elsewhere. Today, they can and do. Governments are therefore under pressure themselves to become "competitive". Competitive government is not necessarily small government; rather it is government that provides services most people and businesses want at tax rates they are willing to pay. Understandably, selective subsidies financed by taxes levied on everybody are seldom seen to fit these categories. How then is government, robbed of its traditional tools, to promote the public interest in this new economic reality? ... The state should focus on providing the legal and institutional environment in which markets and firms are able to thrive. (Daniels and Morck, 1995a, p. 5)

Louis W. Pauly

In such a light, how could we account for the continuing massive effects of national defence expenditures on the U.S. corporate innovation system? How could we interpret the reluctance of Japanese MNCs to cut R&D expenditures even under severe financial pressure, or the freedom from the threat of hostile takeovers that appeared to permit overinvestment in R&D? How could we explain the fact that many cross-border mergers involving German MNCs entailed the extension of the relatively expensive German system of labour-management relations to the new joint entity? How could we understand the aggressive business development operations of the U.S. Embassy in Tokyo? How could we comprehend the internationally uncompetitive salaries of talented Japanese executives, the supine acceptance by German banks of a massive share of the transition costs associated with monetary union, and the evident close harmony between a globalist U.S. foreign policy in the post-Cold War period and the international business strategies of leading American firms?

We concluded that the common wisdom concerning "globalization" and the demise of what used to be called industrial policy were vastly overstated. Our study led us to emphasize, *inter alia*, the importance of new forms of interstate diplomacy to craft new and fairer rules to govern international economic competition in the years ahead; we saw little ground for the hope that market pressures would encourage the automatic adjustment of national rules, at least among the great industrial powers. We contended that the operations of globe-spanning MNCs did not open the path to straightforward mechanisms for rule creation; if anything, they militated against it. In the absence of collaborative market intervention by governments to craft such rules, we did not anticipate a world of more perfect competition and more convergent policies. We expected, instead, the rise of pressures to reinforce sanctuary markets in some countries and regions, the endurance of unwise environmental and labour standards in others, and the fostering of new kinds of cartel-like behaviour and tacit market-sharing arrangements among dominant firms.

Leading industrial states are in fact now involved in an ever-more intricate negotiation over the rules that will govern the future world economy. Certainly questions of grand strategy enter into that negotiation at times. In the main, however, and on the complex agenda posed by the spread of differentially structured MNCs, the negotiation has mainly taken a tacit form. It is an agenda framed by the mutual compatibility or incompatibility of relatively rigid, or very slowly changing, national governing structures and the dense networks of relationships that link states and societal actors at the core of business enterprises (Ostry, 1997). In the United States, Germany and Japan, the insertion of multinational firms into those relationships blurs the fundamentally national orientation of such structures and linkages only on the surface. In the wake of their expansion, however, domestic politics and international markets cannot now easily either be disengaged, nor can they be fully reconciled.

Our analysis suggests the possibility that increasing openness in the corporate markets of leading states will in the future be associated with enhanced official efforts to manage the consequences. Where such efforts fail, measured closure will be a likely response. We see a continuous stream of evidence suggesting that even as tariffs and other barriers to trade are formally dismantled, leading states remain unwilling to stand idly by when basic corporate, capital, and technological advantages are at risk. Leading states will likely be more, not less, involved in steering the industrial activities that take place within their borders and in building opportunities for their industries abroad. We are not saying that the MNCs of the future will be straightforward agents of national governments, like Crown corporations are in Canada. But we are saying that leading MNCs will likely remain deeply marked by national aspirations. The steering of future industrial evolution by political authorities in leading states may not be as overt or direct as it once was, but the subtle interaction, for example, of national budgetary expenditures, subnational government regulations, judicial tribunals, and key corporate strategies will be enough to decisively shape market outcomes. In such a context, the idea that efficient global markets will inexorably and automatically develop through the unhindered operations of multinational corporations is an illusion.

Our research suggests broad differences, even among leading industrial states, on policy fundamentals — the supervision of cartels and other forms of corporate networking, the purpose and direction of national innovation systems, and the nature of the intimate interaction of intra-firm trading and long-term investment strategies. If MNCs reflect such differences in their core structures and strategies, the kinds of nationalist economic policy orientations transparently witnessed early in the twentieth century are not precluded in the modern era of intensifying international competition, only transmuted. The issues thereby raised should not be obscured by the language of globalization. Markets are a tool of policy, not a substitute for it. Their intentional deepening in the post-World War II period was a key element in policies designed to limit the destructive force of xenophobic nationalism. Their liberalization in recent years also reflected deliberate

Louis W. Pauly

political projects. Any contemporary reaction to the consequences of that liberalization translates first and foremost into a political challenge. To assert that corporate markets now "rule" is to forget their origins and most fundamental purposes.

Implications and Speculations

Power may now be shifting within the leading economies of the capitalist world, but the evidence summarized in this paper does not suggest that it is shifting outward. The situation may be quite different, however, for national economies not in possession of a large, diversified, and rooted industrial base. From their point of view, frankly, power may indeed be shifting in the direction of a few leading states and increasingly concentrated commercial hierarchies durably nested within those states. Of course, less powerful states have always found their room for rule-differentiation to be more limited than it is for the more powerful. Such perceptions may help explain the apparently increasing efforts of many smaller states to negotiate adjustments and seek redress through regional and multilateral institutions. At the regional level, the best example of such continuous efforts to recalibrate such a balance of national interests is the European Union (Moravcsik, 1998). Such efforts are needlessly confused, however, by the language of globalization, language that implies inevitability and a sense of powerlessness in the face of a new and faceless form of imperialism. I am willing to concede, however, that such language can provide a useful tactical instrument for states that are capable of compensating for any deficiencies of size with the advantages of flexibility and intelligence. The first prerequisite to success, however, would be policymakers capable of differentiating between rhetoric and interest.

I claim no special expertise on the history or the contemporary political economy of Canada. Living, working and raising a family in the country, however, makes me more than an interested observer. As I reconsider the evidence surveyed in this paper, I am led to question the conventional wisdom concerning the current position of that political economy. Randall Morck of the Faculty of Business at the University of Alberta and Bernard Yeung of the Business School at the University of Michigan very succinctly sum up that wisdom as follows:

Broadly speaking, NAFTA has put competition for investment between the United States, Canada, and Mexico on purely economic terms.... In the new economy, government must be especially resistant to lobbying by special interest groups for government subsidies or other favours.... Multinationals are likely to keep activities that are vital to their competitiveness in the safest economic environment — usually the home country.... However, globalization means that multinationals are fast losing allegiance to their home countries. The economies of scale in centralizing head-office activities can be achieved elsewhere too.... Over time the tangible and intangible assets in a multinationals' home country will depreciate. In a more globalized economy, new assets may well be located wherever the best economic opportunities for the firm are to be found. How can Canada attract these high value-added head-office activities? Specifically, how do we attract spillover-generating activities that initiate a positive feedback loop of innovation stimulating more innovation? The fundamental issue is to *make the Canadian economy more amenable to Schumpeterian creative destruction.* (Morck and Yeung, 1995, pp. 442-450)

If one concludes that much of this wisdom is dubious, does one risk excommunication from the church of the modern market economy?

Canada built its industrial economy partly around branch plants and around resource-based firms encouraged incrementally to add local value to their operations. In such a context, the Canada-U.S. Free Trade Agreement, North American Free Trade Agreement and two decades of macroeconomic mismanagement (or, more charitably, misjudgement) that relegated us, along with Belgium and Italy, to the cellar of the government debt and debt-management league have indeed created a profound dilemma. Canada's original industrial strategy was pragmatic and realistic. In the wake of World War II and the rapid erosion of the legacy of the British empire, Canada needed new tools to build a competitive advantage for itself. A modified national policy did not have as its fundamental purpose the promotion of economic efficiency for its own sake, but the broadening of an economic base capable of holding a fractious society together internally while moderating the political effects of deepening interdependence with the less fractious but more assertive society to the south. This was some trick, but, in retrospect, the first generation of Canadian policymakers after World War II understood the challenge and mastered it. Their efforts were frequently inelegant, not always explicitly defensible, sometimes inconsistent, and sometimes opaque. They would not likely have ever formulated a clear answer to the now famous "Who is us?" question. And to maintain an exquisitely distinctive sense of identity, they built a state that could not adequately be labeled "strong" or "centralized", but which was capable of delivering conservative, balanced, flexible and relatively successful economic leadership.

That comparatively small states with ever more open markets require precisely this kind of leadership, and political structures capable of implementing "smart" policies, has long been recognized by practitioners and scholars alike (Harris, 1985). Effective, nimble states seem particularly necessary when a society is caught between national aspirations and regional economic realities (Courchene, 1998). This has always been Canada's dilemma, a dilemma compounded by the fact that there have always been at least two sets of "national" aspirations. But the recent rise in regionalism within the country as a whole has dangerously coincided an apparent decline in nation-building capabilities at the federal level.

In many ways, the combination of a confederal political structure, geographic size, and vulnerability to an overwhelmingly powerful neighbour rendered postwar Canada unique. I have often been struck, however, by certain comparisons which can be made with countries like Austria and the Netherlands. A few years ago, in fact, a large literature developed within the field of comparative political economy that attempted to draw out important parallels. In the Austrian case, for example, a similar challenge was faced during the past 50 years, namely the challenge of getting the most out of deepening economic interdependence with a powerful neighbour while maintaining a high degree of political independence. At the risk of oversimplifying a complex story, let me simply note that subsidy, explicit negotiation on the internal distribution of adjustment costs, and a fixed exchange rate with its largest trading partner were — and remain — central to the Austrian approach (Katzenstein, 1987). Canada, on the other hand, over the postwar period moved in precisely the opposite direction on all three counts. It is worth re-opening the debate on the economic *and* political impact of such different choices.

The analytical context for such a debate has recently been re-opened by work on "political culture". Under such a rubric, students of international relations and international political economy have once again begun exploring how transnational forces and exogenous shocks are managed differently in different places not only by concrete institutions of governance and social organization but also by the distinctively different cultural norms and orienting ideologies (Berger and Dore, 1996; Risse-Kappen, 1995; Milner and Keohane, 1996). Again, a similar wave of conceptualization a few years ago led some to argue that modern Canadian history made it necessary for the state to compensate for understandable weaknesses in

Canadian society. Conversely, the American state was widely viewed as weak by design in the midst of strong forces binding American society together. Put the two thoughts together, and an effective Canadian state seemed to hold the key to preventing the erosion and likely assimilation of Canadian society.

The distance between such a conclusion and the new orthodoxy well articulated above by Morck and Yeung is stark when it is framed in terms of old debates on industrial policy. In this regard, the evidence of this paper implies *either* the need for a second look at those debates *or* acceptance of the proposition that only leading states have the luxury of building and defending distinctive industrial bases in the era of "globalization". My own view is that the latter proposition is unjustified.

I recently reached a similar conclusion by another route in a separate research project from the one covered in this paper. In a study of the evolution of international monetary and financial institutions, I began with a straightforward summary of the classic theoretical trade-offs countries make between exchange rate stability, capital mobility and monetary autonomy (Pauly, 1997/98). Over the postwar period, I came to the unsurprising (and hardly original) conclusion that Canada wound up in the worst of all worlds when it combined a flexible exchange rate with fully open capital markets *and* fiscal imprudence. In short, it gained precious little of the policy autonomy promised by exchange rate flexibility when it allowed national and provincial indebtedness to get out of hand. In such a context, "industrial policy" became a whipping boy. The fact that the idea of assertive government policies self-consciously steering industrial development remains off the legitimate agenda for national discussion at least partly reflects the continuing challenge posed by a fiscal condition that remains critical in the only relative terms that matter, that is, relative to the United States. To leave it off the table for much longer, however, is to concede that the core challenge of postwar Canadian foreign economic policy has now somehow disappeared. It is to conclude that deepening economic interdependence with the United States no longer needs to be managed. It is to conclude, in short, that even if that deepening now portends integration, it does not matter.

Evidence of the quiet rejection of just such a conclusion is beginning to appear. At the end of a troubled decade, the obvious need is for a movement back towards a new balance between regionalism and national capabilities in the very structure of the Canadian state itself. The pendulum may now be swinging. For all the talk about globalization, as soon as the accounts of the Canadian federal government began registering the effects of a painful turning away from macroeconomic mismanagement, new programs immediately began to be designed to reinvest in the national innovation system and to understand how that system now fit into new regional settings. In such a context, the need to rebuild the national university system, and especially the deteriorating scientific infrastructure still centred on that system, immediately became manifest. Associated programs could, of course, be sold in terms of the still-prevailing orthodoxy, but in comparative historical terms they surely can also be interpreted as strategic in the classic sense of the term. Similarly, decisions on the future of the Canadian financial system, however obfuscating the language of globalization remains in this sphere, have revived old concerns about national control in a strategically important sector. Also once again coming onto the policy radar-screen is the equally ancient issue of how to build and nurture new, Canadian-based multinationals given the incentives in place for entrepreneurs to sell out, mainly to American firms, just at the point where they show the kind of promise that only a large capital injection can exploit (Wolfe, forthcoming; Rugman, *et al.*, 1997). Finally, new and profound questions are being raised as the working out of NAFTA rules impinges ever more intrusively into a range of domestic policy arenas not traditionally implicated by trade and investment regimes.

Nevertheless, new ideas needed to accommodate new facts. In the mid-1990s, for example, less than 1% of Canadian companies invested in research and development, and 25 companies accounted for half of all industrial R&D undertaken in the country. In addition, during the previous decade foreign direct investment (FDI) flows into Canada had doubled and Canadian firms invested more than ever in other countries. Nevertheless, the Canadian share of total FDI flows throughout the world had dropped during the 1990s from around 9% of the total to around 4.5%. Moreover, after dipping to around 63% in the early 1990s, the U.S. share of Canada's own stock of FDI had risen to 70% by 1997 (Investment Canada, 1998; Statistics Canada, 1997). And for all the celebratory talk surrounding an upsurge in Canadian direct investment abroad during the past decade, the notion that excessive economic dependence on the United States now combines dangerously with more open channels through which some Canadians can bail out of their own economy is beginning to find an audience.

Is a movement back towards "closure" the answer, whatever that might mean in some idealized version of Canadian history? No. Even if we could imagine what such a movement might mean, I doubt that its costs would be politically bearable. But is a movement back towards structural balance between centre and region, and a restoration of a degree of nimbleness at the centre too much to hope for? Imagination and a realistic appraisal of new facts will be required.

The research outlined above does not suggest a straightforward trajectory for Canadian policy. It does, however, suggest the legitimacy of bringing basic questions back to the fore. Ensuing debates may well turn on the idea of making the Canadian economy more amenable to Schumpeterian creative destruction. But my guess is that a new generation of pragmatic and non-ideological Canadians, who are not prepared to move to the United States either physically or virtually, have had enough destruction for now. Instead, they look set to rediscover the historical wellsprings of their own creativity. Facing leading states unwilling to play the international economic game by truly neutral rules or to cede real political authority to multilateral institutions, they will begin searching for ways to reopen options for themselves and create new opportunities for their children. Without making a big fuss about it, they will begin rebuilding the capacity of their state to steer industrial development within Canada and to influence the terms of deepening regional and international interdependence. Louis Rasminsky would not have been surprised.

References

Berger, S. and R. Dore, eds. (1996), *National Diversity and Global Capitalism* (Ithaca, NY: Cornell University Press).

Courchene, T.J. (1995-96), "Corporate Governance as Ideology", *Canadian Business Law Journal* 26, 202-210.

_____, ed. (1997), *The Nation State in a Global/Information Era: Policy Challenges*, Bell Canada Papers on Economic and Public Policy, Vol. 5 (Kingston: John Deutsch Institute, Queen's University).

_____ (1998), *From Heartland to North American Region State: The Social, Fiscal and Federal Evolution of Ontario* (Toronto: Faculty of Management, University of Toronto).

Daniels, R.J. and R. Morck (1995a), "Canadian Corporate Governance: The Challenge", in Daniels and Morck (eds.), *Corporate Decision-Making in Canada*, 5.

_____, eds. (1995b), *Corporate Decision-Making in Canada* (Calgary: University of Calgary Press).

Doremus, P.N., W.W. Keller, L.W. Pauly and S. Reich (1998), *The Myth of the Global Corporation* (Princeton: Princeton University Press).

Gerlach, M. (1992), *Alliance Capitalism* (Berkeley: University of California Press).

Harris, R.G. (1985), *Trade, Industrial Policy, and International Competition* (Toronto: University of Toronto Press).

Investment Canada (1998), *Study* (http://info.ic.gc.ca/cmb/welcomeic).

Katzenstein, P.J. (1987), *Small States in World Markets* (Ithaca, NY: Cornell University Press).

Keller, W.W. and L.W. Pauly (1998), *The Limits of 'Globalization': National Firms in World Markets*, MacArthur Transnational Economic Security Working Paper Series (Cambridge, MA: Center for International Studies, MIT and Weatherhead Center for International Affairs, Harvard).

Kester, W.C. (1992), "Governance, Contracting, and Investment Time Horizons", Working Paper 92-003 (Cambridge, MA: Harvard Business School).

Milner, H. and R. Keohane, eds. (1996), *Internationalization and Domestic Politics* (Cambridge: Cambridge University Press).

Moravcsik, A. (1998), *The Choice for Europe: Social Purpose and State Power from Messina to Maastricht* (Ithaca, NY: Cornell University Press).

Morck, R. and B. Yeung (1995), "The Corporate Governance of Multinationals", in Daniels and Morck (eds.), *Corporate Decision-Making in Canada*, 442-450.

Muirhead, B. (1999), *Against the Odds: The Public Life and Times of Louis Rasminsky* (Toronto: University of Toronto Press).

Ostry, S. (1997), *Who's on First? The Post-Cold War Trading System* (Chicago: University of Chicago Press).

Pauly, L.W. (1997/98), *Who Elected the Bankers? Surveillance and Control in the World Economy* (Ithaca, NY: Cornell University Press).

Pauly, L.W. and S. Reich (1997), "National Structures and Multinational Corporate Behavior: Enduring Differences in the Age of Globalization", *International Organization* 51(1), 1-30.

Plumptre, A.F.W. (1977), *Three Decades of Decision: Canada and the World Monetary System, 1944-75* (Toronto: McClelland & Stewart).

Prowse, S.D. (1992), "The Structure of Corporate Ownership in Japan", *The Journal of Finance* 47(3), 1121-1140.

Risse-Kappen, T., ed. (1995), *Bringing Transnational Relations Back In: Non-State Actors, Domestic Structures, and International Institutions* (Cambridge: Cambridge University Press).

Roe, M.J. (1994), *Strong Managers, Weak Owners: The Political Roots of American Corporate Finance* (Princeton: Princeton University Press).

Rugman, A., J. Kirton and J. Soloway (1997), "Canadian Corporate Strategy in a North American Region", *The American Review of Canadian Studies* 27(2), 199-219.

Shleifer, A. and R.W. Vishny (1997), "A Survey of Corporate Governance", *The Journal of Finance* 52(2), 737-783.

Statistics Canada (1997), *Canada's International Investment Position* (Ottawa: Supply and Services Canada).

U.S. Commerce Department, Bureau of Economic Analysis, *Survey of Current Business, Foreign Direct Investment in the United States*, annual series (Washington, DC: Government Printing Office).

_____, *U.S. Direct Investment Abroad*, annual series (Washington, DC: Government Printing Office).

Wolfe, D. (forthcoming), "The Role of Cooperative Industrial Policy in Canada and Ontario", in R.J. Braudo and J. MacIntosh (eds.), *Competitive Industrial Development in the Age of Information* (London: Routledge).

The "Culture" of Multinational Corporations and the Implications for Canada: Comments

Maureen Appel Molot

Introduction

Louis Pauly has written a provocative paper about multinational enterprise (MNE) behaviour which raises, in a very limited way in the Canadian context, an argument he and others have made elsewhere. His argument challenges some of the orthodoxy around globalization, in this instance that globalization is promoting/should be promoting greater similarity in the management decisions of, and reducing the differences among, MNEs of different home countries. He does this through a comparative review of the behaviour of American, Japanese and German MNEs with respect to internal governance and long-term financing structures, their approaches to research and development — in particular how much they do at home and how much abroad — and the kinds of foreign investments they make and the importance they attach to, and the character of, intra-firm trade. Without question we need to unpack the huge number of generalizations and expectations, many of them heavily value-laden, which have emerged around analyses of globalization. Pauly's thesis about the national distinctiveness of the MNEs based in the largest of the developed market economies is not without its own

The assistance of Rodney Lever in tracking down some of the information on Canadian MNEs is gratefully acknowledged.

values and implications for state behaviour. It is thus important to critically examine his analysis in terms of the degree of its novelty as well as where it might lead future research on MNEs, particularly those from smaller economies such as Canada's.

National Characteristics of MNEs

That there are differences in the modus operandi amongst MNEs, certainly MNEs of the largest developed market economies, is not in truth that surprising. A range of more general historical research as well as some of the literature on multinationals should alert us to this. Alexander Gerschenkron's (1962) argument in his *Economic Backwardness in Historical Perspective* presaged Pauly's thesis in some respects. Gerschenkron demonstrates that development does not follow the same pattern everywhere and that states play different roles in the development/industrialization process. The time period of industrialization in conjunction with the degree of differentiation of domestic structures, including the patterns of capital holding, generated differences in the role the state played in the industrialization process. Comparisons were made between Britain, the first industrializer, and Germany and Russia, among others. Although neither the United States nor Japan was included in the analysis we can perhaps extrapolate from our knowledge of history to the experiences of both these economies and appreciate the impact of different national histories on the "national character" of the countries' MNEs. In analyzing different state responses to specific international crises Gourevitch (1986) considers the constellation of domestic social forces as well as the structure of the state (and the international environment); societal actors adopt strategies that reflect their changing evaluation of opportunities and potential alliances as well as their relationship to state institutions.

In terms of the literature on MNEs, there are a number of studies that address issues similar to those considered by Pauly. Kogut, for example, suggests that MNEs are characterized by organizing principles that are reflective of their home countries and that "foreign direct investment is simply the transfer of organizing principles from one country to another" (1994, p. 121). In this instance he focuses more on the organization of production than management structure, but the two cannot be divorced. He notes that U.S. MNEs tend to be much larger than their Japanese counterparts, a function of different production practices, and that foreign direct investment is a means through which national practices are transferred

Maureen Appel Molot

abroad (ibid., p. 123). I will return to this subject below. In examining whether Japanese MNEs are different from western, primarily United States, ones, Westney suggests that firms can be differentiated on at least five characteristics: the number of home country managers in key positions in subsidiaries; high dependence on the parent company for decision making and support activities (including technology development); low level of sourcing in the host country (where sourcing occurs it is from suppliers brought from home); relatively low profitability; and a predisposition to establish multiple subsidiaries in the host country market, each more closely linked to its counterpart in Japan than to other onshore subsidiaries (Westney, 1994, pp. 259-261). These traits are an extension of the management structure of the Japanese parent firms. Westney then questions whether these differences will persist, and, like Kogut, concludes that the strong "country effect" on the structure and operations of Japanese MNEs may evolve, but will not disappear (ibid., p. 266). There may be some value, however, in controlling for comparisons between different home countries' MNEs by industry.

There is one other analysis of the structure and behaviour of MNEs that merits mention. It complements Pauly's thesis, although in critiquing "the myth of the 'global' corporation" it does not distinguish among MNEs by home country. Rather, it argues that collectively these economic behemoths are more tied to their home countries than much of the literature — and the firms' own claims — suggest. In *The Logic of International Restructuring*, Ruigrok and van Tulder assess the degree of internationalization of five key functional areas of management, sales, production, finance, research and development (R&D), and personnel management, across the *Fortune* list of 100 largest firms (1995, pp. 156-159). Three of these — production, finance and R&D — are discussed by Pauly, although not exactly in the same terms. Ruigrok and van Tulder find that large core firms[1] are most

---

[1]Ruigrok and van Tulder (1995, pp. 65-66) cite the following as characteristics of core firms:

    (a) They have sales of at least $1 billion U.S. This trait serves as the basis for the other characteristics.

    (b) A core firm *by definition* (italics in original) has a high degree of independence from other actors.

    (c) A core firm has direct access to domestic and foreign markets and/or customers through subsidiaries and sales offices or through third parties.

internationalized in terms of sales, although for many this means exports; ignoring important differences among sectors in the dependence on overseas sales, over 40 of the *Fortune 100* companies relied on foreign markets for half or more of their sales. Production was much less internationalized: 18 of the 100 MNEs on the *Fortune* list had the majority of their assets abroad and 19 had at least half their employees outside their home country. Firm financing remained primarily in the domestic arena; though many of the MNEs had some of their shares listed on foreign stock exchanges, only a few had more than 10% of their shares held outside their home country. Executive boards and management styles were dramatically national; few firms, regardless of their home base, had many, if any, foreigners on their management boards. And finally, like Pauly, these authors found that most firms did the bulk of their research and development at home. Ruigrok and van Tulder summarize that "on the basis of such overwhelming evidence at the firm level, it would be an understatement to conclude that national borders matter" (1995, p. 159). All firms, even the largest ones, remain embedded in their national jurisdictions as a result of history and the constraints imposed as a result of financing, labour and relations with governments.

If Pauly, like the other authors cited, makes a convincing argument that we need to be very careful in leaping from an analysis of a more internationalized economy to assumptions about similarity in MNE management styles, where does the debate go from here? Two directions come to the fore: first, how can we push/extend the thesis to advance our understanding of how MNEs operate in the current internationalized environment and second, how broad is its applicability? Although Pauly makes a very limited attempt to make his argument relevant to Canada, he does so

---

(d) A core firm owes its relative independence to its control over a series of core technologies and other strategic competencies particular to an industry or industrial activity and/or to its financial capacity.

(e) A core firm has an explicit vision of the organization and management of the value chain and the role external actors (banks, government) should play to facilitate the creation of value added.

(f) A core firm's vision of the organization of its industrial complex serves as an orientation point which it strives to accomplish.

(g) A core firm will often be a user-producer, meaning that it not only produces new products but it is also among the leading users of these technologies.

more in the realm of prescription than analysis. Using Pauly's categories of analysis, a brief effort at comparisons between American and Canadian MNEs will be made (see Table 1).

Advancing our Understanding of MNEs

In none of the work he has published on the national traits of MNEs (Pauly, 1999; Pauly and Reich, 1997; Doremus *et al.*, 1998), is there a discussion of methodology. We are simply presented with the results of the research. We do not know how many corporate executives were interviewed in any of the three countries, nor the size and product line(s) of the multinationals that comprised the research sample. The characteristics of MNEs listed suggest a very heavy emphasis on manufacturing, to the exclusion of the growing service sector. As will be argued below, at least in the Canadian case, size has an impact on management structure. Nor are we told when the MNEs studied began to invest abroad. Are there any within-country differences among MNEs; are all national MNEs in reality as similar as the argument suggests? Finally, the list of questions posed to corporate respondents as a result of which conclusions were drawn about corporate behaviour is not provided. Without some methodological disclosure, it is difficult to assess the meaning of results as well as to consider emulation of the approach in a different context.

The research generates a host of further questions. Are the various components of the national context and of MNE behaviour of equal importance in painting the canvass of national characteristics? Are there any differences in their weight amongst MNEs in each of the three home countries by the age or industry? Have patterns of intra-firm trade and local sourcing changed over the period in which the MNEs have been abroad? Has there been an increase in local sourcing as a result of preferential trading arrangements, with their requirements for regional content? Does length of time in a host country generate pressures for changes in perceptions and thus behaviour? What is the pattern of interaction with host country governments and does this evolve with the length in-country location? And are the patterns of operation consistent across industries? Following Westney (1994, p. 266) it might be useful to do some comparisons controlling for industry, despite the assertion that sector does not account for variation in firm behaviour (Doremus *et al.*, 1998, p. 9). Finally, while corporate governance issues are of interest, would our understanding of the importance of national context be enriched if attention had been directed to the analysis of the same decision across different national MNEs? If there is some growing similarity of production in some industries (such as just-in-time production), indicating that there may be some convergence in how major MNEs see the world, how important is this? In other words is it the outcome of governance that is key, that is, the operating decisions, or the way in which the decisions are made?

While it is dangerous to generalize from one industry, let me refer to some of my own research experience to comment on the behaviour of auto assemblers in the United States, both the Big Three,[2] who are characterized as the "insiders" in the industry, and the transplants, primarily Japanese but also European, who are the "outsiders" (Eden and Molot, 1993). The argument also has applicability to Canada, though for this country it has to be nuanced some because all of the auto assemblers are foreign owned. In a highly competitive oligopolistic industry all players are attempting to position themselves to capture the maximum amount of market share. The outsiders invest in the host country for market access and currency reasons and find themselves under increasing pressure to portray themselves as insiders. The historic insiders adopt a range of strategies to sharpen the insider-outsider distinction, including pressure for policies that initially might be costly for the outsiders, but eventually will result in outsider patterns of operation more similar to those of the insiders. Recalling the discussion by Pauly and others about the different sourcing patterns of Japanese MNEs in host countries and their greater reliance on imports, what is the experience in the auto industry?

First, component production and vehicle assembly now occur in so many locations that the assembler's name plate on a car does not reveal where the vehicle was put together; in other words, the "nationality", of cars, including those sold by the Big Three, is increasingly more difficult to determine. Second, while it is certainly true that the transplants, particularly, though not solely the Japanese, have brought some of their component producers with them, they have been consistently increasing their level of local sourcing in the United States and Canada, both from local parts suppliers and their home country parts producers who have located in North America either on their own or in partnership with host country firms. There are various causes for these changing sourcing patterns, the demands of just-in-time production, for example. But also significant are the content requirements of the North

---

[2] The research was done before the Daimler-Chrysler merger which has made the long-used term "Big Three" no longer appropriate.

Maureen Appel Molot

American Free Trade Agreement (NAFTA) (which will rise to 62.5% North American content by 2003). Given the high level of trade in finished vehicles in North America, assembly firms have a real incentive to expand local sourcing. Third, the number of strategic alliances in the industry has had a significant impact on production strategies; it is blurring status distinctions (the point made above about the difficulties of determining the nationality of a vehicle) and may well be having an impact on management practices. In this regard, it will be interesting to watch the merger between Chrysler and Daimler. Finally, in an effort to keep costs down and to remain competitive, all auto assemblers, to different degrees, are off-loading increasing amounts of engineering and design work to their major suppliers. In short, how are the realities in the auto industry shaping the decision-making patterns management practices of the major players in the industry, MNEs that have the United States, Germany and Japan as their home countries?

Applicability of Analysis to Canada

Pauly makes his argument with respect to the three largest developed market economies: the United States, Japan and Germany. How much of the impact of the argument is a function of national differences and how much relates to the number of MNEs that have their head offices in these particular economies? Would his analysis of national differences in the character of MNEs be so noteworthy if these economies were the home countries of only a few MNEs? Does it resonate elsewhere and in particular in Canada?

The literature on multinational corporations suggests that firms invest abroad for a range of reasons. These include: the search for raw materials; the search for market access (to serve new or expand existing markets, to follow customers, and/or to rationalize production); the search for cheaper production sites; the provision of support to other parts of the MNE already in the host country location; financial motivations; and risk-reduction opportunities (Eden, 1994a, pp. 225-230). These reasons for foreign investment apply across MNEs from all countries, although their importance will vary from one particular case to another, depending among other things on the firm's line of business and the structure and size of its home economy. Ruigrok and van Tulder (1995, p. 160), the OECD and the UN Conference on Trade and Development (UNCTAD) all suggest that MNEs from smaller economies are more internationalized than those from larger countries for reasons that seem obvious — smaller home markets and possibly narrower supply bases, with the need as a result to rely more heavily on foreign suppliers. MNEs from smaller economies also tend to have more of their assets/production abroad.[3] However, "many of them remain remarkably national" with respect to three important areas: they, like their counterparts from larger economies, tend to rely on domestic banks and are no more likely to have shares traded abroad; they still conduct the majority of the R&D at home; and they do not have many non-nationals on their boards (except when cross-national takeovers have occurred) (Ruigrok and van Tulder, 1995, pp. 160-162).

What do we know about Canadian MNEs that might allow us to begin to determine whether they exhibit distinctive national characteristics, in particular in comparison to those of American MNEs? How close do they approximate the pattern suggested for MNEs from smaller economies? Does looking abroad for opportunities alter national character? Is this an area where MNEs from smaller economies have to compromise perhaps more than their counterparts from the large economies?

Any analysis of MNEs in Canada is complicated by historic patterns of foreign ownership, since Canada was a significant host country for MNEs before many of our domestically based MNEs emerged. In fact, Canada was the first foreign location for a large number of American MNEs. When we list the largest firms in Canadian exports, for example, the top three exporters are the Big Three auto assemblers, fourth is IBM, and then comes the Canadian Wheat Board (*Globe and Mail*, 1998). In other words, of the five largest exporting firms in Canada, four are subsidiaries of MNEs and

---

[3]The *World Investment Report 1998* (UNCTAD, 1988, p. 45) list of the world's largest 100 corporations ranks them by transnationality, which is calculated as the average of ratios of foreign assets to total assets, foreign sales to total sales, and foreign employment to total employment. The conceptualization of the transnationality index is based on the dichotomy between foreign and home MNE activity and helps to assess the degree to which the activities and interests of MNEs are embedded in their home economies or abroad. The list of the ten "most transnational" MNEs is comprised of MNEs from smaller economies: Switzerland 3, Canada 2, Sweden 1, Switzerland-Sweden 1, Belgium 1, Netherlands-Br 1, France 1. The transnationality index for these ten MNEs ranges from 97.3% for Seagram down to 84.9% for Michelin. Thomson Corp. is the other Canadian MNE on the list. Nortel and BCE made it into the list of the world's largest 100 corporations, ranking 13 and 64 respectively on the transnationality index. Where these Canadian firms place in terms of size among the largest 100 is a different ranking: Seagram is 34, Thomson 50, BCE 57 and Nortel 85.

the fifth is a state-owned marketing board. There are many other subsidiaries in the top 50 exporters. It is also instructive to compare export sales as a percentage of total sales for some of these companies, whatever their ownership. While selecting percentages as indicators of performance can be arbitrary, exports account for more than 40% of the sales for 33 of these 50 largest exporters (*Globe and Mail*, 1998, p. 96). When we look at Canadian firms by profits, a different picture emerges, in part because some of the major exporters in Canada — including the top four — are wholly-owned subsidiaries and do not trade their shares on the Canadian stock exchanges. When we examine the most profitable Canadian companies, of the top 40, over 30 (if my guess is accurate) are Canadian owned (ibid., pp. 100-101). Most, but not all, of these have investments abroad.

As Rugman *et al.* (1997) suggest, larger Canadian firms have long been operating in a North American, that is, Canada-U.S. environment. Some are also investing in Mexico, but the United States is the main location of Canadian foreign direct investment abroad (CDIA). Moreover, this was the case before the negotiation of the Canada-U.S. Free Trade Agreement (FTA). For some years Canadian direct investment abroad has grown faster than foreign direct investment (FDI) coming into this country. With the growth in Canadian FDIA has come diversification. The United States is a less significant location for investments by Canadian firms in the late 1990s than it was in the previous decade. The United States was the location of 62.9% of the book value of Canadian FDIA in 1989, the year in which the Canada-U.S. FTA was implemented. By 1997 the United States had 51.5% of global CDIA. Using 1997 data, 21% of Canadian FDIA was in the European Union, 21.9% in non-OECD economies (Statistics Canada, 1997, p. 36). Rugman *et al.* point out that although the Canadian economy is approximately one-tenth of the size of that of the United States, our direct investment in that country is six to seven times larger than relative economic size might dictate (1997, p. 207). In keeping with the realities of being a small open economy, to be successful Canadian firms need to be competitive in the major global economy.

How would we characterize the "national context" (Pauly, 1999) of Canadian MNEs and therefore begin to make some judgements about governance and behaviour? The description of each of the categories is derived from the more detailed discussion of each in Doremus *et al.*, *The Myth of the Global Corporation* (1998). The information on Canada is developed from a range of available sources; it is of necessity brief and incomplete, and is put forward in an effort to extend the debate.[4] A comparison of the national context and behaviour of Canadian and U.S. MNEs is presented in Table 1.

(a) *Corporate Governance.* This addresses how firms are managed to ensure the best return on investment. Doremus *et al.* distinguish between firm managers and shareholders (1998, pp. 22-23). In their study of corporate governance, decision making and performance, Rao and Lee-Sing (1996) compare Canadian and U.S. firms across 6 major size classes and 11 major industry groups. They argue that corporate governance structures in Canada differ significantly from those in the United States across a range of criteria, among them concentration of corporate ownership, level of institutional ownership of firm shares, and the composition of the board of directors. The concentration of corporate ownership is significantly higher in Canada, but the level of institutional ownership is higher in the United States (ibid., p. 45).[5] Insider share-holding is higher in Canada than in the United States (ibid., p. 49). The ratio of inside directors (officers of the firm who sit on the board of directors) to total directors is slightly higher in Rao and Lee-Sing's sample of U.S. firms, though the authors note the need to nuance this general statement with reference of the size of firms and sector of operations (ibid., p. 53). The foreign director ratio for Canadian firms varies somewhat by corporate size; what is perhaps most interesting is that the largest firms have the lowest foreign director ratio (ibid., p. 54). Research done using annual reports of some of Canada's largest companies, including the banks, gives a mixed picture on the numbers of corporate directors resident outside Canada (which is the only means of determining national versus foreign directors). Some MNEs — Nortel, Alcan, Inco and Placer-Dome — list close to a quarter or more of their directors as not resident in Canada; others, among them BCE, Noranda and some of the banks have boards comprised solely or almost solely of Canadians.

---

[4]Some of the Industry Canada data used is dated, but more recent information was not available.

[5]See Table 3.7 in Doremus *et al.* (1998, p. 52) for data comparing the ownership structure of American, Japanese and German MNEs.

Table 1: National Context and MNE Behaviour

Context	Canada	United States
Corporate governance	More concentration of ownership than in the United States; managers constrained by capital markets; risk-seeking financial-centred strategies; some state-owned enterprises	Short-term shareholding; managers constrained by capital markets; risk-seeking financial-centred strategies
Corporate financing	Some global funding but utilization of Canadian banks abroad; price sensitive	Diversified global funding; highly price sensitive
Innovation system	Moderate focus on science sensitive high-tech industries; weak linkages across higher education and industry; some government R&D funding; some tax credits	Mission-oriented policy environment; mixed public and private funding and R&D performance; strong linkages across higher education and industry; high foreign R&D funding; national focus on science sensitive high-tech industries
Investment system	Liberal; no constraints on outward and few on inward FDI	Liberal; no constraints on inward or outward FDI
Behaviour		
R&D	Weak R&D performance; affiliate R&D abroad	Centralized; large overseas presence (especially in Germany and UK); Growing slowly; high R&D intensity of foreign affiliates
Technology trade	Limited, trade deficit	Centralized; export-oriented (large trade surplus)
Technology alliances	Some — many outside Canada	Large number; most intra-U.S.
Outward investment	Resources, finance, services telecommunications	Manufacturing, finance, services
Intra-firm trade	High	Moderate
Local production	High integration	High integration

Comments

(b) *Corporate Financing.* This category considers the relationship between corporations and their shareholders, with particular reference to the ties, or lack thereof, between firms and banks (Doremus *et al.*, 1998, 23f). In this area, Canada and the United States are similar. Banks in Canada, like those in the United States, do not hold equity in corporations. However, Canadian MNEs and their managers have close relationships with their banks and many bank executives sit on corporate boards. In a review of banks and corporate governance in Canada, Morck and Nakamura (1996) argue strongly that Canadian banks should not develop a relationship with Canadian MNEs similar to that extant in Germany and Japan. Because Canadian banks are required by law to be widely held, they are subject to corporate governance problems similar to those that often affect widely held entities, with the result that they would not provide appropriate oversight for Canadian firms (ibid., p. 496).

(c) *Innovation System.* This topic captures the national environment for innovation, including national science and technology policies, the source of funds for research and development and the orientation to research across different industries (Doremus *et al.*, 1998, pp. 69-73). The large U.S. defence base combined with the dominance of American MNEs in many research-intensive industries is in striking contrast to the situation in Canada. Investment in research and development in Canada has historically been lower than that in most of the developed market economies. One explanation for this has been the high level of foreign ownership of Canadian industry. The Canadian government has a number of programs in place, such as, Technology Partnerships Canada, to provide R&D support to various industries, among them aerospace. Some provincial governments also have policies to attract research-intensive FDI. Debate is frequent over the value of R&D policies, particularly tax breaks, in stimulating R&D in Canada (OECD, 1998). U.S. business invests about twice as much in R&D as does Canadian business and the public sector in the United States undertakes a larger share of R&D as a percentage of GDP (1.1%) than is the case in Canada (0.7%). Overall the United States has a much higher proportion of personnel engaged in R&D than in Canada.[6] Canada also lags behind other OCED economies in the share of high technology industries in total manufacturing (Industry Canada, 1998).

(d) *Investment System.* What is the national environment for direct foreign investment (Doremus *et al.*, 1998, 76f.)? There is perhaps no subject of Canadian economic policy that has been more analyzed than that with respect to incoming direct investment. For purposes of sketching the national context for MNE for corporate behaviour suffice it to note that Canada currently has no constraints on outward foreign direct investment and very few on inward investment. The restrictions that exist relate to particular sectors, such as banks and the communications media. Under the North American Free Trade Agreement, Canada agreed to common rules for the treatment of FDI from its NAFTA partners and a dispute-settlement mechanism to settle differences between investors from the NAFTA signatories and the NAFTA governments.

(e) *Research and Development.* Here Doremus *et al.* (1998, 86f) examine corporate R&D, with particular attention to R&D by foreign affiliates of MNEs. American MNEs continue to do the bulk of their R&D at home (85%); foreign affiliates do more of their R&D in the United States than do U.S. affiliates abroad (ibid., pp. 95-97). Disaggregating R&D spending by MNEs in Canada requires attention first to R&D levels by MNE affiliates located in Canada and then to R&D undertaken at home and abroad by Canadian MNEs. Data are difficult to get. Of the top 50 R&D corporate spenders listed in *The Globe and Mail's* Report on Business (1998, p. 97), 22 are foreign owned. Of this group, 12 are pharmaceutical companies which, as one of the *quid pro quos* for changes in Canada's patent legislation in the mid-1980s, pledged to spend more on R&D in Canada. If the R&D spending by U.S. affiliates abroad has increased in recent years (Doremus *et al.*, 1998, p. 100), it is not clear whether, with the exception of the pharmaceutical sector, this has been the case in Canada. The major spenders on R&D among Canadian-owned MNEs are those in telecommunications equipment, energy, transportation equipment and software. With the exception of

---

[6]The United States had 7.4 researchers per 1,000 members of the labour force as compared with 4.7 for Canada (Industry Canada, 1997).

Nortel, whose spending on R&D exceeds that of the second-ranked firm by a factor of almost 8, none of the firms listed spends a large sum on research (*Globe and Mail*, 1998, p. 97). Few firms report the percentage of overall R&D done outside Canada. One of the exceptions of Bell Canada Enterprises, which reports that 44.5% of its R&D is done in Canada. Other evidence is more circumstantial, descriptive rather than in percentage terms. For example, Nortel's largest R&D centre is in Ottawa, but it operates a total of 41 research sites in 17 countries; 15 of these research facilities are in the United States. Moreover, the company has research links to more than 120 universities around the world (Olive, 1998, pp. 6-7). Magna International ranked eighth on *The Globe and Mail's* list of top R&D spenders (1998, p. 97). The company's annual report highlights the global sites of its subsidiaries and indicates the number of research and development centres; Magna has 29 different locations where R&D is done, of which six are in Canada (ibid., pp.6-7). As a percentage of GDP, U.S. business overall spends more than twice what Canadian business spends on R&D (1.7% versus 0.6%). Only in the sectors of communications equipment and non-ferrous metals did Canadian firms spend more as a percentage of value-added than American companies (Industry Canada, 1997). Based on their research on firm size and "technological activity", Patel and Pavitt caution against the assumption that large firms are the most active in R&D. Analysis of Canadian R&D activity, admittedly now somewhat dated because it utilizes data from the 1980s, suggests that 11% of technological activity in Canada was undertaken by large firms, 16.9% by foreign-owned large firms, and 72.1% by other sources (Patel and Pavitt, 1991, p. 79).[7]

(f) *Technology Trade.* This refers to the balance of trade in technology. The United States consistently exports more technology than it imports; the other major OCED countries have more or less balanced trade in technology (Doremus *et al.*, 1998, p. 102). Canada imports more technology

---

[7]Comparative percentages with respect to the importance of large firms in national technological activity are: United States 42.8%; Germany 44.8%; Japan 62.5%; Netherlands 51.9%; Switzerland 40.1%; Sweden 27.5%. Only Belgium, with a figure of 8.8% is lower than Canada (Patel and Pavitt, 1991, p. 80). These data suggest that the size of an economy is not necessarily related to the domestic level of R&D.

than it exports. The country has long been an importer of capital equipment. Moreover, Canadian firms have been slower to embrace advanced technologies and commercialize few domestic innovations than their U.S. counterparts (Industry Canada, 1997). CDIA has a rather low technological content (Raynauld, 1994, p. 458). This is not at variance with the overall R&D performance of the largest Canadian firms, which, as noted above, generally lags behind that of the top U.S. firms (Knubley *et al.*, 1994, p. 180). Although the composition of CDIA abroad is changing (see (h) below), McFetridge noted that less than 10% of Canada's net investment position in the United States "would normally be construed as being in R&D intensive industries" (ibid., p. 156). This may have changed some over the decade; moreover it is a statement based on a composite analysis and is not differentiated by sector.

(g) *Technology Alliances.* Technology alliances are arrangements of various types between corporations to share/acquire technology or reduce some of the costs and risks associated with R&D by undertaking it jointly. Alliances have become more important over the last decade. U.S. firms have developed a range of alliances, primarily with each other, in sectors such as information technology, biotechnology and new materials (Doremus *et al.*, 1998, pp. 111-115). While Canadian firms have become more active participants in technology alliances, they have been less active in joint venturing than their U.S. or Japanese counterparts (Globerman and Wolf, 1994, p. 293). Numbers are impossible to determine. Many Canadian MNEs are in the energy and resources sectors where the potential for joint ventures in technology is limited. Companies such as Nortel and Magna, which have R&D sites in a range of different locations, are likely to have some of these alliances. Globerman and Wolf's analysis of Canadian corporate joint ventures in the areas of telecommunications, auto parts and software suggests that these are undertaken for the usual reasons of market access, technology acquisition and risk sharing (1994, pp. 281-292).

(h) *Outward Investment.* This refers to the sectoral composition of FDI by American MNEs as well as MNEs investing in the United States (Doremus *et al.*, pp. 116-122). U.S. FDI is spread across a range of industries, with the largest percentage in manufacturing. The composition of Canadian FDIA has changed over the years, with a decrease in FDI in the resource sector and a dramatic rise in investment in finance and insurance (Rao *et al.*, 1994, p. 70). Data from 1991 indicate that the distribution of Canadian FDI in the United States was then more concentrated in resource and resource-based manufacturing, and in financial service industries (banking, finance, insurance and real estate) than in manufacturing (Knubley *et al.*, 1994, p. 160). This shift to financial services has been at the expense of primary industries and manufacturing. An overwhelming percentage of CDIA belongs to the same industry in Canada and abroad. This pattern can be explained through the exploitation of comparative advantage — Canadian firms utilize abroad the expertise garnered in Canada — and the small size of the Canadian market, which means that Canadian companies have to expand abroad to achieve economies of scale. In keeping with the analysis that MNEs from small open economies are more internationalized than their counterparts from larger ones, research on the top Canadian firms in industries suggests that their orientation is far more outward than that of their American counterparts (ibid., 1994, pp. 183-184). Of the largest Canadian MNEs, depending on what information is available, most have less than half of their assets, or do less than half of their production, in Canada.

(i) *Intra-firm Trade* and (j) *Local Production.* These two topics are addressed in the same section because they are so closely connected. Intra-firm trade constitutes "cross-border transactions" among and between MNE affiliates. Levels as well as composition of intra-firm trade determine affiliate linkages to the local economy. Parent-affiliate or inter-affiliate trade in components suggests that affiliate firms do more sourcing and are therefore more linked to the host country economy than imports of finished goods. Doremus *et al.* suggest that while all affiliates engage in intra-firm trade, U.S. affiliates import a lower percentage of finished items than their German and Japan counterparts and are more integrated into the host country economy (1994, pp. 123-133). We know that a critical amount of Canada-U.S. trade (as much as 70%) (Hart, 1994, p. 20) is accounted for intra-firm trade and licensing and other corporate arrangements. A significant proportion of this is comprised of intra-firm trade within U.S. MNEs. Some of this intra-firm trade is between the parts of Canadian-based MNEs. We have no data that allow us to compare relative sourcing behaviour. Good business practice as well as "Buy America" legislation dictates that U.S.-based affiliates of Canadian MNEs engage in considerable value-added in their U.S. locations.

Conclusion

This brief survey of Canadian MNEs suggests that at least with respect to internationalization to compensate for a small domestic market the behaviour of Canadian MNEs is similar to that of MNEs from other small open economies. Their internationalization is largely limited to sales and production abroad (Ruigrok and van Tulder, 1995, p. 162). Whether Canadian MNEs have had to internationalize to compensate for a narrow domestic supply based is not something the available literature addresses. Resource-based MNEs invest abroad to diversify sources of supply, but that is not unique to corporations from small economies. Some Canadian MNEs, particularly those in manufacturing such as Nortel and Magna, appear to have adopted a multi-domestic strategy, with considerable autonomy given to local subsidiaries to allow them to manoeuvre in different foreign locations (ibid., 1995, p. 161). Canadian MNEs, like their counterparts from other smaller economies, tend to rely on domestic banks and have boards comprised primarily of nationals, although data indicate that some Canadian MNEs do have considerable non-resident membership on their boards. Research on MNEs from other small economies is needed to compare whether Canadian MNEs do more or less R&D at home than their counterparts.

Does the comparison of the national context and behaviour of Canadian MNEs with those that are U.S.-based generate any noteworthy or what might be considered "national" characteristics? Perhaps the most interesting are the differences in shareholder profiles, the continuing relatively low levels of R&D spending as well as questions about the relationship between firm size and expenditures on R&D, the diversification of CDIA, and the importance of exports to corporate bottom lines. Are these characteristics a function of location or size of the economy?

What are the implications of these patterns of national context and MNE behaviour for government policy? Is there, by inference, some suggestion that the long-standing policies of the United States, Germany and Japan, which have promoted the growth of their MNEs, have been appropriate and should be continued? As Susan Strange comments, there is a heavy ideological overlay to the analysis (1998, p. 707). If this is the case, what are we then to make of the prescriptions with respect to Canada with which Pauly concludes his paper? Should the Canadian state develop policies designed to protect the country from the investment activities of MNEs from other states with strong national loyalties or should it be promoting its own home-grown MNEs — recognizing that we do not know whether MNEs from smaller economies have the same sense of national identity as those from the major developed market economies? How much policy space do small open economies have in the current era of globalization? Do we have the capacity to be nimble in the face of growing numbers of challenges under the World Trade Organization and NAFTA? Time will tell. To be innovative in policy we need to know more about Canadian MNEs and how they compare with their counterparts in other small economies than we currently do. Efforts to hark back to an earlier era in Canadian economic life are not sufficient to provide guidance for the future.

References

Daniels, R.J. and R. Morck, eds. (1996), *Corporate Decision-Making in Canada* (Calgary: University of Calgary Press).

Doremus, P.N., W.W. Keller, L.W. Pauly and S. Reich (1998), *The Myth of the Global Corporation* (Princeton: Princeton University Press).

Eden, L. (1994a), "Who Does What After NAFTA? Location Strategies of U.S. Multinationals", in Eden (ed.), *Multinationals in North America*, 193-249.

_____, ed. (1994b), *Multinationals in North America* (Calgary: University of Calgary Press).

Eden, L. and M. Appel Molot (1993), "Insiders and Outsiders: Defining 'Who is Us' in the North American Automobile Industry", *Transnational Corporations* 2(3), 31-64.

Gerschenkron, A. (1962), *Economic Backwardness in Historical Perspective* (Cambridge: Harvard University Press).

The Globe and Mail, Report on Business Magazine (1998), *The Top 1000,* July, p. 96.

Globerman, S. and B.M. Wolf (1994), "Joint Ventures and Canadian Outward Direct Investment", in S. Globerman (ed.), *Canadian-Based Multinationals* (Calgary: University of Calgary Press).

Gourevitch, P. (1986), *Politics in Hard Times: Comparative Responses to International Economic Crises* (Ithaca, NY: Cornell University Press).

Hart, M. (1994), *What's Next? Canada, the Global Economy and the New Trade Policy* (Ottawa: Centre for Trade Policy and Law).

Industry Canada (1997), *Keeping up with the Joneses,* June. (http://strategis.ic.gc.ca/SSG/ra01308e.html)

_____ (1998), *Spotlight on Canada: An Inside Look From an Outside Perspective*, March. (http://strategis.ic.gc.ca/SSG/ra01549e.html)

Knubley, J., M. Legault and S. Rao (1994), "Multinationals and Foreign Direct Investment in North America", in Eden (ed.), *Multinationals in North America*, 143-191.

Kogut, B. (1994), "An Evolutionary Perspective on NAFTA", in Eden (ed.), *Multinationals in North America*, 117-140.

McFetridge, D. (1994), "Canadian Foreign Direct Investment, R&D and Technology Transfer", in S. Globerman (ed.), *Canadian-Based Multinationals*, Industry Canada Research Series (Calgary: University of Calgary Press).

Morck, R. and M. Nakamura (1996), "Banks and Corporate Governance in Canada", in Daniels and Morck (eds.), *Corporate Decision-Making in Canada*.

Olive, D. (1998), "Nortel's Web Sights — Part Two", *Mastering Global Business, Part Four, The Financial Post* and *Financial Times*.

Organization for Economic Cooperation and Development (OECD) (1998), *Technology, Productivity and Job Creation: Best Policy Practices* (Paris: OECD).

Patel, P. and K. Pavitt (1991), "The Limited Importance of Large Firms in Canadian Technological Activities", in D. McFetridge (ed.), *Foreign Investment, Technology and Economic Growth* (Calgary: University of Calgary Press).

Pauly, L. (1999), "The 'Culture' of Multinational Corporations and the Implications for Canada", in this volume.

Pauly, L. and S. Reich (1997), "National Structures and Multinational Corporate Behavior: Enduring Differences in the Age of Globalization", *International Organization* 51(1), 1-30.

Rao, P.S. and C.R. Lee-Sing (1996), "Corporate Governance, Corporate Decision-Making and Firm Performance in North America", in Daniels and Morck (eds.), *Corporate Decision-Making in Canada*.

Rao, P.S., M. Legault and A. Ahmad (1994), *Canadian-Based Multinationals: An Analysis of Activities and Performance* (Ottawa: Industry Canada).

Raynauld, A. (1994), "Rapporteur's Comments", in S. Globerman (ed.), *Canadian-Based Multinationals* (Calgary: University of Calgary Press).

Rugman, A.M., J. Kirton and J.A. Soloway (1997), "Canadian Corporate Strategy in a North American Region", *The American Review of Canadian Studies* 27(2), 199-219.

Ruigrok, W. and R. van Tulder (1995), *The Logic of International Restructuring* (London: Routledge).

Strange, S. (1998), "Globaloney?" *Review of International Political Economy* 5(4), 704-711.

Comments

Statistics Canada (1997), *Canada's International Investment Position* (Ottawa: Supply and Services Canada).

United Nations Conference on Trade and Development (UNCTAD) (1988), *World Investment Report 1998* (New York: UNCTAD).

Westney, D.E. (1994), "Japanese Multinationals in North America", in Eden (ed.), *Multinationals in North America*, 253-275.

Summary of Discussion

Jack Mintz raised the possibility that multinational corporations (MNCs) can have changing identities. For example, Ericsson has recently moved its headquarters from Sweden to the United Kingdom. Has Ericsson changed its national identity? Some corporations are based in Canada, but the bulk of their customers and even shareholders are in the United States. Are these Canadian or American companies?

Louis Pauly countered by saying that cases such as Ericsson are the exception, not the rule. These exceptional cases do not detract from the basic pattern that MNCs retain a national identity. Head-office location, long-standing relationships with national financial institutions and research and development links with the national system are the critical factors forging the national character of a MNC.

Doug Brown cited a recent article in *The Economist* magazine which concluded that a transition to a single corporate culture is under way now that the East Asian model of capitalism has failed. The literature has traditionally distinguished between Anglo-American capitalism, continental European capitalism and East Asian capitalism. Canadian capitalism has been viewed as a hybrid between the American and European models with "Quebec Inc." as a variant closer to the European model. But, *The Economist* sees the old models of national capitalism being overtaken by events. Is it wrong?

Louis Pauly rejected *The Economist*'s hypothesis. Japan will not embrace the American model. Rather, Japan is adapting to a new competitive context. Adaptation is painful, but the current crisis is not as serious as the emergency that prompted the birth of a distinctive Japanese modern state and

social structures. Similarly, the recent Hyundai-Kia merger in Korea proceeded without Ford's participation. This would make for an interesting case study, which might confirm that adaptation in Asia is happening along national lines. Furthermore, it is important to distinguish between the Anglo and American models. Britain is a hollow, hobbled national economy. The City of London is dominant, while the rest of the country has a weak industrial future. But deindustrialization is a uniquely British story. Let us hope that Canada does not inevitably follow the Anglo model just because we have an Anglo culture. The Germans and French have been much more careful about managing the relationship between the industrial and financial sectors. The Americans, despite their free-market rhetoric, are obsessed with maintaining their industrial economy. The U.S. government's defence and health budgets support U.S.-based corporations. State industrial policy is part of America's historical legacy.

Maureen Molot offered support from a reading of U.S. history, which shows the role of the state throughout U.S. industrialization — for example, government investment in the armaments industry during the Civil War. Each country has its unique patterns. As for Japan, the basic patterns of their model will not be dramatically altered. However, we may see more significant changes in Korea, in part because their crisis is more serious. For instance, we may well see increased foreign ownership and participation.

Pierre-Paul Proulx offered an insight from his participation in a recent review of worldwide consulting operations. He came across a proposal at one consulting operation to move towards a virtual headquarters supported by an information technology network. Management would move physically from office to office in the worldwide network every three months or so. What would this sort of development mean for the national character of MNCs? As for Quebec Inc., the old model is dead. But there is a new Quebec International Inc. model with state intervention focused on joint ventures, alliances and partnerships with the private sector. The best example of the new model in action is a series of recent initiatives in the multimedia sector.

Louis Pauly picked up on the reference to Quebec Inc. Canada has always faced a contest between national and regional tendencies. The federal Liberals want to revive the national tendency, but this may not be possible. Ontario is focusing its industrial policy on a regional innovation system centred around the auto industry and linked to Michigan, Ohio and New York. Would Ontario have less room to manoeuvre with this strategy if Quebec secedes? Many people believe that Mike Harris' Ontario would have more room to manoeuvre without Quebec.

Hugh Thorburn raised the examples of Austria, Holland and Switzerland. Small countries can be remarkably successful. But small countries have to do something different from large countries such as the United States, Japan and Germany, which can export their national cultures. To succeed, they must be flexible and highly rational. However, the idea of Canada developing its own MNCs may not work if successful Canadian MNCs are tempted to move to the United States.

Louis Pauly suggested that these small European countries have distinctive national identities born in painful and traumatic circumstances. Austrians had to resolve their identity question. Austrians know that they do not want to be Germans. Canadians are not so clear about what we do not want to be. In this context, developing strong MNCs capable of competing in world markets from a Canadian base would be a good strategy for building a Canadian identity.

Leonard Waverman asked what kind of industrial policy could be recommended for Canada. *Louis Pauly* conceded the impossibility of bringing back old-style industrial policy. However, a state-steering system remains in the financial and telecommunications sectors. This system may have benefited elites, but it built a country. All countries are trying to devise new instruments for steering their industrial futures, rather than surrendering to global markets. If we embrace the rhetoric of globalization, free markets and consumer sovereignty, then we become Americans. The debate should be over whether that is what Canadians want. In any case, even in the United States, where the rhetoric of industrial policy tends to be equated with socialism, there is, nonetheless, a very strong history of successful industrial strategy. Industrial policy is so deeply ingrained that the United States does not even have a word for it.

Peter Leslie raised the issue of regional dimension. What kind of industrial policy can be conceived of which would not be viewed as discriminatory among regions?

Louis Pauly referred to Richard Harris' book, *Trade Industrial Policy and International Competition*, for the Macdonald Commission. We would not be starting industrial policy from *tabula rasa*. Canadians need to be smart in a new context if we want to maintain anything at all that is distinctive. Our only response cannot be: "We surrender. We are inevitably Americans and the Canadian national dream has failed. Our kids are moving to the United States." If that is the case, we might as well join the United States so that we can vote for representatives and senators. The question is: Can we create more Canadian MNCs or do constraints foreclose this? The growth of computer software firms in Ottawa is encouraging, but can we keep those jobs in the face of intense capital market integration? Will it be too easy for entrepreneurs to sell out to Microsoft in Seattle once they reach a certain level? If our children wind up having to go to the United States to work, elite Canadians will be glad their children have that option. There are already an estimated 200,000 Canadians working in New York. There is a new sense of hopelessness that our best and brightest graduates will go south. Can we shift that pattern a bit to create opportunities for them to stay here?

Marvin McInnis found the discussion reminiscent of the situation in post-Confederation Canada. We had the highest rate of emigration of any country in the world. Masses moved south. Perhaps the present situation can also be turned around.

David Slater urged everyone to look at recent U.S. developments. The U.S. government has initiated a "next generation of vehicle" project to ensure that the U.S. auto industry will be competitive in the world economy in light of the Kyoto agreement on greenhouse gas emissions. The government has set a target for the auto industry to develop vehicles that are three times more fuel efficient than today without increasing selling prices. When Canada woke up and Industry Minister John Manley went to Washington to talk about this, he was told that he would need the permission of the "Big Three" auto companies to secure limited involvement for Canada.

Louis Pauly closed the discussion by suggesting that this was exactly the kind of situation in which the Rasminsky generation of Canadian officials excelled in negotiating room for manoeuvre with Washington. New constraints complicate the world, but the task remains the same.

Canadian Information/Culture Policy in the Information Age: Mediums are the Message

Leonard Waverman

The CRTC on Broadcasting Policy:

> *Over the years, the Commission has developed mechanisms designed to strengthen the ability of the private television sector to fulfill its regulatory obligations. These mechanisms include market protection for existing over-the-air broadcasters; non-competitive license renewals and transfers of ownership; priority carriage on distribution systems; and, protection of program rights through simultaneous program substitution requirements ... In addition, the Commission's regulations and policies impose certain restraints on broadcasters. These restraints include a regulatory maximum of 12 minutes per hour of advertising material; the Commission's policy of limiting a person to ownership of no more than one conventional television station in one language in a given market; and, its policy of requiring significant benefits when the ownership or control of a television undertaking is transferred from one party to another.* (CRTC, 1998)

I thank the Future Media Program and the Regulation Initiative at London Business School for their support.

The CRTC on Telecoms Policy:

... competition not only can be expected to increase pressure to reduce rates, but increase choice and supplier responsiveness. (CRTC, 1992, p. 7)

The CRTC on Culture and Competition:

If Canadians are to benefit from increased choice (from the information superhighway) market entry should be regulated in a manner that contributes to the Canadian broadcasting system and the development of quality programing. (CRTC, 1995, p. 6)

Introduction

The Information Age is here. I delivered this paper to Queen's via File Transfer over the Internet, booked my plane and car over the Internet and wrote this paper on my tiny Toshiba Libretto in various parts of the world. I downloaded data from various web sites including Heritage Canada, Industry Canada, the Federal Communications Commission and the European Commission. I saw no "border" when I did all this. The bits and bytes bypassed any national territorial control. Yet, "information/culture policy" is extremely national and in Canada's case, nationalistic. While most countries do not control the Internet, they do control the infrastructure as well as broadcasting and telecommunications services greatly. Telecommunications, broadcasting, satellite services and in Canada, publishing, as well as print advertising are all subject to a variety of controls aimed at making life more "Canadian". The control of content on radio and television (Canadian minimum content) and maximum foreign control for infrastructure as well as content providers are key policies. This entire panoply of policies, I call Canadian Information and Cultural Policy (CICP).

In this paper, I examine whether there is an inconsistency between the universal nature of "The Information Age" and the national nature of its regulation. The question then becomes two-fold. First, what are the underlying instruments of present information policy which are consistent with and those which are inconsistent with the new technology? Second, are there policy instruments which effectively promote these objectives in the new age?

Numerous other academics, including economists, have critically examined Canadian cultural policies. (See Globerman, 1987, 1995, Schultz, 1995; Stanbury, 1998a, b). Many of these authors and most economists are opposed to these policies on various grounds — the policies are inefficient (Globerman, 1987), or extract rent to the detriment of Canadians in general (Schultz, 1995; Stanbury, 1998a, b). In this paper I do not discuss the merits of cultural policies as I feel strongly that economists cum economists have little to say about social goals.[1] What economists can discuss readily and helpfully are the instruments which society can best use to meet these goals.

Therefore, I shall examine the set of Canadian policy instruments involved in the information/culture economy in telecommunications and broadcasting; namely, universal service, Canadian content and ownership controls and ask whether these existing instruments are suitable in the "new information age". Since I do not feel that they are suitable, other instruments are examined.

Technology, Technology, Technology

In the 1970s, telephones could only provide analogue voice point-to-point communications, and cable television distribution systems could only provide one-way broadcast (rather than interactive) television programing. These delivery systems technically could not deliver competing services, and services could not be provided by competing delivery systems.[2] The great distinction between the existing regulation of multimedia, telecommunications and broadcasting markets reflected in the introductory quotations is a holdover from this bygone era when there was a one-to-one correspondence between a service and a delivery system. Since broadcasting and telecommunications were separate services delivered over distinct and separate infrastructures, telecommunications could be liberalized while even greater controls were erected over broadcasting.

The last decade has seen the emergence of a vast number of technological innovations which have ended this one-to-one correspondence

---

[1]In fact, personally, I applaud the CBC, Telefilm and many other Canadian cultural institutions.

[2]Cable TV always faced competition from over-the-air broadcasting.

between a delivery system and a service. Telephony can now be provided by wired, wireless, and soon by satellite technologies, and video delivery can be provided by cable TV, copper wire pairs (ADSL) and soon by wireless — satellite and enhanced or third-generation mobile.[3] The number of services which can be offered over these delivery systems is expanding rapidly. The converged nature of these services is labeled as "multimedia".[4]

Multimedia services can be delivered by many different technologies. Today, telephone calls need not originate from fixed phones using traditional phone lines. Phone calls are increasingly originated from mobile phones (both analogue and digital). Low earth orbit satellite systems as of November 1998 (Iridium) provide phone services. And there is increasing ability by cable TV companies to upgrade their coaxial networks to provide phone services. In the television arena, television signals are now provided by traditional over-the-air broadcast by cable and via satellites (DTH). Technologies appear to allow Near Video on Demand (NVOD) over traditional phone lines and Sprint unveiled plans in the United States on June 2, 1998 to offer high-speed telephony, Internet access and NVOD to businesses in 1998 and to residential consumers in late 1999.

Innovation is increasingly creating new mediums of supply and new services. The potential for several technologies to deliver multimedia services implies that competition is increasing in those markets. Traditional suppliers are being faced with competition from providers that bypass the traditional network and provide services through new technologies.

Thus the competitive interaction between the various service delivery systems (phone lines, cables, over-the-air broadcast, wireless and satellites) is rapidly changing.

Because of multi-product technologies, it is increasingly difficult to differentiate between markets. Market definition depends on demand conditions (the elasticity of demand for a given product and the elasticity of demand substitution between two multimedia products), as well as supply conditions (the cross-elasticity of supply). This confluence of technologies and services means that the traditional division between "broadcasting", and

---

[3]The Low Earth Orbit (LEO) systems of Iridium, Globalstar and Teledesic is designed to provide telephony, but not necessarily to substitute for wired infrastructure in developed countries.

[4]Globerman (1995) discussed similar trends. I have the benefits of four years of additional data.

"telephony" is eroding. Thus, policy convergence will be driven by technological convergence.

Some suggest that convergence is limited because today's costs of provision diverge, that is, there is a low-cost provider. It is undeniable that comparative costs will guide the expansion of specific technologies and services. True competition will really occur between two technologies only if their costs are comparable. Nevertheless, it would be a mistake to rely too heavily on current comparative costs to decide where competition is likely to develop for several reasons. First, costs are changing very rapidly in light of technological breakthroughs, so that current costs may have little predictive power for future costs. More importantly, costs are endogenous. Research and development (R&D) money will flow to technologies that have a potential for market acceptance and which also depend on regulatory restrictions. For instance, the high prices and low quality of local cable systems in the United States has fostered the development of satellite DTH (Direct-To-Home) technologies, with dramatic reduction in costs.

Figure 1 provides a list of services for both communications and entertainment and the multiple technologies capable of providing those services.[5] Thus, for voice messaging nine technologies are listed, whereas for video conferencing only three technologies are shown. The larger the bandwidth requirements of the service, the fewer the available technologies. As was noted, all these technologies may be feasible today.

Figure 2 is similar to Figure 1, but shows the range of services feasible for each technology. Figure 3 provides a concise mapping of technologies and services.

Some services, like television, phone and Internet access, are already provided through several delivery systems. Wireless technologies promise to provide access to many services in the coming years. And in the longer term, satellite communication could revolutionize mobile telephony as well as related services such as long-distance data transmission.

But competition between delivery technologies is not the whole story. In order to assess the extent of competition and thus the ability or need to regulate it is important to know how many providers would likely enter the market using the available technologies. Telecom technologies often have large fixed and sunk costs, which may limit the number of competitors. For

---

[5]Lorenzo Pupillo of Telecom Italia was instrumental in designing these figures.

Figure 1: Delivery Technologies for Multimedia Services

Base Technology	Stationary Telephony	Mobile Telephony	Video	Video on Demand	Internet Access	Video Conferencing	Targeted Advertising	Decentralized Work	High Speed Data
I. Land line									
A.1 Copper-Based, Analog	1				1				
A.2 Copper-Based, ISDN	1		2	2	1	1			1
A.3 Copper-Based, ADSL	1		2	2	1	2		2	2
B Coaxial			1		1				
C.1 Fiber-HFC,FTTC,SDV	1		1	2	1	1	1	1	1
II. Wireless									
A.1 SMR	1	1							
A.2 ESMR	1	1							
B.1 Cellular, Analog	1	1			1			1	1
B.2 Cellular, Digital	1	1			1			1	1
C.1 PCS	1	1			2		2	2	2
D.1 Wireless Cable-MMDS			1		1				
D.2 Wireless Cable-LMDS			1		2				
III. Air Broadcast			1						
IV. Satellite									
A VSAT	2		2		2	2			
B DBS			1		1		(1)		
C Low Earth Orbit		1			2	2		1	
D GEOS	3							1	

Note: 1: Already exists   2: Probable, soon   3: Probable, much later   ( ): Limited use

Figure 2: Technologies and Services

	INTERNET	BROAD BAND NETWORK (HFC, FTTX)	SATELLITE	WIRELESS (DECT, DCS, PCS, FRA)	CELLULAR (TACS+GSM)	MVDS
TECHNOLOGIES						
SERVICES	• VOICE • FAX • CHAT • E-MAIL • VOD* • GAMES • DATA BASE ACCESS • EDUCATIONAL • TELECOMMUTING • HOMESHOPPING • HOMEBANKING	• VOICE • FAX • E-MAIL • VIDEOPHONE • VIDEOCONFERENCE • ANALOG BROADCAST TV • DIGITAL BROADCAST TV • VOD • GAMES • DATA BASE ACCESS • TRANSACTIONS • EDUCATIONAL • TELETRAINING • TELEMEDICINE • TELECOMMUTING • GROUPWARE	• VOICE • FAX • ANALOG BROADCAST TV • DIGITAL BROADCAST TV • HOMESHOPPING • VIDEOPHONE • VIDEOCONFERENCE • GAMES • DATA TRANSMISSION • TRANSACTIONS • EDUCATIONAL • TELETRAINING • TELEMEDICINE • GROUPWARE	• VOICE • FAX • E-MAIL • DATA BASE ACCESS • HOMEBANKING	• VOICE • FAX • E-MAIL • HOMEBANKING • DATA BASE ACCESS • TELECOMMUTING	• VOICE • DATA BASE ACCESS • E-MAIL • FAX • BROADCAST TV • VOD*

(*) Cellular TV

Figure 3: Mapping Technologies and Services

NEEDS	COMMUNICATION					ENTERTAINMENT			
SERVICE / TECHNOLOGIES	VOCE	FAX	E-MAIL	VIDEO PHONE	VIDEO CONFE-RENCE	ANALOG BROADCAST TV	DIGITAL BROADCAST TV (BASIC, PREMIUM, NVOD, PPV)	VOD	GAMES
POTS	✓	✓	✓	✓					
ISDN	✓	✓	✓	✓	✓				
ADSL	✓	✓	✓					✓	✓
INTERNET	✓	✓	✓					✓*	✓
B.B. NETWORK	✓	✓	✓	✓	✓	✓	✓	✓	✓
SATELLITE	✓	✓	✓	✓	✓	✓	✓		✓
TERRESTRIAL						✓	✓*		
WIRELESS (DECT,DCS, PC FRA)	✓	✓	✓						
CELLULAR	✓	✓	✓	✓					
MVDS	✓	✓	✓	✓		✓		✓**	

(**) 28 GHz CELLULAR TV

instance, local phone networks have often been seen as natural monopolies, but the pervasive holding of the price of access below costs has meant that alternative suppliers are constrained because of the below-cost prices (see Crandall and Waverman, 1996). Yet entry for plain old telephone service (POTS) is occurring in a variety of forms. And the telephone delivery system is being altered to provide other services, many of which they could not offer because of regulatory bans. Most probably, switching to a fibre-intensive network will occur in a gradual fashion. Fibre networks to serve the household market will probably be built by expanding fibre in telephone networks and cable television networks. Cable television networks could be upgraded into hybrid fibre coax networks, and then to SDV networks. For the household sectors, it is likely that in the near to medium term, fibre-based networks will be provided mostly by the local cable and telephone companies. Digital Subscriber Loop (DSL) is increasingly viewed as a technology that will be installed in the near future by phone companies, before full fibre networks are developed. All these are alternative delivery systems.

Overall, there is likely to be a significant number of potential delivery systems for multimedia service. As long as competition is allowed to develop using the available technologies, with multiple technologies providing overlapping services, the ability of regulators such as the CRTC to distinguish

Leonard Waverman

telecommunications policy from broadcasting policy will erode. However, one new technology makes this erosion imminent and quick — the Internet.

The Internet

The Internet differs from telephony in several fundamental ways. First, the telephone system involves simple, uncomplicated instruments (the telephone) connected by a sophisticated network with the vast bulk of intelligence residing in the network (the switches). An Internet network links sophisticated terminals (the computer) with a relatively unsophisticated network where off-the-shelf routers replace sophisticated software-intensive telecoms switches. Second, the Internet is digital and sends packets of information across the network, with parts of a message sent across different routes. Third, a voice call involves an open link between the two callers; a transmission link is not held open for an Internet message. Fourth, the Internet is universal, connecting users around the globe. Finally, as Marshall McLuhan might say if he were alive today — "all medium is now the message",[6] that is, on the Internet there is no "voice" or "television", there are only bits. One cannot distinguish easily between a voice call and a video on the Internet. Thus, the Internet, combined with digitalized coding of information makes it extraordinarily difficult for anyone to know what type of information is being transmitted.

The Internet is today mainly used for e-mail, information retrieval, marketing and some voice telephony. There is a good deal of belief that Internet protocol networks will supplant traditional telephony networks and provide greater bandwidth and lower costs. Already one can watch short video clips over the Internet on a computer. Music over the Internet is easy to download. Magazines can be downloaded; advertising is on the search engine or on the web site.

Digital TV and radio have two important attributes. First, as is widely recognized, capacity increases by a multiplicative factor. Second, and crucial for Canadian CICP, since the program is sent in bits and bytes — one cannot distinguish a bit of a TV program passing over cable from a bit of an e-mail

---

[6]McLuhan's aphorism "The medium is the message" relied on non-digital transmission, plus had a deeper message ignored here — the different impacts from oral, visual and print technologies on society.

message. At the distribution and termination ends it is obvious that it is a TV program or e-mail, but the infrastructure provider does not know what the content is.

Canadian policy for the information age was constructed for the non-digital world.

Can it survive?

How should it change?

Existing Canadian Policies

As opposed to the United States and more like the European Union (EU) Information/Cultural Policy,[7] Canadian Information and Cultural Policy (CICP) is based on the perceived need to have Canadian firms, Canadian expression of ideas, Canadian content (Stanbury, 1998a, b provide an excellent review and analysis). U.S. policy is, however, implicitly "American"; for while there are no explicit rules on U.S. content on television, there are foreign ownership restrictions and the set of policies are aimed at developing American industry to maintain world leadership. Hence the attempts by the EU or Canada to assist domestic national identity and culture are not the only examples of intervention in the free market of ideas. I begin by examining the current Canadian policy instruments.

Telecommunications

The CRTC has implemented competitive policies in telecommunications, attempting to move away from its overly restrictive and overregulated regimes of the past.

In 1978, the CRTC began the long march to competition when it permitted CNCP to interconnect with the then federally regulated telecom companies (Bell Canada, BC Tel, Island Tel, etc.) to provide private leased service. However, in 1985 CNCP's application for full long-distance competition was not allowed by the CRTC on the strange notion that the CRTC did not believe that CNCP could survive — a bizarre definition of

---

[7]See Saxby (1996) and Buchwald (1995) for a good description of EU Policy.

regulated competition. Finally in 1992, CNCP and others were permitted to offer long-distance services, eight years after such competition began in the United Kingdom and 17 years after MCI was allowed (by the courts not the regulator, the FCC) to compete in the United States. A new Canadian Telecommunications Act was passed in 1993, enshrining federal jurisdiction over all telecommunications.

In its Local Competition hearing, the CRTC eliminated most restrictions on entry and competition into the telecoms businesses (CRTC, 1997). Importantly, for this paper, the long-held exclusion against telcos providing video transmission services was ended.[8] Now, telcos can offer VDT (Video Dial Tone), where affiliates of telcos and other service suppliers have equal non-discriminatory access to the VDT platform. Telcos are able in addition to apply for broadcasting distribution licences.

Competition in telecommunications has been a long time coming as the CRTC maintained the one firm monopoly model until the 1990s. Now competition is the religion at the Telecoms' side of the CRTC, unlike in broadcasting.

On May 1, 1997 the CRTC, after a three-year discussion and analysis period, devised a framework for local competition in Canada. In its decision, the commission "establishes a framework for local exchange competition that balances the interests and needs of consumers, local competition entrants, toll competitors and incumbent telephone companies while at the same time maintaining universal access to affordable telecommunications services in high-cost areas" (1997, para. 6). Now all aspects of telecommunications infrastructure and service provision are competitive. Entry restrictions do not exist. That is, the main objectives of Telecommunications Policy are met by a competitive market.

However, one important telecoms policy objective continues to be universal service, and it requires regulatory intervention. Residential access, the monthly fee for connection to the network is held below cost for many subscribers.[9] The CRTC has managed the subsidies to local access through "contributions" from long-distance service. The CRTC if it were politically feasible would move to "full rate rebalancing", removing the subsidies, but political intervention has prevented such full cost pricing. Currently, the required subsidy for high-cost loops is calculated as residential average costs

---

[8]See Globerman (1995) for a discussion of the ban.

[9]These consumers are outside urban areas.

plus residential optional local costs minus the associated revenues. The source of the subsidy is long-distance calling, whose "contributions" to the access deficit are frozen at existing levels. All Local Exchange Carriers (LECs) remit their toll contributions to a central fund whose trustee disperses the proceeds to all providers of the subsidized service.

Clearly, the new media, especially the Internet, make bypass of such subsidies possible. What is defined as "toll" services in the era of Internet, private lines and virtual networks? The base for providing the subsidy could easily erode in the face of new services such as these.[10] Therefore, even the limited set of cross-subsidies in Canadian telecommunications is at risk in the new digital age. And if these subsidies erode, what of the complex set of implicit and explicit subsidies for production of Canadian content for broadcasting?

Has competition in telecoms helped consumers? Table 1 provides data on average prices and data on the carrier charges (contributions for access deficits) plus lease of facilities for an entrant Call Net. From 1989 to 1997 Call Net's average price fell from 60 cents per minute to 22.3 cents per minute, a fall of over 60%. Of this 38-cent reduction in average price, Call Net's carrier charges per minute fell by 25 cents per minute. Thus, the fall in average price is both a fall in carrier charges and contributions as well as a substantial decline in Call Net's retained revenue per minute. Customers have benefited from telecoms competition.

Broadcasting

The Broadcasting Act, 1991 defines broadcasting, including what is a program, as follows:

> "broadcasting" means any transmission of programs, whether or not encrypted, by radio waves or other means of telecommunication for reception by the public by means of broadcasting receiving apparatus, but does not include any such transmission of programs that is made solely for performance or display in a public place;

---

[10]These two paragraphs draw heavily on Crandall and Waverman (1999).

Table 1: Call Net Revenue and Access Costs per Minute
(Canadian dollars)

	Revenue per minute	Carrier charges (includes lease of facilities plus access costs)*
1989	$0.596	$0.368
1990	0.578	0.392
1991	0.422	0.255
1992	0.345	0.173
1993	0.312	0.207
1994	0.245	0.174
1995	0.277	0.183
1996	0.254	0.158
1997	0.223	0.124
1998 estimate	0.208	0.113
1999 estimate	0.198	0.109
2000 estimate	0.184	0.104

Note: *The contribution to local access deficits has been an explicit element since 1973 when it was $0.126 per minute falling to $0.036 in 1997. Effective January 1, 1998, local rates increased on average $3.00 a month reducing the long-distance contribution to $0.02 per minute per end where it will stay for four years.

"program" means sounds or visual images, or a combination of sounds and visual images, that are intended to inform, enlighten or entertain, but does not include visual images, whether or not combined with sounds, that consist predominantly of alphanumeric text". (Chapter B-9.01)

The great problem for Canadian broadcasting policy is that new technology and new services make it increasingly difficult to determine, in fact, what is broadcasting or programing. For example, the definition of broadcasting could refer to NVOD over telephone lines where the computer is a "broadcasting receiving device". A program is, I imagine, the Real Video™

images I download on my computer from Fox Sports. However, a joke site on the Internet, while it does entertain, since it is predominantly alphanumeric text, is not a program. In its 1995 analysis, the CRTC appears to distinguish between licensed VOD programing and VOD which "is not scheduled". "These [latter] services will be akin to a bookstore or library" (1995, p. 34). Licensed VOD programing is recommended as offering "the maximum practicable number of Canadian titles ... (and) should be expected to make direct contributions to the development and production of Canadian programs" (ibid.). But how can one tax titles on a shelf or their delivery if the delivery is over the Internet?

Thus, convergence, as described above, and the Internet necessitate a review of these definitions. The CRTC has launched a new Public Notice and Proceeding on "New Media", under both the Broadcasting Act and the Telecommunications Act, to examine the rapidly expanding, and increasingly available, range of communications services collectively known or referred to as new media.[11] The questions the CRTC asks are:

a) In what ways, and to what extent, do new media affect, or are they likely to affect, the broadcasting and telecommunications undertakings now regulated by the Commission?

b) In what ways, and to what extent, are some or any of the new media either broadcasting or telecommunications services?

c) To the extent that any of the new media are broadcasting or telecommunications, to what extent should the Commission regulate and supervise them pursuant to the *Broadcasting Act* and the *Telecommunications Act*?

d) Do the new media raise any other broad policy issues of national interest?

In this proceeding, the CRTC for one of the first times brings together its two sides: telecoms and broadcasting. New media, indeed, has profound effects on broadcasting and telecoms services as traditionally defined and thus on CICP. Moreover, the CRTC may well be behind the curve. As several

---

[11]"New media can be described as encompassing, singly or in combination, and whether interactive or not, services and products that make use of video, audio, graphics and alphanumeric text; and involving, along with other, more traditional means of distribution, digital delivery over networks interconnected on a local or global scale." The commission considers that this may be a useful working description for the purposes of this proceeding.

submissions to the New Media hearings suggest,[12] and with which I wholly concur, it is not likely to be an issue of regulating and supervising the new media, but what existing Canadian policies *survive* the new media.

As we will see below, the present main instruments of Canadian policy — content restrictions and taxes — are not all suited for a "new media" world. How does the Canadian government in a digital world know what broadcasting or programs are being either delivered or viewed?

The CAB and TELUS submissions to the New Media proceeding recommended strongly that the CRTC re-evaluate existing policies. That re-evaluation is absolutely necessary and is required now.

Current Broadcasting Policy for Canada. The relevant statute providing for Canadian broadcasting policy is given in Appendix 3 (note the number of times the word Canadian appears).[13] The key sections are:

3. (1)

(e) each element of the Canadian broadcasting system shall contribute in an appropriate manner to the creation and presentation of Canadian programing;

(f) each broadcasting undertaking shall make maximum use, and in no case less than predominant use, of Canadian creative and other resources in the creation and presentation of programing, unless the nature of the service provided by the undertaking, such as specialized content or format or the use of languages other than French and English, renders that use impracticable, in which case the undertaking shall make the greatest practicable use of those resources;

. . .

(s) private networks and programing undertakings should, to an extent consistent with the financial and other resources available to them,
   (i) contribute significantly to the creation and presentation of Canadian programing, and
   (ii) be responsive to the evolving demands of the public; and

(t) distribution undertakings

---

[12]Canadian Association of Broadcasting (CAB), TELUS, and the Director of the Bureau of Competition Policy.

[13]See Stanbury (1998a, b) for a detailed analysis of these provisions.

(i) should give priority to the carriage of Canadian programing services and, in particular, to the carriage of local Canadian stations,

(ii) should provide efficient delivery of programing at affordable rates, using the most effective technologies available at reasonable cost,

(iii) should, where programing services are supplied to them by broadcasting undertakings pursuant to contractual arrangements, provide reasonable terms for the carriage, packaging and retailing of those programing services, and

(iv) may, where the Commission considers it appropriate, originate programing, including local programing, on such terms as are conducive to the achievement of the objectives of the broadcasting policy set out in this subsection, and in particular provide access for underserved linguistic and cultural minority communities.

Current Canadian broadcasting, as opposed to present Canadian telecoms policy, is based on an elaborate set of entry restrictions, programing requirements and cross-subsidies. Canadian broadcasting rules license infrastructure (network) services and content, establish content rules,[14] tax broadcasters for the production of Canadian content, set maximum permissible amounts of time on advertising[15] and subsidize content production. These policies are the opposite of the thrust in telecommunications where it is competition and markets, not rules and restrictions which maximize Canadian welfare. The thrust of this paper is that convergence of technology also requires a significant convergence of the two policy sides of the CRTC, and renders infeasible the main current regulatory instruments in broadcasting.

Rules on Canadian content are set under the "Television Broadcasting Regulations" SOR/87-49 (see Globerman, 1995; Stanbury, 1998b). Basically, 60% of programing in the hours of 6 PM until midnight are to be

---

[14] "(6) Subject to subsection (9), a licensee shall devote not less than 60% of the broadcast year and of any six month period specified in a condition of license to the broadcasting of Canadian programs. [Television]." Content on radio has rules which define what is "Canadian" music: (the Toronto Symphony recording Beethoven in Ottawa but not Buffalo, Canadian or foreign). See Appendix 4.

[15] "11. (1) Except as otherwise provided in subsections (2) to (4), or by a condition of its license, a licensee shall not broadcast more than 12 minutes of advertising material in any clock hour in a broadcast day."

Canadian.[16] However, since news is Canadian and is low cost, the substitution by broadcasters of news for drama and other so-called under-represented programing[17] itself has had to be controlled by the CRTC by providing drama with a 150% time credit.

Infrastructure providers (cable, DTH) have detailed rules of what programs they must carry — local CBC programs first, then educational programs, then other local programs, regional CBC, etc., before other programing that they may wish to provide. These are so-called basic channels which must be carried before specialty, pay television or pay-per-view channels are carried. The "pay" channels, that is, pay, specialty and pay-per-view have their own "must" carry list. First, each own-language speciality service is carried, then each English-language pay television service, at least one English-language general interest television pay-per-view service, and the ethnic programing service.

---

[16]Manera (1996), reports that for the 1992-93 broadcast year, for the 7pm to 11pm viewing hours the CBC's English television schedule was 85% Canadian, as compared to Canadian content of 24% for CTV and 25% for Global.

[17]"The Commission has focused attention on those categories of Canadian programing that tend to be under-represented in the schedules of Canadian broadcasters. These program categories are primarily drama, music, variety, children's and documentary. Currently, the Commission expects all conventional broadcasters to have appropriate strategies in place to develop programing in these under-represented categories. In recent years, however, regulatory mechanisms have tended to concentrate more specifically on the entertainment categories of drama, music and variety." See DTH Distribution Undertakings.

Canadian programing services are rigorously defined.[18] All networks and infrastructure providers are taxed to pay for the production of Canadian material, basically 8% of broadcasting revenues.[19] These taxes are placed in

---

[18]*Canadian programing service* means

(*a*) a programing service that originates entirely within Canada or is transmitted by a licensed station; (*b*) a programing service consisting of community programing; (*c*) a specialty service; (*d*) a pay television service; (*e*) a television pay-per-view service; (*f*) a DTH pay-per-view service; (*g*) a video-on-demand service; or (*h*) a pay audio service. *(service de programmation Canadien)*

The criteria used in defining a Canadian program are set out in Public Notices CRTC 1984-94, 1987-28 and 1988-105. Most private, conventional English-language broadcasters earning more than $10 million dollars per year in advertising revenues may choose between a condition of licence requiring a minimum level of expenditure on Canadian programs tied to their advertising revenues, or a condition requiring a minimum level of exhibition of Canadian entertainment programs in the evening broadcast period.

[19]*[Contribution to Local Expression and Canadian Programing]*
29. (1) In this section, "contribution to local expression" means a contribution made in accordance with Public Notice CRTC 1997-25, entitled *New Regulatory Framework for Broadcasting Distribution Undertakings.*

(2) If a licensee is required under this section to make a contribution to Canadian programing, it shall contribute
(*a*) to the Canadian production fund at least 80% of its total required contribution; and
(*b*) to one or more independent production funds, the remainder of its total required contribution.
(*b*) in the broadcast year ending on August 31, 1999, and in each broadcast year thereafter, of an amount not less than the greater of
(i) 5% of its gross revenues derived from broadcasting activities in the year, less any contribution to local expression made by the licensee in that year, and
(ii) 3% of its gross revenues derived from broadcasting activities in that year.

The commission seeks to achieve this objective, in part, through its Television Broadcasting Regulations, 1987 (the regulations), through the definition of a Canadian program found in Public Notices CRTC 1984-94, 1987-28 and

central funds available to be drawn on by Canadian program providers. This is the Canadian production fund, and the "independent production fund" now joined and renamed the Canadian Television Fund that meet the criteria listed in the commission's public notice entitled *Contributions to Canadian Programing by Broadcasting Distribution Undertakings*. The networks are the buyers of the programing so produced. The financing of Canadian production is complex, besides the Canadian Television Fund, there are other subsidies, notably Telefilm Canada. There are also barriers to integrated content provision by infrastructure suppliers. If a Pay-TV program which is owned 30% or more by the broadcaster is carried, then at least one other third-party (less than 30% control) program must be carried.[20]

A contentious policy has been the program substitution and deletion. When a Canadian local or regional channel purchases the rights to a program which is shown at the same time on a more distant channel (U.S. channel)[21] in order to allow the Canadian channel to effectively compete, that is, to maximize advertising revenues, the U.S. signal is substituted for by the Canadian signal.

1988-105, and through specific conditions of licence or expectations relating either to expenditures by certain private television broadcasters on Canadian programs, or to the exhibition of Canadian programs in underrepresented categories.

[20]These overly regulated restrictions likely diminish programing.

[21]"(a) shall delete the programing service of a television station and substitute the programing service of a local television station or a regional television station or, with the agreement of the broadcaster operating the local television station or regional television station, shall have that broadcaster carry out the deletion and substitution, if (i) the programing service to be deleted and the programing service to be substituted are comparable and simultaneously broadcast; (ii) the local television station or regional television station has a higher priority under section 17; and (iii) in a case when the broadcaster operating the local television station or regional television station is not to carry out the deletion and substitution under an agreement with the licensee, the licensee has, at least four days before the date on which the programing service is broadcast, received from the broadcaster operating the local television station or regional television station a written request for the deletion and substitution."

A Canadian policy story: the DTH fiasco. The CRTC first published a general approach to Direct-To-Home satellite distribution in 1987.[22] In September 1992 the CRTC issued a Notice of Public Hearing because of the launch of DirecTv in the United States, which has a footprint over much of Canada close to the U.S. border. In its decision in June 1993, the CRTC asserted its jurisdiction over DTH, including that from U.S. services. It backed up its jurisdiction rights by stating that U.S. satellite services (e.g., programing) illegally distributed in Canada via a non-authorized DTH service would lose their authorization for cable distribution. In a response to this decision the two Canadian satellite service providers requested licence exemptions for DTH services distributed via a Canadian satellite, that is, one of the satellites owned by the two providers. Three Canadian groups announced alternative plans to provide DTH services as did a consortium of

---

[22]DTH Directions to the CRTC (Direct-to-Home (DTH) Pay-Per-View Television Programing Undertakings) Order.

5. The CRTC is directed, in the exercise of its powers in respect of the carrying on of a DTH pay-per-view television programing undertaking, (a) to prohibit, by appropriate means, the undertaking from acquiring exclusive or other preferential rights to pay-per-view distribution of feature films and other programing within Canada; (b) to ensure that the undertaking is subject to equitable obligations and makes maximum contributions to Canadian programing, including a significant financial contribution derived from a percentage of gross annual revenues to the production of Canadian programing, and that the financial contribution is administered independently of the undertaking; (c) taking into consideration the total number of channels over which the undertaking's service is offered, to apply rules that are comparable or equivalent to those rules in effect in respect of other pay-per-view television programing undertakings and that pertain to the annual exhibition ratios of Canadian to foreign films and events, the annual minimum numbers of Canadian films and events to be exhibited and the remittances to be paid by the undertaking to rights holders for the Canadian films and events it exhibits; (d) to require the undertaking to be subject to the same generally applicable Canadian policy as other broadcasting undertakings in respect of the use of Canadian and foreign satellite facilities; (e) not to refuse to issue a license to an applicant for the sole reason that the applicant proposes to use foreign satellites for the distribution of non-Canadian programing to subscribers through a DTH distribution undertaking, provided that such use is consistent with generally applicable Canadian satellite policy; and (f) not to refuse to issue a license to an applicant for the sole reason that the applicant holds a license to carry on a DTH distribution undertaking.

DirecTv with the Power Corp. The three Canadian providers (i.e., not DirecTv) agreed in principle to merge their applications. This consortium included the major cable companies and Bell Canada Enterprises. In July 1994, the CRTC exempted DTH undertakings which used Canadian satellites, that is, not DirecTv/Power.[23] The cable companies exited the proposed "all-Canadian" consortium, due to the anti-competitive nature of the grouping of all infrastructure suppliers. The requirements for DTH undertakings (including content, and payments for Canadian productions) were released in July 1995.[24] A number of applications were received by the CRTC in 1995 and in late 1995 two licences were authorized — Express Vu (the original Canadian Consortium minus the cable companies) and Power DirecTv. Five new DTH pay-per-view video channels were authorized and four audio-channels. In August 1996, a third DTH provider, Star Choice, was authorized. Two more applications were received by the CRTC in late 1996. Power DirecTv never got off the ground, largely due to the restrictions of using Canadian satellites. Today, two licence holders compete, each restricted first to replicate what is available on cable. The Canadian border is now many miles high to prevent unlicenced satellite services!

Broadcasting licences. The spectrum for television channels, which is a public resource, is given away free and (until digital TV arrives) the number of slots is limited and controlled by the CRTC for cable and DTH distributors. Therefore, rents can be earned by channel service (content) providers. Hence, applications to the CRTC for these rents leads to numerous competing applications[25] and long drawn out hearings. The CRTC's criteria

---

[23]PN 1994-111.

[24]Orders-in-Council D.C. 1995-1105 and 1995-1106.

[25]Example of a hearing on a license application to CRTC Broadcasting: "Application by TVA GROUP INC., RADIO NORD INC., THOMSON CANADA LIMITED, PUBLICATIONS INTERCONTINENTAL INC., FINTEL INC. and SOBELA IV INC., partners in Le Canal des Affaires, S.E.N.C., a general partnership, for a broadcasting licence to carry on a French-language national programing undertaking (television specialty service) to be distributed via satellite to broadcasting distribution undertakings. The service would provide programing on the economy, the business culture and personal finances. The applicant is seeking a modified dual status carriage and is proposing a monthly wholesale rate of $0.30 per subscriber where the service is distributed on the basic service.

in choosing provider A over B is opaque, easy to criticize and in stark contrast to transparent licensing policy for telecommunications. Clearly, since convergence means that the same content can move over "telecoms" or "broadcasting" facilities, content will move to the regime less controlled. To anticipate that day, the CRTC should move away from beauty contests, where it is the uneven judge, and rely on a neutral market. A first step would be to announce objective criteria — type of programing, desired fee, etc., and then have an auction process where the state, not lucky licence-holders will gain rents. However, such an objective process would require the CRTC to articulate formally its goals and objectives, not an easy or welcome task.

New media review. Only seven years after the major overhaul of the previous 1911 Act, the CRTC is holding public hearings to determine whether the new media requires a re-formulation of Canadian rules — the Canadian Television Policy Review.

The commission's goals for this review of its regulatory and policy framework for television are straightforward to it but are simply a repetition of the past conflicting policy objectives, with little sense of reality. The announced goals are the usual mantra of CICP — to further the development of a strong and viable programing industry; to ensure that Canadians receive a wide range of attractive and distinctive Canadian program choices; to facilitate the growth of strong broadcasting undertakings; to ensure that the Canadian broadcasting system meets the needs of Canadian viewers and reflects their values; and to implement the public interest objectives of the Broadcasting Act (the Act).[26]

The CRTC states; "As the Canadian broadcasting system prepares for a more competitive global environment, it will be necessary to marshal resources from all elements of the Canadian broadcasting system to produce *more* high-quality programing that attracts Canadian audiences and is exportable to world markets. Achieving this will require, among other things,

---

Ottawa, 2 October 1998 Notice of Public Hearing CRTC 1998-7 ISSUE NO. 1, Public Notice CRTC 1998-44, Ottawa, 6 May 1998 MONTRÉAL, QUEBEC 7 DECEMBER 1998, 9:00 A.M."

[26]"A key question asked is: In an environment of increasingly fragmented audiences, what economic model would best ensure the creation, acquisition and exhibition of high quality Canadian programs?"

cooperation between broadcasters and independent producers."[27] Thus the CRTC appears to see that the new media threat requires more subsidies and continued restrictions. This is simply unfeasible.

Phase I of the hearings took place in October 1998. The submission of the Director of the Bureau of Competition Policy to the Final Phase in February 1999 summarizes the submissions made:[28]

1. the new media are not similar to and should not be regulated as "broadcasting" or "content"
2. there are no scarcity elements in the provision of new media services
3. market forces appear to work well
4. "substantial Canadian content is being generated" (page 5)
5. regulation would diminish the provision of Canadian content since content can be provided from anywhere
6. taxation of new media would greatly reduce its supply in Canada.

This appears to be a fair summary of the majority of views.

Yet, the vice-chairman of the CRTC began the oral and final part of this review on February 9, 1999 by referring to two theories that a minority had suggested — first, the necessity of subsidies for the provision of Canadian content on Internet Service Providers and second, more "shelf space" for Canadian content "and methods to draw viewers to this content". These are unworkable ideas and bad policies. For example, Canadian content on radio is defined by points earned as to whether composer, player or producer are Canadian (see Stanbury, 1998b). This is simply impossible on the Internet:

---

[27]Emphasis added. In addition the CRTC states; "Making the transition to digital television will entail major expenditures by broadcasters and producers. It is not clear at this time what additional revenues will be available to assist in defraying these costs. The Commission intends to begin a public process, at a later date, for the purpose of developing a regulatory framework to accommodate the transition to digital television. In the context of the forthcoming review of television policies, however, the Commission will wish to begin to explore issues relating to the impact that the transition to digital television will have on the ability of broadcasters and producers to create, fund and schedule Canadian programs."

[28]Final comments of the director of Investigation and Research to the Canadian Radio-television and Telecommunications Commission re: Broadcasting Public Notice CRTC 1998-82, Telecom Public Notice CRTC 1998-20.

Canadian Information/Culture Policy in the Information Age

how does one "know" or "test" whether the author is Canadian — a Canadian e-mail address? Subsidizing such "Canadian" content would be akin to warming a house with no walls in the Arctic in winter.

The CRTC has already implemented a number of policies which affect "new media" markets. For example, any distributor, except as otherwise provided under a condition of its licence, must ensure that a majority of the video channels and a majority of the audio channels received by a subscriber are devoted to the distribution of Canadian programing services.[29] This would, given the definitions of broadcasting and content apply to all distributors of content. But in the converged world, it cannot. The CRTC wishes to extend its current constraints on Canadian content to the world of digital transmission and cyberspace. As most submissions to the New Media proceeding detail, expanded CRTC regulation will not meet public policy objectives, it will reduce not increase supply. What is not readily apparent is that there is now an increased inability of the current Canadian content and tax policies to provide their goal — Canadian culture.

The Future of Canadian Information/Culture Policy

What does all this technological change mean for the Canadian Information/ Culture policy? Canadian broadcasting policy is designed around one main principle — enforcing Canadian content. To do so, the choice for viewers/ listeners is constrained and taxes are levied to subsidize Canadian content. In telecoms parlance, bypass in broadcasting has been minimized by forcing all infrastructure providers — over-the-air, wires or satellite to show/play Canadian programing and to pay taxes. As long as bypass was relatively easily constrained, CICP was feasible. Note I am not suggesting it was or is optimal. The convulsions in Canada's policy towards DTH broadcasting and magazine publication are examples of inane public policy.

Is this Canadian policy feasible in the world of convergence? In essence, will bypass become so easy that enforcing Canadian content and taxing broadcasting will no longer provide sufficient viewers and support for the Canadian production industry? As I have already detailed, in a digital world with convergence, infrastructure (the delivery system) is neutral with respect to content, that is, the delivery system has no easy way of distinguishing

---

[29]Other than the programing distributed on program repeat channels.

content. In an unconverged world, telephone wires carry telephone calls and coaxial cable carries a TV picture. Thus one can regulate telephony and broadcasting at the delivery system level in different ways. In a truly converged world, delivery system A will not necessarily know what is being carried. In an Internet world, the backbone infrastructure provider has no idea, unless content is monitored and read, as to what is being transported. Two recent issues show how difficult it is to "control" or monitor the Internet. The first issue is the intense public debate on the difficulty of stemming hate and pornographic material on the Web. Some wish to control such content on the Web, others point to the incredible difficulty of doing that but urge the use of existing anti-hate and anti-pornography laws while extending the definition of such literature to include the digital versions of such offensive material (see Saxby, 1996). On a second front, the European Commission has had to assess whether Internet telephony is voice telephony as defined and controlled under relevant EU law. The Commission decided that Internet Telephony, because of the delay in sending and receiving conversations, is not voice telephony.[30] Similarly, the FCC has examined the same issue since Internet telephony bypasses the U.S. contribution scheme, providing subsidies for residential telephone subscribers.

In an Internet world, a TV picture from A to B may go over different routes and not necessarily even be within the nation state where A and B reside. Thus if all infrastructure is Internet protocol, first, there is little control except arbitrary banning of material, for example, television signals that the home at location A can watch. Second, one cannot tax the provider of content, because it is carrying Canadian television since that provider can be anywhere on the backbone system A-B.[31]

Thus in this hypothetical converged world, bypass is easy, one cannot enforce minimum Canadian content on carriage because carriage is universal.[32] Nor can one easily tax broadcasting at the broadcast or carriage levels. Since a "Canadian" broadcast can go via non-Canadian routes from A to B, neither

---

[30]This is a delay in making a decision since new developments greatly diminish delay in delivery.

[31]In 1995, the cable industry contributed $40 million to Canadian program production. (Under CRTC 1993-94, Structural Public Notice.)

[32]Globerman (1995) states "questions arise as to how the regulator will monitor the content of signals carried on computer networks such as the Internet".

the carriage company nor the CRTC would know what broadcasting was being carried in Canada. The CRTC cannot tax U.S. broadcasters or backbone networks for Canadian content. And at the extreme, it is not obvious who is carrying broadcast signals. NVOD over Bell Canada lines is simply the first step. Moreover, what is a television set in this world? What if consumers watch "TV" over the computer?

This hypothetical world may be far away but it will likely appear. The discussion does show that bypass is feasible now and that unlike DTH satellites, the government has little power to prevent it!

But this presents a fundamental problem for Canadian policy. *How does one enforce Canadian content and who does one tax to provide the monies for Canadian productions?* The tax is now levied first, on those entities who gain broadcast licences. The CRTC estimated that in 1993, public and private conventional Canadian broadcasters accounted for 75% of the spending on Canadian programs (CRTC, 1995, p. 39). Part of the economic value of these broadcasting licences comes from the difficulty of Canadian consumers to bypass this programing. In the Internet/converged world with more bypass, licences are less valuable. Therefore, one can surmise that broadcasting revenues/advertising expenditures earned by Canadian licence-holders will fall. There will be less money for Canadian programing. Bypass also threatens the Canadian policy more directly as our hypothetical world showed. Primarily, the "problem" is the inability to enforce content standards.

However, given that the need for the overall social goal of promoting Canadian culture still holds, what policy instruments are feasible?

A User Tax

The United Kingdom, France and other countries primarily tax TV owners, that is, the terminal owner rather than the broadcaster.[33] I suggest consideration of such a tax for Canada. In the ultimate converged world, the TV and the computer are nearly interchangeable. Hence one cannot tax just TV sets since "television programs" can be watched on other types of terminals. Should all computer owners hold TV licences? What if these instruments are

---

[33]The licence tax itself is shifted if less television sets are bought.

in an office in a major corporation? TV sets are normally in homes and primarily for entertainment.

Thus, it is easy to tax TV sets as entertainment tools; taxing all screens is not so easy. One can, however, possibly argue that the TV set tax base is less liable to bypass than the broadcaster tax base since it is likely that the production of material will expand at a faster rate than the computer will replace the TV terminal. Hence, TV licence fees in Canada will be a less risky (less bypassable) tax base than the present broadcasting taxes.

There are other good reasons to prefer a TV licence fee to the present broadcaster infrastructure taxes.

- A per unit TV licence is less shiftable than a broadcast tax, that is, it is a more efficient rent collection device.
- The broadcast tax decreases the revenue to broadcasters and/or raises advertising rates, somewhat defeating the purpose of that tax, which is to encourage the viewing of Canadian programs.
- A TV watcher who only watches U.S. programs on U.S. stations should be excluded from the viewership that establishes Canadian advertising rates.

The arguments against the per unit tax are as follows: first, is its possible inequity, rich and poor pay the same and some poor may decide to exit the TV-watching market rather than pay the tax. Second, administratively, the licence fee is costly to collect.

I turn to an examination of the benefits and costs of increasing the supply of Canadian content by content rules as compared to licence fees. The benefits of lowering the price for the use of Canadian content by increasing subsidies, that is, an increased supply-side rather than demand-side (content rules) policy, can be observed with a simple diagram.

In Figure 4 there are a series of demand and supply curves shown. The solid demand curves are for the viewing of all programs, American, Canadian and others, in Canada. The dashed demand curves are for Canadian programs alone. D_M is the unconstrained demand in Canada for TV viewing, no content rules. B is the demand for all TV viewing, restrained by the 60% rule. The effect of Canadian content rules is to decrease the number of hours watched (see Stanbury, 1998b). The reasoning is simple, unable to watch what they prefer, viewers switch to non-TV alternatives. DC is the demand for Canadian programing with *no* CRTC rules. BC is the

Figure 4: Subsidies for Canadian Programing

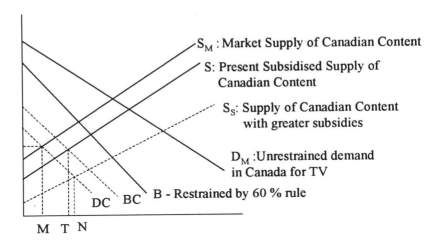

S_M : Market Supply of Canadian Content

S: Present Subsidised Supply of Canadian Content

S_S: Supply of Canadian Content with greater subsidies

D_M :Unrestrained demand in Canada for TV

B - Restrained by 60 % rule

demand for Canadian viewing with CRTC rules. Note BC is assumed to lie above DC. SM is the supply of Canadian programing, no subsidy. S is the supply of Canadian programing with the subsidy. The market, unregulated by CRTC rules, produces M hours of Canadian programing at the intersection of S_M and DC. The imposition of Canadian content rules lowers overall demand for TV but increases that for Canadian content. With a subsidy for Canadian programs, the present actual viewing of Canadian programing is T hours — MT more than in an unconstrained world.

The purpose of this analysis is to suggest that with an increased subsidy *and* a relaxation of the rule over Canadian programs watched, Canadian viewing can *increase* in the figure, to N hours. How can a relaxation of rules on Canadian content increase the demand for Canadian content? In the figure, increased subsidies increase the supply of Canadian programing to S_S. While the relevant demand curve DC (demand for Canadian viewing, no CRTC restrictions) is below BC, the supply response to the increased subsidy levels to *more* Canadian content produced and watched. Whether this figure is realistic would require empirical work, not attempted here.

A UK licence fee is presently £95 or some C$250 per year. There are ten million TV households in Canada and the $250 fee would raise $2.5 billion. This would be sufficient to pay for the CBC and Telefilm; and offset the revenue loss from the elimination of Canadian production taxes. Present subsidies to Canadian broadcasting are approximately $200 million from the production funds;[34] Telefilm's 1998 budget was $150 million, and the CBC's budget for Canadian programs in 1997 was $770 million (Table 2; see also Stanbury, 1998b, p. 225). The total spent on Canadian programing by all Canadian broadcasters in 1997 was $1.6 billion (Table 2). Thus, an annual licence fee of $250 per household would fund the CBC (1998-99 grant, $665 million) and other Canadian programing. These increased subsidies would shift the supply curve for Canadian programing as in S_S in Figure 4. However, who is to be subsidized and who is to be taxed? Convergence means that the supply of content increases and that the meaning of "Canadian" is difficult if at all possible to define. Convergence also means that viewing is not just on a conventional TV. Therefore, a wise policy would be to sunset the subsidies and tax, drawing them down at, say, 10% per year. This allows the "conventional" broadcasting industry time to adjust. In a truly converged world, there are no feasible subsidies and taxes.

Other changes in Canadian broadcasting policy besides the source of the tax, are likely needed to draw broadcasting policy towards telecoms policy — more of a reliance on a market is required. Rather than mandating strict content rules with overrides for some drama, counting 150% of the time to account for its higher cost than news, a variable tax system could be considered, with different tax rates or credits for different types of programs. However, attempting to tax (reduce) U.S. programing in a world of bypass supply passes that programing into modes/over technologies which are more difficult to audit. Thus, U.S. programing would be delivered over the Internet. The present 60% rule works (subject to the stations' use of lower cost/quality programing) because the regulator can count the minutes in prime-time and can observe the station. With thousands of content providers over the converged technology, the CRTC cannot measure minutes of Canadian content.

Conclusion

On the first page of this paper the contradiction between CRTC (Canadian) policy instruments in telecoms and broadcasting is highlighted. What is most

---

[34]Coopers & Lybrand, final report, *Environmental Scan*, to the CRTC on behalf of CAB; p. iv – 7.

Table 2: Canadian Program Expenditures

In $ millions	1993	1994	1995	1996	1997
Private Conventional Television Revenues					
Advertising	1,352	1,380	1,453	1,497	1,600
Other	120	116	123	122	107
Total	1,472	1,496	1,576	1,619	1,707
Profit before interest and taxes (PBIT)	178	166	233	250	267
Canadian Program Expenditures					
Categories 1 to 5 (Information)	259	273	286	283	287
Category 6 (Sports)	43	78	42	55	43
Categories 7 to 9 (Entertainment)	80	78	86	81	81
Categories 10 & 11					
(Games, Human Interest)	52	42	55	58	57
Total Telecast	434	471	469	477	468
Other Canadian Expenses	5	6	5	9	7
Total Canadian program expenditures	439	477	474	486	475
Foreign program expenditures	265	263	291	307	340
Specialty and Pay Television Revenues					
Advertising	98	109	122	155	183
Subscription	325	347	436	489	511
Other	16	16	18	20	22
Total	439	472	576	664	716
PBIT	79	97	98	98	124
Canadian program expenditures	139	153	204	261	263
Foreign program expenditures	54	59	71	79	84
Educational Television					
Canadian program expenditures	n.a.	67	42	77	64
Foreign program expenditures	n.a.	3	6	8	8
CBC/Radio Canada					
Canadian program expenditures	278	276	247	341	353
Foreign program expenditures	33	39	66	29	26
Indirect costs (Canadian programs)	538	581	560	544	414
Total	849	896	873	914	793

Source: CRTC's financial database given as Appendix to Public Notice CRTC 1998.44.

inconsistent is the CRTC's views that one of the benefits of competition is increased choice for telecoms users but that increased choice for information highway users is harmful and thus requires regulating market entry. But convergence essentially means that market entry is ubiquitous and cannot be regulated. Moreover, given that the infrastructures regulated now in such different ways by the CRTC will compete to provide similar services, maintaining varying restrictions on each of several different delivery platforms tilts the playing field, encouraging substitution between systems which may be neither efficient nor equitable. Thus, the CRTC needs to utilize market-based policy instruments relying on increased consumer choice through the market, not CRTC-organized beauty contests and quantitative restrictions. Use taxes and subsidies to guide market outcomes.

My prescription for Canadian broadcasting policy is:

- Rely much more on end-user taxes (i.e., TV licences).
- Relax administrative constraints on program providers.
- Increase subsidies to Canadian conventional programing, but temporarily.
- Use auctions of licences.
- If the revenues from optimal TV licences do not contribute sufficiently to maintain Canadian content, *C'est la vie.*

The responses to the CRTC's "New Media" Public Notice show how Canadian content is growing in the unregulated Internet world. This new media should not be regulated, indeed it shows how market solutions can provide what consumers demand. Thus, liberalizing conventional media rules under a temporarily enhanced subsidy/tax scheme would pave the way for a fully liberalized market.

Appendix 1
DTH DISTRIBUTION UNDERTAKINGS

37. Except as otherwise provided under a condition of its license, a licensee shall distribute as part of its basic service

(*a*) the programing service of at least one of each of the Corporation's English-language and French-language television network affiliates or members; and

(*b*) the programing service of at least one affiliate of each television network licensed on a national basis.

2) Except as otherwise provided under a condition of its license, a licensee shall distribute, to the extent of available channels,

(*a*) each specialty service, other than a single or limited point-of-view religious specialty service;

(*b*) each pay television service, other than a limited point-of-view religious pay television service;

(*c*) at least one English-language general interest DTH pay-per-view service; and

(*d*) at least one French-language general interest DTH pay-per-view service.

40. (1) Except as otherwise provided under a condition of its license, if a licensee distributes one of the programing services referred to in subsection 38(2) or section 39, the licensee shall distribute the service in accordance with the Commission's Public Notice entitled *Linkage Requirements for Direct-to-home (DTH) Satellite Distribution Undertakings*, as amended from time to time.

(2) If a licensee distributes a programing service that comprises the proceedings of the House of Commons, the licensee shall include that service as part of its basic service, unless the licensee and the operator of the programing service agree in writing to the distribution of the service as a discretionary service.

(3) A licensee shall not distribute an English-language DTH pay-per-view service unless it also distributes a French-language DTH pay-per-view service.

Appendix 2
LICENSE TAXES

(2) A licensee shall make a contribution to Canadian programing

(*a*) in the broadcast year ending on August 31, 1998, of an amount not less than 5% of its gross revenues derived from broadcasting activities in the period beginning on the day these Regulations come into force and ending on August 31, 1998; and

(*b*) in the broadcast year ending on August 31, 1999, and in each broadcast year thereafter, of an amount not less than 5% of its gross revenues derived from broadcasting activities in that year.

Appendix 3
BROADCASTING POLICY

It is hereby declared as the broadcasting policy for Canada that

(a) the Canadian broadcasting system shall be effectively owned and controlled by Canadians;

(b) the Canadian broadcasting system, operating primarily in the English and French languages and comprising public, private and community elements, makes use of radio frequencies that are public property and provides, through its programing, a public service essential to the maintenance and enhancement of national identity and cultural sovereignty;

(c) English and French language broadcasting, while sharing common aspects, operate under different conditions and may have different requirements;

(d) the Canadian broadcasting system should

  (i) serve to safeguard, enrich and strengthen the cultural, political, social and economic fabric of Canada,

  (ii) encourage the development of Canadian expression by providing a wide range of programing that reflects Canadian attitudes, opinions, ideas, values and artistic creativity, by displaying Canadian talent in entertainment programing and by offering information and analysis concerning Canada and other countries from a Canadian point of view,

  (iii) through its programing and the employment opportunities arising out of its operations, serve the needs and interests, and reflect the circumstances and aspirations, of Canadian men, women and children, including equal rights, the linguistic duality and multicultural and multiracial nature of Canadian society and the special place of aboriginal peoples within that society, and

  (iv) be readily adaptable to scientific and technological change;

(i) the programing provided by the Canadian broadcasting system should

  (i) be varied and comprehensive, providing a balance of information, enlightenment and entertainment for men, women and children of all ages, interests and tastes,

  (ii) be drawn from local, regional, national and international sources,

  (iii) include educational and community programs,

  (iv) provide a reasonable opportunity for the public to be exposed to the expression of differing views on matters of public concern, and

  (v) include a significant contribution from the Canadian independent production sector;

(l) the Canadian Broadcasting Corporation, as the national public broadcaster, should provide radio and television services incorporating a wide range of programing that informs, enlightens and entertains;

(m) the programing provided by the Corporation should

  (i) be predominantly and distinctively Canadian,

  (ii) reflect Canada and its regions to national and regional audiences, while serving the special needs of those regions,

Appendix 4
RADIO RULES

(2) For the purposes of this section, "Canadian selection" means a musical selection
    (a) that meets at least two of the following conditions, namely,
        (i) the music is or lyrics are performed principally by a Canadian,
        (ii) the music is composed entirely by a Canadian,
        (iii) the lyrics are written entirely by a Canadian,
        (iv) the musical selection consists of a live performance that is
            (A) recorded wholly in Canada, or
            (B) performed wholly in and broadcast live in Canada, and
        (v) the musical selection was performed live or recorded after September 1, 1991, and a Canadian who has collaborated with a non-Canadian receives at least 50% of the credit as composer and lyricist according to the records of a recognized performing rights society;

(3) Subject to subsection (6) and except as otherwise provided pursuant to a condition of its license, an A.M. or F.M. licensee shall, each broadcast week, devote 30% or more of the licensee's musical selections from content category 2 and 10% or more of the licensee's musical selections from content category 3 to Canadian selections and schedule those selections in a reasonable manner throughout each broadcast day.

(4) Where 7% or more of the musical selections broadcast by a licensee during an ethnic programing period are Canadian selections and are scheduled in a reasonable manner throughout that period, subsection (3) shall apply only in respect of those musical selections that are broadcast during that part of the broadcast week that is not devoted to ethnic programs.

(5) Except as otherwise provided pursuant to a condition of its license, an A.M. or F.M. licensee licensed to operate in the French language shall, each broadcast week, devote 65% or more of its vocal musical selections from content category 2 to musical selections in the French language and schedule those selections in a reasonable manner throughout each broadcast day.

6) An A.M. or F.M. licensee may, in any broadcast week, reduce the proportion of its Canadian musical selections from content category 2 to
    (a) not less than 20%, where, in that broadcast week, the licensee devotes not less than 35% and not more than 49% of all its musical selections to instrumental selections; and
    (b) not less than 15%, where, in that broadcast week, the licensee devotes 50% or more of all its musical selections to instrumental selections.

Appendix 5
GLOSSARY

ADSL	=	asynchronous digital subscriber loop
DBS	=	direct broadcast satellite
DSL	=	digital subscriber loop
DTH	=	direct to home
ESMR	=	enhanced specialized mobile radio
FTTC	=	Fibre-to-the-curb
GEOS	=	geostationary earth orbit satellite
ISDN	=	integrated service digital network
LEC	=	local exchange carrier
LEO	=	low earth orbit (satellite)
LMDS	=	local microwave distribution services
MMDS	=	multichannel microwave distribution services
NVOD	=	near video on demand
PCS	=	personal communications services
POTS	=	plain old telephone service
SDV	=	specialized digital video
SMR	=	specialized mobile radio
VDT	=	video dial tone

Leonard Waverman

References

Buchwald, C. (1995), "Canada in Context: An Overview of Information Policies in Four Industrialized Countries", Working Paper No. 2, Information Policy Research Project (Toronto: Faculty of Information Studies, University of Toronto).

Canadian Radio-Television and Telecommunications Commission (CRTC) (1992), *Telecom Decision* 92-12 (Ottawa: CRTC).

_____ (1995), "Competition and Culture on Canada's Information Highway: Managing the Realities of Transition", May 19.

_____ (1997), *Telecom Decision* 97-8, May 1 (Ottawa: CRTC).

_____ (1998), *Television Review* (Ottawa: CRTC)

Courchene, T.J. (1995), *Technology, Information and Public Policy*, Bell Canada Papers on Economic and Public Policy, Vol. 3 (Kingston: John Deutsch Institute, Queen's University).

Crandall, R. and L. Waverman (1996), *Talk is Cheap, The Promise of Regulatory Reform in North American Telecommunications* (Washington, DC: The Brookings Institution).

_____ (1999), *Universal Service in Telecommunications: Who Pays, Who Receives* (Washington, DC: The Brookings Institution), forthcoming.

Globerman, S. (1987), *Culture, Governments and Markets: Public Policy and the Culture Industries* (Vancouver: The Fraser Institute).

_____ (1995), "The Economics of the Information Superhighway", in Courchene (ed.), *Technology, Information and Public Policy*, 243-280.

Manera, T. (1996), *A Dream Betrayed: The Battle for the CBC* (Toronto: Stoddard).

Saxby, S.J. (1996), "Public Policy and Legal Regulation of the Information Market in the Digital Network Environment", Ph.D. Thesis, Faculty of Law, University of Southampton.

Schultz, R. (1995), "The Economics of the Information Superhighway: Comment", in Courchene (ed.), *Technology, Information and Public Policy*, 281-286.

Stanbury, W.T. (1998a), "Regulation and Competition in Broadcasting in the Age of Convergence", in D. Orr and T.A. Wilson (eds.), *The Electronic Village, Policy Issues of the Information Economy* (Toronto: C.D. Howe Institute).

_____ (1998b), "Canadian Content Requirements: Description, Rationale, Politics and Critique", in Orr and Wilson (eds.), *The Electronic Village, Policy Issues of the Information Economy*.

Canadian Information/Culture Policy in the Information Age: Comments

Dale Orr

The Focus of the Waverman Paper

Leonard Waverman's paper is a valuable contribution to public policy. He describes and evaluates the set of policy instruments involved in the information/cultural economy in telecommunications and broadcasting and provides his recommendations for improvement. The point that broadcasting policy is in desperate need of an infusion of economic analysis, and a greater appreciation for consumer sovereignty and competition — is in my view a valid and important point. Broadcasting policy also is in need of solid recommendations on how to achieve the professed objectives in a more effective and more efficient manner. Since I agree with most everything in his paper, I therefore focus on a few points of extension and difference, particularly with respect to broadcasting policy. Specifically I will focus on the central issue raised by the paper: Are the existing policy instruments of broadcasting policy suitable in the new information age?

Waverman clearly spells out the threat of "bypass" of the Canadian communication system arising from technological change, partly due to the possibility of Canadians receiving broadcasting via the Internet and satellite. His policy analysis and recommendations largely flow from the threat to the current regulations posed by technological bypass. I will take one step back from there to examine the effectiveness of existing policy. And then one step beyond, to add to other policy considerations, beyond the challenge posed by new technology, to make my recommendations for the appropriate policy instruments.

Taking One Step Back from Waverman's Assumptions

While Waverman focuses on the challenges to broadcasting policy from the "new information age", I take one step back from there to question whether current policy is effective and efficient, before we even consider the challenges of new technology. I begin by accepting the fundamental arguments made for government protection and subsidization of Canadian content. I accept these policy objectives for purposes of the present discussion — they themselves could be debated. But, like Waverman I do not believe economists are well positioned to contribute to this debate. I do, however, believe economists can contribute to a debate where public policy objectives are taken as given and the issue is: What is the most efficient and effective means of attaining these policy objectives?

For purposes of the present discussion, I accept the following objectives of the Canadian content policies in broadcasting:

- To strengthen national identity.
- To reflect Canadian attitudes, opinions, ideas and artistic creativity.
- To provide information on Canada and a Canadian perspective on international issues.

These are the highest profile, most fundamental objectives provided by the government. I believe that most Canadians accept the above objectives.

I also believe very strongly that the government, in the guise of these publicly acceptable objectives, has protected and subsidized many well-financed, well-organized, "politically sensitive" and "politically correct" groups. These groups have been protected and subsidized in a manner that is unfair to TV and radio consumers, to taxpayers, to the Americans and, more importantly, to other innocent Canadian industries that get broad-sided because the Americans retaliate against our protectionist cultural policies.

I also believe that, in supporting the broad objectives of Canadian broadcasting policy, most Canadians have no idea how they are paying to accomplish these objectives nor how much they are paying. The above points are particularly well supported by the work of the C.D. Howe Institute (Schwanen, 1997) and by William Stanbury (1999).

When one reads the regulations for Canadian content, these regulations go far in identifying as Canadian content, TV programs and music that use workers of the Canadian cultural industry, with little or no regard for the contribution to Canadian culture and identity from the subject matter. This is particularly true of the radio broadcast definitions of "Canadian" music. Details of these regulations which focus entirely on the Canadian citizenship of performers and writers with no regard to whether they are communicating to or about Canadians are detailed in Appendix 4 of the Waverman paper. Like so many regulations, Canadian content regulations have been captured by the producers. As Waverman has emphasized, broadcasting policy does not recognize the benefits of consumer sovereignty or competition.

From another perspective, consider for a moment the themes of current music which does qualify as Canadian content. Many of the songs written and performed by such successful Canadian musicians such as Shania Twain, Celine Dion, Brian Adams and Alanis Morissette have absolutely nothing to do with *Canadian* themes. Fortunately for these artists, Britains, Australians, Americans and many others around the world see much that they can identify with in this music. Few people in Canada or outside consider these songs to be uniquely *Canadian* in their theme.

I conclude therefore that current policies to promote Canadian content in broadcasting are not effective because they do not accomplish the professed objectives of promoting Canadian themes and/or Canadian attitudes. These policies promote the income of those workers in the Canadian cultural industries, without regard to whether their works promote Canadian identity, Canadian attitudes, and/or provide information about Canada.

Threats to Current Cultural Policies

I argue that there are four major policy considerations in Canada today that must be taken account of when identifying the appropriate policy instruments for broadcasting policy.

1. Increasing Technological Bypass

Clearly, as technological bypass increases, protection and subsidization must move sharply to supply-side subsidies and away from demand-side regulations. This is a fundamental result as markets become more competitive; it is not unique to broadcasting. We, therefore, must avoid regulations and/or taxes on the consumer or on the content distributor to avoid bypass. This argument is the theme of the Waverman paper and is well developed there.

2. Retaliation from the Americans

Every piece of protection we provide to our cultural industries costs us something. The cultural protection gained in the Canada/U.S. trade agreement (FTA) and in NAFTA trade negotiations cost us concessions in those negotiations. This is probably the largest source of cost to the Canadian economy of our protection and subsidization of culture. Who is paying this price? Is it our forestry industry? In the recent magazine industry furor the Americans threatened to make the steel industry pay. No one really knows who is paying and how much. This is the typical result of government protection.

3. Competition for the Fiscal Dividend

Even though the downsizing in federal government services is behind us, governments are not going to be a source of growth for years to come. The fiscal dividend over the next several years will be focused on debt reduction, tax reduction and health care. If Prime Minister Chrétien is at all serious about focusing on productivity, as he so explicitly claims he is, increased subsidies for Canadian culture would be near the bottom of his list.

4. Distrust of Detailed Government Intervention

Many in the business community have a distrust of detailed government intervention that goes well beyond the actual dollars and cents involved in such regulations. Detailed government intervention makes it more difficult to conduct business, it increases the uncertainty of any business decision and increases the risk of any business investment. Many businessmen fear, for good reason, that detailed government intervention is contagious. If it is tolerated in another sector it could spread to their sector. Business representations to the government, such as the Canadian Chamber of Commerce "Aim for a Million" and the recent "B.C. Business Summit '98", highlight the costs in jobs and to the investment climate of detailed government intervention.

Many forms of detailed government intervention have been reduced over the past decade. The inefficiency of these regulations, including telecom, has been exposed and eliminated or reduced. However, the current maze of regulations in broadcasting is perhaps the most detailed, convoluted, intrusive area of government regulation remaining in Canada. Canadian content regulations in broadcasting therefore instill a general fear with negative impacts on the investment climate well beyond the communications sector.

How Can We Promote the Objectives of Canadian Content and Culture?

*Focus our promotion of broadcasting entirely on **subsidizing** the production of programing that is directly focused on the cultural objectives professed to be the objectives of current broadcasting policy.*

With this proposal we eliminate protection and move entirely to the supply side with a very up-front transparent cost to our support of our cultural objectives. With this proposal the cultural objective as pursued in broadcasting will have a better chance of rising or falling on its own merits. Let the size of the subsidy be very clear and let it compete for government program expenditures with all the other program needs.

By focusing entirely on subsidization the policy instrument has a much better chance of being *effective*. Subsidies would be given in exchange for programing that contributes directly to the professed objectives.

Since the creation of programing is being subsidized, and the delivery mechanism is not at issue, the threat of bypass from new technologies does not arise. Retaliation from the Americans would not be an issue since the professed objectives are directed at Canadians communicating with Canadians. Exporting the subsidized programs is not a significant issue. Direct, transparent subsidization avoids the issue of detailed government intervention. The reader might argue that the direct subsidization approach will run into trouble because, while avoiding three of the four "threats to cultural policies" noted above, it does run head first into the fourth, "Competition for the Fiscal Dividend".

Indeed, having Canadian culture rely entirely on direct and transparent subsidies does cause this objective to be put up squarely against tax reductions, debt reduction and health care in competition for the fiscal dividend. However, I argue that this is precisely the point. This is the strength of this proposal. Politicians argue that the promotion of Canadian culture is supported by Canadians. This approach to financing Canadian content has the strong advantage that it permits — indeed requires — Canadians, albeit still through the blunt and cumbersome political process, to make the choice.

Granted, competing for the fiscal dividend is a blunt form of consumer sovereignty. However, it is the most appropriate way to deliver a good or service which the government argues is in the public interest but is not commercially viable. Under this proposal it could well be that the quality and quantity of programing that actually does promote Canadian identity, that actually does reflect Canadian attitudes and ideas and provides information on Canada, will increase. Certainly, if there is a strong demand for such programing beyond what is commercially viable and this demand is expressed to the political decisionmakers, this Canadian programing will be provided. If such programing loses out in the competition for the fiscal dividend, that is not a fault of this recommended process. This would be evidence that the Canadian taxpayer has higher priorities for his/her money.

The subsidy should be taken out of general government revenue not collected from TV viewers or radio listeners. The government takes the position that the promotion of Canadian culture is in the national interest. It should, therefore, be financed on a very broad base, such as taxpayers in general.

Eliminate all forms of protection in broadcasting.

By relying entirely on direct subsidization paid to those who wish to produce programing that will serve the objectives of the Canadian content policy, all current forms of "content" regulation of broadcasting would be eliminated. Licence applications would be evaluated on the merits of their business case rather than the current "beauty contests" embedded in their promises to provide Canadian content. Radio broadcasters could select their music — cable companies could select the channels they will carry, and TV networks could select the programs they will carry, with the demands of the consumer, rather than the detailed regulations of the CRTC uppermost in their minds. This would be a breath of fresh air to managers and investors in the communications business and a leap forward for consumer sovereignty.

Commenting on Waverman's Policy Recommendations

Waverman's prescription for Canadian broadcasting policy is:

- Rely much more on end user taxes.
- Relax administrative constraints on program providers.
- Increase subsidies to Canadian programing.
- Use auction licences.

I will focus particularly on Waverman's recommendation of the end user tax, for two reasons. First, this is the proposal which he develops the most fully. Second, I have some reservations about this proposal, whereas I find the others generally acceptable.

Waverman recommends this tax be in the form of a TV licence fee. He recommends this fee be charged to each household that has a TV set. Households with more than one TV set would pay the same as households with one set. Households with no TV sets would not pay the licence fee.

Ninety-seven percent of all Canadian households have a TV set in their home. Waverman notes that an annual fee of $250 per household would raise sufficient revenue to fund the CBC and other Canadian programing. How many low-income households would, particularly over time, decide not to purchase a TV at this higher cost? How many households would be able to bypass or avoid the tax?

As Waverman recognizes, this approach raises some equity concerns. Some low-income families may forego TV viewing due to the tax. And perhaps even more important, some low-income families may forego some other item from their already cramped budget, because they had decided to pay the TV tax.

These elasticities may be very small. In such case, virtually every household may end up paying the TV end user tax. Thus, the TV end user tax would evolve into a "head tax" per household. The debate then becomes: Is it more effective, efficient and equitable to raise the funds to subsidize Canadian content on a flat per-household basis, as opposed to through our progressive income tax structure? A reasonable argument can be made for the per-household tax because these objectives of the Canadian content policy seem to be addressed to all Canadian households. They do not appear to be of more benefit to high-income than low-income households. But should there not be a role for ability-to-pay in terms of financing CICP? Other goods and services in the cultural area, such as museums and art galleries, are financed from general tax revenue. This is a reasonably efficient and equitable way of financing the cultural objectives served by these institutions. I argue the same approach should be used for the cultural objectives to be served by Canadian broadcasting.

References

Schwanen, D. (1997), *A Matter of Choice: Toward a More Creative Canadian Policy on Culture*, C.D. Howe Institute Commentary No. 91 (Toronto: C.D. Howe Institute).

Stanbury, W. (1999), *Canadian Content Requirements: Description, Rationale, Politics, and Critique*, C.D. Howe Institute Policy Study No. 32 (Toronto: C.D. Howe Institute).

Summary of Discussion

Jack Mintz began the discussion by noting that there are instances when a regulation can be more effective than a subsidy. The tax credit for Canadian films is an example of a subsidy that has increased returns for producers, but has not affected the degree to which films made in Canada reflect Canadian culture. In broadcasting, subsidizing Canadian content with production funds and other support programs may not necessarily turn out to be a better solution than regulating.

Leonard Waverman replied that he favours supply-side policies because it will become increasingly difficult to articulate demand-side policies in broadcasting. The problem with the regulatory approach in this field is that it will become more difficult to identify what can be regulated. One advantage of subsidies is that they are perfectly visible. It is very difficult to estimate the total cost of the current regulatory regime. If we move to a more visible subsidy scheme, at least Canadians will know the cost of the broadcasting policy and can debate whether the cost is worthwhile.

Klaus Stegemann supported shifting from regulation to subsidies, but doubted that present and future federal governments would make a change that would antagonize powerful constituencies attached to the current broadcasting policy.

Dale Orr agreed that policy would be hard to change. Protectionist policies always build up clienteles in defence of the status quo. Recent decisions by the Canadian Radio and Television Commission (CRTC) have benefited everyone involved in television except the viewer. Nevertheless, surveys show 95% public support for policies favouring Canadian culture and identity. But this support is based on little or no knowledge of the cost of current policy. Economists have to spread the message about the cost of current broadcasting policy. In the case of airline deregulation, economists played a key role by highlighting the costs of regulation and the benefits of deregulation.

Leonard Waverman hypothesized that as technological bypass makes regulations harder to enforce, the cultural bureaucrats themselves will look for alternatives.

Dale Orr predicted that other industries would lead the lobby for change. The forestry industry is already complaining that U.S. actions against Canada's forestry industry are motivated in part by U.S. retaliation against culture protection.

Doug Brown took the view that economists do not have anything useful to say about cultural policy. If Canadians start worrying about softwood lumber actions led by Jack Valenti, the chief lobbyist for U.S. broadcasters, we might as well throw in the towel on room to manoeuvre. The trouble with economists is that they always focus on the possibility of someone benefiting unfairly and do not consider the possibility of positive spillovers from protection. We should look at our cultural industries as a twenty-first century railway binding the nation together. *Dale Orr* mocked rules that define as foreign content a U.S.-produced documentary on the history of the National Hockey League (NHL) and as Canadian content a Canadian-produced documentary on U.S. history. But as others noted, the truth is that Americans and Canadians have a different view of the NHL. And there is a role for Canadians to say something about the United States from a distinctive Canadian perspective. Similarly, we heard that there is nothing distinctively Canadian about the music of Alanis Morissette. Yet, Morissette emerged out of competition with thousands of artists fostered by the Canadian content rules for radio. Morissette sings with irony, a quality unknown to Americans.

William Watson found it ironic that Canadians would spend billions subsidizing irony at the same time that there are complaints about financial pressures facing hospitals and universities. He cautioned that public good arguments are often convenient because one can hardly ever measure the externality to see whether the degree of protection or subsidy is appropriate. If there is a market failure problem for Canadian cultural broadcasting, he doubted that it was very serious.

Leonard Waverman expressed confidence in Alanis Morissette's ability to survive without Canadian content rules. He warned that radio content rules will be evaded first, because radio is subject to the greatest and fastest bypass. Listeners can design their own radio program with digital programing on the Internet. As a result, we have to think of alternatives to rules restricting Canadians to listening to Canadian radio. He repeated that he was not objecting to the objective of promoting Canadian culture, but was merely asking what instruments can be used if current policies are put at risk by new technologies.

David Baar contributed four comments. First, he warned against basing Canadian content rules on judgements of outputs. Output-based rules would expose regulators to charges of censorship and open up a debate about who is fit to judge what is Canadian. Second, we should not be overly concerned if Canadian content rules support some American-style artists. Canadian content requirements open up opportunities for those with uniquely Canadian perspectives who would not be as successful in the United States as they are in Canada. Kingston's own Tragically Hip, Sarah McLachlan and Spirit of the West are examples. Third, the case for subsidies over regulatory support is strongest in multimedia areas where the delivery mechanism is no longer definable. Fourth, we should not be surprised that film subsidies have not been effective in getting Canadian films on Canadian screens. Film tax credits are not designed to raise Canadian content. Rather, they are job-creation mechanisms.

Robert Wolfe posed two questions. First, given that policies in many areas are opaque, why should we make cultural policy more transparent when it is part of the nation-building enterprise? Second, why should we be concerned that cultural policy serves the interests of producers, when in the preceding session we talked about how desirable it would be to have firms with head offices in Canada?

Louis Pauly supported the points made by Brown and Wolfe and added that we should place the construction of a national identity in a larger context by relating cultural policy and education policy.

Pierre-Paul Proulx could see the logic for more supply-side than demand-side action to support culture as a public good. However, the issue poses special problems in Canada given the cultural distinction between Quebec and English Canada. He would not want anyone defining his national identity for him.

Richard Harris asked whether European countries are resorting to more cultural protectionism and are using demand-side policies to do so.

Leonard Waverman confirmed Harris' surmise, but questioned the sustainability of the European approach. Language acts as a natural barrier for many, but not all, European countries. For example, the Spanish government will have trouble enforcing its policy because Spanish-language broadcasting can be picked up from Latin America.

Daniel Schwanen put forward what he called a middle-of-the-road position. Current policy is problematic even if you adopt the public good/externality argument for supporting Canadian content. We subsidize many products that Canadians never see or hear. Because we define Canadian content on the basis of ownership, we end up subsidizing tycoons. We should develop a simple definition of Canadian content focusing on whether the interpreter is Canadian, rather than on who owns the means of production. We should subsidize identifiable shelf space for radio and TV stations to provide simply defined Canadian content, so that willing customers will know where to find it.

David Slater pointed to other cultural enterprises such as symphony orchestras, visual artists and dance companies, which have greatly enriched Canadian life. We have lots of experience subsidizing these fields and have learned lessons which could perhaps be applied to broadcasting.

Geoffroy Groleau saw asymmetry in production costs as a problem that could justify support for Canadian content. U.S. television programers have a huge U.S. market and can sell their products very cheaply in Canada relative to the costs for Canadian producers aiming at the Canadian market.

Leonard Waverman countered that Canadians can also produce programs to sell in the United States as well as Canada.

Dale Orr rejected the "small market" case for protecting Canadian programing. Most U.S. television programs are produced in New York or Los Angeles and are then broadcast throughout the United States. Yet, America's regions have managed to maintain distinct cultures. Similarly, *The Globe and Mail* is produced in Toronto and sold throughout Canada, but Canadian regions are still distinct.

Harry Arthurs faulted critics of cultural policy for starting with an assumption that no one wants a state-directed culture. Consumer sovereignty has nothing to do with culture. Great music and great books and great theatre need no justification in market terms. Culture lives on its own terms. High culture has always been state-supported. The experiences of lots of other countries show that states can play a positive role in promoting culture. If you believe that France, Italy, the United Kingdom and the United States are right to invest heavily in culture, our policy should be to subsidize culture for its own sake.

Regulatory Diplomacy: Why Rhythm Beats Harmony in the Trade Regime

Robert Wolfe

The title of this volume poses an implicit question: If globalization is a force for policy convergence, do we have room to manoeuvre? This chapter considers one aspect of the question: as more of the economy becomes tradeable, how does the international trading system centred on the World Trade Organization (WTO) accommodate domestic regulation? And as more of life becomes commodified, how do we accommodate ourselves to the trading system? Both questions must be addressed. Incompatible domestic regulations may undermine international openness, but pressures for homogenization undermine political communities. Solving this puzzle has implications for national policy and for how such issues as trade in services and environmental standards are handled in the coming "Millennium Round" of multilateral trade negotiations.

One answer to the apparent inevitability of homogenization would be to create a single global state, but that is an unlikely prospect (Zacher, 1997). Globalization is a constraint, if less of one than is commonly supposed (Weiss, 1998), and transnational capital needs capable states as much or

An earlier version of this paper was prepared for presentation to the ADM Network on Regulation and Compliance at the request of the Canadian Centre for Management Development, September 1998. I appreciate the comments of Harry Arthurs, Nicholas Bayne, Tony Campbell, Peter Carroll, Tom Courchene, Bill Crosbie, Rod Macdonald and Klaus Stegemann.

more than does domestically oriented business (Evans, 1997). Another answer, policy "harmonization", is tantamount to the same thing, and just as unlikely as its counterpart, "deregulation". Regulatory change has been common in all the advanced economies, often associated with liberalization, but "reregulation" better captures what happens (Cerny, 1991). The belief in the inevitability of harmonization, held both by people who welcome and by people who loathe the prospect, reflects what Harry Arthurs (1997a) calls the "globalization of the mind", an affliction that leads elites to think that globalization must be facilitated, just as it leads some social movements to think that it must be resisted. If states in all their diversity will continue to exist, then the traditional option for resolving conflict among them is diplomacy. If we have room to manoeuvre, diplomats, who come from most departments of a modern government, will do some of the manoeuvring. *Regulatory diplomacy* is one manifestation of the social response to the expansion in the role of the market associated with globalization that Polanyi (1944) described as the double movement. The continual reconstruction of the compromise between free trade and the welfare state (Ruggie, 1983) may be characterized as the diplomacy of embedded liberalism.

The chapter proceeds as follows. The first three sections set the stage by defining globalization, regulation, and regulatory diplomacy, or the international relations of policy convergence. The fourth and fifth sections describe an approach to conceptualizing regulatory diplomacy in general, and in the World Trade Organization. The sixth section is an analysis of the techniques of regulatory diplomacy in practice. The seventh section, before a conclusion that tries to bring all these themes together, considers an example of regulatory diplomacy. This example is based on the *Reference Paper* (RP), the key to the February 1997 agreement on trade in basic telecommunications services negotiated in the WTO. The deal involved giant firms, the biggest governments, consumers all over the world, and the latest technology. The RP explicitly creates a regulatory framework in this domain. Understanding how it works is important, for it may well be a model for agreements in other regulatory domains in the next round of negotiations. I will try to show that at least in conception (its operation is still too new for judgement) the RP aims at regulatory rhythm, not harmony.

Globalization and the Singapore Effect

Just as British guns were trained in the wrong direction when the Japanese invaded Singapore, so globalization catches existing policy by surprise. The argument of this paper does not depend on an elaborate definition of globalization or its myriad causes and effects. It will be sufficient to isolate one dimension, trade. By definition, a good (or a service) is non-tradeable if the difference between the local price of the good and its international price is less than the cost of moving it. Declines in the cost of transportation and communications, or associated changes in commercial practices, naturally increase the rate and extent of the division of labour. Such changes may not be caused by policy, but policy must respond. In this respect Canada's problems with *Sports Illustrated* are similar to other problems associated with globalization.

American publications sell in significant quantity in the Canadian market. Since the editorial production costs of these periodicals are covered in the home market, publishers need only cover the additional printing and distribution costs for sales in Canada to be profitable. If the American publisher can create a version that could be printed just for Canada (a "split run"), advertisements could be sold that would be directed only at Canadians. The marginal costs to an American publisher of selling 300,000 copies in Canada using the same glossy editorial content created for the 3,000,000 copies sold in the United States are considerably lower than the gross costs to a Canadian publisher of creating a title of sufficient quality that it could sell 300,000 copies in Canada alone. Given the low marginal costs of the split run, advertising prices can be kept lower than competing Canadian periodicals. Some Canadian publishers would suffer because their periodicals compete directly; others suffer because the pool of money available for advertisements directed at Canadian magazine readers is siphoned out of the country. Canada has long had a policy of supporting a domestic magazine industry by using a variety of regulations to make it difficult for such split-run editions of foreign periodicals to succeed in the Canadian market. The policy could be supported by traditional border measures that took effect when a foreign printed publication crossed the border in physical form. The context changed when satellites were used to transmit complete page proofs of *Sports Illustrated* from American editorial offices to Canadian printing plants. The change in the technology of printing, and of high-speed data transmission, thus led to a change in the industrial organization of the sector. Technological change allowed the creation of the good to be sliced into smaller bits, and then for production to be separated in space and time. Traditional border measures, even where they still exist, have less purchase in such circumstances.

Call it the Singapore effect, when regulatory defences are designed to deal with yesterday's threat. Tariffs were and are a part of domestic regulation: by limiting the role of foreigners in the economy, they give greater scope to national regulation. Agricultural tariffs, therefore, served to protect farm policy. When tariffs come down, or when declines in the cost of ocean shipping integrate formerly distant markets, competition between farmers seems to be affected by differences in everything from marketing arrangements to public relief for crop failures. When something is not traded, or is protected by a tariff, "our" policy decides matters. We get the jobs, we make the rules. But as border measures come down in significance, and as declines in the cost of transportation and communication narrow relative price differences making a wider range of goods and services tradeable, some existing policies lose their purchase, and whole new sets of policies are seen to have the potential to affect international transaction flows.[1] The bundle of policies that we call the welfare state seems to be under threat when the state's right to promote the welfare of its citizens is questioned. Administrative agencies, first created in the nineteenth century, grew rapidly in the New Deal era, and postwar international organizations tried to accommodate them in a open international economy. But now competition, health, safety and environmental regulations are seen in themselves as possible barriers to legitimate market access, precisely because they can be seen as potential replacements for protective tariffs. Some analysts discover the potential existence of "regulation-related trade barriers" or policies that act as "regulatory compensation" for the effects of liberalization (Kawamoto, 1997, p. 83). The trading system adds new barriers to its negotiating agenda as quickly as they are observed, because obstructions of trade are obstructions to growth for individual countries and for the world economy. But the point of negotiations on these new obstructions is more likely to be accommodation than elimination.

---

[1] One of the more insidious effects of globalization is its erosion of the power of informal regulation. Canadian managers of large corporations may do some things without being told, or because everyone in their social network is doing it. This informal regulation does not affect firms that have been "hollowed out" by the relocation of key management functions abroad (Arthurs, 1998), nor does it easily affect operations located outside Canada.

The process of globalization is not smooth. Some factors are mobile — some firms or their executives can shift countries easily. Other factors, notably workers but also sunk costs in plant and equipment, may not be so mobile. In consequence, the effects of new things becoming tradeable are uneven. (See Rodrik, 1997a, pp. 4-5 for a related discussion.) When more of the economy is at least potentially in competition with foreigners, stresses on social cohesion increase at the same time as the fiscal capacity of the state erodes. Rodrik (1997b) finds a correlation between openness for any one economy and the size of government expenditure, another way of expressing the compromise of embedded liberalism. He worries about the possibility that a decline in the ability of individuals to manage risk with the state's help might diminish our collective ability to manage the risks associated with openness. Rodrik understands the embedded liberalism compromise as the ability to spend on domestic concerns, but the state's regulatory role is another one of the ways in which the welfare state can act in favour of its citizens. Embedded liberalism also involves the institutions of global govern-ance that attempt to help states to manage risk collectively by reconciling the actions of the administrative state. Greater global openness, therefore, will be associated with more intensive global governance (Wolfe, 1997). Stable national or international society cannot be based on a decline in the net effects of expenditure and regulation. Canadians can better cope with new competitive pressures if they can still read about their evolving social safety net in Canadian magazines. Both sets of policy tools are needed to reduce the extent of perceived and real exposure to the risks of openness. The challenge is to find ways to do both in ways conducive to international cooperation and domestic growth. It is worth recalling that Singapore's sovereignty and prosperity are more assured now than in the 1940s, but this success was not achieved by building better versions of old artillery.

The Nature of Regulation

The welfare state is an administrative state. It uses the collective power of its citizens to "regulate" outcomes. The conventional story about regulation recalls that we first regulated to correct market failures. In some cases, the aim is managing risks in situations of asymmetric information, where large suppliers know more than individual consumers about whether products are healthy or banks sound. Regulation also uses the power of the state to pursue such collective goals as ensuring that monopoly suppliers provide universal phone service. Then the Chicago School told us that all regulation was really a response to the demands of rent-seeking interest groups, so we deregulated, and where we have yet to deregulate, globalization limits our ability to regulate anyway. The implication of this story is that such regulation as still exists serves only to limit the international contestability of markets, and to reduce global welfare. The goal of policy, therefore, should be to get rid of our regulations and the regulations of significant potential trading partners through international rule-making. At this point international theory takes over the story to explain the circumstances under which the United States as hegemon should pursue its objectives bilaterally or multilaterally. It then explains why small countries have no such options — either they should acquiesce in great power demands, or they should pursue multilateral cooperation for the double reason that it allows banding together with other minnows in a satisfying if futile attempt to constrain the Americans, and that it allows the claim at home that it was an international organization rather than the Americans that forced a necessary change in our policy. When this conventional logic is followed through completely, we can see that even a supposed act of genuine international regulatory cooperation, the Basle Accord on capital adequacy ratios, owes much to American efforts to redistribute wealth from foreign banks to their own domestic banks (Oatley and Nabors, 1998).

A number of things are wrong with this caricature of regulation, one in which the only politics seems to involve vote-seeking politicians, rent-seeking producers and American dominance. The first problem is the illusion that deregulation offers an escape from politics, or from the inevitable conflicts of interests and values that arise in a complex democratic society. The second problem with the conventional story is that its definition of regulation is limited. The OECD (1997) sees regulation as "the diverse set of instruments by which governments set requirements on enterprises and citizens. Such regulations include laws, formal and informal orders and subordinate rules issued by all levels of government, and rules issued by non-governmental or self-regulatory bodies to whom governments have delegated regulatory powers". Such regulations fall into three categories:

- *Economic regulations* intervene directly in market decisions such as pricing, competition, market entry, or exit.
- *Social regulations* protect public interests such as health, safety, the environment, and social cohesion.

- *Administrative regulations* are paperwork and administrative formalities through which governments collect information and intervene in individual economic decisions.

This definition is limited because Crown corporations, agencies, marketing boards and self-governing professions are all forms of regulation, and regulation does not simply take the form of delegated legislation, "rules" as it were. Much regulation could be said to be about the structure of incentives (including subsidies), punishment and institutions (e.g., contract) that can be used to generate desired outcomes (Macdonald, 1985, p. 104). The law can command but it can also provide guidelines for behaviour. Regulation broadly defined is about institutions, providing those that allow the market to function (e.g., property rights), while preserving those essential to a sense of community (e.g., language and culture). The mix of institutions, and their interaction, naturally differs from country to country.

The regulatory reform project popular in many advanced economies during the 1980s and 1990s is similarly limited, being based on a belief that regulation is a visible instrumental activity that can be modified at will. Its focus is the instruments themselves, and not their purposes. Regulatory reform can be understood differently, however. If the market is embedded in society, rather than being seen as a natural entity independent of society, then regulation takes a different role. In Polanyi's (1944) terms, an increase in the role of the market will tend to destroy some existing forms of social organization. The usual response is to use the state to create new social forms, which work to regulate the market in new ways to achieve enduring collective purposes. Vogel found in his case studies of the telecommunications sector, for example, that after competition is introduced, new rules are needed to constrain an established operator who by "rebalancing" local and long-distance rates could use cheap calls to drive out small re-sellers (Vogel, 1996, p. 30). Deregulation is a misnomer. Most often, the introduction of more competition (liberalization) is accompanied not by the reduction of government regulations but by reregulation — the reformulation of old rules and the creation of new ones. The result is "freer markets and more rules" (ibid., p. 3).

Globalization will frequently require liberalization, which in turn will frequently be accompanied by reregulation. In the case of traded services, the growth area in mature economies, liberalization is important because increased openness translates first to increased export opportunities and second to increased competition at home, which can be a source of new ideas and ultimately of higher productivity. Some services on the agenda of the General Agreement on Trade in Services (GATS) are important inputs for other industries. Canadian firms who compete at home or abroad with global firms can be penalized if they do not have access to state of the art business services. The absence of high quality services discourages investment in activities that depend on those services. We cannot provide all advanced services ourselves, and cannot keep improving their quality without competition, but for smaller markets, like Canada, if the barriers to entry are high, foreign suppliers may bypass the market.

Some would see free trade as the simple option for achieving the desired openness in services markets. But free trade is not necessarily a simple policy, nor is it the only policy choice if simplicity is desired. Free trade in services, for example, might have at least two negative consequences for governments. First, is the risk that the service could be interrupted, with disastrous consequences. Food security might be a poor argument for domestic grain production, because grain can be stored, but domestic production of some non-storable services might be sensible. Second, full liberalization might unduly widen domestic inequality by favouring mobile factors (airline pilots) at the expense of immobile factors (daycare workers) (Streeten, 1996, pp. 354, 362-363). Liberalization will be associated with reregulation.

In sum, regulation should be understood broadly as being the linked sets of policies we use to achieve our collective objectives of greater wealth and enhanced social cohesion. In trade terms, regulation will sometimes be used to open the economy, and sometimes for other legitimate purposes. In both cases, the tools may differ between countries. And small countries cannot avoid the consequences when their preferred tools are not those preferred by big countries. The characteristic response to such dilemmas is diplomacy.

Regulatory Diplomacy, or the International Relations of Policy Convergence

Diplomacy is the expected response when states face pressures for policy convergence. The policy studies literature has a positive interest in the origins of policy, including regulation, and a normative interest in the tasks policy might accomplish. International relations can contribute to policy studies when these questions cannot be answered with reference to one country alone. The core questions include understanding what policy in a given domain is, and explaining why it takes the shape it does. Often, regulatory policy in one country seems to resemble or respond to policy in other countries. Sometimes the regulatory convergence mechanism is said to be policy competition (based on the fear that business shops for the least burdensome regulatory jurisdiction), policy imitation (the demonstration effect), direct pressure from powerful states, or change in the intellectual climate, often facilitated by an "epistemic community" of officials and academics or by exchanging information with other states in an international organization (Vogel, 1996, p. 36-37; see also Bennett, 1991; Raustiala, 1997; Haas, 1992; Feketekuty, 1996). International relations can extend these options because the convergence literature assumes that states learn from each other, but does not see policy convergence as something that arises from their relations with each other as states. International relations looks to diplomacy, and to the role of international institutions, or regimes as an explanation for state policy.

Diplomacy is "The conduct of relations between states and other entities with standing in world politics by *official agents* and by *peaceful* means" (Bull, 1995, p. 156). The added emphasis signifies the restriction of diplomacy to state actors, and its definition by opposition to war. Since the ensemble of a country's regulatory framework is likely to differ from that of any other country, *regulatory diplomacy* is an essential means to avoid conflict. Diplomacy is a defining activity for states. Globalization may alter the nature of the policy problem facing states, but it is only through interaction with each other that states come to understand what the changes mean. It is through such interaction, often in international regimes, that policy can converge. A state does not know how to act because it is a state; it acquires its identity through interaction with other states. Bull saw diplomacy as an "institution of international society", along with international law, war and the balance of power. By institution he meant not an organization, "but rather a set of habits and practices shaped toward the realization of common ends" (ibid., p. 71). The international society created after the Second World War is multilateral, marked by formal equality among states: world order is no longer a hierarchy. Much of international life is organized not by treaty or other negotiation among Great Powers, but through international regimes manifested by agreements reached in international organizations. This new multilateral way of managing the most salient aspects of the security and commercial relations among states must be seen as a new form of diplomacy, one characterized by embedded liberalism.

The internationalization of regulation is not a new story. Each era of industrial change brings new needs. *International regimes* are consensually defined as "sets of implicit or explicit principles, norms, rules, and decision-making procedures around which actors' expectations converge in a given area of international relations" (Krasner, 1983, p. 2.; Hasenclever, *et al.*, 1997). They arise wherever there are underlying cross-border transaction flows. Not surprisingly, therefore, they develop first in shipping (for example, on the Danube), telegraph (the International Telecommunications Union), railways (standard gauge in Europe), and trade (when the General Agreement on Tariffs and Trade [GATT] was drafted in 1947, it codified a regime that was already at least a century old). This classic role for international coordination arises when firms, often in response to technological change that makes new things tradeable, find themselves operating in markets that have outgrown existing regulatory boundaries — international organizations have been created to develop essential coordination of standards (Murphy, 1994).

The larger number of international organizations were created after the Second World War, partly in response to the internationalization of domestic policy. The historical evolution of international collective action has three major phases:

- The gold standard era was characterized by implicit limitations on domestic policy, thus less need for international coordination;
- The 1930s were an era of too much self-regarding domestic policy, associated with international collapse; and
- After the resulting catastrophe of the Second World War, states attempted to restore international openness while maintaining space for domestic policy. International coordination in the new postwar system promoted policy convergence without requiring identical policies.

Postwar international organizations embody this paradox of embedded liberalism but it is now harder to maintain this social rapprochement between states and markets, especially in the domain of domestic regulation. Since regulations are highly technical, but also socially constructed, states often need a collective definition of the problem itself before they can regulate in ways that are mutually comprehensible. The aim of regulatory diplomacy is to help the state achieve its legitimate objectives. Sometimes that requires collaborative action abroad; sometimes it requires using international bodies as part of a process of policy learning at home. The activity is broader than what the European Union (EU) calls "regulatory cooperation"[2] because the diplomatic process of officials at all levels talking to each other is in itself an outcome. Regulatory diplomacy depends on an expanded view of diplomacy as well as regulation. The content of much of this diplomacy of embedded liberalism has to do with regulation, but most of the regulatory activity of states is not conducted by officials of foreign ministries. Diplomacy is certainly conducted by ambassadors, who are important symbols of the mutual recognition of states as states in international society (Wolfe, 1998b), and by foreign ministries, who handle these symbolic functions on behalf of the head of state. But no immutable rule of public administration requires the foreign ministry to handle everything "foreign".

Most foreign ministries have a myth of a golden age when interstate relations mattered, the country was an actor in such relations, and the foreign ministry was in control of the interactions between domestic departments and the world beyond. Hocking shows that the myth bears little resemblance to reality. The foreign ministry only came into existence when states disaggregated a previously integrated administrative structure. Without some notion of "foreign" policy as a separate domain, states have no need of a foreign ministry. When such ministries did emerge, their role never went uncontested in the endless rivalry of bureaucratic politics, and they were often kept out of important international negotiations even in such domains as international finance and security. The notion of gatekeeper becomes even more problematic when we accept that linked policy domains engage a multiplicity of "actors" in a variety of arenas whose boundaries span "borders". It is absurd, in other words, to think that it is possible for any foreign ministry to maintain and control a single channel of contact on all issues between its state and all relevant actors (Hocking, 1997). Nor is it realistic to expect the foreign ministry to be accountable for everything the state does that has some impact on foreigners. Regulatory diplomacy is carried out by ministers and officials from many departments of government, and sometimes by firms and non-governmental organizations.

The diplomacy of embedded liberalism is not a diplomacy of harmonization. Harmony as a concept is little explored in international relations. The

---

[2]The term is said to mean both (a) multilateral and plurilateral initiatives for the harmonization or equivalence of standards, regulatory requirements and conformity procedures, or promoting best practices; and (b) bilateral cooperation with trading partners in developing technical regulations, standards for harmonization and regulatory reform (European Commission, 1996).

idea seems to assume that actors have identical interests. Some liberals may believe in a potential harmony of interests, but most students of international relations assume that conflict is always possible and frequently observed in international life. The pressures we observe are not in fact pressures for harmonization. What we really see as a result of globalization is increased incompatibility between national policies. These aspects of globalization can lead to conflict for states, if what they see as their legitimate public purposes are thwarted by others. States worry if pressures from abroad appear to compromise food safety, or if they are asked to consume foreign goods apparently produced in ways that harm the environment. Incompatible policies can also lead to higher than necessary transactions costs for firms. What we face, then, is pressure to minimize *conflict* and reduce *transactions costs*.

This line of argument, that pressures from abroad *require* policy harmonization, embodies two fallacies. The first is the implicit assumption that we can identify the effects of policy on transaction flows and that we can in consequence predict the optimal policy intervention that will reduce such costs. Even when we think we know what works, we can be wrong: allowing different policies may be a good idea, especially in domains where we lack a strong international consensus on the best policy. Reducing transactions costs is no doubt important for small firms in small countries, like Canada, but its significance is not obvious. Firms claim to need the same standard in all markets, whatever it is. But the goal of providing firms with the same rules wherever they do business is neither attainable nor worthwhile. Difference in rules has not hindered the proliferation of firms with activities crossing borders, nor has it impeded an explosion of foreign direct investment. Economies of scale through the reduction of the costs of learning about and meeting a rule can be real, but the significance will vary with the relation between the costs and the profits expected from entering a market. The costs of meeting the rule could be a barrier to entry in some cases and irrelevant in others (Leebron, 1996).

The second fallacy about harmonization is that the only way to avoid policy conflict is to eliminate policy difference. The notion of contestability has recently become popular in discussions of the new issues posed by the apparent salience of domestic regulation for trade policy.[3] Feketekuty argues

---

[3]The concept goes back to work on industrial organization in Baumol *et al.* (1982). For other examples of current usage, see Feketekuty and Rogowsky (1996), Zampetti and Sauvé (1996) and Barfield (1998).

Robert Wolfe

that "global contestability" or "global competition" should be the new way to measure trade policy, which makes domestic regulatory reform central to global liberalization. Graham (1998, p. 205) defines a contestable market as "one in which the barriers to new entrants are sufficiently low that incumbent firms must behave competitively in order to foreclose new entry by rival firms". In domestic terms, contestability is a way to overcome some of the difficulties of regulatory reform; in trade terms, it is a new way of articulating the claim for free trade. The difficulty is that it solves the regulatory overlap problem by moving regulation up to an international organization, and down to markets. It is not a useful device for recognizing horizontal overlaps in jurisdiction. The rhetoric of market contestability is appealing but it obscures the balancing function of trade policy. It would make sense only if the agreed policy objective were allowing markets to be self-regulating, but the WTO is charged with finding ways to *reconcile* difference in the interests of liberalization and stability, rather than with *removing* difference.

How then do we resolve the conflict that can arise when one or more centres of power claim authority over the same transaction? A desire to reduce *both* conflict and transactions costs was the basis for the compromise inherent in the creation of the GATT, but the need to balance national sovereignty and international openness was not new in 1948. The existence of multiple overlapping normative orders operative within the same social, territorial or economic space is an old phenomenon. The current system of states, named for the Peace of Westphalia of 1648, began as an attempt to organize all such normative orders, including those governing religion, property and civil rights, on territorial boundaries. From the moment the states system solidified three centuries before the creation of the GATT, it caused problems. One of the bases for the new states was an insistence on the king's religion being the one practised on his territory. Naturally the king's representatives would have to practise his religion. But how could a Protestant ambassador practise his religion in the territory of a Catholic king? Religion, it turned out, could be regulated but not harmonized. The very basis of extraterritoriality arises from this fact. In short, students of international relations treat harmony as the rare case, the case that is never observed. What we do observe is conflict, and what we study are ways to manage it.

When diplomats were the only entities that crossed borders, resolution of conflict was in some ways easier than it is now when everything moves, everything is fluid. The Westphalian system is undermined by globalization, when some social and economic phenomena transcend borders. The state itself is subject to many such orders, or centres of power, but it can also be the source of (apparent) legitimacy for other normative orders — it can prohibit or shape even private orders. We face incompatibilities between national policies when more than one state attempts to make an authoritative normative claim over the same activity. International regimes are the place where states work together to reconcile normative claims.[4] The regime concept has roots in Mitrany's belief that politics was determined by function (Ashworth and Long, 1999). It implies that regimes are partial orders suited to specific administrative domains, that they are embedded in a broader international order. The kind of reconciliation implied by shifting power upward to international organizations seems implausible. For similar reasons, there seems little prospect of popular support for leaving everything to markets. Regimes allow us to recognize horizontal shifts, allowing power sharing and jurisdictional overlap.

Regimes as sites of regulatory diplomacy are sites where states attempt to understand each other. That effort at mutual comprehension can be a powerful source of policy convergence, but convergence in this sense need not mean "union". Another synonym for convergence is "lines tending to meet at a point". What is the nature of the point where domestic policies converge? Is it a singularity? Or does single point perspective mislead? The notion of "convergent expectations", a pluralist idea central to the definition of regimes cited above, is related to Schelling's focal point, the focus for tacit bargaining (Schelling, 1960/1980). So long as a focal point for expectations exists, actors can converge on a course of action. The force of competing groups, or of convergent expectations, can be thought of as vectors that come together in a new vector, a course of action that no group wanted but that is somehow the result of all their desires. Harmony, as a musical idea, requires everyone to play together to form chords. Rhythm, in contrast, requires only that the players keep the same beat. The idea of convergent expectations may also imply some notion of reciprocity: states who understand their own actions to be shaped by the regime will expect the same of the actions of other actors. The test of the regime, then, is not that any actor is happy with the behaviour called for by the regime, or with the collective outcome, but that the given actor recognizes the legitimacy of

---

[4]By states I mean their officials, but in this paper I do not discuss the thousands of formal and informal meetings of international organizations and associations of various sorts where this work is carried out.

Robert Wolfe

behaviour and outcomes in the context of what is collectively possible; what is collectively possible is what everyone can accept without the system collapsing.

The international relations of policy convergence take place in regimes. The WTO is a central site for regulatory diplomacy, understood as a conversation among governments about how to cope with globalization. (It is not the only site, however, as the illustrative list in Figure 5 shows.) The expansion of the market undermines international rules just as it erodes domestic bargains. The response is a process of discovering new rules; it is not a process of making rules. The distinction matters: new rules are a diplomatic rather than an analytic challenge.

Conceptualizing Regulatory Diplomacy

Regulatory diplomacy is both a normative framework and a set of techniques.[5] The term describes multiple activities, because states face more than one problem in any domain. Understanding the nature of the policy challenge differs from designing new instruments. Knowing how to coordinate action with other states differs from settling disputes. International regimes as sites of regulatory diplomacy can be seen as *regulative* of state action, or of groups within states, which leads to the familiar focus on rules and compliance. But regimes can also be seen as *constitutive* of how states understand cause and effect relations in a domain, which leads in the social constructivist approach (Ruggie, 1998c) to a focus on how values and thus preferences change. The need for any action at all depends on the degree of interdependence between states and their policies. The need for regime rules to be more or less explicit will also depend on how well states understand their collective situation. This approach shares with utilitarian approaches in economics and political science a concern for how people distribute social goods. Unlike such approaches, however, it recognizes that all goods are social goods, because "They come into people's minds before they come into their hands; distributions are patterned in accordance with shared conceptions of what the goods are and what they are for" (Walzer, 1983, p. 7). Constructivists are concerned, therefore, with what Ruggie, after Searle,

---

[5]Regulatory diplomacy is a subset of what many authors call economic diplomacy.

calls "social facts" (Ruggie, 1998a). Traded services such as international telephone calls are social facts. They exist independently of any one person's perception of them, they can be bought and sold, but they cannot be dropped on your foot. In the first years of the GATS we can see in both financial services and basic telecommunications how the obvious attractions of large new markets motivated negotiators, but they needed to learn from each other about appropriate regulatory practices. The *material* push and the available *ideas* generated in organizations like the OECD were both essential to the successful conclusion of WTO agreements in these areas. Such services cannot be regulated until they are understood to be negotiable.

These different regime roles can be encompassed within one international organization, or they can be shared among many international organizations. The choice depends on the context. I see two principal dimensions:

- As *interdependence* between states increases within an issue-area they perceive an increasing *need* for collective action; and
- As the salient dimension of an issue changes from developing an intellectual consensus on improving *allocative efficiency*, to resolving *distributive conflict*, the site and form of action will change.

This dynamic is represented in Figure 1. At the outset, common problems can motivate developing a consensus on good policy. Discussion of *norms* and *principles* is central, but consensus is left implicit. As interdependence increases, an understanding of good policy depends on some consensus on abstract distributive issues, on the location of the contract curve (Young, 1989). The assumption behind Figure 1 is that as inter-dependence increases, and the nature of the problem changes, negotiations shift from *consensual* organizations like OECD or Asia-Pacific Economic Cooperation (APEC) to organizations equipped for distributive negotiations, like the GATT. The *form* of cooperation will shift from definitional problems (e.g., property rights) through *coordination* of national policies, to *collaboration* on joint interstate action (Ruggie, 1998b). We know that coordination is easier than collaboration (Stein, 1983), so the form of agreement will also move from informal understandings to written treaties with recip-rocal obligations (Lipson, 1991). The need for *surveillance* in this context will move from informal mechanisms aimed at transparency through peer review of good practice to more formal dispute settlement mechanisms aimed at compliance.

Figure 1: Regime Roles

	Allocation **Implicit norms**	**Distribution** **Explicit rules**
Low Interdependence	**Box 1** a) Little interaction b) Discussion of comparable policy problems c) Surveillance: create transparency	**Box 3** a) Increasing conflict b) Bargaining: *coordination* of national policies c) Surveillance: promote compliance with agreed norms
High Interdependence	**Box 2** a) Moderate conflict b) "Negotiations" aimed at definitions and norms c) Surveillance: peer review of good practice	**Box 4** a) Greatest risk of conflict b) Bargaining: *collaboration* on joint action or reciprocal agreements c) Dispute settlement bodies essential for enforcement

Action in the top left will always be easier than in the lower right. The closer we get to the lower right, the more rigid policy becomes, the more we are in a one-size-fits-all world. The closer we are to the upper left, the easier it is to accommodate a plurality of normative orders. This formulation applies to the natural history of the Westphalian system of states as well as to that of any particular problem. It describes what we know about life in the society of states: action on the left side is easier and more common than on the right. Globalization does not force a move all the way to the lower right, nor does it make action there any easier. It does increase the need for states not only to learn from each other (left side) but to find ways to avoid distributive conflicts (right side). Before showing how this might work in practice, consider how the WTO handles regulation now.

The Regulatory Diplomacy Principles of the WTO

The WTO is the central organization of the trade regime.[6] Standards, norms, and new ideas (Boxes 1 and 2) can emerge from many multilateral and regional bodies, and from sectoral organizations, but binding commitments on reciprocal liberalization (Box 4) are taken at the WTO. The WTO objective, however, is to help countries stay out of each other's way while facilitating the expansion of international commerce; its objective is not to regulate the world. The WTO follows rather than leads evolving regulatory practice (OECD, 1998, Box 7.1). Where it does lead is in the way its normative framework shapes national policy.

The WTO can follow national practice because that practice evolves in anticipation of what will prove acceptable at the WTO. In other words, states shape and are shaped by the characteristic way in which the WTO seizes an issue. The way the WTO thinks can change over time instrumentally but not normatively. The WTO will always see a new problem in a way shaped by the norms and practices of the regime. It will ask if and why the thing is a trade issue. Oddly enough, given fashionable talk about a "borderless" world (Ruggiero, 1997), it is only borders that give the WTO a role. It cannot conceive of a problem that does not involve sovereign governments and something (goods or services) crossing a border. Governments not firms are the *subjects* of its normative order, even if the topics under discussion are the government regulation of people and firms as well as of goods and services. The WTO always values order over conflict. It sees the benefits of liberalization in allowing the division of labour to increase, because of the gains from trade that come from increasing specialization. But it also values protection of communities, of minimizing the need to change how states do things.

In the way the WTO conceives of regulation, policies that you can see are better than ones that are hidden; price-based measures taken on a non-discriminatory basis at the border are preferred to quantitative measures or the variety of non-tariff barriers (NTBs). What Bhagwati calls "fix-rule" are preferred to "fix-outcome" measures because they let markets rather than governments determine transaction flows. The issue is always the effect of a measure on trade, whether imports or exports. If something does not have an effect on trade, it is not a legitimate focus for WTO action. And the

---

[6]NAFTA is so similar to the WTO in techniques and wording with respect to regulation that it is not of much interest (Sykes, 1995, p. 109).

measure must be *agreed* to have an effect on trade. The WTO is better able to handle problems that arise when states use different means to reach the same ends. Disputes over the goals and purposes of policy are harder to resolve (Sykes, 1995, p. 7). It follows, for example, that health standards based on science are preferred for reasons of transparency. The world cannot "see" the political process by which a country chooses one standard over another, but science is an international language that allows us to understand the logic of a given standard.[7]

This system is sometimes called "shallow" integration, because it looks only at border measures. Some analysts claim that we now need a new system to facilitate "deeper integration". The sort of integration now called shallow was called "negative" by Jan Tinbergen and his colleagues in their early work on the logic of European integration. He was not being critical; he meant integration by doing less not by doing more. For Tinbergen, *negative integration* meant the *reduction of trade impediments* between national economies. In contrast, what he called *positive integration* meant the creation both of new centralized institutions and the modification of existing instruments in order to *avoid a distortion* of the process of free competition (Tinbergen, 1965, pp. 77-78). In the current jargon, positive integration would be called "deep integration", meaning efforts to ensure the regulation of unstable markets bigger than any one country by subjecting formerly domestic regulatory policies to multilateral "harmonization" under the aegis of an international organization. The European Union is the only example at present of an attempt at either deeper or positive integration, which is not surprising given the stringent institutional requirements. We are

---

[7]Science does not always help. Canada is a major producer of asbestos, but major consumers fear the health risks apparently associated with use of the product. The Canadian government decided in May 1998 to initiate consultations at the WTO for the settlement of a dispute with France on the issue of chrysotile asbestos products, which are safe when used properly, according to the safe-use principle of the Canadian government's Minerals and Metals Policy. Since January 1, 1997, however, France has prohibited the manufacture, import and sale of asbestos and products containing asbestos, with rare exceptions (DFAIT Press Release No. 135, May 28, 1998). In this conflict between national standards both sides have appealed to science, with Canada countering a major French scientific study by commissioning a review by the Royal Society of Canada (Expert Panel on Asbestos Risk, 1996). The issue for the WTO will be deciding whether French standards are a sensible health precaution, or disguised protectionism.

unlikely to observe much positive integration any time soon.[8] That being the case, how should WTO proceed?

Calls for deeper integration and contestability notwithstanding, the norms and principles of the WTO are generally applicable to regulatory matters. What some would call the "efficient regulation principles" already present in the WTO agreements — especially the GATS (Article VI), the Agreement on the Application of Sanitary and Phytosanitary Measures (SPS) and the Agreement on Technical Barriers to Trade (TBT) — mostly oblige members to attempt to reach their domestic objectives using sensible instruments and procedures.[9] Good agreements balance reducing barriers and achieving social goals, with flexibility in national decision making. The fundamental principles (see Chart 1) are non-discrimination (most favoured nation [MFN] and national treatment), multilateralism in making rules and settling disputes, reciprocity, respect for domestic imperatives and transparency. In addition, the WTO will typically ask if a measure is necessary to achieve some other goal, if it is based on objective and transparent criteria, and whether some other measure could achieve the objective. In the case of disputes, the WTO prefers either recourse to its own integrated dispute settlement system in the case of conflict between states, and recourse to an independent body for regulatory decisions within states. The dispute settlement system is aimed at resolving conflict not at regulatory control. To say that a measure is subject to the dispute settlement system is not quite the same as saying that it is subject to the courts. The system is not the administrative or criminal law system where punishment is possible, but the civil model, where the aim is helping the parties find an accommodation. The WTO also envisages situations where countries may have to discriminate. These include measures necessary for: protection of health, or the environment; safety; prudential regulation; public order; and national security.

---

[8]Some argue that the closer economic relations (CER) and Mutual Recognition agreements between Australia and New Zealand are also examples of deep integration, as is the North American Free Trade Agreement (NAFTA), though none have the institutional apparatus of the EU. To be clear: the EU is an attempt at positive integration, but the absolute insistence on the absence of central institutions makes NAFTA an attempt at negative integration — and most other forms of institution-building in the world are less intrusive than NAFTA.

[9]For a detailed discussion of these agreements, see Sykes (1995, pp. 77-86).

Robert Wolfe

Chart 1: Fundamental WTO Principles Applicable to Regulatory Cooperation

1. Non-discrimination
Most Favoured Nation (MFN)
National treatment

2. Necessity
Members should ask if a measure is necessary to achieve some other goal, and whether it is the "optimal intervention" or could some other measure achieve the objective.

3. Least-restrictive measures
Can the objective be met by a technically and economically available measure with less effect on trade?

4. Proportionality
The cost of regulation should be proportional to the benefit anticipated.

5. Use of harmonized measures
The general presumption is that international standards rather than national standards should be used wherever possible.

6. Generality
Requirements should be formulated in general terms allowing members and producers to choose an appropriate means of meeting the objective.

7. Mutual recognition
Where members use different techniques to achieve common goals, they should give positive consideration to accepting as equivalent each other's technical regulations, standards, and conformity assessment procedures.

8. Transparency
Measures should be based on objective and transparent criteria. When preparing to draft a national standard that may have a significant effect on trade, members should publish a notice and notify other members through the Secretariat.

9. Open decision making
Members should allow reasonable time for public comment on new measures, including by other members. Tribunals or procedures should allow for the prompt and impartial review of administrative decisions.

Chart 1: (continued)

10. Due process in dispute settlement
Recourse should be possible to the WTO integrated dispute settlement system in case of conflict between states, and to an independent body for regulatory decisions within states.

11. Competition (anti-trust) policy
Reregulation is often needed to ensure that dominant suppliers do not abuse liberalization.

12. Common Principles
These familiar behavioural norms of the trading system are based on the assumption that states share a principled understanding of the goals and objectives of regulation. Where they do not, they should work together in the WTO or other sites of regulatory diplomacy to develop a shared understanding of the regulatory principles on which collective action in the WTO depends.

13. General exceptions
Some of the above norms may occasionally conflict with each other, or with other goals of state policy. The WTO agreements envisage situations where countries may be able to justify a derogation on the grounds of:
- Protection of human life and health and the environment.
- Product and service quality and safety.
- Control of plant and animal diseases.
- The need for prudential regulation to ensure the integrity and stability of financial systems.
- Protection of archaeological treasures.
- Maintenance of public order.
- Prevention of fraud.
- National security reasons.

Source: In addition to the texts of the agreements, this particular formulation of general WTO norms is drawn from Sykes (1995, pp. 118-123); Roessler (1996); Kawamoto (1997); and OECD (1998, Box 7.5). See also Kawamoto (1996); and Feketekuty (1996).

Nevertheless, the WTO envisages the use of voluntary standards as opposed to compulsory regulation wherever possible.[10] The non-discrimination norms of the WTO (MFN and national treatment) work on the presumption that if a state is using an internationally agreed standard, then the action is non-discriminatory and cannot be construed as a barrier to trade. WTO principles do not prescribe a given level of regulation. Countries can impose any needed level of regulation, if it does not discriminate among goods, services, and firms on the basis of nationality. All members face this constraint as importers, and all benefit from it as exporters. The WTO concern is that regulation not be used as an alternative to more transparent means of controlling market access. It is interesting that these principles envisage an intersubjective process between states, and between states and firms, rather than bargaining. They describe ways in which countries can decide if regulation is appropriate in the circumstances, but they do not

---

[10]The distinction between "technical regulation" (compliance is manda-tory) and "standard" (compliance is voluntary) is found in the Annex to the TBT agreement; the definition is itself based on an international standard, ISO/IEC Guide 2. These distinctions are summarized by Sykes (1995, pp. 2-3) as follows: A product *standard* is a specification that relates to some "compatibility" or "quality" characteristic of a product or its manufacture that may or may not be formally promulgated by a private or public standard-setting entity. *Compatibility* is the capacity of products to function in association with others. *Quality* is any other attribute of a product that well-informed users care about. *Product standards* specify attributes of the finished product; *production standards* specify attributes of the process by which it is manufactured or created. *Design standards* specify precisely how a product must be made ("the door must be of steel, one-inch thick"); *performance standards* require the product to meet a certain objective but permit it to do so through alternative designs ("the door must be fire resistant with a 30-minute burn-through time"). The distinguishing feature of a standard is that compliance is voluntary. Regulations differ from standards only in that compliance is legally mandatory. Compatibility tends to be the subject of standards rather than regulations, whereas matters of quality are somewhat more often the focus of regulation. *Conformity assessment* refers to the process through which products are evaluated for compliance with standards and regulations. It encompasses the certification requirements imposed on product manufacturers, testing and certi-fication by third-party laboratories, inspections by customs authorities or other regulatory officials, and so on.

proscribe regulation.[11] Where members do not use an available international standard, they should be able to justify their choice, including showing that it is no more trade restrictive than necessary, and they should offer full opportunity for consultations. In sum, the WTO in principle can handle regulation, but doing it in practice is a major challenge.

Regulatory Diplomacy in Practice

The next step in understanding the practices of the trade regime is to consider the question that states face when domestic regulations overlap: who regulates? Regulation can be carried out by the importing or the exporting country, by neither or by both. This problem is shown in Figure 2, which uses the same implicit format as Figure 1.

Roessler uses the presentation of Figure 2 to illustrate what he calls the WTO's "border adjustment principle", since the rules of the GATT and the GATS do not inherently require a member to have any particular domestic

Figure 2: Who Regulates?

		Importing Country	
		Does not regulate	Regulates
Exporting Country	Does not regulate	Regulatory exemption	Regulation at destination
	Regulates	Regulation at origin	Regulatory duplication

---

[11]This decision is not always easy to make on a consistent basis. Depending on how the National Treatment (Article III) and General Exceptions (Article XX) provisions of the GATT are read together, they can make anything or nothing "unjustifiable" interference with trade (Mattoo and Subramanian, 1998). More criteria are needed to guide panels.

Robert Wolfe

policy (Roessler, 1996). He discusses the table in terms of food inspection, where members could agree to accept the exporting country's inspection, to use an inspector in the importing countries, to require inspection twice, or to have no inspection at all. It is essential to note that the regulations in question apply to products and services, not to the producers or the suppliers. It does not matter how the food was grown if the method does not have an impact on the product itself so long as it passes inspection.

The next layer of complexity is which rule is to be used by the inspectors? It could be a national standard of one of the countries, or an international standard. In the bottom left box, the exporting country could use any one of those three standards, as long as the importing country recognized the testing procedures. In the top right box, the importing country could also use any one of the standards, as long as it applied the MFN and national treatment principles, and as long as the testing agency was not in itself a monopoly that favoured domestic suppliers. In the lower right box, we could have both countries using the same or different standards and recognizing, or not, each other's process. In the meat example, meat could be inspected for conformity to rules for domestic consumption in both countries, which might be little more than an extra expense, or might require different products for the two markets. (The example is not hypothetical. The demands of the U.S. regulatory system are having a profound impact on Canadian meat inspection — see Skogstad, 1998.)

The next step is to consider the "who regulates" question in light of the various possibilities for dealing with the regulation under discussion in the trading system. These possibilities include voluntary or unilateral action, perhaps on the basis of guidelines coordinated at the OECD, multilateral standard setting, as in the International Organization for Standardization (ISO), mutual recognition (or regulatory competition), and harmonization. Many of these techniques were first explored within the EU (Chaitoo and Hart, 1998), and Canada is now developing some expertise with them through its Agreement on Internal Trade. All of these approaches to "regulatory rapprochement" are seen as steps on a continuum to deep integration and greater contestability of markets.

Figure 3 is a first attempt to combine Figures 1 and 2 as a means of sorting out this complexity. In a situation of low interdependence, where states are still trying to understand the issues, it is possible that neither state will regulate, as both learn, perhaps through emulation. At the other extreme, both states might wish to regulate, and the only option would be having a single policy for both, or positive integration. As discussed above, positive

Figure 3: Concepts of Regulatory Diplomacy

	Allocation Implicit norms	Distribution Explicit rules
Low Interdependence	**Box 1** Emulation of best practices/ Voluntary standards	**Box 3** *National treatment* (host country acts)/ *Mutual recognition* (host or home country acts)
High Interdependence	**Box 2** Multilateral standard- setting bodies	**Box 4** *Harmonization*, or "deep integration"

(or deep) integration has stringent institutional requirements, and may be undesirable even if it were possible. Most of the diplomatic action, therefore, is in the lower left and the upper right, but all of the possibilities merit some discussion.

Box 1: Emulation

Global trade needs standards, but they are not the same genre as regulations, though power can be involved in both. Forestry firms, for example, are under enormous commercial pressure to adhere to international standards of good environmental management practice developed either by the ISO (e.g., ISO 14001) or by the Forest Stewardship Council.[12] Voluntary codes are clearly on the rise (Cable, 1996), and some analysts think that "governments should encourage their industries to work with each other and with their foreign counterparts to develop technologies and voluntary standards that will meet

---

[12]Forest certification may not be as valuable as its proponents hope (Haener and Lucker, 1998), and it is already a source of conflict in WTO, though its use is increasingly widespread (Zarrilli *et al.*, 1997).

Robert Wolfe

public concerns about the impact of their activities on various social objectives." Such action "can help meet social objectives at less cost and with less international political frictions than if governments intervene" (Feketekuty, 1996, p. 278). This option of government deference has risks, however, since voluntary action does not necessarily serve a public purpose — nobody elected the environmental and other organizations that comprise the Forest Stewardship Council. A multilateral rule can be easier to accommodate than the rules imposed by the market power of larger states, but the shift to a private forum changes the balance of interests, forces and actors with access to the policy process in ways that may be unproblematic for rich countries while disadvantaging developing countries (Clapp, 1998). Standards for the width of railways can be invaluable for business, but they are not necessarily the means by which a state achieves a policy objective. Nevertheless, voluntary standards are an important form of regulatory diplomacy useful for reducing both interstate conflict and transactions costs.[13]

Box 2: Multilateral Standard-Setting Bodies

One of the most important tasks of regulatory diplomacy is ensuring compatibility between standards, which begins in informal consultations among market actors (Box 1), but can end in coordination and collaboration problems for governments. If the problem is interconnection of 10BaseT Ethernet devices, the market may fail to produce a common plug, but mutual interest in finding a solution, aided by governments, can suffice. These tasks are carried in standards organizations of all sorts. (For a discussion of the

---

[13]The International Conference on Harmonization of the Technical Requirements for the Registration of Pharmaceutical Products (ICH) is another interesting example (see Vogel, 1998). The ICH is a site for some complicated regulatory diplomacy, but it has no right side features: no reciprocal commitments, no surveillance mechanisms. The issues under discussion are not ripe for WTO or for mutual recognition agreements because they do not concern things crossing borders. Distinctive national regulations far from being trade barriers have hurt domestic firms as much as foreigners: drug approvals are long, complex and costly. If countries can share ideas on how to make it simpler, they all benefit. In the process, if they can agree to use similar methods, and to accept data, then the time and costs can be reduced even further.

most important, including the ISO and IEC, see Sykes, 1995, 58ff.) When one player has a preference for one or another outcome, however, voluntary standards bodies cannot do much (Sykes, 1995, 112ff) and so these problems shift to organizations in Boxes 3 and 4.

Box 3: Mutual Recognition and National Treatment

National treatment, as discussed above, is both a fundamental norm of the trading system and an ambiguous tool when applied to regulation. Mutual recognition, the other decentralized form of regulation, is still very demanding, if not as tough as centralized forms such as harmonization, which is difficult, and thus rare. Mutual recognition as a form of coordination is found in Box 3 since it does not require the adoption of identical policies. In the case of which of two countries regulates, the mutual recognition can be of each country's regulations, or of each country's ability to test for conformity to the other country's regulation. The first would only allow a firm to create a single product that would be acceptable in a number of markets if the mutual recognition agreement itself were multilateral. The second would only have this effect if it were based on harmonized standards. Harmonization and mutual recognition, therefore, are compatible but not identical policies (European Commission, 1996).

Mutual recognition is a form of regulatory competition. If one country has a policy that achieves common objectives more cheaply, perhaps by being less burdensome on business, consumers will buy the cheaper products. They might also seek the cheaper products where the less burdensome rule is in practice a less effective rule. Regulatory competition can therefore generate either a race to the bottom or a race to the top, depending on how the competing policies are assessed. Success for the policy depends on having criteria, on the partners having like-minded regulators, and on the risks of catastrophe as a result of potentially inadequate foreign regulation being perceived to be low (Sykes, 1995, pp. 49-51). Even so, it relies upon trust in the existence of reasonable uniformity of enforcement of minimum standards. Mutual recognition is generally seen as a form of home-country control over goods and services. It may yet go as far as home-country control over the suppliers; that is, the home-country authorities would be responsible for any problems caused by a business — when goods or services are sold at some distance from where they are produced, economic agents may well be beyond the effective reach of any authorities but their own. And it suffers

Robert Wolfe

from the risk that national standards can be subject to political or other pressure, especially from dominant suppliers (Bridgeman, 1997, pp. 101-102).

The idea has been developed in Europe over the last 20 years because of the difficulties of harmonization as a means of developing a single market. The 1979 decision of the European Court of Justice in the *Cassis de Dijon* case established the principle that as long as minimum standards are met, a product fit for sale in one EU country can be sold in all the rest. This decision allows the courts to compel a form of mutual recognition in certain circumstances under Articles 30 and 36 of the Treaty of Rome. This expansive use of litigation prompted states to establish a "new approach" to regulation in the Single European Act of 1985. Now the EU can establish "essential requirements" by directive. The process begins with agreement by states to those requirements. After national regulations are brought into conformity with the directive, the mutual recognition principle applies (Sykes, 1995, pp. 87-90 and 97-98). It only works because Europe has a recognized and legitimate central authority, something missing from lesser regional agreements, like NAFTA, and from the multilateral system generally.

The mutual recognition technique is hard even in Europe, where a degree of supranational authority has been established. It may have some application within the Atlantic area generally, usually on a case-by-case basis — within the rubric of the new transatlantic marketplace, for example, the EU has signed product-specific Mutual Recognition Agreements with Canada and the United States. People have been thinking about the applicability of mutual recognition to Canada for many years. In the 1990 Senate report on Financial Services, for example, the Committee thought that a national market could be built on the basis first of agreement on basic standards and principles and second, on respecting regulation of financial institutions as appropriate by host and home provinces (Canada, 1990, p. 71). The concept was then used explicitly in the 1995 Agreement on Internal Trade as one means to "reconcile" differing provincial rules on standards (Article 405) and occupational qualifications (Article 708). The term is defined (Article 200) as "the acceptance by a Party of a person, good, service or investment that conforms with an equivalent standard or standards-related measure of another Party without modification, testing, certification, re-naming or undergoing any other duplicative conformity assessment procedure".[14]

The technique works when countries (or provinces!) see themselves and their policy choices as similar, and when they are prepared to accept a degree of institutional competition among their policies (Kahler, 1996, p. 331). Mutual recognition is first a recognition on the part of the entities of each other. It is a familiar idea in political theory and in discussions of religious tolerance. It turns up repeatedly in discussions of peace in the Middle East, where the first step is said to be mutual recognition by the Israelis and the Palestinians. If such basic mutual recognition does not exist, then the more trivial mutual recognition of standards is not possible. It is based on trust and a belief that the others will regulate as we do — on a "we feeling", in other words. *Home country regulates* is fine, if the importing country likes the home country's standards. If the countries are Bangladesh and Canada, however, Canadians might prefer that their own "higher" environmental standards be applied to anything they consume, even if it is of Bangladeshi origin, and to anything they export, even if it is to be consumed in Bangladesh. *Home country regulates* may lead to convergence over time, but that sort of adjustment can be the result of *de facto* coercion of weaker states.

Box 4: Harmonization

As discussed above, harmonization or deeper integration will be a rare form of regulatory diplomacy because, as noted in Figure 4, it has demanding political requirements that are rarely met, even within the Atlantic area. What we need, therefore, is an alternative way of thinking about Box 3. What do states do in situations where harmonization or formal binding contracts are not possible, but reciprocal agreements subject to surveillance

---

[14]The other means of reconciliation in the AIT is "harmonization", defined as "making identical or minimizing the differences between standards or related measures of similar scope". The required action is similar to that found in the TBT agreement: where national or international standards exist, parties should use them. In the case of the environment, where the Canadian Council of Ministers of the Environment is especially charged in with seeking harmonization, it means (Article 1501) "to adjust environmental measures to minimize unnecessary differences between the Parties without compromising the achievement of the legitimate objectives of each Party".

Robert Wolfe

Figure 4: Forms of Regulatory Diplomacy

	Allocation Implicit norms	Distribution Explicit rules
Inferential reasoning	Box 1 everyday practices/ markets	Box 3 "we feeling"
Formulaic injunctions	Box 2 voluntary bodies	Box 4 common institutions

and dispute settlement in the trading system are needed? It may be possible, however, to stay in Boxes 1 and 2, with enough surveillance that confidence and trust can be established. The OECD has launched a "country review" process, initially involving the Netherlands, United States, Japan and Mexico. The reviews will include a general assessment of the need for regulatory reform, consideration of government capacity and chapters on competition policy, regulatory reform and market openness, and sectoral reviews of electricity and telecommunications. If the technique works at OECD, the WTO Trade Policy Review Mechanism (TPRM) might be tasked with considering whether a country's regulatory structure is either dis-criminatory or an unnecessary barrier to trade.

Finally, Figure 5 is an attempt to map these forms of regulatory diplomacy on to the international organizations where they typically occur, from the exploratory discussions that take place in consensual organizations like the OECD and APEC through agreement on the coordination of standards in major international organizations to the formal integration that takes place in the EU. The WTO could be located in all of the boxes, depending on whether the activity in question was in a working party on a new issue, the notifications process of an existing committee, or in the dispute-settlement system.[15] In the way that all of these figures have been set

---

[15]Regulation is especially pertinent in Agreement on the Application of Sanitary and Phytosanitary Measures (SPS); the Agreement on Technical Barriers

Figure 5: Sites of Regulatory Diplomacy

	Allocation Implicit norms	Distribution Explicit rules
Inferential reasoning	**Box 1** APEC OECD	**Box 3** NAFTA
Formulaic injunctions	**Box 2** UNECE ISO/IEC ITU ICAO FAO/WHO IOSCO	**Box 4** European Union

up, getting to the lower right is always difficult and may not be desirable, while state action in the upper left is always easier and sometimes just as fruitful for minimizing conflict and reducing transactions costs.

The WTO has some form of interorganization relations with over 60 intergovernmental organizations including UN-specialized agencies, regional bodies, and standards organizations; it is also developing extensive relations with civil society organizations (WTO, 1998, pp. 129-136). By comparing the list of organizations and the WTO bodies where they have or have not requested observer status in Table V.9 of the latest WTO *Annual Report*, we can see the variety of shared sites of regulatory diplomacy. It is significant that UNCTAD, which now has a formal mandate to provide WTO-related assistance to developing countries, is an observer to virtually all WTO bodies. The OECD, which has the technical capacity to engage in pre-liminary analysis and discussion of most WTO issues, has almost as wide coverage. The most intensive interorganization cooperation, mandated by the

---

to Trade (TBT); the GATS; and the Agreement on Trade-Related Aspects of Intellectual Property Rights (TRIPs).

Robert Wolfe

WTO Agreement, is with the International Monetary Fund (IMF) and the World Bank.

It remains to try to show how this analytical approach to regulatory diplomacy works in a specific case. In the next section I discuss recent developments in the regulation of global telecommunications. What we find is that the problem of reconciling national regulation of one of the industries most affected by globalization is accomplished through rhythm not harmony.

Example: Regulatory Diplomacy in Telecommunications

The basis for global telecommunications is not a global network, which might require global regulation, but interconnection and interoperability of nationally regulated telecommunications systems (Woodrow, 1991). As technology changed the sector, therefore, the challenge was cooperation among states, not drafting global rules. When this issue was understood to involve the new idea of "trade in telecommunications services", the process moved from the International Telecommunications Union (ITU) to the WTO as part of the creation of the General Agreement on Trade in Services (GATS). In February 1997, Members of the WTO concluded a major negotiation on trade in basic telecommunications services by making additions to the Schedules under the GATS.[16]

The GATS defines services by the four ways or "modes" in which they can be supplied. Two are especially relevant for telecommunications:

1. services supplied from one country to another (e.g., international telephone calls), officially known as "cross-border supply"; and
2. a foreign company setting up subsidiaries or branches to provide services in another country (e.g., a foreign cellular operator setting up operations in a country), officially "commercial presence".

Understanding "market access" in this sector posed two special problems. First, the obstacles to cross-border supply are not necessarily found at the

---

[16]Technically, they adopted the Report of the Group on Basic Telecommunications (WTO: S/GBT/4 15 February 1997). Many of the new Schedules included formal acceptance of the Reference Paper — see below. (This section is based on Wolfe, forthcoming.)

border when the barrier to entry is not a tariff but a domestic regulation. The second special problem affects the possibility of commercial presence. The telecoms agreement requires national treatment, but when domestic regulation enforces a monopoly, national treatment can amount to no access at all.

Negotiating *trade* in basic telecommunications services, therefore, was of necessity a negotiation about *regulation* of telecommunications. Only common principles on domestic regulation could ensure that the new market access was genuine. The deal required investment (foreign ownership) and competition policy provisions, because foreign firms needed assurances that regulation will be fair and even-handed, and that former national monopolies would not abuse their once dominant position. Negotiators decided that these principles should be made a part of the GATS subject to the transparency requirements of the WTO, including the dispute-settlement system, as a way of safeguarding the value of the market access commitments. Principles covering domestic regulation are included in a text called the *Reference Paper* (RP) that elaborates on such GATS principles as transparency (Article III), independent domestic regulatory processes (Article VI), and elimination of anti-competitive practices (Article IX). The RP is not an addition to the GATS; it is a set of principles that has force only to the extent that states incorporated it, in whole or in part, in their Schedules. The text is included in the Appendix.

The first two headings of the RP (competitive safeguards and interconnection) cover the regulation of "major suppliers", with principles designed to ensure that the incumbent and former monopoly telecommunications service providers do not exercise their market power to the detriment of new entrants. The four remaining headings cover universal service, licensing, independence of regulators and allocation of resources. The RP was designed to shape *regulatory institutions* (for example, whether the regulator is independent of the incumbent telecommunications operator and national industrial interests); *regulatory processes* (for example, whether there are measures ensuring that the decision-making process is known and is non-discriminatory); and substantive *regulatory policies* (for example, policies concerning interconnection between carriers) (ITU, 1995).

The RP will shape how states reregulate in this domain. It is not clear whether negotiators would have chosen competition (anti-trust) policy of general application for this task even had such a policy been available in the WTO (Hoekman *et al.*, 1998, p. 116). One advantage of the RP, that might have made it easier to negotiate, is that it is bound in a way that a general competition policy provision could not be. The options for a general provision are either WTO commitments on national enforcement of competition policy rules, or some sort of multilateral competition body (see the special report on competition policy in WTO, 1997). Both are right-side measures implying either coordination (Box 3) or collaboration (Box 4) on competition policy (see Figure 1), and both are subject to rules of interpretation and sources of change that owe nothing to telecoms or services. As in the case of farm subsidies (Wolfe, 1998a), therefore, negotiators seem to have found it preferable to develop rules specific to one sector.

The RP seems remarkably imprecise, to the point where it can only have meaning in the intersubjective interpretations of the participants. Section 3, for example, covers "universal service", a principle recognized by the ITU as being important for most of its members, but the drafting is completely open-ended, with the definition of this concept left to each WTO member. The RP is an agreement among governments, that does not grant any standing to private parties, and it is silent on citizen participation. Firms that think a country is not in conformity with its obligations must induce their own governments to bring a case to the WTO. For some lawyers, the RP is also an inadequate competition law instrument because important terms such as "anti-competitive cross-subsidization" are neither defined nor are they based on commonly understood principles elsewhere. The definition of a "major supplier" is obviously central to the enterprise, yet it is left more general and vague than either of the different definitions used in the telecommunications regulatory frameworks of the major markets, the United States and the EU. Similarly, the term "relevant market for telecommunications services" is crucial, as it would be in competition law generally, yet it is not defined either explicitly or implicitly in other provisions (Bronckers and Larouche, 1997, pp. 26, 43). The regulatory *principles* of the RP, in short, seem to allow enormous national latitude in *practice*.[17] The RP does not require states to have the same rules safeguarding competition in domestic telecoms, only that they have some rules that attempt to achieve certain rather vague objectives. The ISO 14001 standard for environmental management of factories, which requires certification of adherence to national rules (Clapp, 1998), seems similar, in that two like plants can both have ISO 14001 certification and yet face different operating requirements consistent with the policy objectives and capacity of the jurisdiction in which

---

[17]It is not even essential that a state accept all of the RP — four members made no commitments at all, four committed to future adherence, and seven made substantial limitations (Janda, 1998).

they are located. The requirement is one of regulatory rhythm not harmony (for this distinction, see Macdonald, 1997b). Although the RP is meant to regulate the regulator, its rules are constitutive not regulative (for a discussion of this distinction, see Ruggie, 1998a). It does promote policy convergence towards a norm of competition as a regulatory approach, but not specific rules. The RP is in Box 3 though it is in a country's Schedules and it is subject to the dispute-settlement system.

We can also see rhythm in the differing ways countries implement their commitments under Article 22 of the Agreement on Trade-Related Aspects of Intellectual Property Rights (TRIPS) to protect the "geographical indications" that identify a particular good with the reputation for quality or some other characteristic associated with a specific place. The term "champagne", for example, denotes the reputation for excellence and luxury of a particular style of white wine grown in a small region of northern France centred on the cathedral town of Reims. The WTO has found that countries implement this commitment in their laws in considerably different ways, and that in consequence, the criteria for providing protection also differ:

> Some have specific geographical indications laws. Others use trademark law, consumer protection law, marketing law or common law or combinations of these. Some have formal lists of registered geographical indications. Others do not, preferring to rely on court case histories (based on criteria such as consumer protection) to identify where problems have arisen and been sorted out. Some only recognize place names. Others accept other names that are associated with a place.[18]

The WTO operates at the margins, helping states recognize where their own interest lies and to recognize their obligations to each other. It aims to avoid disputes, not to structure massive conflicts. In the case of the RP (or the *Disciplines on Domestic Regulation in the Accountancy Sector* developed by the GATS Working Party on Professional Services, which seem similar in function) excessive detail would be futile, it has no power to coerce, it speaks to form only as an articulation of the objective, and it speaks more to the values of competition than to adjudicable obligations. It is, then, a statement of aspiration. Most of all, it states that using some

---

[18]"Discussion develops on geographical indications" a report on the meeting of the TRIPS Council December 1-2, 1998 on the WTO Web site at http://www.wto.org/wto/new/pu101298.htm.

Robert Wolfe

policy technique, as opposed to some others, is the best way of meeting commonly shared objectives. It recognizes, in sum, that substance and procedure are linked, that it is more important to shape how states understand themselves in this domain than to announce precise rules that all must follow (Macdonald, 1999).

An administrative lawyer schooled in Dicey's or Hayek's contrast between discretion and the rule of law would be appalled. Arthurs observes that "virtually since the beginning of the activist state in Victorian England, public administration has been confronted with two very different visions of the law. One sees law as a 'bridle for leviathan,' a device to hold the administration accountable and protect citizen's rights; the other sees law as a set of norms arising within the administration — as in any site of complex social interaction — in order to organize and facilitate the performance of complex tasks" (Arthurs, 1997b, p. 46). The former perspective might wish to establish one global set of rules for this domain; the latter perspective, legal pluralism as applied to international regimes, welcomes the democratic possibilities inherent in competing normative frameworks. The new normative order in global telecommunications, therefore, adds a mix of overlapping national rules, two international regimes, and the standards set by huge firms. Attempts to impose one method of regulation are futile, because firms evolve too quickly, and because countries are so different. An account of the new telecommunications regime, therefore, would require an account of all sources of normativity in this domain, and it would not presuppose that the trading system requires the establishment of normative hierarchy (Macdonald, 1997b, p. 44).

Conclusion: Rhythm Beats Harmony

Despite extravagant claims for its importance, the telecommunications agreement trails what is actually going on in the global market — it will not itself be the major force for liberalization. In Canada, for example, telecommunications regulation changed in the 1990s for domestic reasons, albeit taking account of international pressure (Schultz and Brawley, 1996). Despite intense pressure from the United States during the basic telecoms negotiations, Canada only relaxed its rules on investment in this domain, maintaining its refusal to allow majority foreign ownership. Similarly, the 1995 European Union offer on market access effectively did no more than offer to extend internationally, and bind, the internal liberalization then planned for January 1, 1998.[19] Often states only agree internationally to changes well underway domestically. The negotiations were as much about learning how to regulate in an era of structural change as they were about bargaining; states adopted the new regulatory mode in *practice* in advance of agreeing to written *rules*; and the new order still attempts to reconcile multilateral openness with national distinctiveness in regulatory means and objectives. The crucial agreement is constitutive not regulative. When the economy is embedded in society, the social response to economic change will have locally specific characteristics. In the compromise of embedded liberalism, states accept that the structure of policy differs by country. The WTO does not impose either central regulation or a common regulatory framework.

The challenge for the WTO is always to understand and reconcile differences, ensuring that the players can get on with things with some degree of predictability. They do not need the same law, or a harmonized law, they just need to have a recognizable rule that structures activity in a fair way. Most important, they need transparency, including the ability to be informed about proposed rules, the right to state views, information on the results of any monitoring exercise, and a forum for settling disputes. All of these elements of transparency are central functions performed by international regimes in their efforts to provide global governance, reconciling the actions of welfare states. In the WTO they correspond to the notification procedures in many agreements, to the TPRM, to the dispute-settlement system, to the TBT requirements, and to the RP provisions.

Some people who have a degree of painful GATT experience think that it is surely better to set the lawyers to work drafting precise rules (and by implication, to set scholars to work studying harmonization) in order to avoid surprises in the dispute-settlement system from panels interpreting a vague provision in an unanticipated way. The desire for certainty is understandable, but the effort to capture quicksilver in a straightjacket must always fail: in the absence of an underlying consensus, no amount of legal precision will bring clarity. Since international harmony is not possible, the question is simply where future disputes will take place, and how they will be structured.

It is an irony that the hardest part of reconciling regulatory structures is understanding our own. Canadians who have to make their federal legislation

---

[19]*Financial Times,* October 4, 1995, 9. EU policy did change on January 1, 1998, but implementation will be slow — for example, in setting up new regulators to replace PTTs (Himsl and Milton, 1998).

equally authentic in French and English know that legal bilingualism imposes a high standard. We have to understand how our own language constructs a problem to be able to translate it into another language, recognizing that both readings of reality have to be understood to be "correct" (Macdonald, 1997a). What the trading system now faces is regulatory multilingualism, in that a regulatory framework is a complex means of ordering social and economic relationships. Understanding the interaction of differing frameworks requires being able to understand each one with a considerable degree of subtlety. No amount of legislative precision can eliminate the need for judgement.

The WTO could attempt to force Bangladesh to agree to have the same rules as Canada for basic telecoms, but that would still require a firm to spend endless amounts of time trying to understand how those rules work when translated to another language in a country with different economic, political, social and religious circumstances, and different technological, geographic and climatic endowments. In short, Bell Canada International will face different regulatory problems in Dhaka than in Ottawa no matter what is attempted in Geneva. The challenge is to frame the problem in such a way that Bell can get on with things without causing undue conflict with or between governments. Worrying about how a WTO dispute-settlement panel might seize an issue is exactly what we pay the lawyers for, but the solution is not to be found in more precise drafting. Efforts to ensure certainty of outcome with rules only provide a reasonable certainty about how the surrogate argument will be framed. And that argument must be democractic. Democracy requires that certain issues that escape the bounds of nation states be brought under some control, though maintaining democratic principles is not easy (Held, 1991). The horizontal dimension of democracy as between states must be served just as much as the vertical dimension of citizen participation. Democracy, in other words, involves not just the precise wording of a rule, but the process of agreeing on and articulating the rule, the organs of government that will give it effect, and the means of adjudicating disputes. We cannot expect these institutions to be the same in every country, nor can we expect the creation of a global institution to take over the task for all countries. Regulatory diplomacy is the institution we have for making democracy work.

In a recent research report on harmonization, Canadian officials argued that "convergence indicates that the rules in individual countries conform to the same, internationally accepted, criteria, while integration implies the adoption of uniform rules across countries" (Canada, 1998). That is a very powerful distinction. The former is worth discussing. The latter is so rare as to be a theoretical curiosity. Even within the EU, states have mostly given up looking for identical rules. North Americans face real limits to our ability to create uniform rules for an integrated market because we have no current intention of pursuing political integration. The idea that convergence requires that national rules conform to "internationally accepted criteria" need not imply harmonization. The simple dictionary meaning of harmony is "agreement", which does not tell us much. A more complex meaning is "combination of simultaneous notes to form chords". Rhythm, in contrast, is determined by the duration of notes. The *Basic Telecoms Reference Paper* could be said to prescribe the regulatory beat while leaving the notes to be determined by each state. When diplomats look for those internationally accepted criteria, therefore, my claim is that rhythm beats harmony. Policy convergence in the era of globalization may require states to regulate to the same beat, but not necessarily to the same tune, which still leaves some room to manoeuvre.

Robert Wolfe

Appendix
Trade Topics: Negotiating Group on
Basic Telecommunications
April 24, 1996

Reference Paper

Scope

The following are definitions and principles on the regulatory framework for the basic telecommunications services.

Definitions

Users mean service consumers and service suppliers.

Essential facilities mean facilities of a public telecommunications transport network or service that (a) are exclusively or predominantly provided by a single or limited number of suppliers; and (b) cannot feasibly be economically or technically substituted in order to provide a service.

A major supplier is a supplier which has the ability to materially affect the terms of participation (having regard to price and supply) in the relevant market for basic telecommunications services as a result of:

(a) control over essential facilities; or
(b) use of its position in the market.

1. Competitive safeguards

1.1 Prevention of anti-competitive practices in telecommunications

Appropriate measures shall be maintained for the purpose of preventing suppliers who, alone or together, are a major supplier from engaging in or continuing anti-competitive practices.

1.2 Safeguards

The anti-competitive practices referred to above shall include in particular:

(a) engaging in anti-competitive cross-subsidization;
(b) using information obtained from competitors with anti-competitive results; and

(c) not making available to other services suppliers on a timely basis technical information about essential facilities and commercially relevant information which are necessary for them to provide services.

2. Interconnection

2.1 This section applies to linking with suppliers providing public telecommunications transport networks or services in order to allow the users of one supplier to communicate with users of another supplier and to access services provided by another supplier, where specific commitments are undertaken.

2.2 Interconnection to be ensured

Interconnection with a major supplier will be ensured at any technically feasible point in the network. Such interconnection is provided.

(a) under non-discriminatory terms, conditions (including technical standards and specifications) and rates and of a quality no less favourable than that provided for its own like services or for like services of non-affiliated service suppliers or for its subsidiaries or other affiliates;

(b) in a timely fashion, on terms, conditions (including technical standards and specifications) and cost-oriented rates that are transparent, reasonable, having regard to economic feasibility, and sufficiently unbundled so that the supplier need not pay for network components or facilities that it does not require for the service to be provided; and

(c) upon request, at points in addition to the network termination points offered to the majority of users, subject to charges that reflect the cost of construction of necessary additional facilities.

2.3 Public availability of the procedures for interconnection negotiations

The procedures applicable for interconnection to a major supplier will be made publicly available.

2.4 Transparency of interconnection arrangements

It is ensured that a major supplier will make publicly available either its interconnection agreements or a reference interconnection offer.

2.5 Interconnection: dispute settlement

A service supplier requesting interconnection with a major supplier will have recourse, either:

(a) at any time or
(b) after a reasonable period of time which has been made publicly known

to an independent domestic body, which may be a regulatory body as referred to in paragraph 5 below, to resolve disputes regarding appropriate terms, conditions and rates for interconnection within a reasonable period of time, to the extent that these have not been established previously.

3. Universal service

Any Member has the right to define the kind of universal service obligation it wishes to maintain. Such obligations will not be regarded as anti-competitive per se, provided they are administered in a transparent, non-discriminatory and competitively neutral manner and are not more burdensome than necessary for the kind of universal service defined by the Member.

4. Public availability of licensing criteria

Where a licence is required, the following will be made publicly available:

(a) all the licensing criteria and the period of time normally required to reach a decision concerning an application for a licence and
(b) the terms and conditions of individual licences.

The reasons for the denial of a licence will be made known to the applicant upon request.

5. Independent regulators

The regulatory body is separate from, and not accountable to, any supplier of basic telecommunications services. The decisions of and the procedures used by regulators shall be impartial with respect to all market participants.

6. Allocation and use of scarce resources

Any procedures for the allocation and use of scarce resources, including frequencies, numbers and rights of way, will be carried out in an objective, timely, transparent and non-discriminatory manner. The current state of allocated frequency bands will be made publicly available, but detailed identification of frequencies allocated for specific government uses is not required.

(The *Reference Paper* may be found on the WTO Web site. It is also reproduced as an appendix to Bronckers and Larouche, 1997.)

Regulatory Diplomacy

References

Arthurs, H.W. (1997a), "Globalization of the Mind: Canadian Elites and the Restructuring of Legal Fields", *Canadian Journal of Law and Society* 12(2), 219-246.

_____ (1997b), "'Mechanical Arts and Merchandise': Canadian Public Administration in the New Economy", *McGill Law Journal* 42(1), 29-62.

_____ (1998), "The Hollowing Out of Corporate Canada?", unpublished paper.

Ashworth, L.M. and D. Long, eds. (1999), *New Perspectives on International Functionalism* (London: Macmillan).

Barfield, C. (1998), "Regulatory Reform and Trade Liberalization", in G. Feketekuty and B. Stokes (eds.), *Trade Strategies for a New Era: Ensuring U.S. Leadership in a Global Economy* (New York: Council on Foreign Relations), 243-258.

Baumol, W.J., J.C. Panzar and R.D. Willig (1982), *Contestable Markets and the Theory of Industry Structure* (New York: Harcourt Brace Jovanovich).

Bennett, C.J. (1991), "Review Article:What is Policy Convergence and What Causes it?" *British Journal of Political Science* 21, 215-233.

Bridgeman, J. (1997), "Regulatory Convergence and Divergence Between NAFTA and the EU: Implications for the Canada-UK Relationship", in R. Wolfe (ed.), *Transatlantic Identity? Canada, The United Kingdom and International Order* (Kingston: School of Policy Studies, Queen's University), 97-111.

Bronckers, M.C. and P. Larouche (1997), "Telecommunications Services and the World Trade Organization", *Journal of World Trade* 31(3), 5-48.

Bull, H. (1995), *The Anarchical Society: A Study of Order in World Politics,* 2d ed. (New York: Columbia University Press).

Cable, V. (1996), "The New Trade Agenda: Universal Rules Amid Cultural Diversity", *International Affairs* 72(2), 227-246.

Canada (1990), "Canada 1992: Toward a National Market in Financial Services", Canada. Parliament. Senate. Standing Committee on Banking Trade and Commerce: Proceedings of the Standing Senate Committee on Banking, Trade and Commerce, Wednesday May 9, 1990, Issue No. 32, 8th Report.

_____ (1998), "Harmonization of Policies, Programs and Standards", Global Challenges and Opportunities Network: Research Report 1, September.

Cerny, P.G. (1991), "The Limits of Deregulation: Transnational Interpenetration and Policy Change", *European Journal of Political Research* 19, 173-196.

Chaitoo, R. and M. Hart (1998), "Reducing Regulatory Barriers to Trade: Lessons for Canada from the European Experience", Occasional Paper No. 18 (Ottawa: Industry Canada).

Clapp, J. (1998), "The Privatization of Global Environmental Governance: ISO 14000 and the Developing World", *Global Governance* 4(3), 295-316.

European Commission (EC) (1996), "Community External Trade Policy in the Field of Standards and Conformity Assessment", Communication of the Commission: COM(96)564 final, 13.11.96.

Evans, P. (1997), "The Eclipse of the State? Reflections on Stateness in an Era of Globalization", *World Politics* 50(1), 62-87.

Expert Panel on Asbestos Risk (1996), "A Review of the INSERM Report on the Health Effects of Exposure to Asbestos" (Ottawa: Royal Society of Canada).

Feketekuty, G. (1996), "Regulatory Reform and Market Openness: An Overview", *Regulatory Reform and International Market Openness* (Paris: OECD), 269-282.

Feketekuty, G. and R.A. Rogowsky (1996), "The Scope, Implication and Economic Rationale of a Competition-Oriented Approach to Future Multilateral Trade Negotiations", in S. Arndt and C. Milner (eds.), *The World Economy: Global Trade Policy 1996* (Oxford: Blackwell Publishers), 167-182.

Graham, E.M. (1998), "Contestability, Competition and Investment in the New World Trade Order", in G. Feketekuty and B. Stokes (eds.), *Trade Strategies for a New Era: Ensuring U.S. Leadership in a Global Economy* (New York: Council on Foreign Relations), 204-222.

Haas, P.M. (1992), "Introduction: Epistemic Communities and International Policy Coordination", *International Organization* 46(1), 1-35.

Haener, M.K. and M.K. Lucker (1998), "Forest Certification: Economic Issues and Welfare Implications", *Canadian Public Policy/Analyse de Politiques* 24, Supplement II, S83-S94.

Hasenclever, A., P. Mayer and V. Rittberger (1997), *Theories of International Regimes* (Cambridge: Cambridge University Press).

Held, D. (1991), "Democracy, the Nation-State and the Global System", in D. Held (ed.), *Political Theory Today* (Stanford, CA: Stanford University Press), 196-235.

Himsl, M. and L. Milton (1998), "Making Good on Access Commitments: Implementation of WTO Commitments on Basic Telecommunications Services by the EU Member States, the United States, and Canada", paper presented to the LSUC/CBA conference on New Developments in Communications Law and Policy, Ottawa, April.

Hocking, B. (1997), "Foreign Ministries: The Myth of the 'Gatekeeper'", paper presented to the International Studies Association, Toronto, March.

Hoekman, B., P. Low and P.C. Mavroidis (1998), "Regulation, Competition Policy and Market Access: Lessons from the Telecommunications Sector", in E. Hope and P. Maeleng (eds.), *Competition and Trade Policies: Coherence or Conflict?* (London: Routledge).

International Telecommunications Union (ITU) (1995), "Trade Agreements on Telecommunications: Regulatory Implications", Report of the Fifth Regulatory Colloquium on the Changing Role of Government in an Era of Telecom Deregulation, http://www.itu.int/pforum/trade-e.htm, December 1995.

Janda, R. (1998), "Benchmarking a Chinese Offer on Telecommunications: Context and Comparisons", paper presented to the China/WTO Accession Project, Geneva.

Kahler, M. (1996), "Trade and Domestic Differences", in S. Berger and R. Dore (eds.), *National Diversity and Global Capitalism* (Ithaca, NY: Cornell University Press), 298-332.

Kawamoto, A. (1996), "Introduction: Regulatory Reform, Market Access and International Market Contestability: An Analytical Framework", in *Regulatory Reform and International Market Openness* (Paris: OECD), 15-26.

_____ (1997), "Regulatory Reform on the International Trade Policy Agenda", *Journal of World Trade* 31(4), 81-116.

Krasner, S.D. (1983), "Structural Causes and Regime Consequences: Regimes as Intervening Variables", in S.D. Krasner (ed.), *International Regimes* (Ithaca, NY: Cornell University Press), 1-21.

Leebron, D.W. (1996), "Claims for Harmonization: A Theoretical Framework", *Canadian Business Law Journal* 27, 63-107.

Lipson, C. (1991), "Why are Some International Agreements Informal?" *International Organization* 45(4), 495-538.

Macdonald, R.A. (1985), "Understanding Regulation by Regulations", in I. Bernier and A. Lajoie (eds.), *Regulations, Crown Corporations and Administrative Tribunals* (Toronto: University of Toronto Press), 81-154.

_____ (1997a), "Legal Bilingualism", *McGill Law Journal* 42(1), 119-168.

_____ (1997b), "Pluralism in Law and Regime Theory", in R. Wolfe (ed.), *Transatlantic Identity? Canada, The United Kingdom and International Order* (Kingston: School of Policy Studies, Queen's University), 37-53.

_____ (1999), "Le droit pédagogue", Montreal, janvier 20 (Law Commission of Canada).

Mattoo, A. and A. Subramanian (1998), "Regulatory Autonomy and Multilateral Disciplines: The Dilemma and a Possible Resolution", Staff Working Paper TISD9802 (Geneva: Trade in Services Division, WTO).

Murphy, C.N. (1994), *International Organization and Industrial Change: Global Governance since 1850* (Cambridge: Polity Press).

Oatley, T. and R. Nabors (1998), "Redistributive Cooperation: Market Failure, Wealth Transfers, and the Basle Accord", *International Organization* 52(1), 35-54.

Organization for Economic Cooperation and Development (OECD) (1997), *Report on Regulatory Reform* (Paris: OECD).

_____ (1998), *Open Markets Matter: The Benefits of Trade and Investment Liberalisation* (Paris: OECD).

Polanyi, K. (1944), *The Great Transformation: The Political and Economic Origins of Our Time* (Boston: Beacon Press).

Raustiala, K. (1997), "Domestic Institutions and International Regulatory Cooperation: Comparative Responses to the Convention on Biological Diversity", *World Politics* 49(4), 482-509.

Rodrik, D. (1997a), *Has Globalization Gone Too Far?* (Washington, DC: Institute of International Economics).

_____ (1997b), "International Trade and Big Government", in B.J. Cohen (ed.), *International Trade and Finance: New Frontiers for Research* (Cambridge: Cambridge University Press), 89-125.

Roessler, F. (1996), "Increasing Market Access under Regulatory Heterogeneity: The Strategies of the World Trade Organization", in *Regulatory Reform and International Market Openness* (Paris: OECD), 117-130.

Ruggie, J.G. (1983), "International Regimes, Transactions, and Change: Embedded Liberalism in the Postwar Economic Order", in S.D. Krasner (ed.), *International Regimes* (Ithaca, NY: Cornell University Press), 195-231.

_____ (1998a), *Constructing the World Polity: Essays on International Institutionalization* (London and New York: Routledge).

_____ (1998b), "Multilateralism at Century's End", *Constructing the World Polity: Essays on International Institutionalization* (London and New York: Routledge), 102-130.

_____ (1998c), "What Makes the World Hang Together? Neo-Utilitarianism and the Social Constructivist Challenge", *International Organization* 52(4), 855-885.

Ruggiero, R. (1997), "Charting the Trade Routes of the Future: Towards a Borderless Economy", September (WTO: http://www.wto.org/new/press77.htm).

Schelling, T.C. (1960/1980), *The Strategy of Conflict* (Cambridge, MA: Harvard University Press).

Schultz, R.J. and M.R. Brawley (1996), "Telecommunications Policy", in G.B. Doern, L.A. Pal and B.W. Tomlin (eds.), *Border Crossings: The Internationalization of Canadian Public Policy* (Toronto: Oxford University Press), 82-108.

Skogstad, G. (1998), "Internationalisation, Regionalisation, and Regulatory Convergence: The Case of Agriculture" (paper delivered to the Canadian Political Science Association, University of Ottawa, Ottawa, June).

Stein, A.A. (1983), "Coordination and Collaboration: Regimes in an Anarchic World", in S.D. Krasner (ed.), *International Regimes* (Ithaca, NY: Cornell University Press), 115-140.

Streeten, P. (1996), "Free and Managed Trade", in S. Berger and R. Dore (eds.), *National Diversity and Global Capitalism* (Ithaca, NY: Cornell University Press), 353-365.

Sykes, A.O. (1995), *Product Standards for Internationally Integrated Goods Markets* (Washington, DC: The Brookings Institution).

Tinbergen, J. (1965), *International Economic Integration* 2d ed., rev. (Amsterdam: Elsevier Publishing Company).

Vogel, D. (1998), "The Globalization of Pharmaceutical Regulation", *Governance* 11(1), 1-22.

Vogel, S.K. (1996), *Freer Markets, More Rules: Regulatory Reform in Advanced Industrial Countries* (Ithaca, NY: Cornell University Press).

Walzer, M. (1983), *Spheres of Justice: A Defense of Pluralism and Equality* (New York: Basic Books).

Weiss, L. (1998), *The Myth of the Powerless State: Governing the Economy in a Global Era* (Cambridge: Polity Press).

Wolfe, R. (1997), "Embedded Liberalism as a Transformation Curve: Comment", in T.J. Courchene (ed.), *The Nation State in a Global/Information Era: Policy Challenges*, Bell Canada Papers on Economic and Public Policy, Vol. 5 (Kingston: John Deutsch Institute, Queen's University), 83-96.

_____ (1998a), *Farm Wars: The Political Economy of Agriculture and the International Trade Regime* (London and New York: Macmillan and St. Martin's Press).

_____ (1998b), "*Still* Lying Abroad? On the Institution of the Resident Ambassador", *Diplomacy and Statecraft* 9(2), 22-53.

_____ (forthcoming), "Farms, Phones and Learning in the Trade Regime", in M.S. Gertler and D.A. Wolfe (eds.), *Innovation and Social Learning: Institutional Adaptation in an Era of Change* (London: Macmillan).

Woodrow, R.B. (1991), "Tilting Towards a Trade Regime: The ITU and the Uruguay Round Services Negotiations", *Telecommunications Policy* 15(4), 323-342.

World Trade Organization (WTO) (1997), *Annual Report 1997*, Vol. 1 (Geneva: WTO).

_____ (1998), *Annual Report 1998*, Vol. 1 (Geneva: WTO).

Young, O.R. (1989), "The Politics of International Regime Formation: Managing Natural Resources and the Environment", *International Organization* 43(3), 349-375.

Zacher, M.W. (1997), "The Global Economy and the International Political Order: Some Diverse and Paradoxical Relationships", in T.J. Courchene (ed.), *The Nation State in a Global/Information Era: Policy Challenges*, Bell Canada Papers on Economic and Public Policy, Vol. 5 (Kingston: John Deutsch Institute, Queen's University), 67-82.

Zampetti, A.B. and P. Sauvé (1996), "Onwards to Singapore: The International Contestability of Markets and the New Trade Agenda", *The World Economy* 19(3), 333-344.

Zarrilli, S., V. Jha and R. Vossenaar (1997), *Eco-Labelling and International Trade* (London: Macmillan Press in association with United Nations Conference on Trade and Development).

Diplomacy and the Discovery of New Rules for the Trading System

Klaus Stegemann

Robert Wolfe in his paper on "regulatory diplomacy" has set himself the task of answering two related questions: (i) As more of the economy becomes tradeable, how does the international trading system, centred on the World Trading Organization (WTO), accommodate domestic policies of member states? (ii) How do we, that is, political communities organized as member states, accommodate ourselves to the international trading system when it increasingly constrains our domestic policies because they are considered "trade-related" by our trading partners? Both questions go to the core of the theme of this volume. Regulatory diplomacy is the instrument that states use to discover new rules which constrain their domestic policies while preserving some room to manoeuvre.

Wolfe deals in greater detail with the first question, sharing with us his insights into the objectives and principles of the WTO as applied to trade-related domestic policies. These are essentially the same objectives and principles as have developed during the history of the General Agreement on Tariffs and Trade (GATT), except that issues concerning domestic policies under the WTO have attained a political and institutional prominence that may amount to a fundamental change in the system (Ostry, 1997, pp. 191-

---

I would like to thank Robert Wolfe for thoughtful comments on an earlier draft.

192). One can distinguish at least five related reasons for this change. First, border policies such as tariffs and quotas have become less important as they were removed (reduced) in eight GATT rounds of trade negotiations and also unilaterally. Non-border policies that affect trade have thus become more important. Second, technological change has made more of the economy tradeable and has stimulated foreign direct investment. In particular, international trade in services became feasible and was recognized as an area of growing importance. But policies regulating markets for services and direct investment are typically non-border policies. Third, certain countries, on behalf of certain interest groups, have moved new domestic policy issues on the trade-policy agenda because the ability to control market access seemed to provide leverage for imposing standards on trading partners' domestic policies. Protection of intellectual property rights, protection of the environment, labour rights and civil rights are prominent examples. Fourth, the Uruguay Round of trade negotiations (1986-94), responding to a combination of the above factors, produced several new multilateral agreements that predominantly constrain domestic policies (Stegemann, 1995). The most important among these are the Agreement on Agriculture, the General Agreement on Trade in Services (GATS), and the Agreement on Trade-Related Aspects of Intellectual Property Rights (TRIPS Agreement). Fifth, the comprehensive and periodically intensive negotiations of the Uruguay Round created new knowledge (possibly new norms) for dealing with diverging domestic policies that are considered trade related. This knowledge transcends the specific agreements that were concluded. The Uruguay Round negotiations seem to have had an economies-of-scale effect as a result of learning by doing. Current negotiations on domestic policy issues benefit from the new knowledge, and the learning continues.

Wolfe views regulatory diplomacy "as a conversation among governments about how to cope with globalization". It is "a process of discovering new rules" in response to changing circumstances. This discovery takes place in the context of international regimes.[1] The WTO is the central organization of the current trade regime and it is the principal site of regulatory diplomacy. Wolfe, therefore, devotes three sections of his paper to the presentation and analysis of norms and techniques of regulatory diplomacy in the

---

[1]As is conventional in the international relations literature, Wolfe follows Krasner (1983, p. 2) in defining international regimes as "sets of implicit or explicit principles, norms, rules and decision-making procedures around which actors' expectations converge in a given area of international relations".

WTO regime, and then applies his general findings to the 1997 *Reference Paper* for basic telecommunications services which supplements the GATS in this area of policy. Some of his findings will be discussed below. At this point, just two general observations: First, Wolfe's presentation of the regulatory diplomacy principles of the WTO warrants careful reading; his insights are based on extensive practical experience as a former career diplomat which has been filtered by the perspective of a political scientist. Second, the view of the trading system which emerges in Wolfe's paper is substantially different from the view held by most economists.

In Wolfe's view, the test of the diplomacy-based regime "is not that any actor is happy with the behaviour called for by the regime, or with the collective outcome, but that the given actor recognizes the legitimacy of behaviour and outcomes in the context of what is collectively possibly; what is collectively possible is what everyone can accept without the system collapsing". This test is more modest than the test one would prescribe for an open trading system with the objective of constraining national policies that hinder mutually advantageous exchange among countries. Reading on, one realizes that Wolfe's regulatory diplomacy serves to make incremental changes in the rules of the system or to discover new rules for new problems. However, regulatory diplomacy cannot change the fundamental objective of the WTO regime, which is to keep markets open, while accommodating diversity of national policies in ways consistent with its norms. "The way the WTO thinks can change over time instrumentally but not normatively. The WTO will always see a new problem in a way shaped by the norms and practices of the regime". The norms or principles applicable to regulatory diplomacy in the WTO are the traditional GATT principles. Under the heading "regulatory diplomacy in practice" Wolfe reviews possible institutional patterns or a set of negotiating techniques. He does not discuss which countries' diplomats are most influential, or why some countries have more room to manoeuvre than others.[2]

As noted above, Wolfe, in his paper, also intends to answer the question how states accommodate themselves to a trading system that increasingly constrains their domestic policies. He does not address this question separately. Rather, his answer is implied in what he tells us about the nature of the trading regime and the role of regulatory diplomacy. Wolfe emphasizes

---

[2]Such questions are discussed in the literature on the history of the Uruguay Round, for example, Croome (1995), or in case studies like Ryan (1998) for the TRIPS Agreement.

that the GATT/WTO trading regime is a compromise between free trade and policies pursued by the welfare state, it is a regime of "embedded liberalism" (Ruggie, 1983). The welfare state uses regulation "to achieve our collective objectives of greater wealth and enhanced social cohesion". But the tools of regulation may differ between countries and the ends may conflict. "And small countries cannot avoid the consequences when their preferred tools are not those preferred by big countries. The characteristic response to such dilemmas is diplomacy." Thus, when Wolfe explains how regulatory diplomacy serves to discover new rules in the context of the WTO regime, he simultaneously explains how states retain room to manoeuvre. "The aim of regulatory diplomacy is to help the state achieve its legitimate objectives." The result of collective diplomacy, the discovery of new rules for the trading system, determines how much room remains for each member state to pursue its national policies. As Wolfe demonstrates in the bulk of his paper, the WTO's objective "is to help countries to stay out of each other's way while facilitating the expansion of international commerce; its objective is not to regulate the world".

One national policy area for which Canada's diplomats have tried to preserve room to manoeuvre for many years is the protection of domestic industries deemed important to Canadian culture. Wolfe introduces the current manifestation of such endeavours: the *Sports Illustrated* case or the problem of designing policies that prevent foreign "split-run" magazines from entering the Canadian market. Most relevant aspects of this problem have been discussed extensively in the media.[3] Moreover, Dale Orr in his comments on the Waverman paper in this volume has given us an illuminating review of Canada's policy choices for protecting culture. Therefore, my comments can stay close to Wolfe's presentation. First, the rhetoric of cultural nationalists often suggests that split-run magazines have an unfair advantage over domestic magazines. As Wolfe states, the "marginal costs to an American publisher of selling 300,000 copies in Canada using the same glossy editorial content created for the 3,000,000 copies sold in the United States are considerably lower than the gross costs to a Canadian publisher of creating a title of sufficient quality that could sell 300,000 copies in Canada alone." This is simply a case of economies of scale and, as economists have realized for some time, scale economies are a source of

---

[3]See the extensive coverage of Bill C-55 in Canada's two national newspapers from mid-January to late March 1999 and especially Ritchie (1999); McKenna (1999); and Roseman (1999).

gains from trade. There is nothing that is unfair about this situation; indeed we never hear of anybody complaining about foreign split-run refrigerators or split-run automobiles. Second, when Wolfe says that the entry of split-run editions would cause domestic magazines to suffer "because the pool of money available for advertisements directed at Canadian magazine readers is siphoned out of the country" he seems to imply that the market for magazine advertising is owned by Canadian publishers. It is common for domestic firms to complain about foreign competition "siphoning" sales out of the country; but it is hard to imagine that this in itself could be an argument to impress foreign diplomats familiar with the norms of the WTO regime. Third, representatives of the Canadian magazine industry have used the term "dumping" to characterize the potential competition of split runs in the Canadian advertising market and have suggested that the United States would be the first to apply anti-dumping measures in such a situation.[4] An editorial in the *Report on Business Magazine* published by *The Globe and Mail* argued that the controversial legislation prohibiting Canadian advertising in split-run magazines (Bill C-55) "aims to prohibit U.S. magazines from dumping cheap editorial product onto the Canadian market. In much the same way that dumped steel hurts our steel companies, U.S.-produced split-run magazines selling in Canada (which use editorial content already paid for by the enormous U.S. print runs) enjoy an unfair trade advantage over Canadian publishing companies" (Best, 1999). The GATT/WTO anti-dumping rules for goods, an early achievement of regulatory diplomacy, make protection relatively easy (Stegemann, 1991). But even if the GATS contained equivalent anti-dumping rules and these were applicable to the Canadian advertising sector, anti-dumping measures could be imposed only following an elaborate investigation and only in the form of anti-dumping duties. The dumping investigation could take place only after split runs have entered and sold advertising in the Canadian market; it would have to determine whether the advertising rates of split-run magazines in Canada are lower than the rates for equivalent foreign regional editions of the same magazines. There is no evidence of this. All the arguments are in terms of cost advantage. Even if the most generous WTO anti-dumping principles could be extended to this case, they would not permit protection of home-grown magazines on the grounds that foreign firms have a cost advantage.

---

[4]The allegation of dumping was particularly prominent in statements by François de Gaspé Beaubien as referred to by Reguly (1999).

It seems useful to speculate what Wolfe could have concluded had he applied his list of "fundamental WTO principles" (Chart 1) to the Canada-U.S. conflict over split-run magazines. Let us begin with Number 10: dispute settlement. In 1997, Canada lost on all counts when the WTO Dispute Settlement Body (DSB) adopted panel and Appellate Body reports in response to a U.S. complaint concerning Canada's magazine protection policies in force at the time.[5] Bill C-55 is part of what Canada claims to be its implementation of the DSB ruling. Canada's previous policies had been found to violate GATT obligations for trade in goods. The ban on Canadian advertising in split-run magazines to be legislated with Bill C-55 is an attempt to utilize the fact that Canada cannot yet be held to equivalent obligations under the GATS. A prohibition of advertising in split runs does, of course, violate the fundamental WTO principle of national treatment or non-discrimination, which is Number 1 on Wolfe's list. But, as provided for in GATS Article XVII, the national treatment obligation applies only to sectors for which members have made market access commitments, and Canada conveniently has not (yet) made such commitments for the advertising sector. Not surprisingly, U.S. officials have said that Bill C-55 is as bad, or worse than, the special excise tax provisions it serves to replace: the new law is designed to prevent entry of split-run magazines into the Canadian market and would thus deprive U.S. magazines of the victory won in the 1997 magazine ruling. The officials have also threatened that if Canada persisted with the legislation the United States would "retaliate" by restricting certain imports from Canada, including steel produced in the Heritage minister's Hamilton, Ontario, riding.

The U.S. threat of retaliation in the magazines case was premature, though not unprecedented. Under the provisions of the WTO Understanding on Rules and Procedures Governing the Settlement of Disputes (DSU), retaliatory measures may be taken only if authorized by the DSB, and authorization will be given only after an elaborate procedure, set out in DSU Articles 21 and 22, has been followed. Where there is disagreement as to whether measures taken to comply with a DSB ruling are consistent with the member's obligations under relevant WTO agreements, the matter shall be decided by referral to the DSB (using whenever possible the original panel) or by third-party arbitration in accordance with DSU Article 25. At the

---

[5]The panel and Appellate Body reports are available on the Internet (www.wto.org/wto/dispute/distab/htm); a summary of the reports (WT/DS31) is published in WTO, *Annual Report 1997*, Vol. I, pp. 129-130.

moment it seems unlikely that one of these procedures will be used to determine the consistency of Bill C-55 with Canada's obligations, because the parties have engaged in regulatory diplomacy to discover a solution with which both sides can live, in the short run (until the next WTO round of negotiations) or in the long run. It did not come as a surprise that in the current bilateral talks all of the components of Canada's magazine policy are on the table, including Canadian tax policies, postal subsidies and restrictions on foreign ownership (McKenna, 1999).

Should these negotiations fail, the dispute could end up in the WTO again, but the final outcome would still depend on regulatory diplomacy. If the WTO panel or arbitrator agreed with Canada that Bill C-55 does not violate Canada's obligations, U.S. diplomats, driven by the need to pacify powerful interests and the U.S. Congress, would almost certainly extract some short-run concessions as they have in the cases of Canadian soft-wood lumber and grain exports. In the longer run, Canada would be under pressure to include the advertising sector in its commitments under the GATS. Both sides also might become active participants in the discovery of new rules that permit limited exceptions to existing rules when the protection of national culture is at stake. In the alternative case, if the WTO panel or arbitrator agreed with the United States that Bill C-55 is inconsistent with Canada's existing obligations, Canadian diplomats would be under greater pressure to negotiate a short-run arrangement that might retain some face-saving features of the current policy in combination with replacement measures, such as direct subsidies, that have the approval of the United States. Almost certainly, Canada could not afford to ignore an adverse WTO verdict on Bill C-55. Even if the Canadian government could politically afford the cost to Canadian export interests of U.S. retaliation, as authorized by the DSB, Canada would not want to be seen as a WTO member flagrantly violating its obligations. Too much of Canada's trade policy rests on the preservation of a rules-based regime for the long term.

Policies like Bill C-55 cannot survive in the WTO regime because they blatantly violate the first four principles on Wolfe's list: non-discrimination, necessity, least-restrictive measures and proportionality. Some derogation of the non-discrimination principle may be inevitable and possibly can be written into the new long-term rules if Canada attains the support of important WTO members with similar concerns for the protection of national culture. For example, it may be acceptable to subsidize magazines that regularly publish a certain percentage of Canadian content, rather than pay subsidies to all magazines on a per-article basis. The principle of least-restrictive measures and the related concept of "optimal intervention" have been discussed by Orr (1999).[6] Other principles on Wolfe's lists, such as transparency and open decision making, will be part of any new rules in this area and pose no problem for Canada. It has become almost impossible for countries to hide protective measures. Indeed, transparency pays because it serves to prevent false accusations. It is conceivable that WTO members will be able to develop a shared understanding of the regulatory principles for the protection of national culture, or certain aspects of it. Wolfe may be right that the *Reference Paper* for the regulation of basic telecommunications services, which he reviews in some detail, could illustrate the approach likely to be taken in other fields of regulation. One should not expect, however, that a separate WTO agreement for the protection of national culture will emerge in the next round of negotiations. New rules are more likely to be discovered on a piecemeal basis, as could be done, for example, by broadening the rules for "non-actionable" subsidies in the Agreement on Subsidies and Counter-vailing Measures or by adding exceptions *cum* regulations for national culture to Article XIV of the GATS.

The *Reference Paper* for basic telecommunications services and other results of regulatory diplomacy that Wolfe has discussed have in common that the rules attempt to facilitate trade and do not go beyond this objective in restricting the members' freedom to pursue diverse national policies. "The issue is always the effect of a measure on trade, whether imports or exports. If something does not have an effect on trade, it is not a legitimate focus for WTO action" (Wolfe, 1999). This characterization of the WTO approach to its members' domestic policies is mostly correct, except it does not fit one important area of recent WTO rule making: the protection of intellectual property rights. As I have explained elsewhere (Stegemann, 1998), the TRIPS Agreement, in spite of the word "trade-related" in its title, almost entirely consists of rules prescribing minimum standards for the protection of intellectual property rights, as well as strict enforcement procedures for such rights. The non-border standards imposed by the TRIPS Agreement are not aimed at regulating domestic policies that affect imports or exports, in contrast with the non-border rules of all other WTO agreements. Regulatory diplomacy created the TRIPS Agreement because interest groups in various developed countries and the U.S. Congress saw the Uruguay Round as an

---

[6]For an illustration of diversity of opinions on this matter, see Browne (1998).

opportunity for a broad trade-off: the developing, newly industrialized, and transition countries had to accept obligations for the enhanced protection of intellectual property rights in exchange for enlarged or more secure access to the markets of developed countries (Ryan, 1998; Stegemann, 1998). Different national standards of intellectual property protection are not per se an obstacle to international trade. Indeed, WTO members would not likely object if other members increased their standards beyond the requirements of the TRIPS Agreement. Certain members would object only if other members had lower standards than the TRIPS Agreement requires. They would object because lower standards reduce the rewards that their nationals can reap on what they consider their intellectual property, but not because lower standards hinder trade. In short, the TRIPS Agreement is a set of rules concerning the protection of intellectual property; it is not an agreement about international trade. Regulatory diplomacy recognized the TRIPS Agreement as a legitimate focus for WTO action because it could be linked to agreements on international trade, historically in the Uruguay Round, and permanently through linked dispute settlement (Stegemann, 1998).

In his characterization of the WTO approach to differences in domestic policies, Wolfe also concludes that "WTO principles do not prescribe a given level of regulation. Countries can impose any needed level of regulation, if it does not discriminate among goods, services and firms on the basis of nationality". Again, the TRIPS Agreement does not fit. Prohibiting discrimination (requiring National Treatment) was not sufficient for the developed countries to obtain higher levels of protection for their nationals' intellectual property. The TRIPS Agreement had to prescribe standards of protection and specific enforcement procedures in order to raise the level of protection in all member countries to the levels that are taken for granted in jurisdictions with leading intellectual property interests.

Table 1 summarizes information on three distinct types of rules being used to constrain the domestic policies of WTO members: (i) prohibition of discrimination (National Treatment), (ii) other prohibitory constraints, and (iii) prescribed positive standards.[7] The purpose of the table is to compare the relative importance of these three types of rules in the GATT, the GATS and the TRIPS Agreement. The table confirms that the TRIPS Agreement (last row) stands apart from the others because it depends on prescribing specific standards for domestic policy, and these are not trade related.

---

[7]The table is nearly identical to Table 4 in Stegemann (1998).

Table 1: Three Types of Rules Constraining Domestic Policies of WTO Members

Agreement	Prohibition of Discrimination (National Treatment)	Other Prohibitory Constraints	Prescribed Positive Standards
GATT[a] (a) constraining importing countries' policies	most important principle prohibiting unequal treatment of imported and domestic goods; internal taxes, laws and regulations not to afford protection to domestic production (Art. III as a core provision)	moderately important to limit forms and extent of domestic subsidies, always related to market access (Agreement on Agriculture, Agreement on Subsidies and CVD); also TRIMS Agreement	transparency of trade-related policies and access to domestic courts (Art. X); exceptional, as for state trading enterprises (Art. XVII) and Agreement on Application of Sanitary and Phytosanitary Measures, only to facilitate market access; future agenda: standards for competition policy to facilitate market access
(b) constraining exporting countries' policies	not applicable, with possible exception of TRIMS Agreement	moderately important to limit forms and extent of domestic subsidies that affect exports (Agreement on Agriculture and Agreement on Subsidies and CVD); also TRIMS Agreement	exceptional, as for state trading enterprises (Art. XVII); future agenda: minimum standards for labour law and environmental protection where applicable to exporting industries
GATS[b]	non-discrimination even more important for market access of services than for goods; National Treatment applicable only in sectors where specific commitments are undertaken (Art. VI and XVII)	important in sectors where specific market-access commitments are undertaken; six types of restrictions are prohibited (Art. XVI:2), as are certain licensing requirements (Art. VI:5)	transparency (Art. III and III bis), access to courts (Art. VI:2), supervision of firms designated as sole providers (Art. VIII) and possibly restrictive business practices (Art. IX); sectoral disciplines set out specific requirements for certain policies, but always to prevent restrictions on market access
TRIPS	prohibition of discrimination moderately important (Art. 3 and 4), but not suitable to achieve the principal purpose of the agreement		core of the Agreement, prescribing comprehensive standards for protection of intellectual property rights and enforcement, as well as transparency and due-process procedures to protect private rights; standards are not trade related

Notes: a. GATT and associated agreements on trade in goods.
 b. GATS and related sectoral disciplines.
Sources: Multilateral agreements named in table.

Klaus Stegemann

Furthermore, the table confirms, consistent with Wolfe, that prohibition of discrimination (National Treatment) is the most fundamental and pervasive constraint in the GATT and associated agreements on trade in goods, as well as the GATS. National Treatment is also likely to become the fundamental principle in a Multilateral Agreement on Investment (MAI), to constrain national policies towards foreign direct investment. Other prohibitory constraints (second column of the table) are not as common, but they are important for various types of subsidies and certain policies that members might use to impede market access for foreign suppliers of services, including foreign investors. The examples of prescribed standards listed for the GATT and the GATS (third column) seem to concern relatively peripheral policies and it could be argued that these rules do not prescribe levels of regulation in detail. On the other hand, even an old provision such as GATT Article X must be seen as a prescription of regulation as it requires members to publish trade-related laws, regulations, judicial decisions and administrative principles and to provide institutions and procedures for judicial or administrative review of actions relating to custom matters. The GATS has similar prescriptions for transparency and judicial or administrative review (Articles III, IIIbis, and VI:2).

The most specific prescriptions for regulation can be found in some of the GATT associated agreements on trade in goods, such as the Agreement on the Application of Sanitary and Phytosanitary Measures (SPS Agreement) and the Agreement on Technical Barriers to Trade (TBT Agreement). In the case of the SPS Agreement, the negotiators recognized that a "strict requirement for non-discriminatory treatment is not possible for SPS measures, since they frequently discriminate against imported goods or goods from a particular foreign country because those goods pose a different risk of a plant or animal pest or disease" (United States, 1994, p. 742). Under the SPS Agreement discrimination is allowed, but SPS measures must not reduce market access for imported goods in an arbitrary or unjustifiable manner. For this purpose, the agreement prescribes the following standard:

> Members shall ensure that any sanitary or phytosanitary measure is applied only to the extent necessary to protect human, animal, or plant life or health, is based on scientific principles and is not maintained without sufficient scientific evidence... (SPS Agreement, Article 2:2)

This general standard requiring necessity, scientific principles and scientific evidence for SPS measures, is made more specific in many cases by the agreement requiring that "Members shall base their sanitary or phytosanitary measures on international standards, guidelines or recommendations, where they exist", in order to "harmonize sanitary and phytosanitary measures on as wide a basis as possible" (SPS Agreement, Article 3:1). Furthermore, the SPS Agreement prescribes in some detail the procedures that members must use to assess risk and the appropriate level of protection; and it also has rules to ensure the "transparency" of a member's SPS measures (United States, 1994, pp. 748-753).[8] The SPS Agreement, by regulating the application of SPS measures to imported goods, is intended entirely to facilitate international trade and to reduce the scope for disputes. As is made explicit in many provisions, the agreement does not and should not constrain national sovereignty for the purpose of establishing SPS standards or to achieve SPS objectives. In other words, the agreement is entirely trade related. Still, if countries choose to pursue SPS objectives, important aspect of their policies are prescribed by the SPS Agreement, and countries have an incentive to harmonize their policies by adopting international standards, because this reduces the scope for disputes.

Similar conclusions are suggested by the latest results of regulatory diplomacy: the 1996 *Reference Paper of the Negotiating Group on Basic Telecommunications*[9] and the 1998 *Disciplines on Domestic Regulation in the Accountancy Sector*.[10] As mentioned earlier, Wolfe has reviewed the *Reference Paper* (RP) in some detail. I agree with him that the RP represents

---

[8]The SPS Agreement was applied, and has received attention in the media, in the dispute over EU restrictions concerning imports of meat and meat products from livestock treated with growth hormones in response to complaints brought by the United States and Canada (WT/DS26 and WT/DS48). See WTO (1998a, Vol. I, pp. 105-106; and 1998b).

[9]The *Reference Paper*, dated April 24, 1996, has been reprinted in the Appendix to Wolfe's paper. It was part of the outcome of sectoral negotiations under the GATS which were concluded in February 1997 by members making additions to their Schedules for basic telecommunications services (Report of the Group on Basic Telecommunications, WTO: S/GBT/4, February 15, 1997). The background and results of these negotiations are discussed by several contributors in Hufbauer and Wada (1997).

[10]The *Disciplines on Domestic Regulation in the Accountancy Sector*, adopted by the WTO's Council for Trade in Services on December 14, 1998, can be found in WTO (1998c, pp. 10-11).

state-of-the-art regulatory diplomacy in the WTO regime. But I do not fully agree with Wolfe's conclusions concerning the potential consequences of documents of this kind for the members' policies in the covered domain. In my opinion, he underestimates the prescriptive potential of the RP. Wolfe acknowledges that the RP was designed to shape national regulatory institutions, regulatory processes and regulatory policies for basic telecommunications services with the purpose of enabling new suppliers to enter markets that are dominated by major suppliers or national monopolies. However, Wolfe discounts the practical impact of the RP, arguing that it "seems remarkably imprecise" lacking workable definitions of central concepts. He calls the document "a statement of aspiration" or an articulation of the objective which "speaks more to the values of competition than to adjudicable obligations". In my view, the RP is about as precise or imprecise as competition law typically is. Wolfe notes the absence of a definition of the term "relevant market" which can, indeed, be as critical for regulatory decisions concerning access to a telecommunications market, as it is for most merger and monopoly cases. Yet, no anti-trust statute or competition law includes a definition of the relevant market; it would be futile to legislate a definition that is presumed to fit all cases.[11]

The RP includes substantive provisions, especially on "interconnection" requirements, which I would call quite prescriptive of national policies in this area. Interconnection rules should enable (new) suppliers to link with (incumbent) suppliers of public telecommunications transport networks or services in order to allow users of one supplier to communicate with users of another supplier and also to access services provided by another supplier. The RP contains a definition of such interconnection which will require some members to liberalize their markets (when others have done so already). The rules are also judiciable, by either a firm having recourse to an independent body or the firm's government availing itself of the WTO dispute-settlement procedures. These procedures can be used to clarify and to enforce the RP only among members who included it in their 1997 Schedules for basic

---

[11]The U.S. Department of Justice and Canada's Bureau of Competition Policy have issued so-called "merger guidelines" which contain lengthy conceptual discussions of market definition and other issues. For Canada's merger guidelines see Canada (1991); this document includes the merger provisions of the Competition Act in an appendix. The definition of relevant markets has been discussed extensively also in the academic literature (Elzinga and Rogowsky, 1984).

telecommunications services. Yet, it is predictable that next time there will be an attempt to extend equivalent obligations to all members who make market access commitments for this sector, and then all members of the WTO.

In another area of the GATS, the Working Party on Professional Services (WPPS) has been busy developing "disciplines" for domestic regulation to facilitate trade in professional services. These follow from the mandate in GATS Article VI:4. The Working Party's first finished output are *Disciplines on the Domestic Regulation in the Accountancy Sector*. This document is remarkably similar in approach and structure to the RP for basic telecommunications regulation and I would also call it prescriptive. The WPPS is aiming to develop general disciplines for professional services, in addition to sectoral ones. "Before the end of the forthcoming round of services negotiations, which commence in January 2000, all disciplines developed by the WPPS are to be integrated into the GATS and will then become legally binding" (WTO, 1998c, p. 10). Thus, regulatory diplomacy is at work filling gaps, adapting established patterns to new issues, making rules more specific and, at the same time, expanding the scope of members' obligations.

The editor has admonished me not to write an essay on "semantic" differences. So, let me say very quickly that I do not agree with Wolfe's narrow definition of "harmonization" of national domestic policies and have no use for his term "rhythm" which in his usage contrasts with harmony. Harmonization, in my view, is a matter of degree, and the term has been used widely and for a long time to describe ways of making different national policies more harmonious, more compatible with trade liberalization, or possibly more similar. For Wolfe, the term harmonization occupies only the extreme end of the spectrum and is almost synonymous with common policy, unified laws and common institutions. His term rhythm then occupies most of the rest (or mostly the other end) of the spectrum covering what most people would call harmonization in the context of a multilateral trading system. By showing that regulatory diplomacy in the WTO regime is likely to bring about mostly the looser forms of harmonization (his rhythm), Wolfe comes to the conclusion that there will remain sufficient room for members to pursue somewhat differentiated national policies in most areas. I agree with him on this, but I believe he could also have come to the conclusion that the room to manoeuvre is shrinking constantly for members other than the two dominant jurisdictions, and particularly for countries considered to be "in the backyard" of a dominant member.

The WTO does not aim to regulate the world. New rules will not constrain all details of its members' domestic policies in a comprehensive manner. Rather, rule making is likely to be driven selectively by the interests of influential firms or groups (euphemistically referred to as non-government organizations or NGOs). Since the Uruguay Round, the process of rule making seems to have acquired a new momentum. Regulatory diplomacy has demonstrated how to discover new rules that constrain or prescribe domestic policies for new issues. The NGOs have discovered how to use this process. The first step is to place an issue on the agenda for negotiations. This could be done by obtaining sufficient support in the U.S. Congress or by persuading the United States Trade Representatives (USTR) to file a complaint under an existing agreement. The next step would be regulatory diplomacy cum NGO activity resulting in a memorandum of understanding or a reference paper possibly with a reference to existing standards under another international agreement (as, for example, for environmental protection or labour standards).[12] At the next stage, adherence to such standards could become a binding obligation for all members. The extent of this obligation can then be clarified through dispute settlement, which would involve further regulatory diplomacy cum NGO activity resulting in more specific rules to impose more specific constraints on domestic policies in the selected domain. All of this is not necessarily detrimental to the interests of a smaller member like Canada. Indeed, new multilaterally agreed rules may occasionally help governments to hold particular domestic interests at bay; other new rules could benefit a small member because they constrain its competitors in world markets, without much effect on its policies which already conform with the new rules. Yet, a small country's influence on the discovery of new rules for the trading system is usually minute, regulatory diplomacy notwithstanding.

---

[12]Virginia Leary (1996) has described the efforts of the Secretariat of the International Labour Organization (ILO) to promote a link between trade and ILO labour standards as a means of increasing compliance with a set of "internationally recognized" workers' rights.

References

Best, P. (1999), "Canadian, not American, Great Stories Must be Told", *Report on Business Magazine* (Toronto), March, 1.

Browne, D., ed. (1998), *The Culture/Trade Quandry* (Ottawa: Centre for Trade Policy and Law).

Canada (1991), Director of Investigation and Research, Competition Act, *Merger Enforcement Guidelines*, Catalogue No. RG54-2/5-1991E (Ottawa: Supply and Services Canada).

Croome, J. (1995), *Reshaping the World Trading System: A History of the Uruguay Round* (Geneva: World Trade Organization).

Elzinga, K.G. and R.A. Rogowsky, eds. (1984), *Relevant Markets in Antitrust* (Washington, DC: Federal Legal Publications) (Vol. 14, No. 2 of *The Journal of Reprints for Antitrust Law and Economics*).

Hufbauer, G.C. and E. Wada, eds. (1997), *Unfinished Business: Telecommunications after the Uruguay Round* (Washington, DC: Institute for International Economics).

Krasner, S.D. (1983), "Structural Causes and Regime Consequences: Regimes as Intervening Variables", in S.D. Krasner (ed.), *International Regimes* (Ithaca, NY: Cornell University Press), 1-21.

Leary, V.A. (1996), "Workers' Rights and International Trade: The Social Clause (GATT, ILO, NAFTA, U.S. Laws)", in J. Bhagwati and R.E. Hudec (eds.), *Fair Trade and Harmonization: Prerequisites for Free Trade?*, Vol. 2 (Cambridge, MA: MIT Press), 177-230.

McKenna, B. (1999), "Thaw in Talks Gives Both Sides Chance to Refocus", *The Globe and Mail* (Toronto), March 16, A4.

Orr, D. (1999), "Canadian Information/Culture Policy in the Information Age: Comments", in this volume.

Ostry, S. (1997), *The Post-Cold War Trading System: Who's on First?* (Chicago: University of Chicago Press).

Reguly, E. (1999), "Death of Magazines Exaggerated", *The Globe and Mail* (Toronto), February 20, B2.

Ritchie, G. (1999), "Don't Let Washington Shred our Magazines", *The National Post* (Toronto), February 9, 18.

Roseman, D. (1999), "How to Protect Canadian Magazines", *The Globe and Mail* (Toronto), February 15.

Ruggie, J.G. (1983), "International Regimes, Transactions, and Change: Embedded Liberalism in the Postwar Economic Order", in S.D. Krasner (ed.), *International Regimes* (Ithaca, NY: Cornell University Press), 195-231.

Ryan, M.P. (1998), *Knowledge Diplomacy: Global Competition and the Politics of Intellectual Property* (Washington, DC: The Brookings Institution).

Stegemann, K. (1991), "The International Regulation of Dumping: Protection Made Too Easy", *The World Economy* 14(4), 375-405.

_____ (1995), "Uruguay Round Results for New Issues", in T. J. Courchene (ed.), *Technology, Information and Public Policy*, Bell Canada Papers on Economic and Public Policy, Vol. 3 (Kingston: John Deutsch Institute, Queen's University), 171-189.

_____ (1998), "The Integration of Intellectual Property Rights into the WTO System", Discussion Paper No. 10-98 (Jena, Germany: Max-Planck-Institute for Research into Economic Systems), (available on the Institute's Website: www.mpiew-jena.mpg.de).

United States (1994), *Message from the President of the United States Transmitting the Uruguay Round Trade Agreements, Texts of Agreements Implementing Bill, Statement of Administrative Action and Required Supporting Documents* (Washington, DC: U.S. Govt. Printing Office, 103d Congress, 2d Session, House Document 103-316, Vol. 1, September 27).

Wolfe, R. (1999), "Regulatory Diplomacy: Why Rhythm Beats Harmony in the Trade Regime", this volume.

World Trade Organization (WTO) (1998a), *Annual Report 1998* (Geneva: WTO).

_____ (1998b), *WTO FOCUS Newsletter*, No. 27 (Geneva: WTO).

_____ (1998c), *WTO FOCUS Newsletter*, No. 36 (Geneva: WTO).

Summary of Discussion

David Slater asked Professor Wolfe how he would respond to Professor Stegemann's view that the high degree of precision in the language of the telecoms *Reference Paper* is more in keeping with international policy harmonization than with Wolfe's concept of policy rhythm.

Robert Wolfe stressed that Article 6, a key provision of the paper, requires countries to have something like our Competitions Tribunal, but does not specify that all countries have to adopt a specific model. Policy harmony implies identical rules, while policy rhythm requires similar purposes but allows countries to set implementation rules consistent with their own national institutional setting.

Louis Pauly drew attention to the dynamic relationship between trade agreements and deeper state and social structures. For example, it is not a coincidence that the North American Free Trade Agreement (NAFTA) embodies legal instruments that work well in a U.S. structural context. The United States is exporting their method of doing business to the world. In Europe, agreements are not always what they seem. Europeans may agree, but then delay implementation. Lack of implementation can be a fallback or safeguard position. The British are increasingly suspicious about lack of implementation by their continental partners. Americans use similar tactics. If Americans have a problem with unanticipated implications of an agreement that they have signed, implementation can be delayed by litigation. Canadians are at a disadvantage because we tend to implement the agreements that we sign, rather than resorting to U.S.-style litigation.

Robert Wolfe agreed that who defines implementation is a key aspect in any trade agreement. For example, the Americans did not like the way the original General Agreement on Tariffs and Trade (GATT) was working and pushed for the 1955 GATT waiver. But it is interesting to note that Canada took advantage of this exception to implement our own farm supply management system.

Klaus Stegemann viewed the Americans' selective reliance on instruments like their section 301 procedure as a bigger problem. When it suits their interest, the United States indulges in bilateral arm-twisting.

Harry Arthurs made three points about Wolfe's framework. First, the ideal models of policy harmony and policy rhythm are likely to be less dichotomized in real situations. Sooner or later, the parties to an agreement have to agree that policies are sufficiently consistent or disputes will arise. This will be true regardless of the degree of precision stipulated in the agreement. The second point is that neither panelist mentioned an important area where we are clearly moving closer to policy harmonization — intellectual property. The third point is that harmonization can come about, not through explicit governmental negotiations, but through standards and modalities of corporate practice.

Robert Wolfe agreed that we are moving towards harmonization in some sectors through non-state mechanisms. In fact, the World Trade Organization (WTO) likes voluntary industry agreements on international standards. Such agreements are often led by industry, not governments. As for the criticism that there is no practical difference between policy harmony and rhythm, the point is that rhythm is a middle ground between harmony and the other extreme of "doing your own thing". Under policy rhythm, it is as if countries are doing a similar dance without having to mimic all of each other's moves. Under policy rhythm, regulatory regimes can remain different so long as they do not cause undue conflicts.

Klaus Stegemann responded to Arthurs' reference to intellectual property. There is no question that the recent intellectual property agreement includes explicit standards that the Americans and Europeans were anxious to get. Countries' procedures do not, however, have to be identical as long as they meet the agreed objectives. This is similar to anti-dumping agreements in which policies have been harmonized for a long time in the sense of meeting objectives, while allowing room for specific procedures to vary. NAFTA binational panels recognize that the three countries have their own procedures.

Chantal Blouin raised the point that the telecoms *Reference Paper* was adopted because the General Agreement on Trade in Services (GATS) was thought to be insufficient for the telecommunication sector. Could the telecoms paper be used as a model for other sectors such as electronic commerce.

Robert Wolfe predicted that electronic commerce will go in a direction similar to telecommunications — policy rhythm, not harmony.

David Slater asked Stegemann if he thought that trade diplomats could be more than pen-holders transcribing the demands of special interest groups. Who would look after consumer interests? Could diplomats represent the broader interest of their national consumers or would we have to look to the WTO to represent the consumer interest? After the last round of trade negotiations, a senior Canadian official involved in the farm trade talks admitted that countries with agricultural protection got together and scratched each other's backs. In that particular trade round, consumers in Canada and in other countries were ripped off. Unfortunately, the consequences would be felt for a long period.

Klaus Stegemann reported that there are forums for representing consumer interests at the Organization for Economic Cooperation and Development (OECD), but they have not been effective to date. The reports of the OECD Committee on Business Practices have not been implemented and the report on anti-dumping policy never saw the light of day.

Globalization and the Meaning of Canadian Life

William Watson

I was delighted when Tom Courchene invited me to give an after-dinner talk about my book *Globalization and the Meaning of Canadian Life*, published by the University of Toronto Press,[1] which deals with many of the themes raised in our discussions here. I am delighted at every invitation to talk about my book. In fact, I am delighted to talk about it even when not invited, as my wife, who has heard my volunteered commentaries on it for several years now, would attest.

Anna Quindlen wrote recently of the joy a writer feels when holding her first cloth-cover book in her hands. "I ripped into the envelope, removed the book, and lifted it up and down in my outstretched hands, just to feel the heft of it, as though it was to be valued by weight. I held it the way I'd seen babies held at religious ceremonies, a bris, perhaps, or a baptism. Hardcovers: every writer's ultimate ambition, whether she admits it or not."

In fact, the parallel with newborns is not exact. Books spit up less. And people are perfectly willing to tell you — with brazen candour and in writing — exactly what they think of your book.

---

[1] This being the text of a speech, rather than an article, I dispense with footnotes and references. Virtually all references can be found in the book itself.

This is my first hard-cover book. Not knowing whether the opportunity will repeat itself, I put into it just about every thought I've ever had. (It was therefore discouraging, upon receiving that first couriered copy from the publisher, to see how slim it was.)

Because the book does cover so many subjects, it is a little hard to précis. But let me try.

To begin with, it really is called *Globalization and the Meaning of Canadian Life*. In his review, David Frum said this was probably the worst title in the history of Canadian publishing. Maybe so, but in this case form fits function. The book comes in two parts: "Globalization" and "The Meaning of Canadian Life". Each is meant to be contrarian. The purpose of "Globalization" is to suggest, first, that economic integration isn't that new, and, second, that national governments will not be as enfeebled by it as many observers suggest. In the language of this conference, they do have and, for a long time, perhaps forever, *will* have plenty of room for manoeuvre.

Given that we are therefore free, if we wish, to continue to build our national identity on the idea that Canadians are the North Americans with the bigger government — which I take to be the recently conventional meaning of Canadian life — the second half of the book argues that this is an unwise premise on which to try to build a nation, not least because big government may ultimately undo the nation. In Harry Arthurs' terms, "There *is* an alternative." It's just not a very wise alternative, and it doesn't really reflect our tradition, if tradition extends back before 1960 or thereabouts, when the idea of *Nous, c'est l'état* (as Richard Gwyn puts it) really took off.

This was, I think, a contrarian idea when the book first occurred to me, in 1988. Harry Arthurs' comments about neo-conservatism made me think that perhaps it still is at least a little bit contrarian. On the other hand, since people with my views now have our own national newspaper, perhaps it isn't. Of course, the *National Post* has many fewer subscribers and readers than the Toronto *Star*. For now, at least.

Let me talk a bit about the first half of the book, "Globalization", before going on to even deeper and murkier questions.

Americans have an excuse for being taken in by the novelty and romance of globalization. They ran an essentially closed economy for most of this century, and have never been on the deficit side of a brain drain. We Canadians have no such excuse. Most of us hail from generations that still studied history in school and we therefore heard about the exciting exigencies of the international trade in furs and then lumber and wheat in our elementary-school history courses. As we all learned, Canada was in large part explored and developed by the world's first transnational corporation, the Hudson's Bay Company. And we heard about the local difficulties created by the British corn laws, by which of course, the British in their endearing way, actually meant "wheat laws". As Michael Hart puts it, "When Sir John A. Macdonald uttered his immortal words, 'A British subject I was born, a British subject I will die', he was not thinking of the Plains of Abraham or Queenston Heights, but of the tariff on ploughs from New York." In sum, we Canadians have been accustomed to the tumult and hard disciplines of international trade for some time now.

Yes, it's true that air travel and the Internet are, quite literally, marvellous, but we are overly smug, I think, in our opinion of how wonderfully modern we all are. I suspect the psychological distance between sea-mail and the trans-Atlantic telegraph was actually greater than that between the long-distance telephone and the Web. And earlier ages have known telecommunications revolutions every bit as profound and dramatic as those now taking place. In 1851, it cost U.S. $5 per word — per *word* — to send a cable from New York to London. That's U.S. $51 in today's currency, which is, what?, three or four thousand Canadian. Just a few years later, the rate was a hundredth of that — a decline in price that rivals the late-twentieth century decline in the price of computation. In the 1850s, it cost £100 and took several months to get a letter from Winnipeg to Montreal (which is at least two weeks longer than it takes now). A quarter-century later, once the telegraph went in, communication was virtually instantaneous. *That's* future shock.

International trade grew by a factor of 25 in the last century, much more than in this. And the rate of migration in the nineteenth century exceeded anything experienced these days. In the 1880s alone, 19% of Canada's population simply picked up and moved, mainly southward — no green card required. In 1900, the U.S. census counted 1.18 million resident Canadian nationals, fully one-quarter of Canada's population at the time. In the first decade of this century, immigration into Canada equalled 24.6% of the population, compared to only 6% in the 1990s, a decade in which, nevertheless, immigration became a hot political topic. In fact, 6% was the lowest rate of immigration — Depression and war years excepted — since the numbers have been kept.

Nor was there any shortage of capital movements in previous eras. Best remember that the world record for foreign direct investment as a share of the investor-country's national income is 9%, set, not by the United States or Japan, but by the United Kingdom in 1913.

But even if we shouldn't be so smug about what a revolutionary age we live in, isn't it still true that open markets and footloose factors will force governments to bid down tax rates in search of investors and immigrants? Since there has been a good deal of trade and investment liberalization since the Second World War, if it were going to happen, there would be signs of it happening already. For the most part, there aren't — though never having been seriously afflicted by econometrics, I have only primitive data to justify that assertion.

- Angus Maddison's 75-year time series on government spending in six big countries shows some convergence before the war, none after.

- A 40-year OECD series on different countries' tax ratios shows slight divergence from the 1950s through the seventies, followed by slight convergence afterward, with the coefficient of variation for 1994 being 21%, versus 22% in 1955. Granted, the same measure does show dramatically increasing divergence in Europe before 1980 and then fairly significant convergence after 1980. But to my mind Europe is a special example of an emerging federation. Europeans actually want to become more alike. (I was glad to see that Bob Wolfe thinks the same thing, arguing that it is the world's only case of positive integration.) But even in Europe, even on such simple things as rules for capital taxation, there is continuing disagreement, in fact "cacophony", according to public finance economist Joel Slemrod.

- In 1994, tax ratios in the OECD varied by almost 30 percentage points of GDP — which I take to be quite a sizeable variation — from just over 20% in Turkey to just over 50% in Denmark.

- In the 29 years between 1965 and 1994, the average tax ratio in the OECD fell in only four years, only one of them a Reagan-Thatcher year. That's worth emphasizing, I think: the considerable economic integration that the world experienced in the first four decades after World War II did not preclude the growth of big government. Between 1955 and 1992, average OECD tax ratios rose from 23.4% of GDP to 38.2%.

- The best evidence that the governments of integrating economies retain considerable room to manoeuvre is, of course, ourselves. The year 1958 was notable in Canada for two reasons. First, it was the last time the

William Watson

U.S. spent more of its GDP through the public sector than we did. (Yes, in the 1950s they had a larger public sector than we did, and it wasn't all just military: we had a big military at that time, too.) And, second, it was the year in which trade hit a postwar low as a share of Canadian GDP. After that, our government grew and our economy became much more open, both at the same time. That should be emphasized: the dramatic economic integration that resulted from the Defence Production Sharing Agreements, the Auto Pact, and the first few rounds of the GATT did not prevent us from taxing ourselves at significantly higher rates than the Americans.

I am no theorist, but I would argue that, experience aside, economics provides good reasons for supposing that even fairly significant differences in fiscal policy can be sustained indefinitely. The economic theory of federalism, which assumes perfect mobility of capital and labour as a matter of course, quite happily contemplates permanent fiscal differences between regions. On the other hand, when factors are mobile, tax revenues can't be wasted. People will stay in a place only if there are offsetting benefits to the higher taxes they pay. That doesn't mean all taxes have to be benefit taxes (i.e., a rough approximation to user charges). If redistribution creates a nicer society, people who value a nicer society will stay. The trouble in Canada is that more and more of us feel that the higher and higher taxes we pay no longer provide high-quality public services or nice-creating income redistribution. Maybe they once did. But those benefits have been sunk, while the interest on them still has to be paid off.

There is also the problem of internal, domestic limits on taxation: even if taxes do provide a nicer society, the higher that taxes go, the more of us there are who will be tempted to stay and enjoy the benefit but not pay the tax, which we can do by going underground, or AWOL from the workforce, or both.

All this talk about high taxes raises the question of the "meaning of Canadian life". Though perhaps I am simply showing my age, or my tendency to listen to CBC, it seems to me that the idea is still quite popular in Canada that what makes this country different from the Americans, apart from snowstorms and a lower per capita GDP, is our larger government. Perhaps the best proof is that Lucien Bouchard himself adopted this very proposition as the Parti Québécois' election platform in 1998's Quebec election.

The second half of the book launches a multi-sided attack on what I regard as a number of false premises underlying our statist self-image. I won't try your patience with all the details of my right-wing screed, but will just hit the highlights.

False Premise 1: The United States is an unregulated, laissez-faire jungle.

I lived in New York City for a year in the early 1990s. My favourite example of U.S. overregulation was a sign I saw under an overpass on the FDR Drive in Manhattan. "Overheight vehicles stop", it said. Well, yes.

The U.S. Federal Code of Regulations is 156,000 pages long, even longer than the Starr Report. When Bill Clinton appointed Al Gore to supervise regulatory reform he said: "I asked him to do it because he was the only person that I could trust to read all 156,000 pages."

False Premise 2: Canadians pioneered statism in North America.

This is the myth of the CPR as our national policy template. In fact, massive subsidization of transcontinental railways was a U.S. invention. Washington gave the builders of the Union Pacific Railway 23 million acres of land and lent them $60 million, fully half the cost of the railway's construction. The one difference was that the Union Pacific was completed in 1869, three years before the first contract was let on the CPR. My favourite quote on all this comes from an 1864 correspondent in the *Atlantic Monthly* who wrote of railway subsidies that while the political ideal was "absolute non-interference of Government in all enterprises whose benefit accrues [only] to a part of its citizens ... facts are not ideal, and absolute principles in their practical application make head only by a curved line of compromise with the facts". A curved line of compromise. Joe Clark couldn't have said it better.

Our National Policy copied the United States on tariffs, too. In fact, Sir John A. only went for tariffs in 1879 because the United States refused to negotiate a new Reciprocity Treaty in the 1870s.

False Premise 3: We are and always have been the kinder, gentler North Americans.

As late as the middle of this century, a strong anti-statist tradition persisted in this country. In 1943, in that wonderful book, *The Unknown Country*, Bruce Hutchison refers to us as the "last surviving rugged individualists" and he describes how distraught federal Liberals then were that they had been forced to mimic the New Deal.

I was shocked to learn, in my reading for this book, that quite respectable Canadians — such as Charlotte Whitton and Harold Innis — had been classical liberals. In 1945, deploring Ottawa's proposed adoption of Keynesianism and the welfare state, Innis quoted Goldwin Smith approvingly: "The opinions of the present writer are those of a Liberal of the old school as yet unconverted to State Socialism, who looks for further improvement not to an increase of the authority of government, but to the same agencies, moral, intellectual, and economical, which have brought us thus far."

False Premise 4: We are bunglers in the market, compared to the Americans and never have had a private sector worth speaking of.

In fact, we have had our share of shrewd operators. The private syndicate that built the CPR made its capital in a leveraged buy-out of the St. Paul, Minneapolis, and Manitoba Railway, a transaction in which the general manager of the railway may have connived in order to understate its true value. In any case, he later complained that he had not received his fair share of the impressive profits. (George Stephen's original investment of $100,000 turned into $21 million — almost as good a return as earned by that famous commodity futures trader, Hillary Rodham Clinton.)

The Toronto Stock Exchange, which now seems as grey and unexciting as, say, *The Globe and Mail*, was the VSE of the 1920s, ridden through with sharp and shady practitioners.

False Premise 5: It is crucial that Canadian policy be different from American.

I have a long section on this in the book but will simply assert that it isn't crucial at all. What's crucial is that Canadian policy be right. Yet, too often, alternatives are dismissed because "That's the American way of doing things. We Canadians don't do things that way. It's not our tradition."

Now, a respectable argument can be made that the world needs lots of policy diversity, so that maybe we should self-consciously do things differently here. But it would be very hard to calculate the optimal amount of policy diversity for the world. And it's not clear that if Noah had a policy ark, a country so similar to the United States as we are would be invited on board. A world that has Islamic fundamentalism, Chinese communism and Tony Blair may not actually need the marginal increase in policy diversity that Canada provides. Which brings me to:

False Premise 6: We are quite a distinct society from the United States.

In fact, across a wide range of variables we are very similar to the United States. In many cases, it's us and the United States over here, and the rest of the world over there. We aren't *exactly* like the Americans. There are obviously differences between us. Our penchant for existential self-doubt is an example. Our self-consciousness in regard to the Americans is another. At the end of the day, I find these qualities actually rather endearing, if also often infuriating.

But it should not be a goal of policy — not even an implicit goal of policy — to multiply these differences. Too often, we have tolerated unwise and excessive intervention on the grounds that "That's the way we do things here." Or: "We've always had a tradition of state intervention or joint public and private ownership", and so on.

It is especially unwise to pursue large government when it involves obvious costs, only three of which I'll mention.

Cost No. 1: High Marginal Tax Rates. As calculations by Jim Davies at Western and Bev Dahlby at Alberta have made clear, just about everybody in Canada faces a marginal tax rate in excess of 50%. And rates are a lot higher than that for people with incomes of $10 or $20 thousand, who face

William Watson

clawbacks of various social benefits and tax credits. The disincentive effects on work and investment are obvious and have been enumerated on many occasions by many people. I won't dwell on them.

But there is another effect that should give pause, particularly to those who like intervention. It is that high taxes and administrative over-reach put the state — which we all agree is a bulwark of civilization — in a bad odour. Anti-state populism isn't simply the mobilized ignorance of red-neck Albertans (if that term isn't oxymoronic). Times have changed: the state doesn't commandeer a quarter of GDP any more, it commandeers a half. Some commentators would have us feel guilty that we no longer have an appetite for ambitious social programs. Well, of course, the reason for that is that we have already had our fill. Gluttony is not a virtue. Our parents, who built the welfare state, may well have felt differently had they started from a base of 50% of GDP instead of 25%.

Cost No. 2: We Become a Confederacy of Beggars. When the state intrudes in virtually every area of life, too much of life comes to wait upon the minister — as universities know well — and to depend on pleasing the minister. One of the most frustrating parts of being a Canadian neo-conservative — or classical liberal — is trying to get business people to speak out. They are always working on their next deal with the government, or petitioning for a special regulatory favour. In 1932, Charlotte Whitton, then a social worker, wrote that "There is a grave danger of the development, as a matter of course, of a general tendency to reliance on social aid [that is] so disruptive of the very basis of initiative, enterprise, and strength of character that must be the greatest resource of any people." The temerity she worried about is no more evident than in the government relations departments of the large firms that supposedly run our public policies these days. Many of our academic colleagues who consult with governments suffer the same syndrome. Which brings me to:

Cost No. 3: The Corrosive Effect on our Politics of Consuming Jealousies. George Orwell wrote that "A man receiving charity practically always hates his benefactor; it is a fixed characteristic of human nature." Hatred — or shall we use the milder term, jealousy — among Canadians is not the result of big government. Blair Fraser wrote in 1967 — our golden year, supposedly — that "never in their history have Canadians demonstrated any warm affection for each other. Loyalties have always been parochial, mutual hostilities chronic." Two decades earlier, Harold Innis put it this way: "The hatreds between regions in Canada have become important vested interests. Montreal exploits the hatred of Toronto, and Regina that of Winnipeg, and so one might go through the list. A native of Ontario may appear restive at being charged with exploitation by those who systematically exploit him through their charges of exploitation, but even the right to complain is denied to him." Innis could not know, of course, that Ontarians would seize this right in the 1990s, after the cap on CAP, as Tom Courchene terms it.

Big government did not cause this problem, but big government obviously does not help. The definitive example of this was the awarding of the CF-18 repair contract to Canadair Ltd. of Montreal, rather than Bristol Aerospace of Winnipeg, in the 1980s. At the time, the federal government argued that this was done for economic reasons, but during the 1995 referendum the truth came out: as westerners had believed at the time, the contract *had* gone to Quebec for political reasons. The consequences for the Meech Lake Accord, and therefore possibly for the Confederation, had been dire.

A philosopher-king put in charge of a loose confederation in which interregional jealousies were already pronounced might well decide to do as many things as possible outside the political system, according to market rules. If we are not good at deciding things collectively, if we are perpetually envious and petty, as we seem to be, then continuing to do so much through the public sector may end up literally consuming the country in jealousy.

That's it for the right-wing screed.

The book then concludes with a speculative rumination about what seems to me to be a greater danger to national sovereignty than the liberalization of trade and investment. And that is the new communication technologies. The danger here is not so much that nation states will be *forced* to become alike, but that they will *want* to be alike because everyone in all countries will have become culturally American, whatever their passports may say.

I go on at great length about this in the book, but the main point I make is simply that this isn't a foregone conclusion. Yes, satellite technology means that everyone in the world can see the same images at the same time. (Eventually Larry King will be available in the rudest Himalayan hut. "Go ahead, Katmandu! Do you think Bill Clinton should be impeached?") But Internet technology pushes us towards having almost no simultaneous experiences (except on special occasions such as the publication of the Starr

Report). What seems certain is that these effects will not precisely cancel, but which will predominate is impossible to say.

Canadian cultural nationalists worry that Canadians will not have enough common experiences to sustain themselves as a nation, and they therefore wish to subsidize common cultural experiences, particularly those delivered by television — if it is not too unseemly to use the words "culture" and "television" in the same sentence. But their view of how countries sustain themselves depends far too heavily on idealized recollections of the in fact very untypical age that lasted a few fleeting years in the 1950s, after CBC television went on the air but before its monopoly was ended by antenna, cable and, in 1961, CTV. That age is gone now, forever. With the advent of the 500-channel universe and the Internet, it's never possible to know what "cultural products" your fellow commuter was consuming the night before. But that's a normal situation for our species. For most of history, human beings have not simultaneously experienced the same things. And yet we had nations before we had network radio and TV. We may well have them afterward.

So, will nation states survive? I close the book with an economic analysis. There are lots of people who want them to survive (which is why the status quo is always a sort of tyranny). They still perform many useful functions, including deep economic integration. And, finally, a Breton-Scott style analysis, which looks at the optimal size of jurisdiction as being a result of balancing-off administration costs, coordination costs, mobility costs and signalling costs, doesn't give any strong clues as to whether technology is making the optimal jurisdiction bigger or smaller. So there is always the possibility that it may stay more or less the same.

And then there is the question of our affection for our nation states. Let me close by reading the book's final paragraph.

No doubt all this calculation sounds quite bloodless to non-economists. In this bloodiest and most nationalist of all centuries, that may not be a bad thing. There is more to countries than accounting, including the not-unimportant fact that many of us have become very fond of our nation states. In his first inaugural address, Lincoln spoke about the "mystic chords of memory, stretching from every battle-field and patriot grave to every living heart and hearthstone all over this broad land". Canadians fought neither a revolutionary nor a civil war, but after four centuries of European presence, we, too, are a community based on memory, albeit sometimes imperfect and conflicting memory. An essentially utilitarian approach to the question of countries need not preclude emotional attachments of this sort. A ship is primarily a means of transportation, but this does not mean that those who sail her cannot be fond or proud of her or even love her, especially when she has served well through heavy seas. So it is with our own ship of state, even if the English-Canadian tradition, like the sailor's, is not to speak of such things too openly or often.*

William Watson

Towards a North American Common Currency: An Optimal Currency Area Analysis

Thomas J. Courchene

Within Canada, far too little attention has been devoted to the question of the costs and benefits of exchange rate stability or to the possibility of moving toward a fixed exchange rate regime. North American free trade and currency stability within the continent go hand in hand — free trade and flexible rates are inherently inconsistent.

Richard Harris (1993, p. 59).

Research on this paper began when I was a visiting scholar at ZEI (the Centre for European Integration) in Bonn, Germany. In this regard, I wish to acknowledge Jürgen von Hagen and his ZEI associates for providing a stimulating research environment. The current version of this paper differs from the Conference version in several respects. First, aspects of the march of events over the intervening period (e.g., the introduction of the Euro) have been incorporated. Second, and far more important, Richard Harris and I have written two post-Conference papers (1999a, 1999b) which have extended the analysis in several ways. In several places in what follows, I have drawn heavily from these joint papers. Finally, I have benefited substantially from comments by, among others, Bill Robson, Finn Poschmann, Daniel Schwanen (all of C.D. Howe Institute), and from Ted Carmichael and Peter Kirkham. And, of course, the imprint of Rick Harris is all over this version of the paper.

Fiscal discipline, cooperative monetary discipline, and a fixed exchange rate regime constitute the only internally consistent policy package (each part needing the other two) that can successfully achieve low inflation, full employment and sustained growth at the same time. All smaller, macroeconomically successful, countries have adopted it. I think Canada should go that way too.

Pierre Fortin (1994, p. 102).

The exchange rate is the most important price in the Canadian economy.

Robert Mundell (1990/1991).

Introduction

In line with these quotations, the thrust of the ensuing analysis is exchange rate fixity (defined to span the spectrum from fixed exchange rates to a common currency) should be the cornerstone of Canada's macroeconomic future within the emerging North American and global economic order. Indeed, the ultimate goal of this paper is to make the case for a North American monetary union (henceforth NAMU), along the lines of Euro currency integration. An important element in the analysis is the proposition that the introduction of the Euro signals the advent of a new monetary order, one in which national currencies are being superseded by supranational currencies. Phrased differently, the Euro represents a move towards currencies becoming an international or supranational "public good". To the extent that this is true, the longer-term currency option for Canada is not the traditional choice between a fixed or a flexible exchange rate, but rather between dollarization (i.e., using the U.S. dollar as legal tender) and a supranational Canada-U.S. or North American currency.

Analytically and politically, this is a tough "sell". Neither the summer 1998 sharp decline in the Canadian dollar nor the advent of the Euro in January 1999, appears to have shaken the commitment of Canada's macro authorities or the majority of Canadian economists to the monetary status quo, namely price stability and a freely floating exchange rate.

Accordingly, the paper has to address three broad issues or challenges. The first of these is that the prolonged fall in the Canadian dollar (from 104 U.S. cents in the early 1970s to 63.5 cents in the summer of 1998) as well as the associated volatility (from 104 cents in May of 1974, to 71 cents in January of 1986, to 89 cents in October of 1991, to the low-to-mid 70-cent range for much of the rest of the 1990s, near 63 cents at one point during the summer of 1998 and to the 65-67 cent range at the time of writing) represents a policy error of the first magnitude for a country that ships over 80% of its exports to the U.S. market. Hence, the role of the paper's next section, "A Critique of the Monetary Status Quo" is to demonstrate that the Bank's price stability/flexible-exchange-rate philosophy was, and continues to be, an inappropriate macro strategy.

The second goal or challenge is to make a case for a formal link between the Canadian and U.S. dollars both on traditional analytical grounds and in the context of the emerging geo-economics of North America. This is the role of part three, "The Case for Exchange-Rate Fixity".

But what sort of exchange-rate fixity? Focusing on the alternative approaches to exchange-rate fixity is the third goal of the paper and the resulting analysis constitutes part four, "Toward Exchange-Rate Fixity: A Menu of Options". Over the shorter term, the analysis will argue for a fixed-exchange-rate regime. However, three other options, more long term in nature, are also presented and assessed — a currency-board arrangement, a common Canada-U.S. currency (NAMU) and "dollarization". Among these three, the NAMU option emerges as the clear winner.

Of necessity, this paper is in the nature of a polemic, that is, an essay in persuasion, since as already noted both the policy authorities and most of the mainstream of academic and business analysts have fully bought into the monetary policy status quo. Indeed, as John McCallum asserts, in the context of rationalizing the dollar's recent plunge: "the idea that we should, at this juncture, either fix our currency to the U.S. dollar or simply 'use' the U.S. dollar is, if you'll pardon the pun, one of the looniest ideas to hit the air waves in quite some time" (1998a, p. 4). With respect, however, the folly appropriately rests with those who have bought into the conception of the Bank of Canada as the Bundesbank of North America, replete with an inflation target considerably below that pursued by the Federal Reserve and with exchange rates determined by the interplay of international capital markets.[1] Indeed, the Bundesbank analogy, although oft-cited in the early days of Canada's shift towards price stability, is not appropriate. Whereas the Bundesbank delivered low inflation and a "hard" currency, the Bank of

---

[1]It is, of course, true that if Canada pursues monetary independence (via targeting price stability or employment or a monetary aggregate) this perforce requires a flexible exchange rate. This is not at issue. What is at issue is that Canadian monetary independence is the wrong paradigm in the emerging global economic order.

Canada has delivered low inflation but a "soft" currency. In any event, the net result of this policy constellation is that it has distorted Canadian resource allocation and predetermined the path of macro variables (e.g., the debt) so that the core of McCallum's analysis (detailed below) is correct — the legacy of Canada's macro policy is that a less-than-70 cent dollar has indeed become the "policy-induced" equilibrium value of the Canadian/U.S. exchange rate. This is part of the later argument to the effect that a floating rate is not serving Canada well.

Thus, the time has arrived for a comprehensive review in terms of the conception of Canadian monetary policy, and macro policy in general. An integral part of this is a rethinking of the role of the exchange rate in the context of a progressively integrating North America. The place to begin is by recognizing, à la Mundell in the frontispiece, that "the exchange rate is the most important price in the Canadian economy" and, as such, cannot be left to the whims of the "kids in red suspenders". But the equally integral corollary of exchange rate fixity must be a rethinking of the role of the rest of the macro arsenal and in particular the fiscal stances of both levels of government.

Prior to addressing the case for more formal exchange-rate fixity and the alternative institutional arrangements that can deliver this, attention needs to be devoted to the past and current failings of Canada's monetary and exchange-rate stance.

A Critique of the Monetary Status Quo

Governor John Crow's February 1988 Eric J. Hanson Memorial Lecture at the University of Alberta publicly[2] launched Canada into an era of price

---

[2]In an earlier draft, the word "formally" was used instead of "publicly". However, in his October 1998 Gibson Lecture at Queen's University's School of Policy Studies, Governor Gordon Thiessen notes that price stability had been the Bank's *modus operandi* since 1982:

> In response to the persistence of high inflation during the 1970s, the Bank of Canada adopted a narrowly defined monetary aggregate (M1) as a target in 1975. When this aggregate became increasingly unreliable and turned out not to have been all that helpful in achieving the desired lessening of inflation pressures, it was eventually dropped as a target in 1982. Subsequently, the Bank embarked on a protracted

stability. However, it was not until 1991 that the Bank of Canada and the government formally (and jointly) adopted inflation targets — 3% by the end of 1992, 2.5% for mid-1994 and 2% by the end of 1995, where these targets have a band of ±1 percentage point around them. The 1%-3% target band was extended on several later occasions and, in particular, the February, 1998 federal budget extended this target range (again with the agreement of the Bank) until the end of 2001:

> This extension reflected the fact that the economy had not yet reached full capacity in the current upswing. It would, therefore, be helpful to have the economy demonstrate more fully its ability to perform well under price stability. The government and the Bank now plan to determine this long-term target before the end of 2001. (Thiessen, 1998, p. 4)

In terms of achieving price stability (or, more correctly perhaps, low and stable inflation), the policy has surely been successful. Beginning in the early 1990s, Canada's inflation rate fell below the U.S. inflation rate and has remained below ever since — the August 1998 three-month inflation rate in Canada was 0.4%, compared with 2.2% in the United States, with yearly rates equal to 0.8% and 1.6% respectively (from the *Economic Indicators* page of October 3-9, 1998 issue of *The Economist*). Over the years, support for the price stability stance has come from many quarters, with the C.D.

---

empirical search for an alternative monetary aggregate target, but no aggregate was found that would be suitable as a formal target. *Thus, from 1982 to 1991, monetary policy in Canada was carried out with price stability as the longer-term goal and inflation containment as the shorter-term goal, but without intermediate targets or a specified path to the longer-term objective.* (1998, p. 3, emphasis added)

As noted in the ensuing text, official inflation targets have been in place since 1991. Hence, from the Bank's perspective, Governor Crow's 1988 Lecture is probably best viewed as more formally alerting the public to the Bank's on-going price stability goal. This redating (at least from my vantage point) of the price stability era has important implications for this paper. In particular, it means that the depreciation of the exchange rate from over 80 cents in 1981 to 71 cents in 1986 (see Figure 4 below) is now an integral part of Canada's experience with price stability as the monetary strategy. Nonetheless, much of the analysis of price stability and exchange-rate flexibility will focus on the post-1988 era.

Howe Institute leading the way via a series of edited volumes[3] (Lipsey 1990; York, 1990; Laidler, 1997) as well as Laidler and Robson's 1993 monograph, *The Great Canadian Disinflation*. Beyond this, David Laidler and William Robson have performed a more or less continuous monitoring role in terms of their numerous C.D. Howe *Commentary* pieces on Bank policy. While they have frequently challenged the Bank's short-term stance, their criticisms have always been framed in the context of full support for the underlying price stability philosophy.

To be sure, there has also been pointed criticism of the Bank's price stability and floating exchange rate stance (e.g., Courchene, 1990; Mundell, 1990/1991; Harris, 1993; Grady, 1993; Fortin and Osberg, 1996; and, at the popular level, McQuaig, 1995), the most pointed of all being Pierre Fortin's 1994 paper, "Slow Growth, Unemployment and Debt", and his 1996 Presidential Address to the Canadian Economic Association.[4]

To revisit these analyses in any detail would take us too far afield.[5] Nonetheless, as part of making the case for moving towards greater exchange rate fixity, including options for a common currency, we need to make a corresponding case that price stability and a freely floating exchange rate have not served Canada well. While the ensuing analysis has not been triggered by the summer 1998, Asian-led currency crisis, the decline in the Canadian exchange rate over this period does serve as a convenient entrée to assessing our overall macro strategy.

---

[3]While not all the authors in these edited volumes are on side with the price stability strategy, the overall thrust of the volume is clearly supportive of the Bank's ongoing strategy.

[4]In the most recent volume (August 1998) of the *Canadian Journal of Economics* the Bank's Charles Freedman and Tiff Macklem offer a rebuttal to many of Fortin's contentions.

[5]In passing, it is instructive to note that the core of the Fortin critique (based on his own empirical evidence and drawing support from the Akerlof *et al.*, 1996, simulations) is that the Bank's target range is too low with the result that our real-side performance is much inferior to that in the United States. This is consistent with the earlier quotation from Governor Thiessen to the effect that "the economy had not reached full capacity in the current upswing".

The 1998 Currency Crisis

From a value of 71 cents in March of 1998, the Canadian dollar plummeted to near 63 cents before the Bank of Canada, having already spent roughly $6 billion in August alone in defence of the dollar, finally raised interest rates a full percentage point and stemmed the fall. This episode leads to several important deductions/implications.

The first has already been alluded to — McCallum's recent analysis. Writing in the Royal Bank's *Current Analysis* series, McCallum (1998a) utilizes a version of Bank of Canada's own econometric equation for forecasting the value of the Canadian dollar. According to his preferred equation, the equilibrium value of the currency in 1998 Q2 was 67.7 cents (versus a then-actual value of 69.1 cents). In this model, the principal "driver" of recent exchange-rate movements is global commodity prices. McCallum's general conclusion with respect to the exchange-rate decline is that the response to that time (i.e., no response) of the federal government and of the Bank was appropriate — after all, the value of the dollar had fallen only a couple of cents beneath its equation-determined equilibrium value. In September, McCallum published an update (1998b), where he notes that the "value added of this new analysis is that we now have some reason to believe that Canada's rising level of public debt over the past quarter century, whether in absolute terms or relative to the United States, has contributed to our sinking currency" (1998b, p. 1). In terms of his new econometric results, which build on the earlier research by Chandler and Laidler (1995),[6] the 31 cent fall from parity in 1973 to 69 cents in the first half of 1998 is due to relative (to the United States) inflation differential (10 cents), relative debt levels (10 cents), global commodity prices (10 cents), with 1 cent due to the interest rate differential. Given that the inflation differential now works in favour of a stronger Canadian dollar, the debt and commodity price variables emerge as the proximate determinants of the dollar's recent plight. A corollary of this analysis is that there really was and is no currency crisis.

---

[6]A large part of the link between debt (and particularly external debt) and the exchange rate is that with rising interest payments to foreigners, Canada will require a larger trade surplus as the current account offset, which in turn requires a lower dollar. Utilizing a methodology embodying this causation, Chandler and Laidler (1995) found that what they defined as the fundamental equilibrium exchange rate (FEER) was in the range of 69-72 cent range in 1995, a value well below the then-existing exchange rate.

Hence, McCallum remains opposed to the Bank's interest rate hike (which occurred between his two papers) although he acknowledges that "the situation became quite scary in the 24 hours preceding the Bank of Canada's recent one percent hike in interest rates" (1998b, p. 3).

These results beg several key questions that merit further analysis. Why is Canada's debt so high? and Why are we allowing falling global commodity prices to drive the exchange rate when Canada's resource exports are not much more than one-third of total exports, and when the overall terms of trade (as distinct from commodity prices) could not rationalize the extent of the depreciation?[7] Moreover, the expectation, implicit if not explicit in the context of the 1988 shift to price stability, was surely that achieving price stability and a lower inflation rate than in the United States would lead to a corresponding *appreciation* of the dollar. Why, then, have international capital markets abandoned the Canadian dollar while, say, the Austrian and the Netherland pegs to the German mark are holding and, even more impressive, the U.S. dollar and Argentinian peso remain perfect substitutes under the Argentine currency-board arrangement.[8] Finally, and although only indirectly related to the currency crisis, Canadian policymakers spent much of the past year in fear of a U.S. interest-rate hike because the United States was further along in this cyclical boom than we were. And in the summer 1998 currency turmoil, the authorities were hoping for a U.S. interest-rate decline to remove pressure on the Canadian dollar. This suggests, as elaborated upon later, that flexible exchange rates do not isolate us from U.S. monetary policy. It also raises the issue of why we have allowed our respective business cycles to get out of sync when over 80% of our exports are destined for the U.S. market.

----

[7]The sum of exports of wheat, other farm products, energy, lumber and sawmill products, pulp and paper, and metals and minerals is just under 35% of total exports for the third quarter of 1997, the latest available data from Table J.5 of the Bank of Canada *Review*, Summer 1998.

[8]I was in Argentina at the very time that the Canadian dollar fell below 64 cents. In a small store in the centre of the business district I purchased a $50 item with a hundred peso note (Argentina uses the $ symbol for pesos). My change consisted of a $5 bill and $20 bill (U.S. currency) and $5 bill and $20 bill in pesos. No currency crisis here, in spite of the fact that the Argentines had just been granted a $6 billion emergency loan to buttress their fiscal mess. More on currency boards later in the analysis.

Thomas J. Courchene

While the factors triggering the ongoing currency turmoil related to the Asian financial meltdown and the implosion of the Russian economy, the fundamental problems relating to the Canadian dollar, as reflected in the McCallum analysis, have much of their origin in the philosophy, timing and implementation of price stability, to which I now turn.

Price Stability: Triggering an "Identity Crisis"

The monetary discipline associated with price stability may well have been the correct medicine for the 1970s, characterized as it was by runaway nominal magnitudes. However, the macro dysfunction of the mid-1980s was not inflation. Rather it was the shortfall of aggregate savings and in particular the emergence of twin deficits — a persistent *government deficit* in the midst of one of the longest postwar booms (at least for Central Canada) on the one hand, and a *current account deficit* ($25.5 billion in 1988) in order to draw in foreign savings to finance the boom, on the other. The adoption of price stability in 1988 exacerbated these twin deficits. To see this, consider the national-income-accounting identity, expressed in its "twin-deficit" form:

$$(G-T) \equiv (M-X) + (S-I) \tag{1}$$

where the fiscal deficit (G-T) is identically equal to the current account deficit (M-X) plus private sector net savings (S-I). This identity can also be expressed as:

$$(M-X) \equiv (G-T) + (I-S) \quad \text{or} \tag{2a}$$

$$(M-X) \equiv A-Y \tag{2b}$$

which states that the current account deficit (or net foreign savings) equals domestic dissaving (equation 2a) or, more simply, net foreign savings equals the difference between domestic absorption, A, and output, Y (equation 2b). This latter identity suggests that if a country is intent on absorbing more than it is producing, then it will incur a balance-of-payments deficit on its current account. Alternatively, the capital account inflows will offset the shortfall in domestic savings.

Admittedly, these relationships are identities and as such imply little about causation. Nonetheless, the following stylized facts with respect to the impact of price stability are fully consistent with the aggregate savings formulation. The transition to price stability generated higher nominal rates (Figure 1) and, more importantly, higher real interest rates throughout the early 1990s recession. While our inflation rate fell below the U.S. rate after 1991 (Figure 3), this was more than offset by Canada's higher nominal rates (which would be more evident were Figure 1 cast in terms of long-term interest rates). Compounding all of this was the dramatic appreciation of the exchange rate (Figure 4).

The result of the interplay of these factors led to the rather disastrous scenario captured in the four panels of Figure 5. Canadian unit labour costs (measured in U.S. dollars) rendered Canadian manufacturing non-competitive (lower left panel), productivity growth lagged our G7 partners (upper left panel) and fell way below U.S. productivity growth (upper right panel). Not surprisingly, Canadian corporate profits plummeted (lower right panel) with the result that the 1990s recession in Canada was the most severe since the Great Depression.

Figure 6 places all of this in the context of the aggregate savings relationship. The dotted line in the figure represents the government deficit (G-T) and the solid line depicts net private savings (S-I). The vertical distance (measured as a percent of GDP) between these two is, from equation (1), the current account deficit (M-X). As the upper panel of Figure 6 reveals, post-1988 the government deficit (as a percent of GDP), rose once again to the 6% level. Net private savings (S-I) also rose, but by a lesser amount so that the current account deficit also increased, that is, the vertical distance between lines G-T and S-I grows larger after 1988. The underlying economics here are reasonably straightforward. The increase in G-T was triggered by both a revenue collapse (the severity of the recession decreased tax revenues) and by the interplay of automatic stabilizers (Unemployment Insurance [UI] and welfare payments soared). However, thanks to high real-interest rates, debt-servicing also spiralled upward. In terms of equation (2b), then, A-Y increased substantially — Y clearly fell and, arguably A increased via the stimulus coming from the government sector. In any event, the result was to increase net foreign savings (M-X), both in absolute terms and relative to the U.S. situation where the U.S. current account was in balance in 1991 (from the lower panel of Figure 6, the G-T and S-I lines for the United States are equal for 1991).

Thomas J. Courchene

Figure 1: Canadian and American Short-Term Interest Rates and Differential

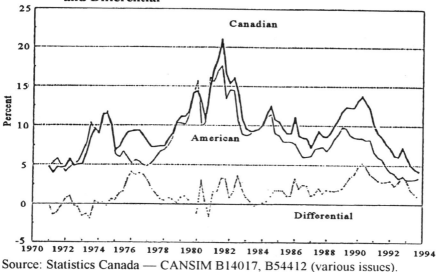

Source: Statistics Canada — CANSIM B14017, B54412 (various issues).

Figure 2: Canadian and American Short-Term Real Interest Rates

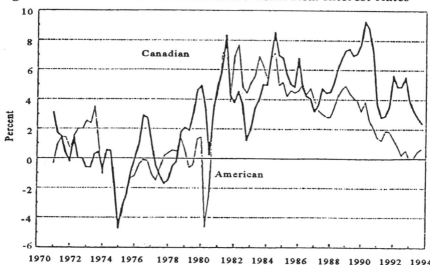

Source: Statistics Canada — CANSIM B14017, P484000, B54412, D139105 (various issues).

Reproduced from Courchene (1997, Figures 15.6 and 15.7).

Towards a North American Common Currency   *281*

Figure 3: Canadian and American Inflation Rates

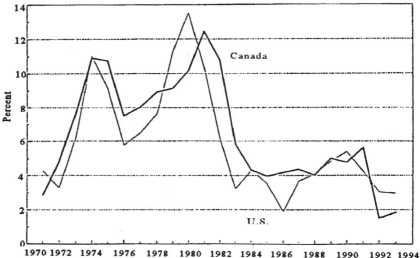

Source: Statistics Canada — CANSIM D139105, P484000 (various issues).

Figure 4: Canadian-U.S. Exchange Rates

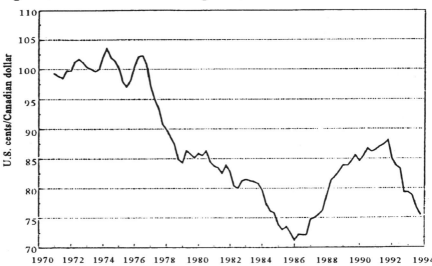

Source: Statistics Canada — CANSIM B3400, D751986, D750952 (various issues).

Reproduced from Courchene (1997, Figures 15.9 and 15.8).

Thomas J. Courchene

Figure 5: Manufacturing Competitiveness

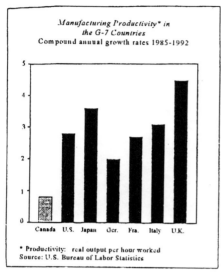

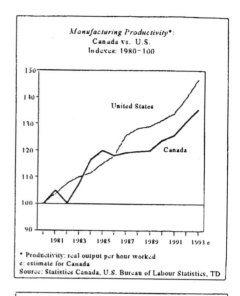

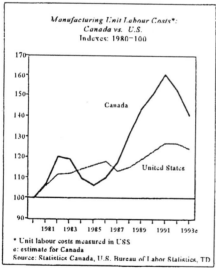

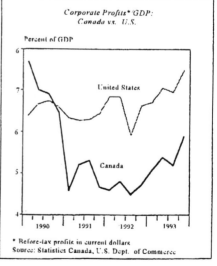

Source: Reproduced from Toronto-Dominion Bank, Department of Economic Research.

Reproduced from Courchene (1997, Figure 15.13).

Figure 6: Aggregate Savings Imbalances

Panel A: CANADA

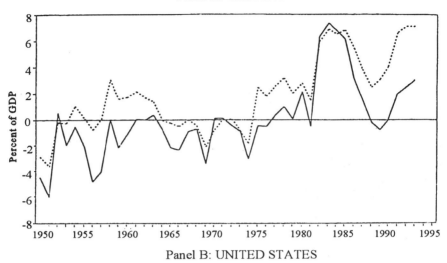

Panel B: UNITED STATES

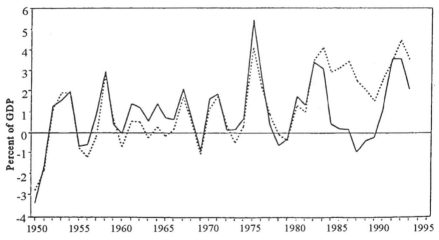

Note: —— = $(S - I)$; ---- = $(G - T)$. Vertical distance between $(G - T)$ and $(S - I)$ equals $(M - X)$. For example, if $(G - T) > (S - I)$, then vertical distance is the current account deficit.

Source: Designed and produced by Bill Robson of the C.D. Howe Research Institute in Toronto. Source: National Accounts data from CANSIM and CITIBASE.

Reproduced from Courchene (1997, Figure 15.1).

Figures 7 and 8 cast these twin deficits in even bolder relief, with the former tracing the deterioration of the Canadian current account deficit and the latter revealing the relative explosion in Canadian government debt vis-à-vis the U.S. debt.

These results feed directly into the McCallum analysis. His econometric estimates indicate that one-third of the fall in the dollar is due to the debt overhang. Chalk much of this impact up to the surge in the debt in the wake of price stability. However, the impact does not end here. The rise in the debt and especially the foreign-held component of the debt means that interest payments to foreigners in the "invisible" component of the current account have increased significantly — from $15.2 billion in 1987 to $20.5 billion by 1990 and eventually to a peak of $30.3 billion in 1995 (Table J1 of the Bank of Canada *Review*, Summer 1998). In turn, this requires an increasingly large merchandise trade surplus in order to achieve current account balance. Phrased differently, current account balance requires a lower "equilibrium" exchange rate. Moreover, the large ongoing current account deficit (over $26 billion in 1998.Q1) arguably makes the Canadian dollar more susceptible to falling commodity prices. This is so even though resource exports are not a major proportion of total exports, because as a consequence the required merchandise trade surplus is larger and the equilibrium value of the dollar for current account balance is lower. In this sense, there probably is an indirect relationship in the eyes of the international capital markets between high foreign debt levels and the influence of commodity prices on the exchange rate. (As an important aside, this analysis strengthens the hand of our fiscal authorities in their recent move towards making debt reduction a more prominent fiscal goal.)

To this point, our assessment of price stability has been that it generated an "identity crisis", as it were, in terms of the aggregate savings (or, more correctly, dissavings) relationships reflected in equations (1) and (2), the impacts of which are still reverberating in terms of the exchange rate dynamics. As already noted, others have found price stability wanting because it targeted on an inflation level that was too low (e.g., Fortin, 1996 drawing from the work of Akerlof *et al.*, 1996), with the result that Canada's unemployment rate significantly diverged from the U.S. unemployment rate. While Figure 9 reveals the all-Canadian unemployment rate diverged from its U.S. counterpart during the early 1980s recession, the Ontario unemployment rate veered off from the U.S. rate only when the impacts of the late 1980s exchange rate appreciation took their devastating toll on the Ontario economy and particularly its manufacturing sector. Relatedly, Robert

Figure 7: Current Account and Trade Balance as a Percentage of Output

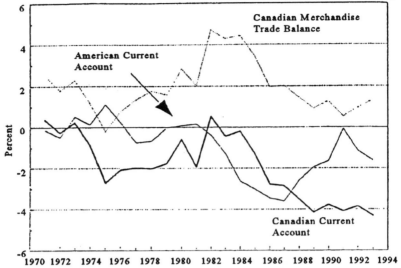

Source: Statistics Canada (various issues) — CANSIM (various series) D20000, D72002, D72003; CITIBASE (various series) — BPCR, GDP: Survey of Current Business.

Figure 8: Gross Public Debt as a Percentage of Output

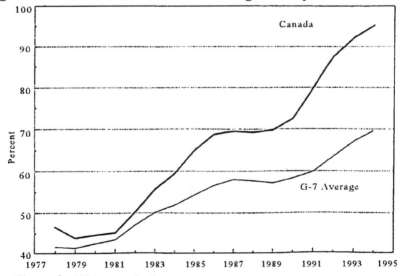

Note: Figures for 1994 are projections.
Source: Organization for Economic Cooperation and Development (OECD) (1994).
Reproduced from Courchene (1997, Figures 13.10 and 13.11).

Figure 9: Unemployment Rates
Percent unemployed of labour force

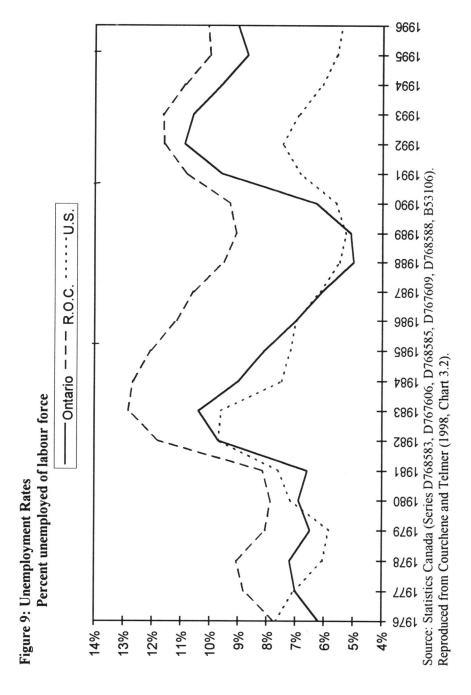

——— Ontario — — R.O.C. ······ U.S.

Source: Statistics Canada (Series D768583, D767606, D767605, D768585, D767609, D768588, B53106).
Reproduced from Courchene and Telmer (1998, Chart 3.2).

Mundell (1990/1991, p. 25), among others, noted that one of the striking features of the shift to price stability was that accompanying tight money policy disassociated Canadian policy and the policy cycle from that in the United States: "it is very unusual for Canadian monetary policy to make such a sudden departure from U.S. policy in view of the intimate connection between the two economies and their financial systems".

Not only did both of these features depart significantly from our traditional approach to macro management in the upper half of North America, but they played a role in the volatility of the exchange rate over the 1986-92 period — from 71 cents in 1986 to 89 cents in 1991 and back to the mid-to-low 70 cent range in the early 1990s. Harris explains this exchange-rate "misalignment problem" in terms of the "rationale bubbles model":

> [The bubbles model] attempts to explain how an exchange rate can move away from its underlying fundamentals for a considerable period of time. To give an example; for a country with high interest rates, an appreciating currency attracts more and more short-term investment as speculators see both a rising currency and high yields. The growing investment drives up the currency further, which confirms the belief that it is appreciating and attracts more investment. Ultimately, this bubble must come to an end as fundamentals begin to weigh more heavily on the market. (A deteriorating current account and contraction of the export- and import-competing sectors are the most immediate evidence of an overvalued currency). It bursts when some event triggers a sudden dumping of the currency and sets up a rapid depreciation with self-confirming expectations now driving it in the opposite direction. (1993, p. 34)

The conditions for a Canadian exchange-rate bubble were clearly ripe. From Figure 1, Canadian nominal interest rates in the transition to price stability went from roughly 7.5% in 1986 to over 13% in 1990, with the Canada-U.S. differential reaching five percentage points in 1990. When combined with the rapid appreciation of the dollar, the returns to foreign investors/speculators were rather spectacular. And when the interest rate differential began to close, among other factors, and the exchange rate began its dramatic recoil, returns turned sharply downward, if not negative, and foreigners quickly abandoned the Canadian dollar.

As an important aside, one of the major achievements of the price stability era, namely having Canadian nominal interest rates dip below U.S. nominal rates and, therefore correspond to the lower Canadian inflation rate, came with a considerable cost. Part of this cost was that Canadian real

Thomas J. Courchene

interest rates have exceeded U.S. real rates (Figure 2) from 1986 onward and remain higher today. This was alluded to earlier in the context that the pursuit of Bank of Canada "credibility" was and remains costly.

However, in 1996, we did achieve "interest-rate crossover" — Canadian nominal rates below U.S. nominal rates for a significant portion of the maturity spectrum.[9] But this created a further problem for the exchange rate. This is clearly evident in terms of the "safe-haven" argument for the recent decline of the dollar. Investors fleeing the Asian and Russian monetary turmoil were looking for a safe haven for their money. And because U.S. nominal rates were higher than Canadian nominal rates, this made the safe-haven decision obvious. There is an important practical point at issue here, one that I have raised elsewhere (1990), but expressed more succinctly by Harris:

> [Safe-haven investors] do not care about the Canadian inflation rate; rather they are interested in Canada's nominal interest rate relative to their own and in the future course of the [Canadian] exchange rate. (1993, p. 55)

In the event, the international investors chose wisely: the sharp decline in the Canadian dollar during the summer of 1998 and the prime minister's declared "indifference" to the decline, punished those few who sought safe haven in the Canadian dollar.

The essence of the argument thus far is that the Bank's decision to target a lower inflation rate than the Americans meant that exchange rates were no longer determined by real-side factors but rather by what Drucker (1986) has referred to as the "symbol economy" — asset prices, credit flows and international capital markets. The problem here is that at the best of times "floating exchange rates provide inherently volatile and unpredictable cost structures" and, as such, are wholly inappropriate in a Canada-U.S. Free Trade Agreement (FTA)-North American Free Trade Agreement (NAFTA) environment which "requires stable and predictable rates of international exchange and cost calculations to support the volumes and trade and degree

---

[9]While nominal rates were lower than U.S. rates, so was our inflation rate, with the result that at the long end of the maturity spectrum (where the "cross-over" did not occur) Canadian real rates were substantially higher. And with the recent interest-rate hike, real rates are higher across much if not all of the maturity spectrum.

of specialization associated with it" (Harris, 1993, pp. 39, 40). But these were hardly the best of times.

Exchange Rates and NAFTA

Prior to addressing the merits of fixed exchange rates, or, more generally, a more formal link to the U.S. dollar, it is intriguing to focus on why there was not more concern at the time with the Bank's public conversion to price stability and its benign neglect for the external value of the dollar, coming as it did during the run-up to the FTA. There are really two questions here. The first relates to exchange-rate flexibility. While economists had done their homework well in terms of the likely impacts of the FTA (Harris, 1983; Whalley, 1986; among others), there remained considerable uncertainty, probably best reflected in the Macdonald Commission's opting for free trade as a "leap of faith". In this uncertain context, flexible rates were viewed as the essential buffer. Should free trade not go as well as had been anticipated, the exchange rate would depreciate and compensate for any forecast error. This assumes, of course, that exchange rates would be driven or determined by real-side fundamentals, a realistic assumption during the run-up to the FTA negotiations.[10]

The second relates directly to the Bank's (public) price stability conversion. Other things being equal, it is easy to make a case for price stability, so that the policy attracted many adherents. But other things were not equal — we already had an emerging twin-deficit problem and we were embarking on an "open-borders" policy with the United States. Moreover, it was not entirely clear in the context of 1988 just what price stability meant. Was it zero inflation? Was it a gradual process towards ever lower inflation rates?

As it turned out, the transition towards price stability was far more draconian than anticipated, compounded as it was by the introduction of the Goods and Services Tax (which had the potential for some tax pass-through to prices) and the errant fiscal behaviour of the Ontario government. As already noted, what this meant, however, was that exchange-rate determination was no longer driven by real-side fundamentals: rather, it became driven

---

[10]Although perhaps not as realistic as many of us anticipated, given the evidence in footnote 2 that the Bank was already on a price-stability track.

by the capital or asset side. In other words, the exchange rate would not (and did not) serve its potential buffer role in terms of accommodating the uncertainty associated with the FTA. It was marching to a new drummer and this drummer was price stability.

Beyond this, two other factors came into play. The first was that many, if not most, price-stability adherents recognized that debts and deficits were a problem. And they did make the case for more fiscal restraint (e.g., Purvis, 1990). However, on balance they tended to take the position that the Bank should not be constrained from doing what it could do best (namely, deliver price stability) simply because the fiscal authorities were following inappropriate budget stances. However, the problem with this approach is that the empirical evidence is overwhelming that the abandoning of fixed exchange rates was tantamount to removing fiscal discipline from the operations of virtually all developed nations and Canada was no exception (McKinnon, 1997).[11]

The second had to do with establishing the Bank of Canada's "credibility". The argument can be expressed in the following way. Sure there are costs to price stability. But these are short-term in nature and the promised benefits are sure to materialize soon. Thus, we must stick with the policy, that is, we must establish "credibility", which will in turn hasten the emergence of good times. Unfortunately, this credibility refrain became an ongoing chorus. In the 1990s the credibility issue arose in a different guise. Specifically, the argument became: while our real interest rates have been well above those in the United States since the inauguration of price stability, we are almost at the "interest-rate crossover point" (where Canadian nominal interest rates will fall below U.S. nominal rates). The implication here was that domestic credibility was well established and all that was now required was that the international capital markets be made aware that the Bank of Canada was really North America's Bundesbank. As it turned out, the interest-rate crossover point only came after the 1995 Referendum and once the 1996 Ontario budget began to put that province's fiscal house in order (Courchene and Telmer, 1998, Chart 3.6). However, what the recent

---

[11]It is important to note that several nations which maintained fixed exchange rates with a larger trading partner also had mushrooming deficits and debts. Perhaps the more general point is that the demise of Bretton Woods coincided with the rise of real interest rates relative to real growth rates which, *ceteris paribus*, in turn tilted the balance in favour of deficits, especially for those countries that already had substantial deficits.

currency turmoil indicates is that international capital markets have little confidence in the Canadian dollar, the result of which is that we may well end up with a major real interest-rate misalignment — higher nominal interest rates and lower inflation rates than the Americans. Phrased differently, the costs of price stability are still with us.

In the event, critics of price stability were slow off the mark. My critique of price stability and freely floating exchange rates only appeared in early 1990 and Mundell's case for fixed exchange rates in the Canadian context appeared in the spring of 1990. Nonetheless, these and other policy critiques served to make a case that Canada would have been much better served for the emerging FTA reality with a fixed-exchange-rate system. In particular, there was a recognition that fixed-exchange-rates systems carried important implications for the conduct of fiscal policy — even at the provincial level (Courchene, 1990). One example will suffice. While the Bank of Canada now argues that the very expansionary fiscal policy of the David Peterson Liberal administration in Ontario (with public spending well in the teens in the midst of the province's most vigorous and prolonged postwar boom) severely complicated the transition to price stability, the Bank governor made no public comments at the time. Under a fixed-exchange-rate regime, it would have become much more obvious that Ontario's policy could compromise exchange-rate stability and, arguably, the governor would not have remained silent since the Bank's role would have been to ensure that exchange-rate parity was sustainable. Admittedly, counterfactuals have limited value. Nonetheless, in terms of this paper, the proposition that the appropriate monetary conversion in 1988 ought to have been fixed exchange rates rather than price stability serves as an instructive lead into the remainder of the analysis — the positive case for fixed exchange rates.

To round out this section, the conclusion is rather straightforward — price stability, defined as Canada attempting to run a lower inflation rate than the Americans, was inappropriate in 1988 and it remains inappropriate today — indeed more so, since in the interim the Canadian economy has become increasingly more intertwined, trade-wise, with the U.S. economy. More to the point, the legacy of price stability is, as McCallum notes, that the equilibrium value of the exchange rate is under 70 cents.

One final caveat is in order. Aspects of the above analysis, of and by themselves, need not lead to an argument for exchange-rate fixity. Rather, the conclusion could be that the real problem relates to Canada's chosen approach to price stability, not price stability itself. For example, had we opted to target the same inflation rate as the Americans, the resulting

Thomas J. Courchene

exchange-rate volatility may have been much ameliorated. The thrust of the rest of the analysis, however, is that exchange-rate flexibility, per se, is inappropriate, regardless of the rest of the monetary order. For this reason, *From Fixing to Monetary Union: Options for North American Currency Integration* (Courchene and Harris, 1999a) does not bring the Bank of Canada's policy into the case for exchange-rate fixity. Rather, it focuses directly on the analytical arguments for a formal link between the Canadian and U.S. dollars. My rationale for including an assessment of recent Bank policy as an integral part of the present analysis for exchange-rate fixity is to emphasize that monetary independence (price stability and exchange-rate flexibility) not only has not served Canada well but, in addition, the appropriate "conversion" in 1988 should have been to fixed exchange rates, not to price stability.

But since we cannot re-run history, the remainder takes the past as given and focuses on the forward looking case for exchange-rate fixity.

The Case for Exchange-Rate Fixity

The analysis now shifts away from a critique of the existing monetary policy thrust and towards making a case for a fixed exchange rate as an integral part of Canada's present and future monetary and macro strategy. The first part of this section addresses Canada's altered geo-economy — in particular the increasing integration, post-FTA and NAFTA, of the Canadian and American economies. This will be followed by a more analytical discussion focusing the merits (and the challenges) of a regime of fixed exchange rates. Having thus set the case for exchange-rate fixity, the section following will outline the alternative ways in which this formal Canada-U.S. exchange-rate link can be implemented.

North-South Economic Integration

Table 1 presents data, by province, on interprovincial and international trade in goods and services in 1984 and in 1996. The evidence is startlingly clear — trade is rapidly shifting north-south. Focusing first on the aggregate (or all-province) data (which appear as the last row in the table), in 1984 international (ROW, for *Rest Of World*) exports were 113% of exports to

Table 1: Domestic and International Exports, 1984 and 1996 Goods and Services ($ million)

| | 1984 | | | 1996 | | | 1996 Openness | |
	ROC $	ROW $	ROW/ROC (ratio)	ROC $	ROW $	ROW/ROC (ratio)	ROW/GDP %	(ROW+ROC)/GDP %
Newfoundland	653	1,811	2.77	992	3,026	3.05	30.06	39.91
PEI	408	193	0.47	782	442	0.57	16.69	46.22
Nova Scotia	2,580	2,011	0.78	4,108	3,650	0.89	19.39	41.21
New Brunswick	2,459	2,628	1.07	4,696	5,702	1.21	35.41	64.57
Quebec	22,915	21,368	0.93	34,500	56,249	1.63	32.07	51.74
Ontario	39,441	56,286	1.43	64,169	140,658	2.19	43.5	63.41
Manitoba	4,847	3,205	0.66	7,311	7,733	1.06	28.29	55.03
Saskatchewan	4,073	6,448	1.58	6,272	10,444	1.67	39.50	63.22
Alberta	22,178	13,924	0.63	23,069	33,500	1.45	37.20	62.82
BC	6,835	14,018	2.05	13,580	30,344	2.23	29.2	42.39
All Provinces	106,389	121,892	1.15	159,479	291,748	1.83	36.57	56.56

Notes: ROC relates to exports from the given province to all other provinces.
ROW relates to international exports.
Source: CANSIM Data Base (Matrix 4255).

Thomas J. Courchene

other provinces (ROC exports, for *Rest Of Canada*).[12] By 1996, however, ROW exports were running at 183% of ROC exports.[13] At the individual province level, in 1984 five provinces had ROW exports in excess of ROC Exports (Newfoundland, New Brunswick, Ontario, Saskatchewan and Alberta). In 1996, eight provinces (all except PEI and Nova Scotia) exported more internationally than to the rest of the provinces. And the ROW-ROC ratios for *all* provinces in 1996 exceeded those for 1984.

The last two columns of Table 1 present measures of "openness". Overall international exports represented 36.57% of aggregate GDP, with ratios ranging from 16.69% for Prince Edward Island and 19.39% for Nova Scotia on the low side to ratios of 43.5% for Ontario and 37.2% for Alberta on the high side. If one adds in interprovincial exports, then the combined ROW-ROC exports-to-GDP ratios exceed 60% for four provinces — New Brunswick, Ontario, Saskatchewan and Alberta.

While ROW exports in Table 1 relate to exports to all countries, with over 80% of Canada's overall exports destined to U.S. markets it is clearly the case that trade with the United States now exceeds interprovincial trade.

Figure 10 presents the Ontario trade patterns in more detail. From a position in 1981 where both ROW and ROC exports (and imports) were running at about $40 billion, Ontario's ROW exports in 1994 were more than double its ROC exports and were growing nearly a magnitude faster. Given that Ontario's exports to the United States account for about 90% of its overall ROW exports, the 43.5% ROW/GDP entry in Table 1 means that roughly 40% of Ontario's GDP is exported to the United States. More recent data (Eves, 1998) indicates that nearly 44% of Ontario's GDP is destined for U.S. markets. As well, the impact of the FTA on Ontario's ROW exports did not materialize until after 1991, arguably reflecting the exchange rate and unit-labour cost implications alluded to in the previous section.

Apart from noting that Canada-U.S. exchange-rate volatility becomes highly problematic for a province that sends 44% of its output to the United States, the implications of the relative shift from east-west trade to north-

---

[12]Had this table begun in 1981, ROW exports would have been only 87% of ROC exports (Courchene and Telmer, 1998, Table 9.1). This increase over 1981-84 reflected the enhanced Canadian penetration of U.S. markets triggered by the sharp appreciation of the U.S. dollar over 1982-85.

[13]And more recent data (Grady and Macmillan, 1998) indicate that international exports are now more than twice as large as interprovincial exports.

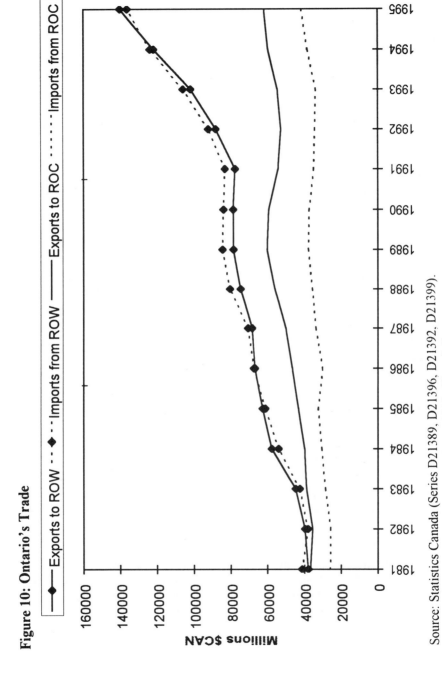

Figure 10: Ontario's Trade

Exports to ROW · · · ◆ · · · Imports from ROW ——— Exports to ROC · · · · · · Imports from ROC

Millions $CAN

160000
140000
120000
100000
80000
60000
40000
20000
0

1981 1982 1983 1984 1985 1986 1987 1988 1989 1990 1991 1992 1993 1994 1995

Source: Statistics Canada (Series D21389, D21396, D21392, D21399).
Reproduced from Courchene and Telmer (1998, Chart 9.1).

Thomas J. Courchene

south trade will be detailed later. In the interim, the analysis casts these results in a broader context, beginning with a comparison of the trade links between the 15 members of the EU.

Intra-European Trade. Table 2 presents data on intra-European trade for the so-called EU15 nations. The first column of figures relates to the proportion of EU exports to the country's total exports. These ratios are quite high, ranging over 80% (Netherlands and Portugal) to the 50% range

Table 2: Intra-EU Trade and Openness (1996)

	EU Exports as % of Total Exports (%)	EU Exports as % of GDP (%)	Total Exports as % of GDP
Belgium/Luxembourg	76.6	48	63
Denmark	67.4	20	30
Germany	57.1	13	23
Greece	52.0	5	10
Spain	66.8	12	18
Finland	54.5	18	32
France	62.1	12	19
Ireland	71.1	49	69
Italy	55.2	11	20
Netherlands	80.6	42	52
Austria	64.1	17	28
Portugal	80.0	18	23
Sweden	57.0	18	32
United Kingdom	57.8	13	32
Europe 15 Total	62.9	16	25
Canada	82.0*	30.0**	36.57***

Notes: *Canada's exports to the United States as a percent of its total international exports.
** This is calculated by multiplying the 36.57% all-provinces figure for ROW/GDP in Table 1 by the 82% share of aggregate Canadian exports to the United States.
*** Reproduced from Table 1.

Source: *Eurostate Yearbook '97: A Statistical Eye on Europe 1986-96* (Luxembourg: Office of Official Publications of the European Commission), pp. 208, 451 and 450 for the 3 columns respectively.

for Greece, Finland, Italy and Sweden. The EU15 aggregate ratio is 62.9%. *However, all of the individual country ratios are less than the 82% concentration of Canada's share of exports going to the United States* (last row of the table).

The second data column presents EU exports as a percent of GDP. Here, three countries — Ireland (49%), Belgium/Luxembourg (48%) and the Netherlands (42%) have ratios in excess of the 40% figure for Ontario's exports to the United States. At the aggregate EU15 level, (second last row), however, the ratio of EU exports to total GDP is only 16%, in comparison with the 30% figure for Canada's ratio of U.S. exports to GDP.

The final column is comparable to the "openness" data in the final column of Table 1. Ireland has an openness (total exports/GDP) of 69%, above any of the comparable provincial ratios, although the four provinces with ratios in the 60% range are not far off. However, the lowest Canadian province ratio (Nova Scotia with 39.91%) is above 11 of the 14 European countries and the all-Canada ratio without including internal trade (i.e., 36.57% from the last figure in Table 2) is well above the 25% aggregate European ratio.

To be sure, these comparisons must be treated with caution. For one thing, it may be more relevant to compare, say, the province of Ontario to the German province (Land) of Bavaria, but inter-Länder trade data do not appear to be available.[14] For another, larger countries tend to be more "closed" than smaller countries. For example, the aggregate openness ratios for France, Italy, Germany and the United Kingdom all fall between 19% and 23%. Nonetheless, the evidence is clear — Canada is more integrated trade-wise to the United States than the EU countries are to Europe. The obvious

---

[14]Nonetheless, aspects of the Bavaria-Ontario comparison may be instructive. Roughly 50% of Bavaria's international exports are to EU countries. This represents 10.2% of its GDP, with total international exports equaling 20% of GDP. Hence, internationally, Bavaria is much less "open" than Ontario with its international exports equaling 43.7% of GDP (Table 1). Intriguingly, Bavaria's largest single trading-partner (at least for exports) is the United States, accounting for 11.3% of Bavaria's total trade. Given the fact that Bavaria is about the size of Ontario (population-wise), and that Germany has more than twice Canada's population, one would assume that Bavaria's interländer trade might be quite large. But no data are available on these trade flows. The above data are from *Statistics on Bavaria, 1996* (Munich: Bayerishes Ländesamt für Statistik und Datenverarbeitung).

observation that follows is that if 11 of these EU nations are opting for a common currency, the case for a formal link between the Canadian and U.S. dollars on transactions-cost grounds and the resulting certainty-of-trading relationships is even more pressing. Again, caution is no doubt warranted since there is more to the Euro than minimizing transactions costs and, in any event, we are talking about 11 different currencies rather than two. However, if the Euro succeeds, as I assume it will, the case for a more formal Canada-U.S. link will become more persuasive. Part of this will be that with two competing reserve currencies, many more nations will contemplate linking their currencies to one or the other. This is rather obvious for the Eastern bloc nations waiting for access to the EU. But even the Swiss will be placed in a difficult position. Another reason for keeping a close watch on the process of moving towards the Euro is that the internal price revaluation that the Germans, for example, will have to go through in terms of converting the mark to the Euro is very similar to the process that would be required under a common Canada-U.S. currency and, under some version of a Canada-U.S. currency board arrangement. But this is getting ahead of our story.

East-West Asymmetry. Returning to the Canadian situation, the enhanced north-south integration is complicated by the fact that the Canadian internal regional/provincial business cycles are not synchronized. This is evident from Figure 11 which focuses on the recessions of the 1980s and 1990s and their implications for employment recovery. From the upper panel of Figure 11, four years after the onset of the 1980s recession, employment in Ontario was 105% of its pre-recession peak, whereas employment in Alberta and especially British Columbia was still well below their respective pre-recession peaks. The 1990s recession was entirely different. British Columbia skated through the recession with nary a negative impact — four years after the 1990s recession its employment was nearly 110% above the pre-recession peak (although it appears to be heading for rougher economic times in the current environment). In sharp contrast, Ontario's employment was still well below its pre-recession high. More quantitatively, the highest two-province correlation in terms of changes in provincial GDPs over the 1961-95 period is 87%, for Ontario and Quebec (Kneebone and Mackenzie, 1998, Table 1). On the other hand, "Alberta stands out in particular with changes in output negatively correlated with five of the other provinces, including Ontario and Quebec, and low positive correlations with the other provinces, except Saskatchewan [which presumably relates in part to the fact that fossil energy is also important for Saskatchewan, TJC]" (ibid., p. 10). In passing, one

Figure 11: Employment and Recovery after Two Recessions

A: 1980s Recession
Employment Recovered Four Years Later?

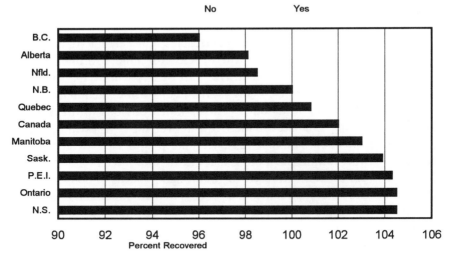

B: 1990s Recession
Employment Recovered Four Years Later?

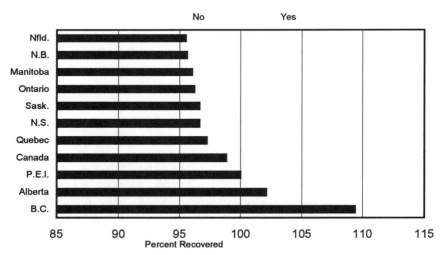

Sources: Statistics Canada, TD Bank, Department of Economic Research.
Reproduced from Courchene and Telmer (1998, Chart 9.2).

Thomas J. Courchene

might note that the movements of the exchange rate over this period served, if anything, to exacerbate these employment patterns.

North-South Trade and East-West Asymmetry: Implications for the Exchange Rate. In *From Heartland to North American Region State*, Colin Telmer and I (1998) drew some rather controversial implications from this combination of east-west asymmetry and enhanced north-south integration. Specifically, we asserted that Canada is less and less a single east-west economy and more and more a series of north-south, cross-border economies (with British Columbia also a Pacific Rim economy). And for Ontario, the conclusion is that it is emerging as a North American region state, replete with an arsenal of policies designed to pursue a provincial-international interface, or to make Ontario a more attractive location in the integrating North American economic space. Presumably, this also applies to Alberta, British Columbia, Quebec and even New Brunswick as this province vies for North American leadership in digitization technology and call-centre activities, among others.

The essential point here is that Canada's regional economies are becoming progressively integrated with their cross-border counterparts. In turn, this serves to provide a quite different perspective with respect to one of the key arguments for flexible exchange rates, namely the role of the exchange rate in buffering the asymmetric shocks hitting the Canadian and U.S. economies. Prior to addressing the issue, it is important to reconcile the above analysis with the new research on the economic role of the Canada-U.S. border, initiated by McCallum (1995) but carried much further by John Helliwell.

The Economic Role of Borders. In *How Much Do National Borders Matter?* Helliwell (1998) consolidates and extends the analysis of the role of the Canadian border as a "dividing line" in North American economic space. Utilizing a gravity model in which flows are assumed to respond positively to mass (typically measured by GDP) and negatively to distance, Helliwell derives estimates for interprovincial and international (usually Canada-U.S.) flows of goods, services, people and capital. By inserting a "border" variable in the various regressions he can ascertain the differing degrees of domestic and international integration. Very succinctly, among his results are the following:

- Over the period 1993 to 1996, the border affect in terms of goods is about 12. That is, within-Canada trade is 12 times more integrated than cross-border trade;

- For services, the border effect is such that "interprovincial trade in services is between thirty and forty times more intense than that between provinces and states" (Helliwell, 1998, p. 116);

- "After allowing for the effects of distance, population size, and income differentials, a resident of a Canadian province is almost one hundred times as likely to have been born in another province than in the United States" (ibid., p. 117);

- Pooled OECD and Canadian interprovincial data "show a high correlation of savings and investment rates across countries coupled with a zero correlation across provinces" (ibid., p. 117). Note that this result is also obtained by Hanson and Waller (1999).

By way of explaining these results, Helliwell draws on the work of Oliver Hart (1995) among others. For example, Helliwell notes that:

> as the economic and institutional development proceeds in a society, more attention and importance are transferred from the family to the rules and expectations set by larger units. All of these units may improve the efficiency of economic exchange by using reciprocal long-term rights, expectations, and responsibilities to supplant the need for expensive and complex contracts that would be required to support cooperation and exchange if the world were at once more impersonal and uncertain.
> ... What is [clear] is that as long as national institutions, populations, trust, and tastes differ as much as they do, the industrial organization and other institutional literatures would predict that transactions costs will remain much lower within than among national economies, even in the absence of any border taxes or regulations affecting the movements of goods and services. (1998, pp. 122-123)

In an earlier article, Stanley Hartt (1992, p. 5) makes essentially the same point: east-west trade is privileged in part because of the high degree of legal, institutional and social *comity* that prevails within Canada, where he defines comity as "reciprocal courtesy extended by one jurisdiction to another in friendly recognition of each other's laws" which, in turn, "oils the wheels of commerce". Hartt then adds:

> The least-noticed aspect of the [Canadian] economic union is not mandated by the Constitution at all, but results instead from a myriad of laws based on comity among provinces. These courtesy laws enable individuals and firms that conduct business in one province to enjoy a favoured status in other provinces in relation to such matters as obtaining licenses to carry on business, having a standing in the courts for legal actions, registering security interests against poverty, enforcing judgements, and like matters that function as the workaday tools of economic man ... Canadians have advanced, established rules about such things, but above all they enjoy a system that affords advantages to all those partaking in the economic union called Canada. (1992, p. 14)

Thus, borders do matter. This is not in doubt. The more interesting issue is how Helliwell's analysis squares with the above assessment on North American integration.

At one level, the two sets of analyses are fully consistent. Helliwell is surely correct in emphasizing that the east-west union is much more tightly integrated than the Canada-U.S. economic space. Yet it is also true that, because the United States is so large, cross-border trade is now dominating east-west trade. Indeed, Helliwell's estimated value of 12 for the border effect from 1993 onward was, for 1988, estimated to be in the range of 17. Since these are annual snapshots, the fall from 17 to 12 for the border effect is consistent with the rapid North American integration depicted in Table 1 and Figure 10 above, that is, if the "average" border rate falls by roughly one-third, the "marginal" changes must be (and are) rather dramatic. More significant for present purposes is Helliwell's conjecture that the factor of 12 may well incorporate the full (equilibrium) impact of the FTA and NAFTA. He bases this on the response to the U.S.-Canada 1965 Auto Pact, where the impact ran its course in about five years. While this is, at the base, an empirical issue that future data will sort out, my view is that cross-border integration will intensify. In part, this is because I view the FTA and NAFTA as arrangements that serve to increase "comity" across the Canada-U.S. border. In other words, the FTA was and is much more than a trade agreement — it is also a framework for establishing more common and predictable institutional, legal and administrative procedures on both sides of the border. The other part is related. Refocusing east-west on Ontario's part, for example, will place its footloose industry in the balance since the open borders as part of the FTA and NAFTA imply that these industries can operate from locations south of the border. Hence, Ontario has little choice but to pursue policies that will privilege Ontario and Ontarians within North American economic space since the *status quo ante* no longer exists.

Over the medium term the more intriguing implication of the Helliwell analysis is whether or not enhanced cross-border trade and comity might undermine east-west integration. Although not addressed in detail by Helliwell, this is an important issue for purposes of this paper since some versions of a common currency (e.g., dollarization) may serve to tie selected Canadian regions more to their U.S. counterparts than to their sister Canadian regions. Indeed, this is a concern that has dominated much of my recent research. In particular, since I have assumed that Canada is now more an east-west social policy railway than an economic policy railway, as it were, we need new instruments or governance structures to ensure that the east-west social contract or human-capital union remains intact. Albeit controversial, this was and is the rationale for my ACCESS model (Courchene, 1996) with its call for bringing the provinces more fully and more formally into the preservation and promotion of the east-west social union. The fact that Ontario and Alberta have been active participants in the revitalized Annual Premiers' Conferences and in the APC's call for more co-determination across a range of economic and social fronts is a very significant development, since these are the very provinces that could strike out on their own in terms of their approach to the east-west social union. Needless to say, I very much welcome the February 4, 1999, Framework Agreement on the Canadian Social Union.

There is a larger context that is relevant here as well. A shift to a fixed-exchange-rate regime involves much more than a mere pegging of the exchange rate. It also has very significant implications for fiscal policy at both levels of government. This need not take the form of Maastricht-type guidelines in terms of debts and deficits, but some degree of fiscal co-ordination or harmonization across governments is a necessary requisite. This is another reason why the recent social union agreement represents a novel and creative governance instrument in the context of integrating North American economies.

While enhanced North American integration is an argument in its own right for greater exchange-rate fixity (Harris, this volume), it also informs most, if not all, of the other rationales for an integrated North American currency area, to which I now turn.[15]

Exchange Rates and Living Standards

In 1974 (i.e., shortly after we abandoned our 1960s experiment with fixed exchange rates), the Canadian dollar was worth 104 U.S. cents.[16] Now it is worth roughly 67 cents, dipping as low as 63.5 cents in the late-summer 1998 currency crisis. This represents an enormous fall in our living standards vis-à-vis the Americans. This not only puts Canadian asset prices at bargain-basement levels for American investors but as well provides significant incentives for skilled Canadians to ply their human capital south of the border, as they are doing in increasing numbers. Why did we do this to ourselves? The traditional argument is that Canadian monetary in- dependence and a floating dollar enhances our policy sovereignty and economic flexibility, the former because we can implement a made-in- Canada inflation and nominal interest rate policy and the latter because a floating rate can isolate Canada from unwanted global policy and price shocks. Apart from noting that Fortin (1994, 1996) has effectively countered the supposed virtues of Bank of Canada monetary independence, it is instructive to emphasize that the loss of Canadian assets, both physical and human, arising from a value of the Canadian dollar two-thirds of what it was 25 years ago represents a powerful counter to the sovereignty argument.

Exchange Rate Volatility and Misalignment

The Canadian dollar has not only fallen: it has, en route, also departed both upward and downward from underlying fundamentals for long periods of time. In the literature, this is typically referred to as the "misalignment"

---

[15]Some of the following arguments for greater exchange-rate fixity are cast, in the first instance, in terms of the problems associated with flexible rates. As such, they could have been included in the second section.

[16]While the analysis in this section, and others that follow, were part of the original Conference version of this paper, they have been updated to reflect the augmentation in the more recent papers with Richard Harris (1999a, b).

problem or, in popular parlance, as the volatility issue. As already noted, the dollar went from 104 cents in 1974, to 71 cents in 1986, to 89 cents in 1991, to the low 70-cent range for most of the 1990s and then to 63.5 cents in the summer of 1998, rebounding to the 65-67 cent range recently. The problem here is that within the integrating NAFTA context, "floating exchange rates provide inherently volatile and unpredictable cost structures" when what is really required are "stable and predictable rates of international exchange and cost calculations to support the volumes of trade and degree of specialization associated with [this trade] (Harris, 1993, pp. 39, 40). This is especially the case as we move from a resource-based economy to a human-capital-based economy, since this is a move away from organized commodity spot markets priced in U.S. dollars and towards a regime where [generally unhedgeable] long-term bilateral contracts loom large within an economy with a substantial import competing manufacturing sector. On both these latter counts, exchange-rate volatility is bound to be problematic.

In more detail, Harris assesses the problems associated with both down-side and upside misalignment:

> One consequence of an undervalued exchange rate is that it protects inefficient operations from otherwise appropriate market signals. In the Canadian case, the robust demand growth in the [mid-1980s] recovery plus the low exchange rate probably delayed appropriate productivity-improving investments in our manufacturing industry until much later in the decade (1993, p. 36).

> [In terms of the overshooting of the Canadian dollar associated with the transition to price stability] the FTA presented [agents] with an option other than lowering costs or shutting down; they could now move to a U.S. location, and a number of highly publicized moves did occur. No doubt some of these relocations were made in the expectation that the overvalued exchange rate was permanent (1993, p. 37).

As Harris and I (1999a) emphasize, the longer-term legacy of repeated bouts of misalignment is likely to result in Canadian comparative advantage shifting towards industries that are resource-based and/or capital intensive, and with an employment base that is both less diversified and less-human-capital intensive than would be the case with exchange-rate stability. This is not an appealing future in a world where we all agree that human capital will be at the cutting edge of competitiveness.

Thomas J. Courchene

Flexible Rates and Productivity

Complementary with the above reflections on the implications of exchange-rate volatility are the likely associated problems on the productivity front. John McCallum refers to this as the "lazy dollar" hypothesis. Writing in the *Current Analysis* series of the Royal Bank, he notes:

> The idea that a weak currency induces "laziness" on the part of the manufacturing sector is not one that appeals to this author, but it seems to be broadly consistent with the data, [which] suggests a "double-dip" in Canada's relative manufacturing productivity or the first half of the 1980s and then in the period 1994-97. Both of these periods correspond roughly to times of weak currency. Indeed, there is a positive and significant correlation (R=.45) between the Canada-minus-U.S. productivity growth gap and the lagged value of Canadian unit labour costs in manufacturing relative to the United States (expressed in the same currency). So it may be that a weak currency has been a *cause* rather than a *consequence* of poor productivity growth in our manufacturing sector (1988b, pp. 3-4) [emphasis not in original].

In his more recent 1999 paper, McCallum quantifies this relationship — a 10% reduction in the Canadian currency is associated, two years later, with a 7% reduction in the ratio of Canadian to U.S. productivity in manufacturing. Since Canada's future living standards depend on productivity growth, this is an ominous finding indeed.

Admittedly, productivity measurement is immensely complicated (Harris, 1998), so that this evidence is probably best viewed in the nature of an hypothesis that merits further research. Nonetheless, it does accord well with anecdotal evidence. More to the point, it suggests that the ongoing federal review of Canadian productivity issues must address the relationship between exchange-rate volatility and our productivity performance.

Asymmetric Shocks and the "Buffer" Role of Flexible Rates

Those who defend the floating dollar always (and sometimes *only*) point to the potential safety-valve or "buffer" role of the exchange rate in addressing the asymmetric shocks that hit Canada and the United States. The purpose of this section is to argue that the assumed virtues of floating rates as a buffer in the face of asymmetric shocks are overrated — fixed exchange rates also have adjustment mechanisms that can accommodate such shocks.

As a prelude to this analysis, we note that the Bank of Canada, among others, has emphasized that allowing the exchange rate to track the downward trend in commodity prices is insulating our commodity-producing sectors from the fallout of falling prices. No doubt it is, but with what implications. The first is that if, say, agriculture has a problem, let's tackle this problem head-on: the exchange rate is the wrong instrument! The second and related comment draws from the recent paper by Grady and Macmillan (1998). They note that over the FTA/NAFTA period (1989-97) the top five export sectors in terms of recording increases as a percent of GDP were, in order, transport equipment (including autos), machinery and equipment, electrical and communication products, lumber and wood, and chemical and chemical products, followed by several service categories. The five exports groups that contracted as a share of GDP were, again in order, grains, utilities, metallic ores and concentrates, non-metallic minerals, and petroleum and coal products (Grady and Macmillan, 1998). Only one of the former group falls into the commodities category, whereas all five of the latter group do. Clearly, Canada's wealth-generation process is shifting away from resources and towards human capital and high technology activities and processes. This provides a quite different perspective on the wisdom of allowing the exchange rate to track commodity prices.

The third, and again related, point is that the index of commodity prices has fallen much more than Canada's overall "terms of trade", that is, the ratio between export prices and import prices. Over the 1990s the latter have fallen only about 3%, way less than the commodity-price-linked exchange-rate depreciation. As Mundell noted:

> Canada is a multi-region country. Some of its regions are export-oriented raw material producing, whereas other areas are industrialized. *The intra-Canada terms of trade are more volatile than Canada's international terms of trade because prices of the exports of different regions often fluctuate in opposite directions.* (1990/1991, p. 9, emphasis added)

The traditional argument for exchange-rate buffering relates to offsetting terms of trade shocks, not to shocks related to only one component of the terms of trade. Following Harris (1993), Grubel (1999) has argued that the exchange-rate tracking of commodity prices is compounding the productivity challenge by serving, via exchange-rate movements, to entice labour and capital to remain in declining sectors. One could very well ask whether this is the latest version of Canada's repeated approaches to regional economic development. As noted earlier, if commodity-related sectors are falling on hard times, we may well have to design or redesign aspects of our national economic strategy with these sectors in mind, but the exchange rate is the wrong instrument for this.

Now that I have broached the Mundell proposition, namely that Canada's interregional terms of trade are much more volatile than Canada's international terms of trade, it is appropriate to combine this with the earlier proposition that Canada can best be viewed as a series of regional, cross-border economies rather than a single national economy. In tandem this leads to a quite different approach to the issue of asymmetric shocks, one that represents an update of Mundell's seminal 1961 contribution.

A Fresh Approach to Asymmetric Shocks

I approach the asymmetric shock issue by conceptually parsing asymmetry into two components — regional asymmetry and national asymmetry. The former refers to the manner in which external shocks affect Canada's regions vis-à-vis comparable regions in the United States. National symmetry will relate to the fact that external price shocks in, say, the commodities or resource sector will have a larger overall impact on Canada because commodities/resources are a larger component of GDP in Canada than in the United States.

With respect to regional asymmetry, consider the following thought experiment. British Columbia aligns its policies to become competitive in the American northwest and the Pacific Rim. Likewise, suppose Alberta sets its domestic cost and tax parameters so that they are on par with its competitors in the Texas Gulf. And Ontario and Quebec gear their economic policies to match those of the U.S. Great Lakes states. Ditto for the Canadian and American bread-baskets and also for Atlantic Canada as it pursues its more complicated economic future with respect to the New England states, the Atlantic Rim and presumably central Canada as well. In any event, the scenario assumes that each province or region has aligned itself to be competitive with its cross-border counterpart.

Now comes a commodity price shock (say a positive shock from Canada's vantage point). *Initially, this shock affects each side of the regional cross-border economies similarly,* that is, there is no cross-border regional asymmetry. BC lumber is affected in the same way as northeast

U.S. lumber. Alberta oil faces the same price change as Texas Gulf oil. Oshawa/Windsor are still in step with Detroit in terms of autos, and so on. However, if Canada takes the commodity shock out in terms of an appreciation of the Canadian exchange rate (vis-à-vis the U.S. dollar), *then all of the Canadian provincial/regional economies are now offside with respect to their American counterparts.* This is inappropriate policy, especially if this exchange rate "buffering" is also associated with volatility. Arguably, each Canadian trading region would prefer to maintain exchange rate and transactions certainly with *both* east-west and north-south trading partners. This requires exchange-rate fixity.

But we are not out of the woods yet, since there is still the issue of "national" asymmetry. There are two components to what we refer to as "national asymmetry". One is a north-south component, since any change in, say, commodity prices will have a larger overall impact on Canada because commodity-based goods and services are a larger component of Canadian GDP than U.S. GDP. The second component relates to "east-west" asymmetry. This is so because while the initial price shock does not affect the Alberta/Texas Gulf or the Oshawa/Detroit cross-border regions differentially, it *does* affect the relative prices between commodities and manufacturing, that is, between Alberta and Ontario. Both require some "buffering", to use the Bank's term, but not necessarily of the exchange-rate variety. What are the adjustment mechanisms under exchange-rate fixity?

The answer is at least three-fold. The first mechanism is, of course, the internal adjustment of prices. Note that this is not as significant a challenge as might at first be imagined, because the external shock affects both of the cross-border sides of the regional economies in a similar fashion, that is, it is the exchange-rate response, not the commodity price shock, that triggers the cross-border disequilibrium for Canada's regional economies. Phrased differently, we allow Ontario and Michigan (and Alberta and the Texas Gulf, etc.) to adapt in the same way.

Second, if there is a significant commodities price shock, fiscal stabilization will have to come to the rescue. But this has always been an integral part of the philosophy underpinning fixed rates. Indeed, it is under fixed exchange rates that fiscal policy becomes a potent stabilizer. Moreover, it is probably important that individual provinces/regions also become involved in the fiscal stabilization of the exchange rate. In particular, and as argued in Courchene (1990), one would expect that economies that are beneficially affected by a favourable terms of trade shock to their own region would use their fiscal levers to temper their booms. Had Canada been under fixed exchange rates in the late 1980s, the pressure on Ontario to temper (rather than *fuel*) its boom would have been much more transparent and intense, since one and all would have understood the implications for the fixed exchange rate. (As an important aside, in any process of convergence related to adopting a common currency or a committed exchange-rate fix, it is important that Canada ensure that its debt/GDP ratio is brought down at least to the U.S. ratio in order to ensure that there is room to manoeuvre on the fiscal stabilization front).

The third accommodating aspect is arguably the most important, since it addresses the east-west or *internal asymmetry* within Canada. In the case of region-specific shocks *we already have in place mechanisms to deal with this* — the national tax-transfer system, unemployment insurance, equalization, internal migration, and the like. And apart from internal migration, all of the rest are triggered automatically, that is, they operate as automatic stabilizers.

Hence, it is simply not the case that adjustment to external price shocks requires a floating exchange rate. Indeed, the adjustment mechanism underpinning exchange-rate fixity is, arguably, more appropriate for an integrating North America. At the very least, this distinction between "regional" and "national" asymmetry merits further research.

The Transactions-Costs or Integration Benefits of Fixed Rates

While the transactions and efficiency gains associated with a larger currency area will depend on the nature of the currency integration (i.e., the gains will be larger under an irrevocably fixed currency such as that under dollarization and NAMU), they will nonetheless be substantial. The estimates of currency conversion gains are typically set in the range of a few tenths of a percent of GDP. However, there is a much broader range of potential benefits. For example, Canadian firms operating in the North American market could eliminate the accounting costs that arise from using two currencies. Companies which currently hedge exchange-rate risk would no longer find it necessary to do so, and most of the costs associated with providing exchange-rate-related derivatives would no longer be necessary. Menu costs associated with providing price information and invoicing in two currencies would be eliminated, which might prove particularly important to the development of "e-commerce" in Canada. Capital markets would be deeper and interest rate spreads on government and corporate debt would be reduced, thereby improving the efficiency of financial intermediation and reducing borrowing costs in Canada. Canadian issuers of new equity offerings would find a larger market in the absence of exchange-rate risk. In product markets, price discrimination by national market would be less prevalent, given better price comparison information on the part of consumers.

Beyond these transactions-related benefits, there are a host of other efficiency and operational gains for exchange-rate fixity.

- Canada's trade elasticities for both exports and imports are among the highest in the OECD countries, so that avoiding misalignment of the real exchange rate becomes especially important to Canada (Harris, 1993, p. 43);

- Fixed exchange rates give Canada a realistic chance of getting its fair share of North American investment based on the competitive advantage of its firms and its industries (in contrast to location decisions being made in terms of the size of the market in order to isolate firms from unhedgible exchange rate volatility) (ibid., p. 44);

- Finally, but not exhaustively, the certainty associated with a fixed rate regime means that any reductions in the real exchange rate are likely to have a greater impact in terms of increasing exports and decreasing imports than would be the case under floating rates.

Recapitulation

The thrust of the above analysis is that Canada is no longer appropriately viewed as an optimal currency area, in the sense of justifying a stand-alone, freely-floating currency. On grounds of enhancing transactions efficiency, of accommodating external shocks, and of maximizing the opportunities presented by increasing North American integration, among others, the appropriate currency reach for Canada and Canadians includes the U.S. dollar area.

Thus far, I have used "exchange-rate fixity" as a generic term to encompass a broad range of alternatives — pegged rates, fixed exchange rates, currency boards, dollarization and NAMU. In the remainder of the paper, I shall focus on each of these in turn. This will be followed by some

Thomas J. Courchene

brief observations on the likely impact of these alternatives on the important and delicate issues of sovereignty and the evolution of social policy.

Towards Exchange-Rate Fixity: A Menu of Options

The operating assumption in this section is that the Canadian currency must be formally linked to the U.S. currency. The issue thus becomes: What sort of link? As noted in the introduction, four separate options will be described and assessed.[17] The first and most obvious is a fixed exchange rate with the U.S. dollar (where I distinguish between a pegged rate and a truly fixed rate). Attention will then be directed in turn to a currency board arrangement, dollarization (using the greenback as the Canadian currency) and a common Canada-U.S. (or NAFTA) currency. Note that this ordering does not imply anything about which is the preferred option. For example, I shall argue that NAMU is much preferable to dollarization. To anticipate aspects of the ensuing analysis, readers can refer to Table 3, which provides a comparative assessment of some of the key features of the four options.

As backdrop to the more detailed discussion of each of the alternatives, a few general comments are in order. First, what all of the options have in common is the need to decide upon the value of the exchange rate to make the link or conversion, as the case may be. This will be referred to as the "entry point" issue. As we shall see, this is a non-trivial issue given the current undervaluation of the dollar. Second, some options will require more lead time (and negotiations) than will others. For example, while I probably am in the distinct minority in believing that some version of a Canada-U.S. common currency is a real possibility, the required lead time will be upwards of a decade if the Euro experience is a guide. In this sense, the practical value of some of what follows may well be to stimulate needed further research on the feasibility and design issues related to a common currency.

---

[17]There is, of course, another option, namely that the Bank of Canada target the same inflation rate as the Federal Reserve. As Fortin argues (1996), this would have represented a marked improvement in terms of implementing an inflation-targeting regime. And in principle, it should lead, over the longer term, to greater exchange-rate stability. From the vantage point of this paper, however, this strategy does not remove the exchange-rate volatility and misalignment problems, which the above analysis views as key to successful integration under the FTA and NAFTA. Hence, this option does not fall in our preferred choice set.

Table 3: Assessing Alternative Approaches to Exchange-Rate Fixity*

Options	Own Currency	Seigniorage	Bank of Canada?	Exchange Rate Variability	Policy Flexibility	Implementation Costs	Implementation Time	Clearings	Reversible	Access to U.S. Capital Markets	Maintain Financial Sector Policy
Fixed-Exchange Rates	Yes	Yes	Yes	Fixed, within a narrow band.	Full, subject to gearing policy to maintaining the fixed rate.	Minimal; need to select "entry point".	One to three years to establish credibility	Status quo plus smaller transactions costs for U.S. clearings.	Yes	Enhanced access vis-à-vis flexible rate status quo.	Yes
Currency Board	Yes	Yes, but less.	Yes, but under currency-board rules.	Fixed at one-to-one.** No band.	Less. Bank is a passive actor. Can run deficits only by taxing or borrowing.	Requires internal revaluation of prices and a new currency.**	Several years, presumably preceded by fixed exchange rates.**	More integration with U.S. clearings systems.	Yes, but, expectation must be that it will not be reversed.	Larger still.	Yes, but will be more U.S. banks operating in Canada.
Canada-U.S Common Currency	Yes	Yes	Yes, but under the Euro arrangement.	None (common currency).	Somewhat more than currency board. And Bank has some say in Canada-U.S. policy.	Same as above.	Probably a decade, as in Euro process	National clearings and then full integration into Canada-U.S. clearings (along the Euro Target scheme, presumably)	Yes, we still maintain a central bank and our own currency.	Full	Yes, but may be greater harmonization over time.
Dollarization	No	No	No	None (no Canadian currency).	Minimal, and Canada may be drawn into U.S. policy orbit.	Minimal in that it could be triggered by private sector agents, but societal costs could be large.	Variable, depends on private sector agents	Progressively integrated into U.S. clearings systems	Not without major problems (no central bank, no separate currency).	Full	Will likely be drawn more into U.S. financial policies.

Notes: *For all options, Canadian price level would be tied to U.S. price level and Canada would follow the U.S. business cycle more so than under the status quo.
**This need not be the case. If a currency board were implemented at, say, 75 U.S. cents to the Canadian dollar this would not require the issuing of a new currency. The implementation time would be much reduced.

Third, the options are not mutually exclusive. Indeed, the opposite is true — the route to a common currency would surely go through a period where the Canadian dollar is fixed to the U.S. dollar, just as exchange-rate fixity is an integral part of the transition to the Euro.

An Exchange Rate "Peg"

In his analysis of exchange rate alternatives currency arrangements for Canada, former Bank of Canada Governor John Crow notes that the mechanics of fixing the exchange rate are straightforward — "in Canada, all that is needed is a government declaration that its Exchange Fund Account will intervene in unlimited amounts to defend a given exchange rate" (1996, p. 14)[18]. Typically, the exchange rate is allowed to fluctuate within a narrow band (± 1% or perhaps 2%) of the par value. If this is all that is contemplated, we would refer to this as a "pegged" exchange rate. We agree with John Crow that a "pegged regime invites attack and is demonstrably brittle under pressure" (ibid., p. 13). Indeed, the pressure could well come from *within* since under our definition of a pegged note there is no concerted effort on the part of overall macro policy to defend the peg. While pegged exchange rates can prove valuable as temporary stopgaps, this is not what we have in mind in terms of a fixed exchange rate.

Fixed Exchange Rates

Unlike a pegged rate, a full-blown fixed-rate regime would perforce require the full coordination of fiscal policy (both federal and provincial) as an integral component of a fixed-exchange-rate regime. As I have noted earlier (1990), what is involved here is in the nature of a policy "paradigm shift". Conducting overall macro policy under a fixed-rate system is quite different from that under a floating rate system. Among other items, provinces with booming economies would be expected to "temper" their booms via their fiscal stance, if this were what maintaining the exchange rate fix required.

---

[18]The core of John Crow's analysis is to make a case for the floating dollar. In the process, however, he provides a valuable overview of some of the pros and cons of the various options.

It is, of course, still possible that fixed-rate regimes can get caught in "one-way" bets by international capital markets. Indeed, Crow's earlier quote to the effect that a pegged exchange rate would "invite attack" and is "demonstrably brittle" was actually in reference to a fixed-rate regime. Yet there are several fixed-exchange-rate success stories — Austria/Germany and Netherlands/Germany for example. Crow views these as special cases:

> The Netherlands guilder, which might seem an exception since it shadows the German mark within an explicit tight band, is to all practical intents fixed, rather than adjustable. This is because successive Dutch governments have made attachments to the mark a keystone of national economic policy within the broader framework of strong support for the political goal of European Union. Austria and Belgium are close to being in the same camp as the Netherlands because of their overriding political commitment to shadowing the mark. (1996, p. 17, note 12)

Apart from the fact that these fixed-exchange-rate regimes operated successfully well before the notion of political union emerged (let alone that it still is not on the horizon), this quote does provide the secret to a successful fixed-rate regime, namely that our attachment to the U.S. dollar must be the keystone of our national economic policy within the broader North American framework. Indeed, a comprehensive policy commitment to "shadow" the dollar, backed up by a full understanding of what this means on the fiscal front and in the context of already high and increasing north-south trade integration should make a Canada-U.S. fixed rate the most stable and viable such regime anywhere. This does not mean that it cannot be toppled by unforeseen events: after all, in August 1998 alone, we apparently spent $6 billion of international reserves defending a floating rate! What it should mean is that international capital markets will come to view the Canadian dollar as fully integrated into the U.S. dollar area and, therefore, a near-perfect substitute for the U.S. dollar.

As Harris and I (1999a) emphasize, the convergence to a fixed exchange rate, and in particular to a fixed-exchange-rate mentality cannot occur overnight.

Drawing on the Dutch example, we note that the monetary authorities must first demonstrate that they are willing to use monetary policy as an instrument to deliver an exchange-rate goal in the form of a target band for the exchange rate, rather than simply intervene in the foreign exchange-rate market. Once this credibility is established, foreign exchange speculation becomes stabilizing and interest rates between the two countries should tend to converge. Over time the exchange target band can be narrowed and the requisite intervention will diminish. This is the "shadow" policy referred to by John Crow. In short, credibility has to be earned and, therefore, it would be unwise to move suddenly to a fixed exchange rate. How long would such a transition take? No one can know for sure, but it took the Dutch about three years from their initial shift to "fixed rates" before they achieved interest rate convergence with Germany.

Currency Board Arrangements

Because currency board options are not fully integrated into mainstream analysis (i.e., into the optimal currency area literature), my approach to these arrangements is to begin by casting them in a very favourable light, leaving the associated problems until later. Fortunately, Hanke and Schuler (1993, pp. 14-16) exactly fit this bill and I quote them at length:

> A currency board is an institution that issues notes and coins convertible into a foreign "reserve" currency ... at a fixed rate (in contrast to a pegged rate) and on demand. It does not accept deposits. As reserves, the currency board holds high quality, interest-bearing securities denominated in the reserve currency ... A currency board's reserves are equal to 100% or slightly more of its notes and coins in circulation, as set by law ...

> *Convertibility:* The currency board maintains unlimited convertibility between its notes and coins and the reserve currency ... at a fixed rate of exchange. Although the currency board does not convert local deposits denominated in its currency onto reserve assets, the board's swap offer on currency will be arbitrated to local deposits at commercial banks. *No currency board has even had problems maintaining its fixed rate of convertibility.*

> The unrestricted convertibility into the reserve currency that characterizes the currency-board system means that both current-account and capital-account transactions are unhindered ...

> *Seigniorage:* ... the only economic difference between using currency issued by a currency board, rather than reserve currency notes and coins, is that by using a currency board's currency, the seigniorage is captured

by a domestic currency board, instead of the foreign central bank that issues the reserve currency ...

In addition to that economic difference (seigniorage), use of a domestic currency board issue, rather than a foreign currency, satisfies national sentiment.

Monetary policy: By design, a currency board has no discretionary powers. Indeed, its operations are passive and automatic ... Under a currency-board system, government expenditures can only be financed by taxing or borrowing.

Historical Record: The currency board system has an excellent record ... It has existed in 60 countries: in all cases, convertibility was maintained at a fixed exchange rate ... Even though currency boards performed well, most fell victim to the intellectual fashion which favoured central banking in the 1950s and 1960s ...

Protecting a Currency Board: Although the currency-board system was a great economic success, most currency boards have disappeared because they lacked the political independence required to prevent them from being converted into a central bank ... The currency board must be insulated from any possible government manipulation and the threat of conversion to a central bank. To that end, the board's constitution should specify that a majority of the board of directors should be appointed by foreign governments or foreign private institutions ... The currency board should also keep its assets in a safe-haven country such as Switzerland, and should be incorporated as a private entity under the law of the safe-haven country ... Another way for the currency board to strengthen its credibility would be to use its notes to contain a statement that they are convertible into the reserve currency at whatever fixed rate had initially been established. The currency board's notes should be printed outside of the country where the board operates.

The authors conclude with the observation that "for the Americas, the currency-board system offers a means to establish sound money in the region and facilitates the regions' natural tendency to evolve toward a common currency area" (ibid., p. 20).

One can raise concerns with and/or elaborate on the Hanke-Schuler analysis. For example, one can take issue with their definition of seigniorage since it does not take account of the fact that the reserves have to somehow be "purchased" in the first place. (Presumably, Canada's international

Thomas J. Courchene

reserves would be applied towards this end.) Moreover, as Williamson (1997, pp. 7-8) notes, it is a misrepresentation to think that the danger of a speculative run is eliminated by a 100% reserve against notes and currency since bank deposits can be converted freely (by the banks) into currency. He looks favourably on the Hong Kong experience in not monetizing 100% of its reserve-currency inflow, thereby creating a foreign exchange reserve over and above that constitutionally needed and, in the process, allowing some scope for a lender of last resort in any future crisis. Along similar lines Perry offers the following observation:

> Turning to the case of Argentina, we see that permitting the inter-nationalization of the financial sector can help both to reduce the vulnerability of banks to negative external shocks and to smooth out capital flows, because foreign-owned subsidiaries can draw from credit lines to their parent banks when confronted with negative external shocks. Although for good reasons, such as better client knowledge, countries like Argentina are likely to maintain a sizable domestic banking system, they also may obtain such "cushion effects" from swap arrangements, such as the one that the Argentine Central Bank signed recently with some foreign banks. (1997, p. 2)

Another issue that frequently arises in the currency board literature is the degree of discipline that appears to result. Mundell is most emphatic about this:

> Make no mistake about it. The adoption of an unabrogable currency-board system is a major step. If it means anything, it means monetary and fiscal discipline. If governments move to a currency board system (or any other unabrogable fixed exchange rate system), budget deficits become possible only to the extent that the public, at home or abroad, buy government securities to finance the deficit. Of course, movement to an unabrogable currency-board system would enormously strengthen the market for government bonds, up to the point of saturation. If fiscal deficits proceed beyond this point of saturation, a default premium will enter interest rates. Devaluation risk has been removed by the intro-duction of the currency board, but default risk replaces it. (1993, p. 27)

Finally, Calvo emphasizes another type of discipline — "in some countries, and Argentina is an example, the existence of a straightjacket like this [a currency board] is focussing the politicians' attention on perfecting the labour market as they never have before" (1997, p. 17).

Towards a North American Common Currency

In terms of this paper, a Canadian currency board would represent an "unabrogable" commitment (to use Mundell's term) to the U.S. dollar. It represents a more formal commitment to the U.S. currency area than a fixed-rate regime because it takes monetary policy right out of the picture (although Argentina is often viewed as maintaining a quasi-currency board since it kept its central bank in place, albeit governed by a new legal framework). Moreover, there is a precise exchange-rate value — one-to-one in the peso-dollar Argentinian regime so that the currencies are perfectly substitutable (American Express charged me a 20 cent fee for converting a $100 U.S. travellers cheque into 100 pesos).

In terms of Table 3, currency boards represent a quite dramatic departure from fixed exchange rates. First of all, there is no independent monetary policy — indeed, no Bank of Canada under the strict version of a currency board. More generally, overall policy flexibility is much more constrained. On a "flow basis" seigniorage still exists, since the U.S. dollars can be held in easily-convertible U.S. bills or bonds, but there is a once-and-for-all cost of acquiring this U.S. dollar reserve in the first place. On the positive side of the ledger, there would no longer be any transactions costs associated with Canada-U.S. trade, and our access to U.S. capital markets would be much more thorough. Presumably, U.S. banks would find it easier to do business in Canada and, in the process, integrate the Canadian dollar more fully into the U.S. clearings process (although Canadian clearings would proceed as usual).

How relevant is this option for Canada? There are several ways to approach this. The first is that we would presumably opt for a currency board only after a period of fixed exchange rates. Indeed, a currency-board-type regime might be part of an optimal path towards NAMU, a Canada-U.S. common currency. (The unabrogable link of the EU11 countries' currencies to the Euro in January 1999, is a variant of a currency-board arrangement). Second, a currency board regime may be an effective way to forestall a move towards "dollarization", since currency boards are more consistent with maintaining national symbolism and flexibility. In terms of this last point, if something went totally awry with U.S. monetary policy, we would still have our own currency in place.

In general, however, a currency board arrangement does not represent a first-best option for Canada. A currency board is much more appropriate for a country that has a history of monetary instability. Canada clearly does not fall into this category. However, if a common currency along Euro lines is not possible and if dollarization is unacceptable, a currency board does

Thomas J. Courchene

represent a fallback approach for permanently fixing the exchange rate. At the very least, including currency-board arrangements as part of the fixed-rate spectrum should serve to stiffen the resolve of our macro authorities to ensure that a fixed-exchange-rate system will hold.

Dollarization

Dollarization is, in a sense, the ultimate fix — we simply abandon the Canadian dollar and use the U.S. dollar. However, we also abandon much of our monetary institutional framework, the Bank of Canada included (see Table 3). It is convenient to distinguish between "market dollarization" and "policy dollarization" (to use the convenient terms suggested by Ted Carmichael in his comments on Courchene and Harris, 1999a). Policy dollarization is highly unlikely since it implies a conscious decision by our policy authorities to opt for the U.S. dollar as Canadian legal tender. On the other hand, market dollarization – use of the dollar by the private sector — is alive and well. As noted in the concluding section, the British (and to a lesser but still significant extent, the Swiss) are well launched on the EU-equivalent path of "market Euroization".

A willy-nilly drift into dollarization, triggered by an unstable Canadian exchange rate, would be enormously costly to the country. In this context, I disagree with the position of many economists and financial analysts that, during the summer 1998 currency crisis, we should have allowed the value of the dollar to be determined by the whims of international capital. In this context, the uncertainty associated with, and the expressed indifference of our policy authorities towards, the movements of the dollar were especially inappropriate. While it is no doubt the case that an interest rate hike in the then economic environment was problematical, it was far more important to stem the flight from Canadian-dollar-denominated assets. The international capital markets had clearly lost confidence in the Canadian currency. Not to put too fine a point on this, we were heading, domestically, in the direction of market dollarization. Hence, I support fully the Bank of Canada's 1% interest-rate hike in the "scary" situation (McCallum, 1998b) associated with the dollar's free fall in later summer. Private agents, whether domestic or international, *will* act in their self-interest to protect their investments. If the volatility of the exchange rate places these interests at risk, rationale agents will shift to more certain transactions and store-of-value alternatives and in the Canadian context this means using the U.S. dollar. It would be an enormous mistake on the part of analysts and authorities alike to assign this scenario a zero probability.

While dollarization may well end up as a default option, there is a much more preferable longer term alternative — NAMU. This option differs from all of the earlier alternatives because it cannot be unilaterally implemented by Canada: it requires the consent and participation of the Americans. Whether this will be forthcoming is part of the ensuing analysis of NAMU.

North American Monetary Union (NAMU)

NAMU would be the North American equivalent of the Euro. In the case of the Euro, this means an overarching (supranational) central bank with a board of directors selected in part from the still-existing national banks. Hence, the Bank of Canada would have a role (at a minimum one-fourteenth, complementing the 12 federal reserve banks and the Mexican central bank), in designing North American monetary policy. Since the U.S. dollar is already the world's foremost reserve currency, the Americans would presumably maintain their "greenback". But European experience suggests that Canada would have some flexibility in terms of our own currency. One side of our NAMU currency (say the $5 bill) would proclaim that this is North American legal tender and a perfect substitute for a U.S. $5 bill (or words to this effect) while the other side (the Europeans call this the "landscape" side) could be emblazoned with Canadian symbolism. (Note that this approach to the EU currency, a common side and a country-specific side, was only abandoned at the eleventh hour. Now all bills will be identical. But the Euro coins will differ on one side.) Since the national currencies would be perfect substitutes there would be no exchange rate.

Implicit in all of this is an *internal revaluation* of Canadian wages and prices in order that one new Canadian (NAMU) dollar will exchange for one U.S. dollar. But this process of currency conversion is exactly the same process that all 11 European countries are undergoing in preparation for the launch of the new Euro currency. The process towards locking in the precise exchange rates would presumably follow some European approach to the Euro.

Obviously, the Americans would have to be fully on side. Is this in their interest? I do not know the answer to this. However, with the Euro currency reach now exceeding the formal[19] U.S. dollar reach, the Americans would presumably be in favour of a larger formal dollar area, especially given their proclivity to run current account deficits. Moreover, the Americans cannot be too thrilled with the ongoing currency implosions in Latin and South America and their having to arrange bail-outs. But it is probably the case that they will not initiate a move to a NAMU. We Canadians initiated the FTA negotiations and, with Mexico, spearheaded NAFTA. The same will have to be true for a NAMU. Since it is unlikely that politicians or the Bank of Canada will take the lead, the task will have to fall on the rest of us, and especially on the business community.

Would Canadians be in favour of NAMU? Again, I do not know the answer to this. But the issue is wrongly posed. If currency integration of some sort is highly likely in North America, the question for Canadians is whether they would prefer a NAMU to dollarization. Here, I think the answer is clear and positive.

Nonetheless, there is one important issue relating to NAMU that remains a stumbling block for many Canadians, namely that the governance of North American monetary policy will remain in the hands of the U.S. Federal Reserve since it will probably have a dominating influence on the board of directors of the North American Federal Reserve Board, as it were. Hence, North American monetary policy will, for all intents and purposes, be U.S. monetary policy. At one level this is, of course, inevitable — the necessary implication of moving to exchange-rate fixity is to adopt U.S. policy with respect to inflation and interest rates. At another level, however, the issue becomes one of raising concern with respect to the inherent difference between multipolar Europe and the Euro on the one hand and the hegemonic United States and the NAMU on the other. The European Central Bank (ECB) is a federation of 11 central banks whereas NAMU would be a federation of three, with the United States likely having the overwhelming voting power. Actually, and as noted above, it is probably more correct to say that

---

[19]Intriguingly, there has even been discussion in academic circles that the Euro could displace the U.S. dollar as the currency of choice in the underground and illegal market. Part of this is related to the fact that there will be a 200 Euro bill, whereas the largest widely-circulated U.S. note is $100. Obviously, the solution here would be to issue a larger U.S. dollar note, assuming, of course, that the Americans want to continue receiving the considerable seigniorage from the underground economy.

NAMU will have 14 constituent banks if one counts the 12 U.S. federal reserve banks.

While this is surely the NAMU reality (although less so if the common currency eventually extends to all the Americas), there is another way to approach the comparison between NAMU and the Euro. The first point to be made here is that a comparison between Canada and Germany or Canada and Italy is not fully appropriate. The Europeans needed to join together to form a currency that could compete in global portfolios with the U.S. dollar. In other words, the appropriate comparison is not between the Euro and NAMU but between the EURO and the U.S. dollar. In this light, now consider the currency choices facing Canada and Britain. Both have to weigh the economic benefits and costs of maintaining a separate currency or adopting the common currency. In Canada's case, this means sharing a voting membership in a North American Federal Reserve with the 12 existing U.S. federal reserve banks and the Mexican central bank. In Britain's case, this means joining the Euro with a similarly small voting role — one vote in the face of the eleven existing central banks. It is probably the case that the 11 European central banks are likely to exercise more policy independence than are the 12 U.S. federal reserve banks. However, we would hazard a guess that Canada would be more likely than Britain to garner a seat on any Executive Council. In any event, the mandate of these supranational central banks is likely not only to be driven by price stability, but these supranational banks themselves will appoint a further number of "independent" directors to the board (as in the ECB).

To be sure, this does not counter the concern that policy under NAMU would be U.S. driven, but it does provide an alternative vantage point for viewing the Euro-NAMU comparison for those nations that are currently outside these arrangements.

NAMU: Operational Considerations

As already noted, the transition to NAMU would presumably follow the Euro model.[20] Canada, Mexico and the United States would, having agreed to a NAMU in principle, engage in a EU-type exchange-rate mechanism which would set their currencies on a convergence path for entry in NAMU.

---

[20]This section is taken directly from Courchene and Harris (1999b).

Thomas J. Courchene

We have already noted aspects of this convergence in terms of the Dutch example, that is, gradually calibrating policy to embrace the common exchange rate. Presumably, there will exist some "convergence" criteria, along Euro lines. In any event, Canada will presumably want, as a run-up to establishing a NAMU "entry point", to bring its debt/GDP ratio down to U.S. levels. This will ensure that we have similar fiscal manoeuvrability under NAMU as will the Americans. More importantly, as we bring our debt/GDP ratio down, our exchange rate will rise (along the lines of McCallum's exchange-rate equation, where the value of the Canadian dollar is negatively related to the debt/GDP ratio). In other words, part of the NAMU conversion process will be to generate an appropriate equilibrium entry point for the common currency.

Unlike dollarization, which would mean the disappearance of the Bank of Canada and the likely integration of our financial infrastructure into the American institutional environment, NAMU will preserve our financial environment. The Bank of Canada will remain. So will our existing clearing system, since the North American equivalent to the European "Target" system would serve to provide cross-national clearings. In principle, at least, we should be able to extend NAFTA's governing principle, namely "national treatment" to the operations of financial institutions and regulation. In other words, Canada could and would maintain its existing approach to its financial sector (e.g., branch banking and ownership rules). Under the Euro the national banks will still be responsible, among other things, for monitoring and research functions. This will also carry over to NAMU: indeed under the existing U.S. system, the 12 federal reserve banks already play an important research and advisory role. Seignorage would be shared across the member banks of NAMU, and on and on.

The key difference will be in terms of how Canada adjusts to any shocks to the system. Obviously, the exchange rate no longer exists as an instrument, so that adjustment must take place in other ways. As noted earlier, this means that Canada will have to adjust to exogenous shocks in much the same way as California and New York will have to adjust, that is, via price and wage flexibility and internal migration among other avenues. And for shocks that have different impacts across Canada's regions, our east-west transfer system (income taxes, equalization and Employment Insurance) will provide "buffering". At the aggregate level, we will still have scope for stabilization policy, especially if in the convergence to NAMU we bring our debt/GDP ratio down to American levels.

Sovereignty, Social Policy and Exchange-Rate Fixity

It is undoubtedly the case that any move to fix the Canadian exchange rate will generate concern from certain quarters that we are selling out to, or perhaps "buying into" the American philosophy. Harris offers the following comments on the loss-of-sovereignty issue in the context of fixing the exchange rate to the U.S. dollar:

> Undoubtedly, fixing the Canadian dollar to the U.S. dollar would be seen as compromising a sovereign monetary policy, a symbol of Canadian independence from the United States. There are two answers to the sovereignty issue. First, it would be Canada's own unilateral decision to undertake such a policy — no treaty would be signed with the United States, and future governments could always choose to unpeg the exchange rate. Therefore, no formal loss of sovereignty is contemplated. Second, many other countries have fixed their exchange rates to one of the major currencies (the U.S. dollar, the Japanese yen, or the German mark) without an apparent loss of political sovereignty. Austria and the Netherlands, for example, have both fixed their exchange rates to the mark without political integration with Germany. (1993, pp. 44-45)

In line with Harris's first point, it seems to me that the issue is not sovereignty, per se, but how we choose to act as a sovereign nation. We can, of course, continue with our made-in-Canada inflation rate and a freely floating and volatile dollar. What the above analysis suggests is that there is a far better way to exercise our sovereignty on the monetary policy front, namely to tie our dollar to the U.S. dollar and reap the resulting export, investment and productivity gains. Moreover, it is not as if the status quo allows us to be free of U.S. influence. It clearly does not. Thus, the monetary policy choice is ultimately one of choosing the preferred way to live next to a superpower. By adopting their inflation rate, we do indeed give up on a made-in-Canada inflation rate. But we also gain important degrees of freedom (sovereignty?) in other policy areas and in terms of other policy instruments since we do not have to employ them in rearguard action, as it were, to counter the considerable problem of being out of sync with the U.S. business cycle, to give but one example.

Once one proceeds beyond a fixed-exchange rate system, the sovereignty issue alters considerably. Assuming that, over the longer term, there will be enormous pressures for Canada to enter into a common currency area with the United States, then NAMU is far more sovereignty-preserving than is dollarization. As indicated in Table 3, under dollarization we will inevitably be drawn into the U.S. financial orbit, beginning, of course, with the disappearance of the Bank of Canada. This is not the case with NAMU — the Bank of Canada will play a role in the North American Federal Reserve System similar to the role of the Bank of France under the European Central Bank. Indeed, one can envision a "national treatment" provision under NAMU for financial institution policy similar to the national treatment clause under the FTA/NAFTA.

Turning now to social policy, will fixed exchange rates serve to unwind Canada's east-west social contract? While this is an extremely complex issue, my answer is that it will not, or, probably more correctly, need not. The first point to make is that Canada adopted its continental European-type social contract in precisely the time frame when we were progressively integrating trade-wise with the Americans. In this sense, North American integration, per se, is not the culprit. Indeed, Canada's medicare program offers firms a comparative advantage vis-à-vis U.S. locations. However, globalization writ large is admittedly wreaking havoc with our social envelope: the returns to education are rising and those for routinized work are falling with the result that incomes are polarizing. Moreover, the increasing internationalization of production means that many manufacturing activities are being "contracted-out" off-shore. But this development is complicating social policy everywhere, not only in Canada, and under any and all exchange-rate regimes.

The second point is that the current anxiety with respect to the ongoing downsizing of the social envelope has its origins not in the FTA or NAFTA but rather in the concerted effort on Ottawa's part to put its fiscal house in order. And, as argued earlier, some of this deficit/debt overhang stems from our price stability experiment and the pressure to pare down our social envelope becomes particularly intense when the Canadian dollar is overvalued. With the 1999 federal budget, some of these cuts to transfers have now been restored.

The third point relates more directly to the exchange-rate fixity issue. The "golden era" of Canadian social policy was surely the Pearson years. Much of what we Canadians hold near and dear in terms of our social programs emanated from this period. *But throughout this creative social policy era, Canada had a fixed exchange rate with the United States.* Quite obviously, the Canadian government did not view its decision to fix the Canadian dollar as an impediment to asserting our identity in terms of a comprehensive social policy infrastructure. Indeed, it may be time to make the opposite case — with currency issues out of the way, as it were, the policy agenda can focus on issues that really matter to fostering a distinctly Canadian identity for the twenty-first century.

To conclude this section on sovereignty, it is instructive to note that Bank of Canada Governor Gordon Thiessen has raised a variant of the sovereignty issue in his assessment of the relevance of a Euro-equivalent for North America: "The Euro is not a blueprint for North America. The political objectives that motivated monetary union in Europe do not have a parallel in North America" (1999, p. 6). Now I grant that NAFTA is largely a trade and economic blueprint, whereas EU integration does incorporate, in addition, aspects of a confederal and, in some areas, a federal overarching structure. But to link the Euro only to the potential *political* evolution of Europe is to ignore the compelling *economic* rationales for a supranational currency. It is highly unlikely that the British will ever buy into the overarching European political project, but it is highly likely that they will embrace the Euro. Even Switzerland, not a member of the EU, is embracing "market Euroization". As Tagliabue (1999) noted:

> The reasons for this [Swiss] enthusiasm for the Euro are clear. Switzerland, with just seven million people and an area a little larger than Maryland's, is surrounded by four Euro nations — Germany, France, Italy and Austria — and conducts about 70 percent of its trade with the 15 nations of the European Union.

But, as noted, Canada ships over 80% of its exports to the U.S. market!

The essential point here is that it is wrong to link NAMU to some sort of eventual political evolution of North America. The preferred approach to this issue is to view the Euro as the first concrete exemplar of the trend towards currency unification worldwide. Phrased differently, the monetary order of the twenty-first century is likely to be characterized by a few super currencies and the issue becomes one of whether Canada will be able to maintain a stand-alone currency in this environment. In other words, national sovereignty in the millennium will be fully consistent with the emergence of currencies as "supranational public goods".

Thomas J. Courchene

Conclusion

The conclusions of the foregoing analysis are rather straightforward, although admittedly controversial:

- Price stability with freely floating exchange rates was and continues to be a sub-optimal policy;

- The resulting degree of exchange-rate volatility is inconsistent with the geo-economics of the FTA and NAFTA. And this inconsistency extends well beyond the issue of transactions uncertainty per se; it also imperils our productivity performance and our ability to attract foreign investment designed to serve the NAFTA market.

- Phrased differently, Canada is no longer a stand-alone optimal currency area. Rather, the optimal currency area for Canada includes the United States dollar area. This implies Canada-U.S. exchange-rate fixity. The traditional argument that a flexible rate is useful to offset terms-of-trade shocks does not apply to a country with very diverse, cross-border regional economies. We have a more-than-adequate set of policy instruments which can accommodate these shocks. Indeed, it is the existence of these instruments in the context of regional economic diversity that makes exchange-rate fixity optimal;

- The obvious and preferred approach to exchange-rate fixity over the shorter term is an exchange rate fixed to the U.S. dollar. If we make the fixed rate the cornerstone of our policy under NAFTA, we can hold the fix, just as Austria and the Netherlands have been able to hold their fixed rates against the German mark;

- A currency board will also deliver fixed rates, but this option only makes sense in the event that we cannot adhere to a fixed-rate regime. Since I believe that exchange-rate fixity is an integral part of our North American economic future, the principal value of a focus on a currency-board arrangement is to ensure that the authorities stiffen their determination to make a fixed-exchange-rate system sustainable.

- Dollarization is not an appealing alternative, but private sector agents could begin to transact in U.S. dollars as a means of avoiding the on-going exchange-rate uncertainty.

- Over the longer term, a Canada-U.S. or Canada-U.S.-Mexico common currency (designed roughly along Euro lines) is an appealing option. Accordingly, we need to embark on a comprehensive research agenda that will focus on design, implementation and operational aspects of such a North American Monetary Union.

- Finally, and speculatively, NAMU will be consistent with what sovereignty will mean in the millennium.

One could conclude on the above note. However, the march of events elsewhere in the Americas is such that a degree of urgency is now associated with this issue. Argentina's President Carlos Menem recently proposed that his country move from its currency-board arrangement to full dollarization. More importantly, in January of 1999, the head of the Mexican Bankers' association called for the spread of the U.S. dollar area to Mexico. And in March of 1999, the Mexican equivalent of Canada's BCNI called for full dollarization of the Mexican economy.

Intriguingly, U.S. economist Robert Barro (1999) suggested that the United States could (and should) find creative ways to support these dollarization initiatives. For example, Barro suggested that the U.S. Federal Reserve could simply "give" the Argentine Central Bank a one-time allotment of $16 billion of newly issued U.S. currency. This would provide Argentina with the required amount of U.S. currency to embark on full dollarization. In return, the Fed would get $16 billion of non-interest-bearing pesos (the peso and the U.S. dollar already exchange on a one-to-one basis) which the Fed would hold as collateral. This transfer of U.S. dollars to Argentina would cost nothing (except paper and ink) and over the longer-term the United States would garner the seigniorage arising from an expanding supply of U.S. dollars in Argentina.

Barro then goes beyond this to note that one of the problems with dollarization is that it would remove the existence of a lender-of-last-resort facility. No problem here — the United States could become a lender of last resort for its dollar-zone clients. He even suggests that the United States should take the lead in promoting this monetary integration.

Thomas J. Courchene

To be sure, Robert Barro is not the U.S. government. But it is significant that this issue has now been raised in the foremost financial paper in the United States.

My concern with all of this is that *the emphasis is on dollarization, not on NAMU*. What are the prospects for NAMU if Mexico, let alone the rest of Central and South America are fully dollarized? (As intriguing: What are the larger economic implications for Canada within NAFTA if the Mexicans decide to use the U.S. dollar as their currency?) If we want to keep the NAMU option alive, we must become party to these discussions and any resulting deliberations. The "we" in the previous sentence includes academics on both sides of the border, but more importantly, it should include our peak business associations. It would be most unfortunate indeed if, when we Canadians finally realize the virtues of a NAMU, this avenue was no longer open because dollarization had already spread to the rest of the Americas.

References

Akerlof, G.A., W.T. Dickens and G.L. Perry (1996), "The Macroeconomics of Low Inflation", *Brookings Papers on Economic Activity* 1, 1-59.

Barro, R. (1999), "Let the Dollar Reign from Seattle to Santiago", *Wall Street Journal* (March 8).

Calvo, G. (1997), "Argentina's Experience after the Mexican Crisis", in Perry (ed.), *Currency Boards and External Shocks*, 15-18.

Chandler, M. and D. Laidler (1995), *Too Much Noise: The Debate on Foreign Exchange Rate Volatility and Policies to Control It*, Commentary No. 72 (Toronto: C.D. Howe Institute).

Courchene, T.J. (1990), "Zero Means Almost Nothing: Towards a Preferable Inflation and Macroeconomic Policy", *Queen's Quarterly* 97(4), 543-561. Earlier versions were presented at the Universities of Waterloo and Toronto.

_____ (1996), "ACCESS: A Convention on the Canadian Economic and Social Systems", Working Paper (Toronto: Ministry of Intergovernmental Affairs).

_____ (1997), "The International Dimension of Macroeconomic Policies in Canada", in M.U. Fratianni, D. Salvatore and J. von Hagen (eds.), *Macroeconomic Policies in Open Economies*, Handbook of Comparative Economic Policies, Vol. 5 (Westport, CT: Greenwood Press), 495-537.

Courchene, T.J. and R.G. Harris (1999a), "From Fixing to Monetary Union: Options for North American Currency Integration", Commentary No. 127 (Toronto: C.D. Howe Institute).

_____ (1999b), "North American Monetary Union: Analytical Principles and Operational Guidelines, paper presented to the Western Washington University Conference, "Should Canada and the U.S. Adopt a Common Currency?".

Courchene, T.J. and M. Laberge (1999), "The Future of the Canadian Currency Union: NAFTA and Quebec Independence", in J. von Hagen and C. Waller (eds.), *Common Money: Uncommon Regions*, proceedings of a conference sponsored by the Centre for European Integration, University of Bonn (forthcoming).

Courchene, T.J. and C. Telmer (1998), *From Heartland to North American Region State: The Social, Fiscal and Federal Evolution of Ontario* (Toronto: Faculty of Management, University of Toronto).

Crow, J., Governor of the Bank of Canada (1988), "The Work of Monetary Policy", Eric J. Hanson Memorial Lecture, University of Alberta, Edmonton, reprinted in *Bank of Canada Review*, February.

_____ (1996), "The Floating Canadian Dollar in our Future", in T.J. Courchene (ed.), *Policy Frameworks for a Knowledge Economy*, Bell Canada Papers on Economic and Public Policy, Vol. 4 (Kingston: John Deutsch Institute, Queen's University), 11-36.

Drucker, P. (1986), "The Changed World Economy", *Foreign Affairs* 64, 1-17.

Eves, E., Ontario Minister of Finance (1998), *Ontario Economic Outlook and Fiscal Review* (Toronto: Queen's Printer for Ontario).

Fortin, P. (1994), "Slow Growth, Unemployment and Debt: What Happened? What Can be Done?" in T.J. Courchene (ed.), *Stabilization, Growth and Distribution: Linkages in the Knowledge Era*, Bell Canada Papers on Economic and Public Policy, Vol. 2 (Kingston: John Deutsch Institute, Queen's University), 67-108.

_____ (1996), "Presidential Address: The Great Canadian Slump", *Canadian Journal of Economics* 29(4), 761-787.

Fortin, P. and L. Osberg (1996), *Unnecessary Debts* (Toronto: Lorimer).

Freedman, C. and T. Macklem (1990), "A Comment on the 'Great Canadian Slump'", *Canadian Journal of Economics* 31(3), 646-665.

Grady, P. (1993), "Making Free Trade Work by Fixing the Dollar", *Canadian Business Review* 20(2), 29-32.

Grady, P. and K. Macmillan (1998), "Why Is Interprovincial Trade Down and International Trade Up?" *Canadian Business Economics* 6(4), 26-35.

Grubel, H.G. (1999), "The Case for the Amero", (mimeo), forthcoming from the Fraser Institute.

Hanke, S. and K. Schuler (1993), "Currency Boards for Latin America", in N. Liviatan (ed.), *Proceedings of a Conference on Currency Substitution and Currency Boards* (Washington: The World Bank), 13-21.

Hanson, S. and C. Waller (1999), "Intranational Financial Integration: Evidence from the Canadian Banking System", in J. von Hagen and C.Waller (eds.),

Common Money: Uncommon Regions, proceedings of a conference sponsored by the Centre for European Integration, University of Bonn (forthcoming).

Harris, R.G. (1983), *Trade, Industrial Policy and Canadian Manufacturing*, Ontario Economic Council Study No. 31 (Toronto: Ontario Economic Council).

_____ (1992), *Exchange Rates and International Competitiveness* (Ottawa: Economic Council of Canada).

_____ (1993), *Trade, Money and Wealth in the Canadian Economy*, 1993 Benefactors' Lecture (Toronto: C.D. Howe Institute).

_____ (1998), "Long-Term Productivity Issues", in T.J. Courchene and T.A. Wilson (eds.), *Fiscal Targets and Economic Growth* (Kingston: John Deutsch Institute, Queen's University), 67-90.

Hart, O. (1995), *Firms, Contracts and Financial Structures* (Oxford: Clarendon Press).

Hartt, S. (1992), "Sovereignty and the Economic Union", in S. Hartt *et al.* (eds.), *Tangled Webb: Legal Aspects of Deconfederation* (Toronto: C.D. Howe Institute), 3-31.

Helliwell, J.F. (1998), *How Much Do National Borders Matter?* (Washington, DC: The Brookings Institution).

Kneebone, R. and K. Mackenzie (1998), "Stabilizing Features of Fiscal Policy in Canada", in T.J. Courchene and T.A. Wilson (eds.), *Fiscal Targets and Economic Growth* (Kingston: John Deutsch Institute, Queen's University), 191-235.

Laidler, D., ed. (1997), *Where Do We Go from Here: Inflation Targets in Canada's Monetary Policy Regime* (Toronto: C.D. Howe Institute).

Laidler, D. and W.B.P. Robson (1993), *The Great Canadian Disinflation: The Economics and Politics of Monetary Policy in Canada, 1988-93* (Toronto: C.D. Howe Institute).

Lipsey, R.G., ed. (1990), *Zero Inflation: The Goal of Price Stability* (Toronto: C.D. Howe Institute).

McCallum, J. (1995), "National Borders Matter: Canada-U.S. Regional Trade Patterns", *American Economic Review* (June), 615-623.

_____ (1998a), "Drivers of the Canadian Dollar and Policy Implications", *Current Analysis* 2(9) (Toronto: Royal Bank of Canada).

_____ (1998b), "Government Debt and the Canadian Dollar", *Current Analysis* 2(10) (Toronto: Royal Bank of Canada).

_____ (1999), "Seven Issues in the Choice of Exchange Rate Regimes for Canada", *Current Analysis* (Toronto: Royal Bank of Canada), February.

McKinnon, R.I. (1997), "Monetary Regimes, Government Borrowing Constraints and Market-Preserving Federalism: Implications for EMU", in T.J. Courchene (ed.), *The Nation State in a Global/Information Era: Policy Challenges*, Bell Canada Papers on Economic and Public Policy, Vol. 5 (Kingston: John Deutsch Institute, Queen's University), 101-142.

McQuaig, L. (1995), *Shooting the Hippo: Death by Deficit and Other Canadian Myths* (Toronto: Viking Press).

Mundell, R.A. (1961), "A Theory of Optimum Currency Area", *American Economic Review* 51(4), 657-665.

_____ (1990/1991), "The Overvalued Canadian Dollar", paper prepared for the first meeting of the Canadian Monetary Policy Review Board, McGill University, Montreal, (April 4-5) (mimeo) and (1991), "De la surévaluation du dollar canadien", *L'Actualité économique* 67(1), 5-36.

_____ (1993), "Currency Boards, Fixed Exchange Rates and Policy Rules", in N. Liviatan (ed.), *Proceedings of a Conference on Currency Substitution and Currency Boards* (Washington, DC: The World Bank).

Perry, G., ed. (1997), *Currency Boards and External Shocks: How Much Pain, How Much Gain?* (Washington, DC: The World Bank).

Purvis, D.D. (1990), "The Bank of Canada and the Pursuit of Price Stability", in R. Lipsey (ed.), *Zero Inflation: The Goal of Price Stability* (Toronto: C.D. Howe Institute), 29-66.

Tagliabue, J. (1999), "Switzerland's Enthusiasm for Euro Grows", *New York Times*, February 24.

Thiessen, G.G., Bank of Canada Governor (1998), *The Canadian Experience with Targets for Inflation Control*, J. Douglas Gibson Lecture (Kingston: School of Policy Studies, Queen's University).

_____ (1999), "The Euro: Its Economic Implications for Canada", remarks to the Canadian Club of Ottawa, January 20.

Whalley, J., ed. (1986), *Canada-United States Free Trade* (Toronto: University of Toronto Press).

Williamson, J. (1997), "Features and Implications of Currency Boards", in Perry (ed.), *Currency Boards and External Shocks*.

York, R.C., ed. (1990), *Taking Aim: The Debate on Zero Inflation* (Toronto: C.D. Howe Institute).

Towards a North American Common Currency: Comments

Richard G. Harris

It is always a pleasure to comment on one of Tom's papers. This paper is classic Courchene containing a deft mix of fact, theory and his usual slightly radical views on what is otherwise regarded as conventional wisdom. In this particular case, I happen to agree with his views on the costs of flexible exchange rates, so I am complicit in his guarded attack on what in Canada is the orthodox view on these matters. Given the wide range of issues discussed in the paper, my comments will be narrow and address only a few issues.

The emergence of a European Monetary Union and the Euro as a new international currency has raised the issue, mentioned occasionally during the North American Free Trade Agreement (NAFTA) debate, as to whether North America might ever contemplate a currency union. By and large this is dismissed by most as extremely unlikely given the political dominance of the United States in the region. Nevertheless the debate on the currency union also re-opens the debate on exchange-rate "policy" within Canada, including the possibility of a fixed-exchange-rate regime. As the author notes, most of the issues regarding the virtues of fixing versus floating are part of the larger debate on optimal currency areas. In teaching this material I have relied in the past few years on a text by Paul De Grauwe, *The Economics of Monetary Integration.* As this has not been a hot topic within Canada recently, I recommend this book as a place to start to see what has happened to Optimal Currency Area theory and empirical analysis since Mundell's seminal piece in 1961.

The general analytical framework in the optimal currency area (OCA) literature is based on a cost-benefit analysis of the benefits of a single currency, or a relatively permanent fix, versus the macroeconomic costs which may occur by giving up an instrument of stabilization policy, monetary policy. This can be represented in a simple diagram with costs and benefits on the vertical axis and the degree of economic integration on the horizontal axis, running from 0 to 100, with 0 corresponding to no integration and 100 corresponding to "full integration". In the case of geographically separated regions the latter case would be an impossibility. The Integration Benefits curve which slopes up measures the benefits of having a common currency, or permanently fixed exchange rate. The Macroeconomic Cost curve represents the cost of sacrificing monetary independence when the exchange rate is fixed. It slopes down under the presumption that as regions integrate, their cyclical behaviour becomes more closely linked. At a critical level of integration indicated by x^* where the two curves cross, the cost-benefit

Figure 1: Cost-Benefit Analysis of Currency Unions/Fixed Exchange Rates

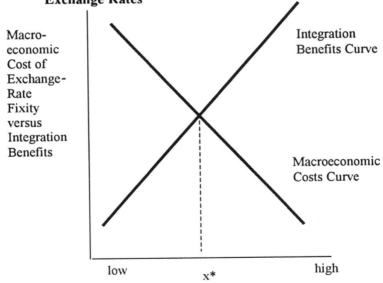

Richard G. Harris

analysis would imply indifference between the two regimes. For integration levels x>x* OCA cost-benefit analysis would indicate that a single currency/fixed-rate regime would be preferred. For x<x*, monetary independence and therefore flexible rates would be preferred. This framework provides a convenient device to discuss arguments about the relative merits of the two regimes in the Canadian context: the benefits from fixing the Canadian to U.S. dollar, or alternatively a currency union. These benefits arise from a variety of microeconomic factors including notably the benefits due to the elimination of exchange-rate volatility. These benefits rise as the degree of economic integration between Canada and the United States rises. They are traded off against the potential loss of macroeconomic control that fixed rates would involve. It is important to emphasize that the choice of exchange-rate regime is a matter of balancing costs versus benefits, and that different countries will come out differently in such calculations. "Different strokes for different folks." What is crucially important for a small country fixing to a large country is the degree of bilateral integration.

The paper undertakes a careful review of the case for fixing. Most interesting is the analysis of recent trade data which attempts to make the case that (a) on a north-south trade basis Canada and the United States have become more integrated and (b) they have levels of integration that are greater than those found within the European Union. In a sense then he is arguing that Canada has moved along the Integration Benefits curve to the right. He goes on and argues the controversial view that Canada is becoming more a north-south economy than east-west. This is a direct attack on the conventional view that Canada is a highly integrated national economy east-west that often faces asymmetric shocks relative to the U.S. economy. In the Courchene view the monetary response to perceived national shocks under a flexible-rate system destablilizes the regional terms of trade, and thus possibly aggravates cyclical instability. This is an important idea and one that deserves additional research. It also ties in directly with his subsequent argument, due in part to Mundell and others, that with a diversified export base Canada should not use the exchange rate as a "shock absorber" to terms of trade shocks. Some recent work by Cuddington and Liang (1998) provides some important evidence on this point. In an international comparisons study they contrast commodity-exporting countries in terms of the exchange-rate regime. They find that countries with flexible-rate systems have more volatile internal relative prices between commodities and manufactured goods than do fixed-rate countries. This supports both the Courchene and Mundell view that flexible rates have actually exacerbated regional instability within

Canada by increasing the volatility in internal relative prices between regions.

The latter part of the paper turns to alternative currency arrangements. I would agree that in the medium term a fixed-rate regime is the only realistic policy alternative for a Canadian government. As he notes, quoting John Crow, a fixed-rate system can only be sustained with a strong degree of political commitment to the system. Exactly right, and this is precisely why a national debate will be necessary if Canada is to move towards a fixed-rate system. The Bank of Canada alone could not unilaterally move to such a regime. In the discussion of currency boards, one point that bears emphasis, is how credible this arrangement would be as a discipline device on economic policy. It is often argued that currency boards are the only realistic mechanism to support a fixed rate. I disagree and would point to the alternative models used in Europe during the 1980s and 1990s, such as the Netherlands. Furthermore, I remain unconvinced that either currency boards or flexible rates insulate countries from the consequences of bad economic policy. The International Monetary Fund (IMF), for example, in its review of banking crises (see Caramazza and Aziz, 1998) found that the incidence of such crises was independent of the exchange-rate regime. As to the prospects for a North American currency it seems at the moment admittedly unlikely, but who knows. The success or failure of the Euro, together with reform of the international financial architecture will be important determinants of the single North American currency debate.

In the last part of the paper "dollarization" is discussed — the abandonment of the use of the Canadian dollar by Canadian firms and residents. It may well be that globalization ultimately means that a national currency issued by a small country will lose its value as a unit of account and as a medium of exchange, and assets issued in that currency will lose their role as a store of value. There are some troubling signs that this may be happening with respect to the Canadian dollar. The loss of confidence in the currency during the summer and fall of 1998 undoubtedly aggravated the problem. From a macroeconomic perspective, loss of confidence in a currency translates into an unstable demand function for domestic money which ultimately creates problems for domestic monetary control. The literature on exchange-rate economics tells us very clearly that exchange markets can move for a long period against fundamentals in periods of either sustained appreciation or depreciation leading to serious exchange-rate misalignment. In the case of undervalued currencies, the longer the period of misalignment the greater the incentive for individuals to switch to an international currency (i.e., the U.S. dollar in our case) as both a medium of exchange and store of value. If there is anything to these arguments they are certainly troubling and call into question the wisdom of the Bank of Canada's response to the recent depreciation.

References

Caramazza, F. and J. Aziz (1998), "Fixed or Flexible: Getting the Exchange Rate Right in the 1990's", *Economic Issues*, No. 13 (Washington, DC: International Monetary Fund).

Cuddington, J. and H. Liang (1998), "Commodity Price Volatility Across Exchange Rate Regimes", Working Paper (Washington, DC: George Washington University).

De Grauwe, P. (1994), *The Economics of Monetary Integration*, 2d ed. (New York: Oxford University Press).

Summary of Discussion

Robert Lafrance reported on Bank of Canada research on the choice of exchange-rate regime. The Bank hosted a conference on the subject in 1992. In one of the papers delivered at that conference, a similar schemata to that just set out by Professor Harris was used to analyze the macroeconomic and microeconomic implications of flexible and fixed rates. Bank research has focused on the nature of asymmetrical shocks between Canada and the United States as well as on interregional asymmetries within Canada. While it is true that north-south trade has increased, the asymmetry across the border is still greater than asymmetries within Canada. Canada's economic cycle is not that closely linked with the U.S. cycle. The nature of shocks differs in the two economies. Canada's economy is still more commodity-based. Thus, the Bank's analysis leads to the conclusion that a flexible exchange rate is the best choice for Canada. In the context of the conference theme, if you want room to manoeuvre, you want flexible exchange rates and an independent monetary policy.

Thomas Courchene replied that the question is room to manoeuvre on what. With a fixed exchange rate, Canada can get Greenspan-type price stability instead of Thiessen-type price stability and we would have more room to manoeuvre on other fronts. There are trade-offs on where we want the room to manoeuvre. We would not lose anything on the price stability side and we would gain other benefits. As for asymmetrical shocks, we cannot just look at the American and Canadian economies as national aggregates. We have to look at regions and compare shocks. If we lump the two countries' regions together into two national economies, we may see asymmetry between Canada and the United States, but that may not be relevant.

David Slater provided some historical perspective on the issue. The U.S. monetary policy record is a mixed bag. U.S. postwar monetary policy has faced a dilemma reconciling the U.S. dollar's dual role as the international reserve currency and as a domestic currency. This dilemma is still not resolved. The United States has made gross monetary policy mistakes in the past and we have to assume that they will make gross mistakes in the future. Do we want to tie ourselves to that currency when this will tie us to their mistakes? Could we do better with our own monetary policy? Courchene makes a strong case that we have not done better over the past ten years. We should also remember that during the 1970s and early 1980s Canadian inflation averaged two to three percentage points per year higher than U.S. inflation.

Richard Harris did not dispute the historical facts about U.S. monetary policy. But he argued that a U.S. policy mistake will affect Canada under any exchange-rate regime.

William Watson asked whether the development of financial derivatives over the last 15 or 20 years has affected the microeconomic implications of the exchange-rate choice. Are firms in a better position to handle the risk of exchange-rate volatility or is volatility so large that it cannot be effectively hedged?

Stuart Wilson also wondered why we could not rely on the financial sector to provide futures contracts if the trade sector needs to be insured against exchange-rate risk.

Richard Harris said that the interesting point to emerge from studies is how little exchange-rate hedging goes on even by large corporations. In addition, access to hedging is limited. For example, Canadian workers cannot insure against exchange-rate risk. The cost of hedging ensures that the financial sector is the only sector making money out of flexible rates. Financial institutions are collecting foreign exchange transaction costs amounting to about 0.5% of GDP.

Dale Orr asked whether we should wait five years until we see how the Euro works for small European countries. Some sceptics of fixed exchange rates also argue that if the Euro reduces the role of the U.S. dollar as a reserve currency, this may not be a good time to fix to the U.S. dollar. Alternatively, another argument sometimes put forward against fixing the Canadian dollar to the U.S. dollar is that this would make it easier for Quebec to separate.

Thomas Courchene agreed that, on one level, a North American currency would make it easier for Quebec to sort out the monetary implications of separation, just as a European currency and increasing European integration may make it easier for Scotland to separate from the United Kingdom. But there is an offset in the Quebec case. The Parti Québécois' (PQ) priority is partnership — a broad economic arrangement with Canada after sovereignty. The lesser the role for the Canadian dollar, the lesser the rationale for a post-sovereignty partnership deal. So a move toward monetary union may be a disadvantage for the PQ in terms of reassuring voters that sovereignty will be based on a partnership arrangement with Canada. As for the need to watch what happens in Europe, everyone agrees that Canada cannot move rapidly to a fixed rate. There are important lead times. However, it is important to start thinking now about our options. We were able to take advantage of the free trade "window of opportunity" because we had done our homework. We need to do the same for monetary union.

Claude Lavoie asked whether there is good empirical evidence that exchange-rate variability harms the economy.

Richard Harris cited a book by Paul De Grauwe which summarizes the studies of European economies. We know that, under a fixed-rate regime, real exchange-rate variability is less. We should also keep in mind the fundamental distinction between the effects of exchange-rate volatility and the effects of exchange-rate misalignment. Misalignment can have large effects on resource allocation. For example, the U.S. dollar's strength during the Reagan years had a negative impact on the industrial northeast.

Robert Lafrance agreed that exchange-rate misalignment can have an impact. However, it is not clear that the Canadian dollar has been grossly misaligned except perhaps for brief periods. Movements of the Canadian dollar can be explained pretty well by looking at a small number of variables.

Pierre-Paul Proulx pointed to studies showing that intra-firm and intra-industry trade are driving transborder regional integration in North America. In a recent Industry Canada study, Serge Coulombe estimates that interprovincial convergence in production per capita stalled in the late 1980s. The factor mobility which had previously been generating interprovincial convergence seems to have diminished. If shocks affect Canada's regions differently, the old adjustment mechanisms may not be working as well. These trends strengthen the case for bringing the exchange-rate regime into line with the new realities. However, it is interesting to note that the Euro is associated with a tendency to centralize more power in Brussels, since the Euro countries have given up an important domestic policy instrument. This contrasts with Courchene's argument that fixed rates should go along with greater decentralization in Canada.

Thomas Courchene noted that many people now think that something similar to Canada's interregional transfer system is necessary in Europe under the Euro. If asymmetries within Canada are serious, the east-west transfer system will continue to handle this problem under fixed rates and will allow provinces to exercise their powers in our decentralized federation.

Leonard Waverman took the view that there is a strong case for fixing the exchange rate and that a ten-year lead time will be required. He noted that the British are also moving in this direction. Chancellor of the Exchequer Gordon Brown recently stated that Britain's adoption of the Euro is a question of when, not if.

Louis Pauly differentiated between a fixed-rate regime and a monetary union. European countries are moving to a monetary union because they are engaged in a political construction. Canadians would not be interested in a monetary union with the United States because there is little interest in political union. But a fixed exchange rate might help us rebuild a national identity. Bay Street executives have wallets and bank accounts full of U.S. dollars. This U.S. dollarization has insidious effects on Canada's national identity. There is a constituency for a solution to the costs of holding a depreciating Canadian dollar. However, the constituency for fixing the exchange rate may be largest at the bottom of the dollar cycle. It might be difficult to hold political support for the peg during different economic circumstances from those prevailing today.

Thomas Courchene responded by challenging the notion that a monetary union requires a political union or even movement towards political union. This is not to deny that political factors played a role in the creation of the Euro. But whether the British formally adopt the Euro will have much more to do with the economic benefits then any political implications. Indeed, the FTA and NAFTA, especially given the national treatment principle, work against political union. This is because we can now get from the Americans what we really want from them — their market — without having to also take what we do not want — their institutions and their values. A monetary union would allow us to maximize the economic benefits arising from the FTA/NAFTA.

Michael Abbott asked what other countries' experiences in the postwar period could tell us about where to peg the Canadian dollar and what would be necessary to maintain the peg?

Thomas Courchene made two related points in response. First, since the conversion process towards a NAMU would presumably take a decade or so, the process of exchange-rate convergence towards equilibrium rates would presumably follow the European EMS route. Beyond this, as a Canadian strategy, it would make sense (in terms of maximizing future fiscal flexibility under a monetary union) for Canada to reduce its debt/GDP to U.S. levels prior to locking into an equilibrium exchange rate. If one believes in a FEER approach to exchange-rate determination, this would increase the entry-point value of the Canadian dollar in any currency integration.

Richard Harris said that we could draw on a lot of historical experience to manage the transition to a fixed rate. For example, the Delors report on European monetary union includes an important study on the Dutch transition to a fixed rate. Norway is going through a transition to a fixed rate right now. In principle, we should shoot for a PPP peg, but PPP estimates are all over the map. This does present a problem and highlights the need for more Canadian research.

Robert Lafrance raised Statistics Canada's estimate that the PPP value of the Canadian dollar is about 80 cents U.S. No one would want to peg at 80 cents at this time. Where to peg is always the key issue in moving to a fixed rate. Fixing the exchange rate could pose special problems because the nature of future shocks is not predictable. Economies should equilibrate to the real exchange rate. Suppose we have fixed the currency about where it is now, but we need real appreciation in future. We would need price deflation to generate real appreciation. No one wants deflation because it is hard to end deflation. The Bank of Canada view is that the currency will appreciate over time if commodity prices come back. In the Bank's long-term projection model of the Canadian economy, a decline in the debt/GDP ratio reduces the twin deficits and helps the Canadian dollar. No one can predict when this will occur, but appreciation looks to be the underlying trend. As Professor Harris pointed out in his *National Post* article, Canadians are experiencing a welfare loss because of the low currency. But that loss will be recovered over time if the dollar appreciates. It is not clear that the weak dollar is the cause of weak productivity growth in Canada. The conclusion at the first Bell Canada conference was that there is no consensus explanation of the decline in productivity in Canada or indeed in other countries. Since this remains a puzzle, the Bank of Canada will be doing research on the linkages between unit labour costs, the exchange rate and productivity.

National Tax Policy for an International Economy: Divergence in a Converging World?

Nancy Olewiler

Introduction

What kind of economy do Canadians want? Most people's list would include: output and productivity growth, high average incomes and an acceptable income distribution, low unemployment, a skilled labour force, strong social and physical infrastructure, low real interest rates, sufficiently high savings to generate investment, stable and low inflation, a healthy population and high level of environmental quality. Government activities are a major part of this picture. Governments assist in providing a human and physical capital infrastructure through education and public works. They provide social safety nets for health, unemployment and retirement. Fiscal and monetary policy can help stabilize swings in economic activity. Governments regulate economic activities to correct distortions such as underpricing the environment, non-competitive behaviour and natural monopolies.

Does globalization threaten all this by restricting our tax policies, lowering tax revenues, and hence, lead to reductions in expenditures by national and subnational governments? The world's economies are linked by communications, international trade in goods and services and technology transfers. Many markets for capital and labour are international, not just local, regional and national. Some argue that these forces of globalization will constrain economic decisions in countries, especially choices with regard to the level and nature of government activity. Globalization poses some tough questions for Canadian tax policy: Does globalization mean we will have to change our tax structure? Is the size of government inevitably smaller due to a smaller tax base and lower tax rates? Can Canada pursue a national tax policy that diverges from that of our trading partners and competitors? This paper will examine trends in taxation for Canada and its major trading partners over the past 20 years and use that information to help answer these questions.

The outline of the paper is as follows. The second section briefly notes the stylized facts of globalization and considers whether globalization is having an impact on tax rates and tax revenues. I look for evidence of convergence of tax rates, a shift in the tax mix from taxes on mobile to less mobile factor inputs, and reductions in tax revenues as a share of GDP. Section three looks at the pressures globalization may place on the Canadian tax system, with a particular focus on the links between taxation in Canada and the United States, and considers tax policy implications for Canada. The following section notes some of the domestic and regional challenges to tax reform in Canada.

Globalization and Taxes: Evidence for Convergence

Globalization can be characterized by the following stylized facts:

- Increasing openness of economies to international trade in goods and services and factor flows.
- Greater mobility of factor inputs.
- Global sourcing of production.
- Deregulated financial markets.
- Significant reductions in transactions costs due to technological change in information flows.
- Increasing concentration of industry and a larger percentage of world output produced by multinational enterprises.
- Global economic agreements over trade, investment, the environment and taxation.

There are many implications for a national tax policy:[1]

- It will be harder to sustain significant tax rate differentials for mobile factors. Tax rates will have to converge. Mobile factors such as portfolio capital and highly skilled labour will be more difficult to tax. Therefore, reliance on profits-based taxes and a progressive income tax will decline. If tax revenues are to remain constant, taxes will have to be shifted to less mobile factor inputs including land, fixed capital and unskilled labour. Greater reliance will be placed on tax bases such as consumption, payroll and user charges and fees for service. If shifts in the tax mix do not occur, the tax base will erode in response to tax differentials. This would mean tax revenue as a share of GDP would fall.

- It will be more difficult to collect taxes on activities that take place outside a country's tax jurisdiction. This will affect both the volume and the nature of cross-border activities. The tax base will erode because it is now easier for individuals and corporations to find ways of avoiding and evading taxes. It will become harder to identify the location of transactions and the residence of taxpayers. Examples include transfer pricing of multinational enterprises (MNEs), arranging business activity so that debt and the resulting interest charges are incurred in high-tax countries, while profits are reported in low-tax countries, the use of flexible financial instruments, creation of offshore trusts and electronic commerce.

- Tax competition will intensify. Preferential treatment of industries has always existed, only some of which is justified on market-failure grounds. Globalization increases the likelihood of tax competition as pressures will intensify to "race to the bottom" by providing incentives for mobile factors to locate in one's jurisdiction. These pressures will be felt most by provincial and municipal governments. If governments succumb to tax competition, economic inefficiency increases, total tax revenues may decline, and with them, government expenditures. All countries are made worse off from the distortions that result from tax incentives.

---

[1]See Mintz (1998); McKenzie (1998); Hogg and Mintz (1993); and Owens (1993) for additional discussion of the impact of globalization on tax policies.

- Deregulation will affect social well-being. It will be harder to preserve environmental quality, health and safety legislation, social health insurance and other employment benefits because these add to the costs of doing business and governments will be loathe to use their tax and regulatory powers to enhance the quality of life.

- While the benefits from coordination of tax policies within and across countries increase, so too does the incentive to free ride on tax changes of other countries. This is particularly a danger in our tax systems. Changes to the federal income tax bases affect the tax revenues of the provinces. If the federal government cuts corporate and personal income tax rates, while expanding the tax base, provincial revenues will be affected. Similarly, changes in provincial taxes that are deductible from federal tax bases affect federal revenues. Analogous changes can occur across countries with the myriad of features in tax agreements. The free-rider problem will make it difficult to achieve agreement within and among countries as to what sort of tax changes are desired.

The impact of these trends on national tax policy for Canada will be discussed more fully in the third section. It is important to remember at the outset that resource allocation and locational decisions of people are dependent on many non-tax factors. The extent to which globalization affects Canada will depend on both tax and non-tax factors. Non-tax factors include: the size of the market, transportation links to other markets, the business and legal climate as influenced by governments, unions, and communities, communications and physical infrastructure, financial markets and their regulation, availability of a skilled labour force, political stability, low crime rates and a healthy natural environment. Note that many of these non-tax factors can be affected by government expenditures, and hence, are dependent upon tax revenues. There is potential for a vicious cycle of globalization pressures leading to tax cuts that in turn contribute to declining levels of human and physical capital and other non-tax variables. Conversely, countries with relatively high taxes may continue to be a desirable location for business investment and residence if the balance between taxation and government expenditures is seen as favourable. A key question is how much latitude does Canada have in choosing the size and activities of its public sector and, hence, the type of economy it has.

The points raised above are well known. I turn now to a discussion of the empirical evidence on tax rates, the mix of taxes, and the share of tax revenues in gross domestic product (GDP) for the OECD.[2] Discussion above suggests a number of hypothesis. Globalization will:

1. Lead to a convergence of tax rates on mobile factor inputs across countries.
2. Shift the tax mix (the share of each tax in total tax revenue) towards relatively higher taxes on less mobile factor inputs.
3. Decrease tax revenues as a share of GDP if tax competition occurs.

The data reveal some interesting trends and some potential paradoxes. I begin first with an examination of evidence for convergence of tax rates on mobile labour and capital.

Taxes on Mobile Factor Inputs: Labour Income

Research on the extent of labour mobility is still in its infancy. A number of factors have made some sectors of the labour market more mobile literally or effectively. These include: trade agreements such as NAFTA which allow people in a number of skill classes to move across borders (at least temporarily), the European Union and its creation of a single market and removal of barriers to professional certification, and technological change in communication which blurs the distinction between workplace and residence. Consultants can work for countries around the world without leaving their homes. Two issues emerge for tax policy. The first is that differences in marginal tax rates on income across countries will be more important than in the past. Second, it will be harder for governments to measure and tax personal income if people earn income for services performed in different countries. Tempering all this is the fact that people have to live somewhere. What matters to them is not just their marginal tax rate or how easy it is to shelter income, but their communities, family, the goods and services they consume.

---

[2]Information is restricted to OECD countries due to data availability. The usual caveats apply: it may be too soon to measure the impact of globalization on taxes, and the data are highly aggregated.

Globalization is expected to lower marginal income tax rates, especially at the top end of the scale, and to lead to convergence of these rates across countries. What is the evidence?

The broad pattern for OECD countries over the period 1978-95 is that tax bases broadened (via elimination of deductions, exemptions, and special rates) and the average top marginal rate fell from 59 to 42% (OECD, 1997). This supports the view that globalization reduces maximum marginal tax rates on high-income and, likely, mobile individuals. But information on maximum marginal tax rates does not indicate at what income level the maximum rate applies. For example, in Canada, the maximum marginal rate (ignoring surtaxes) is reached at an income level for an individual of $59,180, while in the United States it is not reached until household income reaches U.S. $278,000 (for a household filing a joint return). To get around this problem, Table 1 shows marginal tax rates by income level and household characteristics for 15 countries for the years 1978 and 1995. The taxes included in these calculations are income taxes for all levels of government in the country plus social security contributions paid by the employee. High-income earners (defined here as those earning twice the income of an average production worker), faced the same (couples) or higher marginal tax rates (singles) on average across the OECD in 1995 than in 1978. Globalization does not necessarily bring down marginal tax rates on high income earners. However, the dispersion in tax rates across countries for high-income earners declined from 1978 to 1995. Standard deviations fell from 17.5 to 11.1 for single people and 18.6 to 14.1 for couples with children. This suggests greater convergence in marginal tax rates over the period.

These averages hide some significant variation across countries. For the United States, Germany, Norway and Sweden the marginal tax rate for high income couples with children fell considerably. Canada and Denmark had little change over the period, while marginal tax rates increased in the remaining countries. The most mobile people should be those who are single with no children. Yet, the data show that the single high-income earners faced higher marginal tax rates in 1995 than in 1978 for all countries in this sample except the United States, Denmark and Sweden. Although the evidence suggests that rates are converging, they converged as of 1995 to a higher rate for these potentially very mobile people — single people without children. The data also do not indicate whether the "high-income" people

Table 1: Marginal Tax Rates by Income Level (OECD Countries)

Country	Single Person						One-Earner Couple with 2 Children					
	Low Income		Middle Income		High Income		Low Income		Middle Income		High Income	
	1978	1995	1978	1995	1978	1995	1978	1995	1978	1995	1978	1995
Canada	29.8	31.4	33.1	45.9	46.1	48.1	28.4	31.4	30.2	50.9	51.1	51.7
United States	31.6	29.9	37.6	29.9	46.5	42.9	28.4	50.1	31.6	50.1	34.5	29.9
Japan	10.1	15.0	13.7	19.4	24.4	28.1	0.7	9.7	0.7	19.4	20.4	28.1
Germany	38.2	51.2	53.2	52.6	48.6	49.6	38.2	19.6	38.2	42.4	37.5	32.1
France	23.0	35.0	29.2	35.6	30.1	43.3	10.0	20.9	19.8	20.9	19.5	22.5
Italy	19.8	34.3	25.3	34.3	32.7	41.1	19.8	34.3	25.3	34.3	32.7	41.1
United Kingdom	39.5	35.0	39.5	35.0	33.0	40.0	39.5	35.0	39.5	35.0	33.0	40.0
Australia	33.5	39.5	33.5	35.5	47.5	48.5	33.5	48.0	33.5	35.5	47.5	48.5
Belgium	35.5	54.8	46.1	54.8	48.8	61.8	9.7	46.0	43.9	49.2	47.1	59.4
Denmark	41.5	51.7	55.9	54.5	66.7	66.3	41.5	47.0	55.9	47.0	66.7	66.3
Finland	37.5	46.7	49.3	53.1	57.9	58.7	34.1	48.6	49.3	53.1	57.9	58.7
Netherlands	44.3	48.4	50.8	55.9	50.0	60.0	39.5	48.4	50.8	45.0	50.0	60.0
Norway	42.6	35.8	47.6	45.3	69.6	49.5	31.6	35.8	42.6	35.8	69.6	49.5
Spain	20.7	30.3	21.7	32.5	23.6	30.4	20.7	24.1	21.7	24.1	23.6	28.5
Sweden	41.7	37.2	59.7	37.2	81.7	56.5	41.7	37.2	59.7	37.2	81.7	56.5
Average	32.6	38.4	39.7	41.4	47.1	48.3	27.8	38.4	36.2	38.7	44.9	44.9
Standard Deviation	10.1	10.6	13.5	11.1	17.5	11.1	12.9	18.3	15.5	10.9	18.6	14.1

Source: OECD (1997, p. 36, Table 20).

identified in Table 1 are paying the maximum marginal rate. Twice the income of a standard production worker may still be too low to put individuals or households into the highest tax bracket in some countries (e.g., the United States). This evidence on the taxation of labour income is thus somewhat inconclusive. The other thing we do not yet know is whether the tax differentials that exist are affecting factor flows. Data on marginal tax rates cannot tell us whether people (and which people) are actually moving in response to tax rate differentials. We will have to await the results of a number of studies underway on the "brain drain"; the current evidence is largely anecdotal.

While the results for high-income people are somewhat inconclusive, Table 1 indicates that marginal tax rates for low-income people (single or couples) have risen since 1978. The averages have increased from 32.6 to 38.4% for singles and 27.8 to 38.4% for couples. Rates on low-income earners have also diverged over the period, though very slightly so for single households. Low-income people are likely to be much less mobile than those with high incomes due to lower education and skill levels. These trends support the hypothesis that with globalization, less mobile labour will face higher marginal tax rates.[3]

Table 2 offers some evidence that the tax burden on middle-income workers in the G7 countries has risen. A tax wedge — the difference between the cost of the worker to the employer and the consumption that persons are able to support on their income — is calculated for an average production worker for 1978 and 1994. While the average tax wedge has changed little over the period, falling in the United States and Norway, it has risen in all other G7 countries. The standard deviation also has risen.

Figure 1 provides some evidence that payroll tax burdens have increased for employees relative to those for employers, that is, there is a shifting of the tax towards a less mobile factor input. The panels show the employees' shares of GDP plotted against employers' social security contribution rates in OECD countries for the years 1986 and 1994. The figures indicate that the share of wages in total output is lower in countries with higher employer social security contribution rates. The negative relationship is consistent with

---

[3]The averages hide some diverging moves. Marginal tax rates for single people in the United States fell for all income levels. The UK and U.S. rates for low-income earners fell during 1978-95. It also would be interesting to examine the share of total income tax revenue paid by low-income people for different countries. A recent tax incidence study for Canada is by Vermaeten *et al.* (1995).

Table 2: Overall Tax Wedge,* 1978-1994
Percentage of the Earnings of an Average Production Work (G7 Countries and Mexico)

	1978	1985	1994
Canada	31	37	40
United States	36	37	35
United Kingdom	44	48	44
France	37	40	41
Germany	50	53	59
Italy	51	56	57
Japan	21	26	26
Mexico			34
Average	41	43	42
Standard Deviation	10.6	10.7	11.3

Note: *The difference between the cost to the employer and the consumption
      which can be supported from that wage.
Source: OECD (1996a, p. 53, Table 22).

shifting of the payroll taxes to workers over time (through higher prices of goods and services or lower nominal wages). As many countries have income ceilings on contribution rates for employees, this suggests the impact will be felt least by high-income earners, allegedly the most mobile of labour.

Table 3 presents effective tax rates on consumption for the G7 countries from 1978-88. These rates have been rising gradually over the period, thus supporting the hypothesis that immobile factors are facing higher tax rates. But note that significant divergences in rates persist over the period and the standard deviation is rising, not falling. The United States and Japan have low rates; Canada, the United Kingdom, Italy and Germany are in the middle, and France is at the top of the scale. The evidence on consumption tax rates is thus mixed.

Figure 1: The Wage Share and the Employer Social Security Contribution Rate in OECD Countries*

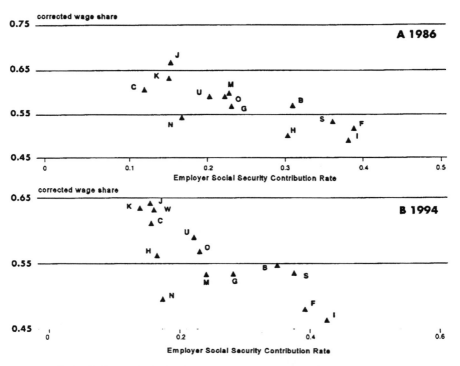

O = Austria J = Japan B = Belgium H = Netherlands C = Canada N = Norway M = Finland S = Sweden
F = France K = United Kingdom G = Germany U = United States I = Italy W = Switzerland (1994 only)

Note: * The wage share is the ratio of wages and salaries to GDP divided by the ratio of dependent (employee) employment to total employment. The employer social security contribution is the ratio of total employer compulsory social security contributions and voluntary pension contributions to total wages and salaries.

Source: OECD (1990, p. 158, Chart 6.3), as cited in TCBT (1998, p. 3.16, Chart 3B). Data updated by TCBT Committee Secretariat.

Nancy Olewiler

Table 3: Consumption Tax Rates, 1965-1988
      (G7 Countries)

G7 Country	1965	1970	1975	1980	1985	1988
Canada	12.8	12.6	11.0	10.5	12.2	13.1
United States	6.4	6.4	5.8	5.4	5.5	5.2
United Kingdom	13.2	15.1	12.1	15.1	17.8	16.9
France				22.2	21.6	21.4
Germany	15.9	17.3	14.6	15.9	14.9	14.7
Italy		13.3	10.8	11.6	11.8	14.3
Japan	5.7	5.8	4.3	4.8	5.2	5.3
Average	10.8	11.8	9.8	12.2	12.7	13.0
Standard Deviation	5.1	5.3	5.5	5.7	5.8	5.9

Source: Mendoza, *et al.* (1994, p. 306, Table 1).

Business Taxation and Capital Flight

This is a complex topic. Capital comes in a variety of forms from very mobile portfolio capital to foreign direct investment to relatively immobile fixed capital assets. It is the former that is of most concern, but note that all capital ultimately becomes mobile as fixed capital depreciates over time either physically or through technological obsolescence. Complexity in analyzing the impact of business taxation is compounded by the ability of firms to change their tax liability through, for example, transfer pricing, foreign affiliate designations and financing methods.

Governments, especially at the federal level, have a wide range of tax policies that influence business investment and location. These include: the statutory corporate income tax rate (or rates), tax incentives (e.g., accelerated depreciation allowances, R&D tax credits, tax holidays), the treatment of losses, what is included in the tax base, withholding rates on payments to non-residents, how double taxation is alleviated, international tax treaties (e.g., sourcing rules, deferral arrangements, branch arrangements), and the administration of taxes — tax complexity and compliance costs. It is beyond the scope of this paper to examine each of these policy variables.[4] Evidence on the potential for capital flight focuses on an examination of marginal effective tax rates across different inputs. Globalization should lead to equal marginal effective tax rates across the most mobile assets.[5]

Capital taxation should be the most harmonized type of tax in a globalizing world. Some even argue it should (or will) be eliminated because it tries to tax the most mobile factor input. The data suggest that capital tax rates have not converged in developed economies. Explanations for why not include the persistence of institutional and regulatory barriers to the flow of financial capital (financial institutional regulation), and high transactions costs in the form of complying with very complex tax legislation in every country in which one does business.

Table 4 provides the statutory maximum corporate tax rates for the G7 countries for 1983, 1990 and 1997. Rates have fluctuated since 1983. From 1983 to 1990, they fell on average approximately five percentage points, but by 1997, they had risen again by the same amount. The standard deviation rose over the period, indicating greater, not less variability in the maximum rates across countries. This is evident from looking at individual countries. Canada's maximum rates are below those of Germany, Italy and Japan, but above those of the United States, United Kingdom and Mexico. This evidence does not support hypotheses of rate reductions and convergence for corporate income taxes in the G7 countries.

As noted above, corporate tax rates may not be that meaningful an indicator for several reasons. Statutory rates are generally not the company's effective rate. Corporate income taxation is complex; rates vary by sector (e.g., in Canada, manufacturing and processing face lower statutory rates than transportation and communications industries). Tax expenditures (R&D, resource allowances, accelerated depreciation) lower effective rates. A better measure is the effective marginal tax rate. Effective tax rates for

---

[4]There is a large literature examining the impact of various tax policies on investment. See, for example, Cummins *et al.* (1995), Brean *et al.* (1991), Lyon (1996), Cummins (1996), Mendoza *et al.* (1994), Feldstein *et al.* (1995), Tanzi (1995), and Gentry and Hubbard (1998) for recent contributions.

[5]This is also known as capital export neutrality.

Table 4: Maximum Corporate Income Tax Rates
(G7 Countries and Mexico)

Country	1983	1990	1997
Canada*	44.9 - 52.9	35.3 - 45.8	38.1 - 46.1
United States*	48.7 - 51.4	34.0 - 41.9	35.0 - 42.5
United Kingdom	52	35	31
France	50	37.0**	41.6
Germany	56.0**	50.0**	57.4**
Italy	38.8	46.4	53.2
Japan	53	52	51.6
Mexico			34
Average	49 - 51	41 - 44	49 - 51
Standard Deviation	5.7 - 5.5	7.8 - 6.4	10 - 9.3

Notes: *Rates vary by province or state.
   **Tax rates on retained earnings. Rates on profits distributed to stock-holders are lower in all cases except France, in 1990, when the rate of dividends was higher (42%) compared to the rate of 37% on undistributed profits.
Source: TCBT (1998, p. 2.16, Table 2.5).

1995 are shown for manufacturing industries for the G7 plus Mexico in Figure 2. Canada's rate is in the middle, above that of the United States, United Kingdom and Mexico. Table 5 has a more detailed breakdown of effective tax rates on factor inputs for Canada and the United States. The United States has lower effective rates in virtually every category. Therefore, while the economies of Canada and the United States are closely linked, a substantial divergence of effective marginal tax rates exists. I do not have data to investigate whether the divergence in marginal effective rates has changed over time. But we are now almost ten years into a Free Trade Agreement (FTA) with the United States, and one might have expected greater convergence in tax rates between our two countries.

Figure 2: Effective Tax Rates on Marginal Investments for Manufacturing, G7 Countries plus Mexico (1995)

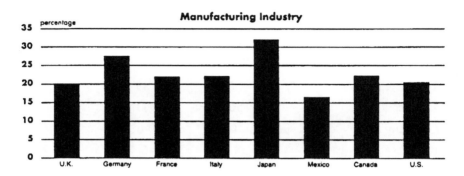

Notes: Effective tax rates reflect income and capital taxes on investment in tangible capital for large firms. The effective tax rates are calculated relative to gross-of-tax rates of return on capital.

Sources: Calculations by the TCBT Committee Secretariat with the technical assistance of the Department of Finance, Canada, and Ken McKenzie, as cited in TCBT (1998, p. 3.12, Chart 3A).

From the data above, considerable variation in tax rates on capital remains in the OECD. While the trend is generally towards declining statutory rates, some countries continue to move in the other direction. The available evidence does not suggest a trend towards convergence of tax rates.

The Tax Mix: An Increasing Burden of Taxation on Immobile Factors?

The second hypothesis is that the tax mix — the share of each tax in total tax revenue — should be shifting towards relatively higher taxes on less mobile factor inputs. I examine this for Canada, the United States, OECD countries

                                                             Nancy Olewiler

Table 5: Canada - United States Effective Tax Rate on Costs for Large Business (1996)

	Canada			United States		
	Labour	Capital	Total	Labour	Capital	Total
Forestry	-5.2	45.4	0.9	0.1	25.4	3.5
Mining	2.7	13.3	5.7	-0.3	1.9	0.4
Oil and Gas	1.4	8	4.5	-0.3	3.9	1.9
Manufacturing	3.2	27	8.8	-0.5	22.5	5.2
Construction	-0.6	59.9	5.5	-0.6	30.1	2.8
Transportation	3.2	39.5	8.3	0.4	14.3	2.5
Communications	4.4	35.2	15.4	0.4	8.3	3.4
Public Utilities	4.5	44.4	26.9	0.4	17.8	10.5
Wholesale Trade	3.6	51.7	10.4	0.3	28.6	4.5
Retail Trade	3	53	7.5	0.5	27.6	3.1
Other Services	2.7	39.5	9.7	0.4	26.1	5.5
Total	**2.8**	**33.3**	**9.4**	**0.2**	**22.7**	**5.2**

Note: Effective tax rates are expressed relative to costs excluding taxes. Excludes financial sector.
Source: TCBT (1998, p. 3.11, Table 3.5).

as a whole, and the countries in the European Union (EU). Table 6 presents tax revenues over the past 20 years for the personal income tax (PIT), corporate income tax (CIT), social security taxes (includes employment and social insurance), property taxes and goods and services taxes (all excise and value-added taxes) as a percentage of total tax revenue. Globalization should increase the shares of taxes applied to less mobile factor inputs relative to the more mobile factor inputs. These numbers are aggregates and therefore cannot differentiate between mobility within a tax class. As proxies then, the

Table 6: Taxes Collected as a Percentage of Total Tax Revenue (1975-1996)

	Canada					United States				
	1975	1980	1985	1990	1996	1975	1980	1985	1990	1996
PIT	32.8	34.1	35.2	41.0	37.7	34.6	39.1	37.8	37.7	37.6
CIT	13.6	11.6	8.2	7.0	8.9	11.4	10.8	7.5	7.7	9.6
Social Security	10.0	10.5	13.5	14.3	16.3	20.5	21.9	25.2	25.8	24.7
Property	9.5	9.1	9.3	10.0	10.4	13.9	10.7	10.7	11.4	11.0
Goods & Services	32.0	32.6	31.8	25.9	24.9	19.5	17.6	18.8	17.3	17.2
PIT + CIT	46.4	45.7	43.4	48.0	46.6	46.0	49.9	45.3	45.4	47.2
Sum of Others	51.5	52.5	54.6	50.2	51.6	53.9	50.2	54.7	54.5	52.9

	European Union					OECD				
PIT	28.6	28.1	28.1	27.2	26.0	30.0	31.3	29.8	29.4	26.8
CIT	6.0	5.8	6.3	6.8	7.5	7.5	7.6	7.9	7.9	8.2
Social Security	28.4	29.0	28.7	28.2	28.9	22.1	22.3	22.4	22.8	25.1
Property	4.9	4.1	3.8	4.2	4.4	6.2	5.2	5.1	5.6	5.4
Goods & Services	31.3	31.0	31.6	31.6	31.2	32.6	32.3	33.5	31.9	32.5
PIT + CIT	34.6	34.9	34.4	34.0	33.5	37.5	38.9	37.7	37.3	35.0
Sum of Others	64.6	64.1	64.1	64.0	64.5	60.9	59.8	61.0	60.3	63.0

Source: OECD (1998).

PIT and CIT are taxes on mobile factors, while social security, property and goods and services taxes are on less mobile factors.

Looking at the "mobile" category, we see a slight downward trend in their share of total tax revenue for the European Union and the OECD as a whole. Canada and the United States follow a cyclical pattern, with the shares falling from 1975 to 1985, then rising again in 1990 and 1996. Canada's 1996 shares are back to their 1975 level, while those in the United

Nancy Olewiler

States exceed their 1975 level. The CIT and PIT are income-sensitive taxes. Business cycles are probably as (if not more) important than changes in tax policy over this period. While the CIT and PIT shares fluctuate for Canada and the United States, the trend is basically downward for the CIT and upward for the PIT. Recall from Table 1 that marginal tax rates have gone up for all income levels in Canada, while in the United States, they have fallen for all but the low- and middle-income couples. PIT rates in these two countries have (recall Table 2) declined since the early 1980s. If the PIT is seen primarily as a tax on immobile labour, the share of total taxes paid by immobile inputs rose in Canada and the United States, fell in the EU, and remained constant over the entire OECD. Thus, there is no conclusive evidence that globalization significantly alters the tax mix. However, these numbers suggest that tax mixes are similar in regions where a country's economies are integrated. The aggregate tax shares in Canada and the United States have been similar over the time period shown.

Tax Revenues as a Percentage of GDP

The final hypothesis is that globalization can lead to tax competition. If so, governments will lower tax rates on mobile factor inputs to attract them to their country (or region). This can lead to the "race to the bottom". I have already presented evidence on tax rates in Tables 1 and 2 for labour and business income. Tax rates on corporations in the G7 have changed very little, while the maximum marginal rate for individuals has declined.

If tax competition is occurring, we might expect to see an increase in tax revenues as a percentage of GDP for taxes on less mobile factor inputs, as governments have to depend more on these taxes to raise tax revenue. If tax competition is particularly fierce, then tax revenues as a whole may be declining if governments reduce their size in response to globalization. Table 7 presents data on tax revenues as a percentage of GDP for Canada, the United States, the European Union and the total OECD. First note that total tax revenues have risen as a share of GDP. There is no evidence that globalization is making governments reduce taxes as a share of GDP. The data also suggest that globalization is only modestly shifting the tax mix towards less mobile factor inputs. The sum of PIT plus CIT shares have risen, but at a lower rate than that of the tax shares of less mobile bases for the European Union and the OECD as a whole. In Canada, taxes on both bases have risen equivalently, while in the United States, the shares on

Table 7: Taxes Collected as a Percentage of GDP (1975-1996)

	Canada					United States				
	1975	1980	1985	1990	1996	1975	1980	1985	1990	1996
PIT	10.9	10.9	11.7	14.7	13.9	9.3	10.5	9.9	10.1	10.7
CIT	4.5	3.7	2.7	2.5	3.3	3.0	2.9	2.0	2.1	2.7
Social Security	3.3	3.4	4.5	5.2	6.0	5.5	5.9	6.6	6.9	7.0
Property	3.1	2.9	3.1	3.6	3.8	3.7	2.9	2.8	3.0	3.1
Goods & Services	10.6	10.4	10.5	9.3	9.1	5.2	4.7	4.9	4.6	4.9
PIT + CIT	15.4	14.6	14.4	17.2	17.2	12.3	13.4	11.9	12.2	13.4
Sum of Others	17.0	16.7	18.1	18.1	18.9	14.4	13.5	14.3	14.5	15.0
Total	**32.4**	**31.3**	**32.5**	**35.3**	**36.1**	**26.7**	**26.9**	**26.2**	**26.7**	**28.4**
	European Countries					OECD				
PIT	10.7	11.4	11.2	11.5	11.3	10.0	10.8	10.8	11.0	10.4
CIT	2.1	2.2	2.6	2.7	3.1	2.3	2.5	2.8	2.8	3.1
Social Security	9.3	10.6	11.4	11.5	12.2	7.0	7.7	8.2	8.6	9.8
Property	1.6	1.5	1.5	1.7	1.8	1.8	1.6	1.7	1.9	1.9
Goods & Services	10.5	11.3	12.5	12.8	13.0	9.9	10.3	11.2	11.2	12.0
PIT + CIT	12.8	13.6	13.8	14.2	14.4	12.3	13.3	13.6	13.8	13.5
Sum of Others	21.4	23.4	25.4	26.0	27.0	18.7	19.6	21.1	21.7	23.7
Total	**34.2**	**37.0**	**39.2**	**40.2**	**41.4**	**31.0**	**32.9**	**34.7**	**35.5**	**37.2**

Source: OECD (1998).

mobile factors have risen more rapidly than those on fixed factors. Shares for the CIT taken alone have fallen in Canada and the United States, but increased in the European Union and OECD. Shares for the PIT and social security taxes have risen for each country, the EU and OECD. This could be evidence that globalization has shifted taxes to less mobile factors. However, goods and services and property taxes do not show a consistent pattern across the countries. Consumption taxes (in all but the United States) have

Nancy Olewiler

grown in importance over the past 30 years. Many countries now use value-added taxes (VATs), some at fairly high rates. The number of countries having a VAT rose from 9 in 1960 to 28 in the 1970s, 48 in the 1980s, and by the mid-1990s numbered over 90 (Tanzi, 1995, p. 46). Overall, the evidence is therefore inconclusive. Tax competition does not appear to be driving down tax revenues as a share of GDP, but tax mixes have changed for some countries/regions. The data suggest the tax burden on immobile factor inputs has risen relative to that on mobile factor inputs. Globalization may therefore be affecting who pays the tax, but thus far has not greatly affected the size of government tax revenues relative to total output in the economy.

The differences among countries can obviously stem from very different domestic conditions with respect to debt and deficits (and policy targets for them), economic growth and a host of other non-tax factors. Figure 3 shows a major divergence in the relationship between taxation and government expenditure for OECD countries. Cumulative changes in tax revenues for Canada from 1990 to 1998 have risen, but primary government expenditure has fallen. The rest of the OECD is all "all over the map". One can infer that pressure to raise tax revenue will vary considerably across the OECD. This is one reason why we might expect divergence in tax rates to continue despite pressures from globalization.

Globalization and the Canadian Tax System

Data from the previous section paints an equivocal picture about the effects of globalization on taxation in OECD countries. Tax rates have not converged, but taxes on immobile factors appear to be rising relative to those on mobile factors. I turn now to a more detailed look at globalization and taxes in Canada, and look particularly at our taxes relative to those of the United States.

The last section presented the following picture of Canadian taxes compared to other OECD countries.

- A total tax/GDP ratio below the EU and OECD average, but higher than the United States.
- Higher personal income taxes than the others.

Figure 3: Changes in Tax Revenues and Primary Government Spending
(Projected Cumulative Changes between 1990 and 1998 as a Percentage of GDP)

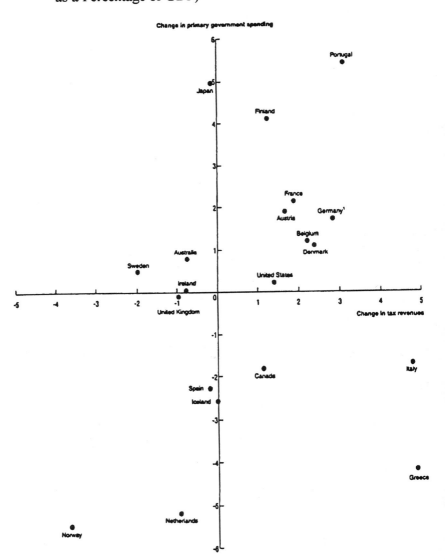

Source: OECD (1996b, p. 13, Figure 4).

Nancy Olewiler

- A corporate income tax a bit higher than the others relative to GDP, but with much higher marginal effective tax rates on labour and capital than those in the United States.
- Higher goods and services taxes than the United States and Japan, but lower than the others.
- Lower payroll taxes than most countries.

In terms of their shares of tax revenues, Canada and the United States are similar with respect to taxes on relatively mobile versus immobile factors. Canada and the United States have a significantly higher share of their tax revenues coming from the PIT plus CIT (and thus a lower share from the remaining taxes) than do the EU and the OECD as a whole. What does all this imply for tax reform in Canada? In this section, I consider the implications for tax reform of personal, business, payroll and consumption taxes in Canada.[6] What taxes should be changed and how? The general prescription is for reductions in marginal tax rates on the most mobile inputs, combined with base broadening on the business tax side and modest increases in payroll and consumption taxes.[7] I do not view these as revenue-neutral changes. The overall level of taxes should be reduced. As our

---

[6]It is beyond the scope of this paper to examine other complexities of the tax system, such as the intricacies of international taxation. See the *Report of the Technical Committee on Business Taxation* (1998) for a detailed examination of tax reform in this area. In addition, there are other tax instruments available to governments — for example, user fees and property taxes. Discussion of all these taxes is beyond the scope of this paper. However, some general principles can be noted: user fees should be linked to benefits received. There is considerable scope for increasing these fees to cover damages to the environment, better pricing of water use, congestion of urban roads, etc. Property taxes do represent a tax on a fixed factor. As such, they could be a target for higher levies in a globalizing world. However, property taxes are linked to local public services, so any increase should, in principle, be connected to funding of these public activities. Health-care financing is another important item for reform.

[7]Another way to state these principles of tax reform is to minimize the marginal efficiency costs of the tax. While there is debate over the measurement of marginal efficiency costs, most studies rank the taxes in ascending order of marginal efficiency costs as: property, sales, payroll, corporate income, personal income, all capital income and capital income in the personal income tax. See, for example, Jorgensen and Yun (1991).

economy continues to grow, there is room to bring tax rates down without greatly affecting total taxes as a percent of GDP.[8] If economic growth does not occur and cuts to tax rates are not offset by base broadening, tax revenues will decline. This will make it more difficult for Canada to provide important social goods in an era of balanced budgets. Governments would then have to look for ways of providing essential public goods and services more efficiently and scale back their activities that have a dubious connection to economic and social well-being.

Personal Income Taxes

Maximum marginal tax rates on personal income have to come down if Canada is to retain its most mobile people.[9] The minister of finance has said so, and even British Columbia is beginning to phase in a reduction of high-income surtaxes. Ontario has started the process of cutting marginal tax rates (but has kept its surtaxes). Alberta has recently announced major cuts to its PIT. Marginal tax rates on personal income are so significantly above those in the United States for middle- and upper-income couples that there is widespread feeling that we will lose mobile workers to the United States and other lower-tax jurisdictions such as the United Kingdom. The fact that we cannot yet tell if this has happened should not be comforting. Recall that our maximum marginal rate applies at just over $59,000. A married person in the United States earning an equivalent (in purchasing power parity terms) income faces a marginal tax rate of 28%. American taxpayers also have more exemptions and deductions than their Canadian counterparts, which include exemptions for dependants, mortgage interest deductibility, and standard or itemized deductions.

---

[8]See Wilson *et al.* (1998) for calculations of the "room for tax cuts".

[9]Other changes to the personal income tax such as indexation of the tax brackets will reduce taxes for low- and middle-income taxpayers, as well as high-income earners. Marginal tax rates are, of course, not the only factor that affects mobility of labour. Individuals will look at net fiscal incidence — their total taxes versus government expenditure programs that affect them, community variables, and so on.

If maximum marginal rates do come down, PIT revenues will decline and taxes on other income levels will have to rise.[10] However, reducing the maximum marginal tax rate might not lead to as significant a reduction in tax revenue as imagined. After the major tax reform of 1986 in the United States, reported income of those at high-income levels rose, at least for a short period of time. This was due to changes in capital gains taxation as well as the very large reduction in the maximum marginal tax rate (from 50 to 28%).[11] Second, notwithstanding the gloomy news about economic activity in the short run, forecasted economic growth will generate more income, which leads to more tax revenue. In other words, there will be tax room created if the Canadian economy continues to grow. Tax revenue losses due to rate reductions can be offset if the tax base is broadened. I am not convinced that there is much scope for base broadening of the PIT, although others might disagree (see Ruggeri and Vincent, 1998). Reducing tax expenditures such as retirement savings plans would be counterproductive from the viewpoint of keeping the most mobile people (and their capital) in Canada.

High marginal tax rates also create an incentive to evade taxation even if one doesn't emigrate. Trade and other agreements give individuals more freedom to work in foreign countries for short periods of time. People can also work for foreign entities without leaving their residence because of electronic commerce and the other technological changes in communications. Self-employed individuals find it easier to evade taxes than salaried workers, and more Canadians are now self-employed than in the past. From 1976 to 1996, the number of self-employed people relative to total private sector

---

[10]There are many ways to lower effective tax rates in Canada. In addition to reducing the tax rates, the federal government could adjust the brackets, for example, apply the maximum marginal rate at a higher income level. For more discussion of these options, see Kesselman (1998); and Davies (1998a, b).

[11]See Auerbach and Slemrod (1997). The reduction in the maximum marginal rate to 28% lasted for four years, although people did not know at the time that the reduction was "temporary". The statutory rate was subsequently increased to 39.6%. Effective marginal tax rates are higher than that because at high-income levels (recall these are significantly higher income levels than those at which the maximum marginal rate applies in Canada), a taxpayer loses personal exemptions and itemized deductions. The United States thus lowered rates and broadened the base.

National Tax Policy for an International Economy   *367*

employment has risen from under 14 to over 19% (TCBT, 1998, p. 3.19). This change is due to a number of factors, including labour shedding and outsourcing of business services begun in the last recession.

Business Taxes

Globalization suggests that a small open economy should not impose a source-based tax such as Canada's corporate income tax (CIT) on capital income.[12] If capital is mobile and the country is a price-taker in world capital markets, capital will not bear the incidence of the tax. Firms will continue to locate in the country only if the return to other factor inputs (presumably labour and land) declines enough to compensate firms for the larger amount of before-tax income they have to earn to be able to offer the owners of capital the world rate of return after tax. If this is the case, why not simply tax the immobile factor inputs directly and therefore eliminate the distortion introduced by the tax on capital?

As we saw in the second section, all OECD countries have corporate income taxes with non-zero rates that in some cases are close to the maximum marginal tax rate for individuals. So why is there the gap between theory and reality? First, not all capital is highly mobile. Second, mobile capital may not actually pay the statutory rates. Multinational enterprises, for example, use transfer pricing to minimize their tax liability. Companies with subsidiaries can also arrange their financing to record deductions from taxable income in high-tax countries and declare their profits in low-tax countries. The higher a country's marginal tax rates, the greater the incentives to minimize tax liability by these and other means. One of the negative side effects of globalization is the increased complexity of tax systems as governments respond to these income-shifting strategies with tax legislation. This in turn leads to greater incentive to engage in tax planning to get around the new rules. Convergence of CIT rates will help reduce these non-productive activities.

Corporate income taxation is also necessary to minimize opportunities for individuals to shift their labour income to an otherwise untaxed corporate base. If there were no CIT, the owners of closely held firms would not take

---

[12]See Gordon and MacKie-Mason (1995); and the TCBT (1998) for further discussion of the issues raised in this section.

wages from the firm. They would put the firm's (their) income into retained earnings, sell their shares in the corporation, then pay capital gains tax on the return. As capital gains are taxed preferentially in Canada, and were in the United States, the person ends up paying a rate lower than their personal tax rate. Even if capital gains are taxed at a rate identical to that of personal income, individuals can use their business income to defer taxation as long as their earnings are retained in the company.[13] The existence of a CIT would help to eliminate this as it serves as a backstop for the PIT. If personal and corporate taxes were fully integrated, the tax rates facing the owner/wage earner would be the same. In Canada, integration occurs approximately for small businesses via the dividend tax credit. Integration of the personal and corporate taxes would also minimize double taxation of income.

Corporate income taxes are thus seen as necessary even in a global economy. But there is definitely pressure to have rates across countries converge to a lower level. One of the key recommendations of the Technical Committee on Business Taxation for Canada was to lower the statutory CIT rate. Our maximum corporate rate is above that of the United States for most non-manufacturing industries, and well above Mexico's and the United Kingdom's (see Table 4). From Table 5, recall that the effective tax rates on capital are higher in Canada than in the United States for all industries. The divergences between Canadian and U.S. rates create an incentive for capital and profits to leave Canada and for companies to deduct expenses in Canada while declaring profits in the United States. This erodes Canadian tax bases.

Rate reductions, however, are just one part of corporate tax reform. There are many non-neutralities (or inequities) in Canadian business taxes.[14] Taxes on income from capital vary substantially across industries. Businesses in the service sector face marginal effective tax rates that are much higher than those in the primary sectors and manufacturing. Figure 4 shows these rates by industry. Tax expenditures such as accelerated depreciation

---

[13]Having a CIT also ensures that non-resident and tax-exempt owners of the corporation pay some tax. These owners benefit to some extent from publicly-provided programs, and the CIT allows them to pay for a share of these costs. Corporate income taxes in Canada are also credited against foreign taxes in countries such as the United States, United Kingdom and Japan. If there were no CIT, a transfer of revenue from Canadian governments to foreign governments would result.

[14]See the TCBT (1998) for a detailed discussion of these issues.

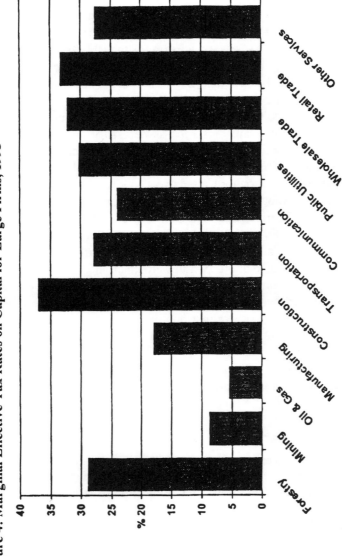

Figure 4: Marginal Effective Tax Rates on Capital for Large Firms, 1995

Note: Effective tax rates covers federal and provincial corporate income taxes, corporate taxes, and sales taxes on capital purchase.

Source: TCBT (1998), estimates prepared for the committee.

Nancy Olewiler

allowances and research and development tax credits vary in their impact across industries, favouring certain industries over others.[15] Provincial governments have a number of regional and activity-based investment tax credits. All of these non-neutralities have economic costs: lost output, high compliance costs, and misallocation of resources. The good news is that reducing these non-neutralities will broaden the tax base and help alleviate the impact on government revenues of any reductions in CIT rates.

Unfortunately, globalization pressures may make it difficult to engage in tax reforms that broaden the base. Industries complain about government intervention when it is in the form of taxation, but are generally quite mute when it comes to tax expenditures that give them preferential treatment. Everyone wants a rate reduction, but no one wants to pay the bill in the form of elimination of non-neutralities. All levels of government may find it difficult to avoid succumbing to industry pressure to let their preferential treatment persist. Tax revenues as a share of GDP could then fall if economic growth does not make up the difference.

Consumption Taxes

Value-added taxes (VATs) are thought by most economists to be an ideal tax on consumption in a globalizing world. They guarantee a country independence in setting its tax rates because the tax is based on the destination principle — where the good is consumed, not produced. Imports are taxed, exports are not. VATs are thus highly compatible with trade liberalization and trade agreements. Savings and investment decisions are not distorted, and economic growth is not dampened. They can also raise a tremendous amount of revenue. As noted above, the number of countries using VATs has increased ten-fold since the 1960s. Canada has the Goods and Services Tax (GST) as well as provincial sales taxes. Will globalization put pressure on us to shift more of our tax base to consumption and away from income and profits?

---

[15]If employment insurance benefits also are included in these calculations, marginal effective tax rates for Canada's primary sectors, construction and transportation would be much lower than shown in Figure 4.

Much has been written on the theoretical and practical aspects of substituting consumption taxes for income taxes.[16] While there may be many benefits of doing so, the basic problem may be: "We can't get there from here." Unless the United States undertakes similar tax reforms, we will not be able to raise consumption taxes here by any appreciable amount. Looking first at consumption-based taxes on individuals, note that from Tables 6 and 7 that the United States has significantly lower goods and services taxes as a percent of total revenues and GDP than Canada. They do not have a VAT. Their sales taxes are at the state level, with some states levying no sales tax. The tax differential within U.S. states and between Canada and the United States generates "cross-border shopping". This puts a limit on the extent to which our GST can be raised.[17] Tax evasion, already a problem with the GST, will intensify. Consumers are very intolerant of sales taxes, in part because they are so visible. Income-distribution problems would also intensify. A major shift to consumption-based taxes could only be done for Canada by coordinating this change with the United States.

A consumption-like tax could also be applied to business, as a replacement for the corporate income tax or an add-on tax imposed if CIT rates were lowered substantially. This sort of tax has a variety of names, including the flat tax and the cash-flow tax. The tax base of the cash-flow tax is gross income minus expenditures on all inputs (including investment in depreciable assets). Thus, compared to the CIT, financial income and expenses are not included in the tax base. Interest is not deductible and capital is expensed, not depreciated. When an asset is sold, its full value is taxed. Under the CIT, only the capital gain (or loss) is added to (or subtracted from) income. The tax base under a cash-flow tax could be larger or smaller than that of the CIT. The cash-flow tax is thus similar to the GST because both exclude financial income and interest deductions and the GST tax base is revenues net of costs of current and capital purchases from other businesses. The two taxes are similar because both have to define financial transactions. Financial transactions are typically excluded under most proposals for cash-flow taxes, and would have to be taxed in some other way. There are, however, differences between a VAT and cash-flow tax. As noted above, the GST is

---

[16]See, for example, Grubert and Newlon (1995); McLure (1992); Musgrave (1992); Milesi-Ferretti and Roubini (1998).

[17]Recall the cigarette tax episode in eastern Canada.

Nancy Olewiler

a destination-based tax, while most proposed cash-flow taxes are origin-based. Export revenues are taxed, while the costs of imports are deducted from the tax base. The tax applies to the return on business activities regardless of where the goods produced are consumed.

The Technical Committee on Business Taxation (1998) considered whether a cash-flow tax could be substituted for Canada's CIT. A potential cash-flow tax base was compared to the CIT base by industry using 1993 data. The tax base under the cash-flow tax is likely to be smaller than that of the CIT, although more revenue would be raised from certain industries (manufacturing, transportation, communications and public utilities) than under the existing CIT. The cash-flow tax has many appealing character-istics, but it is unlikely to be introduced without a major change in the whole tax system in Canada and other countries. Substituting a cash-flow tax for the CIT, but retaining the PIT is a bad idea because the tax bases would be very different. Individuals could, for example, avoid personal taxes on finan-cial income by shifting those assets to a corporation they own. Inefficiency and inequities would result. The cash-flow tax is also not consistent with income taxes used by the United States and other countries. A multinational enterprise could finance capital in Canada with foreign debt, expense the capital in Canada, then deduct interest expenses on the foreign borrowings in another country. This could certainly help attract business to Canada, but would also receive a very cold reception from other countries. The cash-flow tax would also encounter difficulties under the current U.S. foreign tax rules. It is not likely to be treated as a creditable tax (corporate income taxes are). For a tax to qualify for crediting, gross income must be subject to tax and costs must be deducted. The cash-flow tax does not do this. Thus, a U.S. multinational operating in Canada would be allowed to deduct the cash-flow taxes paid in Canada, but not take them as a tax credit. This would increase their tax liability and discourage investment in Canada. Finally, the transition to a cash-flow tax would require complex arrangements. Unless there is a major move to adopt cash-flow taxes in the United States and elsewhere, Canada would find it extremely difficult to proceed on its own.

Payroll Taxes

The last major tax considered is the payroll tax. Payroll taxes in Canada have been used to finance social security programs, health care (in some provinces), and employment insurance.[18] Federally, both employees and employers contribute to these taxes. As noted above, our payroll taxes are lower than those of most G7 countries and the OECD as a whole. Are they a candidate for rate increases?[19] Unless benefits from social programs are expected to change beyond the current plans for social security taxation, there is no economic rationale for increasing these taxes if they are to remain insurance taxes. However, the employee's portion is a candidate for higher rates on the grounds that increasing this rate would not significantly affect the most mobile people unless the ceiling on payments was raised considerably. The burden would fall most heavily on lower income people. As Tables 6 and 7 indicate, Canadian payroll taxes are low relative to the United States, EU and the OECD as a whole.

The economics literature takes the general view that payroll taxes on employers are shifted back in the long run to labour in the form of lower after-tax earnings. In the short run, they may in part be borne by capital in the form of higher costs of labour. It may take several years for labour markets to fully adjust to an increase in the employer's portion of the tax due to multi-year wage contracts. If the tax is shifted to labour, an increase in the employer's portion may not inhibit mobile capital from flowing into Canada, or create incentives for mobile labour to leave the country. However, certain labour markets may have characteristics that dampen the shift of the employer's portion back to labour. Examples include strong unions that can prevent firms from reducing wage rates and the inability of employers to cut the wages of workers at provincially mandated minimum wages. Finally, recall that in Canada (and elsewhere) the self-employed are an increasing share of the labour force. They only make contributions for their pensions, not employment insurance. An increase in employer payroll taxes will not raise as much revenue if employers respond by increasing the amount of work they contract out to self-employed people. Following the principle of

---

[18]Lately, the link between EI premiums and expected benefits has become tenuous as far more is being collected in revenue then expected to be paid out in benefits. The EI tax is now serving more as a general source of revenue. The recent announcement of reductions in EI premiums are unlikely to have any impact on the most mobile workers due to the modest extent of the reduction and the ceiling on insurable earnings.

[19]See Kesselman (1997) for an extensive discussion of payroll taxes and their reform.

taxing the least mobile factors (and ignoring the requirement to balance EI premiums with payouts over the business cycle), it would appear that there is scope for modest increases in payroll taxes on employees if one needed to raise revenue to offset reductions in other taxes.[20]

Tax Reform for Canada?

Economists view efficiency and neutrality as major goals of tax reform whether the economy is operating in autarky or in a globalizing world. These goals typically require a reduction in the disparity between tax rates across different classes of assets and types of investment, the tax base to be broadened, and marginal tax rates on mobile factor inputs reduced. These policy goals are just as important within a country as between countries. Tax reform could improve the efficiency and equity of our economy. Aggregate measures of economic welfare would rise. Some people would, of course, be hurt. It is not possible to undertake tax reform without creating winners and losers. But the aggregate pie would be bigger because the economy's resources would be used more efficiently. This would allow some redistribution of income to those made worse off by tax reform.

In principle, globalization does not change any of the fundamentals of tax reform. These are still good ideas. However, if we do not undertake these sorts of tax reform and other countries do, globalization will impose changes on our economy and our tax system that we may have been able to prevent. If mobile factors flee because our tax rates exceed those of other developed countries, the tax base will decline and the tax burden on remaining factors must rise or tax revenues will fall. There will still be losers. If mobile inputs flee, the ability of the economy to generate growing output and incomes may be threatened. If we ignore the forces of globalization and do not alter our tax structures, we will have fewer choices in the future about the type of country

---

[20]The Technical Committee on Business Taxation (1998) recommended that partial experience rating be incorporated into the employer's portion of the payroll tax to enhance the efficiency and fairness of the EI system. As the EI account now has a large surplus, and to phase this in so that no company pays a rate above the current level, a company's premiums would then either remain constant or fall, depending on their employment experience.

we want to have. If we do nothing, it will be harder for the Canadian economy to prosper.

What are the prospects for undertaking tax reform in Canada? The confounding issues are:

- The federal and provincial governments may have very different, and conflicting, agendas.
- We cannot rule out a race to the bottom within Canada.
- Interest groups for corporations and individuals may thwart tax reform.
- Income inequality may rise.
- We cannot count on cooperation from the United States.

I look at each of these briefly.

Any tax reform in Canada requires at least some degree of coordination and cooperation between the federal and provincial governments. In a globalizing world it is even more important than before to have a united front within the country. This means more harmonization of taxes and tax bases, less variation in tax rates across the country, and mitigation of tax changes that affect the tax bases of other jurisdictions. We have co-existed with differing tax rates across the country for years. Capital and labour flow fairly freely across provincial borders. Not everyone lives in Alberta (but capital and labour are leaving British Columbia). Why push for greater coordination and harmonization now? There are many reasons, including: reducing the costs of doing business in Canada and making it more desirable for investment, improving efficiency by reducing distortions introduced by the tax system, reducing the complexity of the tax system and minimizing the risk that provinces will engage in competitive reductions in tax rates.

Canadian provincial governments think of themselves as autonomous, able to pursue paths different from others. This is why the tax structure of British Columbia is different from that of Alberta. In a world of increasing factor mobility, it does not make sense to have significantly different taxes and tax burdens across the country. Will globalization be the glue that binds Canada together? I hope so, but I doubt it. Unless there is a recognition and acceptance of the argument that we would have a better chance of staying a wealthy country if tax policy was coordinated and harmonized internally, provinces and the federal government will continue to bicker about long-standing disputes such as equalization, block transfers for social programs, independence over tax bases, and so on. Unless all believe they face a common threat from outside the country, I cannot see any change in behaviour on the part of any level of government. I am not suggesting that the federal/provincial conflicts are trivial squabbling — they represent real issues that require action. But, there has to be a spirit of cooperation among the levels of government that is not generally present in this country. My fear is that globalization will make provincial governments more likely to engage in a destructive race to the bottom. The federal government could make a number of changes on its own. However, given the integration of the federal and provincial tax systems, unilateral changes by the federal government still affect provincial revenues. The provinces in turn can make changes to their tax rates and bases that affect federal tax bases and/or offset the federal actions.[21] Whether threats to alter each other's tax revenues would keep the parties bargaining constructively is anyone's guess.

Base-broadening measures are particularly difficult to initiate. Federal and provincial governments may find it too difficult to withstand the lobbying pressures of those industries made worse off, particularly if they have mobile capital. A number of the sectors adversely affected by the tax reform discussed are in the primary industries. Their capital is somewhat less mobile than other industries. Will governments succumb to their complaints? Due to the regional concentration of these industries, it will be difficult for governments to impose base-broadening measures that raise effective tax rates for these industries, especially with the resource sectors (forestry, mining, fisheries) facing significant pressures (e.g., lower tax rates abroad, declining markets, declining stocks of the resource). Alternatively, the government could forego base broadening and let income tax revenues from businesses decline or hope for strong economic growth. The trade-off will be between efficiency and neutrality losses (if base broadening does not occur) and political expediency. There would be as well, many winners from a rate reduction and broadening of the CIT. Among these are some of the most mobile sectors of the Canadian economy including communications, wholesale trade, and the traded goods component of the service sector. Tax

---

[21] An example of this is the introduction of capital taxes at the provincial level. These taxes are deductible from the federal CIT and thus have led to an erosion of the federal base and a shift in the tax mix between the federal and provincial governments. The federal government could respond by removing deductibility of provincial capital taxes from the CIT. The TCBT has recommended this action. The provinces do have the credible threat to take up any tax room vacated by the federal government.

reform could be done on the corporate side that would benefit Canada as a whole and strengthen its international competitiveness.

The types of tax reform discussed in this paper will undoubtedly increase tax burdens on less mobile factors — land, fixed capital, and immobile labour. Tax reform may affect adversely the less well off individual in Canada — a troubling prospect, but hard to prevent. Measures such as low-income exemptions (for PIT and GST) would have to be increased. Public debate on tax reform will continue. There will be some who want to "fight globalization" by trying to close our economy's doors. Governments may also find it difficult to withstand pressure from these groups and others representing individuals who are made worse off. Those made worse off may not believe the argument that doing nothing or fighting these changes is not an option.

Many others have advocated that in the face of globalization, we increase our efforts to coordinate tax policies with other countries (see Mintz, 1998). Of course we should do this, and I hope people are correct in believing that globalization will bring us closer to more harmonized and coordinated tax systems, but not necessarily with converging tax rates. Europe certainly seems to be moving in that direction. With U.S. governments preoccupied with internal matters and Congress shifting away (perhaps temporarily) from trade arrangements, Canada may have a long wait to see some tax cooperation with our local neighbours. This is a subject for another paper.

Conclusion

Globalization is having an impact on taxes and tax reform. Tax rates, levels, and the tax mix have changed to a modest extent over the past 20 years. The evidence is mixed — some tax rates have converged, but considerable divergence still exists. The changes are not yet large, but we have no reason to expect that the forces of globalization will not continue unless the economies of the world take a step back from integration due to recent events. But I suspect even that would be short lived. There are and there will continue to be pressures on Canadian governments to adjust their taxes. If we do not manage our own tax reforms, changes will result from the movement of factor inputs in response to international prices and rates. We will find our tax bases affected, quite possibly in ways more destructive than if we plan for and implement tax reforms which make Canada competitive with other countries. But this does not mean that no divergence is possible. The data presented suggest that countries can have different mixes of taxes, different rates, and still retain their mobile inputs. We do not have to look exactly like the United States. Our tax revenues on mobile versus less mobile inputs as a percentage of total tax revenue have been close to those of the United States for the past 20 years, and we have managed to create a different climate in our public sector. What we need to change now are those taxes that affect mobile inputs and to engage in international cooperation on taxation. We cannot afford to wait until the data show us that we have lost labour and capital to other countries.

Where does this leave us? I believe that tax reform for Canada should lower rates for personal income taxes, especially those at the high end of the personal scale. Corporate income tax rates should decline to reduce the divergence between different sectors within Canada and to make our rates competitive with those in the United States, United Kingdom and Mexico. There is considerable scope for base-broadening measures that reduce preferential tax treatments of industries, but less so for individuals. These measures should improve economic efficiency because there will be fewer distortions and greater incentives to work and invest in Canada (and keep one's income, rents and profits here as well). I would make these recommendations even if there were no pressures from globalization. Tax reforms that increase efficiency, decrease distortions, and yet preserve sufficient revenues to supply public goods and services and have some redistribution of income will enhance Canadian growth and quality of life. Globalization may intensify the pressures to make these changes, and could be the catalyst that forces greater harmonization of federal and provincial taxes in Canada. If so, rather than fearing globalization, we should embrace it. This sort of tax reform is welfare enhancing even in a world of autarky. Of course, Canada should also heed the advice of many to cooperate in international tax discussions.

Globalization could lead alternatively to greater tax competition within Canada and between Canada and other countries. We have enough domestic tax competition given the variety of tax incentives still prominent in all provinces. If Canadian governments do not cooperate in setting tax policies, globalization could set off this destructive competition. Tax rates and bases will have to adjust in response, and many people will be made worse off. If we can resist this sort of tax competition at home, globalization does not mean that Canada has to succumb to a race to the bottom with large reductions in taxes and giveaways in the form of tax incentives to compete with other countries. We can maintain tax rates that are somewhat higher than those in the United States (and comparable to other G7 countries) if we use those tax dollars to invest in human capital, infrastructure, a healthy environment and other public goods and services that improve the quality of life and our investment climate. We are in the enviable position now of having eliminated the federal budget deficit, so despite recent world events, there is room to adjust tax rates and bases. There is scope for divergence in a converging world, just not too much.

References

Auerbach, A.J. and J. Slemrod (1997), "The Economic Effects of the Tax Reform Act of 1986", *Journal of Economic Literature* 35, 589-632.

Brean, D.J.S., R.M. Bird and M. Krauss (1991), *Taxation of International Portfolio Investment* (Ottawa: The Centre for Trade Policy and Law).

Cummins, J.G. (1996), "The Effects of Taxation on U.S. Multinationals and Their Canadian Affiliates", Working Paper 96-4 for the Technical Committee on Business Taxation (Ottawa: Department of Finance).

Cummins, J.G., K.A. Hassett and R.G. Hubbard (1995), "Tax Reforms and Investment: A Cross-Country Comparison", NBER Working Paper 5232 (Cambridge, MA: National Bureau of Economic Research).

Davies, J.B. (1998a), *Marginal Tax Rates in Canada: High and Getting Higher*, Commentary No. 103 (Toronto: C.D. Howe Institute).

_____ (1998b), "Personal Income Tax: Directions for Structural Reform", *Policy Options* 19(10), 17-19.

Feldstein, M., J.R. Hines and R.G. Hubbard (1995), *The Effects of Taxation on Multinational Corporations* (Chicago: The University of Chicago Press).

Gentry, W.M. and R.G. Hubbard (1998), "Fundamental Tax Reform and Corporate Financial Policy", NBER Working Paper 6433 (Cambridge, MA: National Bureau of Economic Research).

Gordon, R.H. and J.K. MacKie-Mason (1995), "Why is There Corporate Taxation in a Small Open Economy? The Role of Transfer Pricing and Income Shifting", in Feldstein, Hines and Hubbard (eds.), *The Effects of Taxation on Multinational Corporations*.

Grubert, H. and T.S. Newlon (1995), "The International Implications of Consumption Tax Proposals", *National Tax Journal* 48(4), 619-647.

Hogg, R.D. and J.M. Mintz, eds. (1993), *Tax Policy for Turbulent Times*, Policy Forum Series 28 (Kingston: John Deutsch Institute, Queen's University).

Jorgensen, D.W. and Kun-Young Yun (1991), "The Excess Burden of Taxation in the United States", *Journal of Accounting, Auditing & Finance* 6, 487-508.

Kesselman, J.R. (1997), *General Payroll Taxes: Economics, Politics, and Design* (Toronto: The Canadian Tax Foundation).

_____ (1998), "Priorities for Cutting Canadian Taxes", *Policy Options* 19(10), 13-16.

Lyon, A.B. (1996), "International Implications of U.S. Business Tax Reform", Working Paper 96-6 (Ottawa: Technical Committee on Business Taxation, Department of Finance).

McKenzie, K.J. (1998), "Tax Cutting in a Global Economy", *Policy Options* 19(10), 28-32.

McLure, C.E. (1992), "Substituting Consumption-Based Direct Taxation for Income Taxes as the International Norm", *National Tax Journal* 45(2), 145-154.

Mendoza, E.G., A. Razin and L.L. Tesar (1994), "Effective Tax Rates in Macroeconomics: Cross-Country Estimates of Tax Rates on Factor Incomes and Consumption", *Journal of Monetary Economics* 34, 297-323.

Milesi-Ferretti, G.M. and N. Roubini (1998), "Growth Effects of Income and Consumption Taxes", CEPR Discussion Paper No. 1979, forthcoming in *Journal of Money, Credit and Banking*.

Mintz, J.M. (1998), "Is National Tax Policy Viable in the Face of Global Competition?" Institute for International Business Symposium, October 23, 1998, Rotman School of Management, University of Toronto.

Musgrave, P.B. (1992), "Substituting Consumption-Based Direct Taxation for Income Taxes as the International Norm: A Comment", *National Tax Journal* 45(2), 179-184.

Organization for Economic Cooperation and Development (OECD) (1990), *Employment Outlook* (Paris: OECD).

_____ (1996a), *Economic Outlook* 59 (Paris: OECD).

_____ (1996b), *Economic Outlook* 60 (Paris: OECD).

_____ (1997), "Fiscal Consolidation and the Effectiveness of the Public Sector", *Economic Outlook* 61 (June), 31-37.

_____ (1998), *Revenue Statistics 1965-1997* (Paris: OECD).

Owens, J. (1993), "Globalisation: The Implications for Tax Policies", *Fiscal Studies* 14(3), 21-44.

Ruggeri, G.C. and C. Vincent (1998), "Can We Unload the Personal Income Tax?" *Policy Options* 19(10), 20-23.

Tanzi, V. (1995), *Taxation in an Integrating World* (Washington, DC: The Brookings Institution).

Technical Committee on Business Taxation (TCBT) (1998), *Report of the Technical Committee on Business Taxation* (Ottawa: Department of Finance).

Vermaeten, A., W.I. Gillespie and F. Vermaeten (1995), "Who Paid the Taxes in Canada, 1951-1988?" *Canadian Public Policy/Analyse de Politiques* 21, 317-343.

Wilson, T.A., P. Dungan and S. Murphy (1998), "What is the Room for Tax Cuts?" *Policy Options* 19(10), 7-12.

National Tax Policy for an International Economy: Comments

Robin Boadway

This paper first examines international evidence on the presumed effects of globalization on domestic tax comparisons, and then goes on to discuss some implications of globalization for the Canadian tax system. Let me consider these briefly in turn. I can be very brief since the data speak for themselves, and the implications/proposals are for the most part fairly non-controversial. I shall then spend some time complementing Professor Olewiler's remarks with some of my own observations and concerns about Canadian tax policy in a competitive world.

In the first part of the paper Nancy Olewiler examines three reasonable consequences of globalization, and ones with which most economists might agree: the convergence of tax rates on mobile factors of production, the shift in tax mixes towards less mobile factors, and decreased tax revenues as a share of GDP. She might have added a fourth — the tendency for tax systems to become less distributive, though no doubt the evidence here would be every bit as inconclusive as that which she reports. Roughly speaking she finds the following:

- inconclusive evidence about convergence of tax rates on high labour income recipients (although the numbers rely entirely on comparisons of top marginal income tax rates, when the appropriate comparison should be between average tax rates of all sorts based on residence: income, sales, payroll and property);

- no trend towards convergence of capital income tax rates, or even a general decline in rates;

- no evidence that globalization has significantly altered the tax mix in favour of less mobile factors, though the tax mixes are somewhat more similar between Canada and the United States than vis-à-vis other countries;

- no evidence that globalization is causing reductions in tax rates; and

- no evidence that taxes on mobile factors have converged.

At the outset, it is worth flagging a potentially important caveat. These comparisons are largely based on *marginal* tax rates — the marginal tax rate in the top income bracket for individuals and the marginal effective tax rate (METR) on investments by corporations. The problem is that, in theory, mobile factors should respond to *average* tax rates rather than marginal ones, and they can be very different than average ones. For example, marginal income tax rates for the top bracket are likely to show much scarier dispersions than average tax rates. Moreover, the relevant average tax rates should include all taxes borne by a resident, including income, sales and payroll taxes. This may well generate the same qualitative story as marginal tax rate comparisons, but the policy implications are likely to be very different. Concern with mobile factors will translate into concern with bringing average rather than marginal tax rates down, and that constitutes a completely different tax reform agenda. Let us, however, suppose that the same story as the above would go through with the use of average tax rates.

These findings, which confirm what many others have noted in the past, might be viewed as very surprising, and indeed disappointing, for those who would push the theme that globalization severely constrains domestic tax policy. It amounts to at least a lukewarm shower for part of the existing tax policy agenda, although it does beg the question of whether governments have just been stupid not to recognize the forces of globalization as constraints on good tax policy.

Let me take a slightly different perspective. Should we be surprised at these data? We in Canada probably should not be. Our federation has been a "mini global economy" for decades. There are virtually no internal barriers to labour and capital mobility, and no tariff-like distortions on interprovincial trade. Moreover, there is also a fairly extensive system of redistributive

Robin Boadway

federal-provincial transfers which is highly effective at equalizing the tax capacities among provinces, implying that they need not use differential tax rates to provide a given level of public services. Yet, despite the opportunities for conforming, there is clearly no convergence of tax systems among Canadian provinces, even on highly mobile factors. Personal income tax rates, including those on the highest income persons, differ considerably across provinces, and corporate tax rates even more. There is no evidence of tax rates on mobile factors being competed away. Tax mixes are vastly different across provinces, with different provinces relying to very different extents on sales taxes, payroll taxes and income taxes. What is even more surprising, though perhaps not to the sophisticated economist, is the persistence of high tax rates on capital income and on capital more generally, the most mobile of the factors of production. Most provinces maintain relatively high corporate tax rates, they show no reluctance to levy significant capital tax rates, and they have amongst the highest property taxes in the world.

Is this stupidity? Perhaps, perhaps not. For one thing, maybe some factors are not as mobile as we think they are. There have been a series of studies of interprovincial mobility in Canada, which estimate that fiscally-induced mobility is of second-order importance; and, it is not clear that studies of international labour mobility are showing any different. But capital is presumably much more mobile than labour (though innumerable efforts to attract capital to high-unemployment regions by subsidies and preferential tax rates rather belies that presumption). Perhaps the real problem is that, once in place, capital no longer is mobile. Governments worldwide seem unable to resist the urge to tax accumulated capital and its returns, given that the stock of existing capital is much larger than the flow of new capital. Economists are virtually universal in their agreement that capital income tax rates are too high, given the many good things that flow from investment and savings. Of course, taxing old capital will be anticipated by potential investors and will discourage them from investing. But governments may not have the credibility or the length of time horizons to discipline themselves into not tapping into old capital. Fortunately, most governments behave the same way, with the consequence that there is an uneasy equilibrium with high capital tax rates, albeit one in which incentives exist to compete for new capital. Maybe the lesson from this, if I can borrow from Buchanan and Brennan's argument in *The Power to Tax*, is the following: If one wants to tame the revenue-grubbing instincts of government, perhaps we should not broaden the corporate tax base and make it more simple: a narrow, messy tax system with lots of loopholes gives Leviathan less opportunity to grow. (Of course, you will realize that my tongue is in my cheek.)

I would be tempted also to downplay the importance of the tax mix, at least as an element of the tax competition/mobile factor scenario. There is a very large overlap in base among the major taxes — income, sales and payroll. A shift in the mix of taxes probably has relatively little impact on the incidence of the tax burden as a whole, at least that is what incidence studies have led us to believe. I would have thought that what is perhaps more important is what potential migrant gets on net from government services less taxes, the so-called *net fiscal benefit* (NFB). A consensus is emerging that a lot more redistribution takes place on the expenditure side of the budget than on the tax side. A recent study of the incidence of health system in Manitoba showed that the pattern of NFBs is extremely progressive, owing mainly to progressivity on the benefit side. We may want to focus on more than revenue-neutral tax reforms as a response to globalization if the real action is taking place on the expenditure side of the budget.

Despite the complete absence of alarm bells that come from looking at the raw tax data, Olewiler nonetheless takes the position that we still need to adopt our tax system to the reality of being next to the United States. If the loss of mobile factors is eventually going to be a problem, it is certainly with respect to the United States that it will be relevant. So conditioning our tax system on that possibility is, of course, prudent. There is also undoubtedly an important demonstration effect at work here that suggests that we might want to emulate the tax system in a successful country. Moreover, the tax reforms that are likely to come out of that are probably sensible ones in any case. Her suggestions are actually fairly modest in the main, although there is likely to be much more action in the details. She proposes a revenue-neutral reform which lowers the top marginal personal tax rates, lowers the corporate tax rate and eliminates many of the remaining sources of prefer-ential treatment, and perhaps increases payroll taxes moderately. These are proposals that are hard to argue with. But will they accomplish what needs to be accomplished?

We might want to go much further than this. I would argue that the main concerns we have with our tax system do not stem primarily from the imperatives of globalization, but are those which hamper our economy's efficiency, productivity and fairness. They might be exacerbated by the pressures of globalization, which might enhance the case for reform. But they do not stand or fall on globalization alone. My list of issues would include the following.

- First and foremost, it seems clear that when it comes to inefficient tax systems, the provinces are the big villains. Among the broad-based taxes, their sales taxes are the most distortionary — biased against goods in favour of services, biased against foreign-produced versus domestic-produced products, and biased against goods that use business inputs. As I already mentioned, Canadian property taxes are among the highest in the OECD, especially taxes on business, and this is not going to cure itself in the wake of massive deficit down-loading. Resource taxes are a complete jungle. Taxes and other forms of levies on oil and gas, mining, forestry and other resources bear no relationship to rents, and have much wider divergences in marginal effective tax rates than for other sectors. (Here is where the argument for a cash-flow-type tax, rightfully dismissed by Olewiler as a replacement for the corporate tax, comes into its own.) And provincial business taxes do more than mirror the federal one; they add their own special interprovincial distortions and preferential treatment of favoured activities.

- This is all related to what I would regard as an out-of-whack federal-provincial mix of taxes. One of the costs of the extensive fiscal decentralization the Canadian federation has undergone over the postwar period is that the provinces occupy significant amounts of income tax room. The consequence of this is a noticeable increase in tension and disagreement over the Tax Collection Agreements, reflected in an increasing number of special provincial measures and various threats to pull out. It would not take much for the Tax Collection Agreements to disintegrate, in which case, income tax disharmonization and all that it entails would ensue. Although there is a lot of wishful thinking about interprovincial cooperation solving this and other interprovincial disputes, there is virtually no reason to be sanguine. If one were starting from scratch, one might want to re-jig both the degree of vertical imbalance and the allocation of major taxes between federal and provincial governments. It seems nonsensical to have provinces levying taxes on the most mobile of factors, capital, and the federal government occupying so much of tax fields that might be more efficiently used by the provinces, such as payroll and sales taxes. Made-to-measure federations would not assign corporate taxes to the provinces. As an aside, a mischievous observer might also note the absence of wealth transfer taxes in these international comparisons. These taxes, though common among

OECD countries, are conspicuously absent in Canada. Apparently, globalization would not prevent us from adopting such a tax.

- The business income tax system, despite its fairly recent reforms, is still quite deficient in many ways, including those which are of relevance for productivity growth. The Mintz Committee focused on a number of non-neutralities of the business tax system, such as those arising from excessive write-offs and special incentives which give rise to differential METRs. But, the number one problem in my mind is something that is not easily captured in conventional METRs of the sort reported, and that is that the tax system is not as conducive to risk and entrepreneurship as it could be. There is no effective system of full loss offsetting, so that firms engaged in highly risky activities, especially young firms, face discrimination. (It has been argued in the United States that this is offset by the fact that entrepreneurs can remain unincorporated and obtain write-offs for risky investments at higher personal tax rates and then incorporate if profits emerge — this, however, presumes refundability at the personal level, which does not apply, at least in Canada.)

- Related to this is the fact that the business tax system, by the way it treats financial income, effectively favours large, mature businesses over small, immature ones. This is because internal equity finance (retained earnings) is treated preferentially to outside equity finance. This simply compounds the problem faced by entrepreneurs.

- Open economy considerations do have some important implications for income tax systems, in particular for the treatment of capital income. These issues have, of course, been around much longer than globalization: our economy has always been open to international capital flows, and the design of our corporate tax system has been cognizant of that. Olewiler has mentioned some issues involved in taxing capital income in an open economy, basically pointing out that one can end up shooting oneself in the foot. The Mintz Committee spent some time considering the reform issues surrounding the treatment of cross-border capital flows, and I defer to their report for the gory details. But one outstanding and anomalous issue remains even after the dust clears on their report and that concerns the mechanism that exists for integrating the corporate and personal tax systems. Our integration system fits well into the schema of the Carter Report, where the taxation of comprehensive income was the norm, and openness of the economy was not a concern. But our tax system is not a tax on comprehensive income, and capital markets are highly open. The combination of these two factors implies that our system of integrating personal and corporate taxes does not fit, and may be costing us tax revenue unnecessarily. On the one hand, giving dividend tax credits to Canadian shareholders of Canadian corporations at least partly amounts to an unnecessary windfall: in an open economy, shareholders will not have borne the burden of the corporate tax, so there is no need to give them relief. On the other hand, giving it selectively to shareholders who hold non-sheltered assets and not to those which are sheltered is discriminatory. If we are in the game of mimicking the U.S. tax system, perhaps re-evaluating the dividend tax credit is one good place to start.

- Finally, to the extent that it is the overall level of taxation rather than the tax structure that is a concern (and it will be if average tax rates are important rather than marginal ones), we cannot avoid re-visiting the expenditure side of the budget: taxes cannot be cut without cutting expenditures. Olewiler is rightly concerned about getting enough revenues out of the tax system to finance important social programs. The challenge here is to know how we can accomplish our social objectives in a more cost-effective manner. That, much more than tax policy design, is probably the most pressing concern. But, here again, is globalization the main driving force? Given that the bulk of taxes are borne by residents, and that the international mobility of residents is really quite limited, it is not at all clear to me that, apart from the demonstration effect, there is any real need for nations to conform in levels of taxation and hence the public services that they provide to their citizens.

Summary of Discussion

Nancy Olewiler picked up on Robin Boadway's reference to the lack of evidence that factor flows within Canada have been influenced by tax differentials between Canadian provinces. She raised the possibility that intra-Canadian factor flows in response to tax differentials may start to show up once threshold differentials are breached. So far, higher tax rates have not induced people to leave British Columbia, but the tax differential between Alberta and British Columbia is now huge and growing and may now be inducing movement out of British Columbia.

Jack Mintz agreed with the presenters that the data do not show a lot of tax policy convergence. Perhaps the theory suggesting convergence is wrong. We should keep three things in mind about mobile factors. When a government tries to tax a mobile factor, it might leave and go to another jurisdiction. But when factors are mobile and governments have imperfectly competitive powers in international markets, there are incentives to export taxes. We see examples in tourism. Another example is the Saskatchewan potash tax. Almost all of Saskatchewan's potash production is exported out of Saskatchewan and they are responsible for a large share of world production. They have purposely levied an origin-based tax knowing that foreigners will bear the burden of the tax. Historically, the size of the foreign-owned business sector in Canada was an important rationale for the corporate income tax in Canada.

Mintz's second point was that the key globalization issue for tax policy is not so much the mobility of factors, but the problem of determining where income is earned for tax purposes or where a transaction takes place for sales tax purposes. With the internationalization of business, it is no longer as easy to determine the source of income. For example, tax authorities have given up trying to apply arm's length transfer pricing rules to intra-firm global financial trades and have moved to allocation formulas. This is leading to international cooperation. Governments will be forced into cooperating in order to levy certain types of taxes. For many professional services provided by multinational consulting operations — for example, architects — it is difficult to determine where a service takes place and where you should impose the value-added tax (VAT). VAT harmonization in Europe has been driven precisely by the difficulties of determining where the VAT base is.

The third point made by Mintz is that, while capital may not be all that mobile, reported profits of multinational companies (MNCs) are the most mobile and elastic of the tax bases. This is why statutory corporate income tax rates have fallen over the past ten years or so in most member countries of the Organization of Economic Cooperation and Development (OECD). For example, Canadian rates were reduced in the 1987 tax reform. Most OECD countries are now in the 30-35% range. Sweden, Norway and some of the other Nordic countries have moved to a new dual-income tax system with lower tax rates of about 25-30% on capital income and higher rates on labour income.

Mintz also commented on factor mobility within Canada. The Winer-Day paper for the Ontario Fair Tax Commission showed that anglophone labour is more responsive to tax rate differentials than francophone labour. Also, James Hines' recent study is an example of econometric work with panel data at the firm level showing that capital is more mobile than appears to be the case in studies looking at aggregate data. It is not entirely clear how much integration between corporate and personal taxes you want in a small, open economy. But there are two issues that have to be borne in mind. First, empirical studies show that the Canadian equity market is not perfectly integrated with world markets. Dividend tax changes do seem to affect equity prices. Second, integration plays a big role in minimizing transaction costs when it comes to estate planning and liquidation of small companies. These considerations would apply even if Canada fit the profile of a small, open economy perfectly.

David Slater asked whether tax reform is necessary now to prepare for demographic pressure that may push up the tax revenue-GDP ratio in future.

Robin Boadway agreed and said that in this regard an important development was the shift to targeted benefits and away from universal benefits. On the tax side, the key has been the advent of the refundable tax credit to target transfers to those who most need them.

David Crane observed that much less attention was being paid to taxation of the working poor than to taxation of rich people. Should increasing the child benefit to help the working poor also be on the tax policy agenda? Second, before Canadians talk about reducing the tax/GDP ratio, would it not be better to start by reducing the debt/GDP ratio to create room for a permanent reduction in the tax/GDP ratio?

Nancy Olewiler responded that she is not too worried about the debt/GDP ratio in the current climate given favourable long-term projections. Therefore, the tax/GDP ratio should be the focus of attention. She pointed out that she did report in her paper that the tax burden on the working poor had increased over time. Pressures to shift taxes to the working poor will continue if we do not reform our tax system. If we try to help the working poor without an efficient tax reform, the working poor will bear the tax burden in the long run because they are the least mobile factor of production.

Robin Boadway agreed that the tax treatment of the working poor and of the disabled are important issues. However, they are not related to the globalization theme of the conference. He observed that imaginative uses of refundable tax credits to increase incentives are more likely now that the federal and provincial governments are free from the constraints of the Canada Assistance Plan funding arrangement.

Gene Lang asked the panelists to put themselves in the shoes of the federal finance minister facing a choice between reducing personal income tax rates and restoring greater indexation of tax credits and tax brackets.

Nancy Olewiler would opt to get marginal tax rates down rather than adjust tax brackets. For brain drain issues, the maximum marginal tax rate is important. Where the top bracket starts may also be a consideration. In a low-inflation environment, the lack of full indexing is not that important.

Robin Boadway concurred and said that he has never been very concerned about the lack of full indexation. Yes, de-indexing acted as a hidden tax, but it was a relatively painless way to address the debt problem. He would let fiscal drag run its course and pay down the debt. However, he could see a stronger case for indexing credits.

Neville Nankivell asked whether the panelists would recommend raising the income threshold for starting the top marginal rate.

Nancy Olewiler thought that, while raising the top marginal rate bracket would be costly, it would be an important step forward. By starting the top rate at an annual income of $59,180, we effectively treat middle-income people as if they are rich.

Summary of Discussion

Adil Sayeed asked whether the 1986 U.S. tax reform has reduced our room to manoeuvre on the corporate income tax side because U.S. corporations have more trouble claiming foreign tax credits.

Jack Mintz replied that there is now less room on the U.S. foreign tax credit side to accommodate relatively high Canadian corporate income tax rates, especially our high rates on service sector businesses. Other aspects of the 1986 U.S. tax reform such as measures to broaden their corporate tax base were just as important. For example, their changes to interest allocation rules induced U.S. corporations to shift interest expenses to foreign subsidiaries. As a result, debt-asset ratios of foreign-owned companies in Canada — 80% of which are U.S.-owned — have risen.

Richard Harris posited the following scenario. A more protectionist Europe starts using tax policy as part of an activist industrial strategy with tax subsidies for favoured sectors such as aerospace, computers and biotechnology. The U.S. responds with selective tax instruments focusing on their own favoured industries. What would Canada's room to manoeuvre be in such a scenario?

Robin Boadway pointed out that attempts to implement strategic industrial policy under the guise of industry-specific tax subsidies could run up against World Trade Organization (WTO) rules.

Richard Harris responded that WTO rules have not stopped this sort of thing in the past. The potential for more EU-U.S. conflict is real. For example, the Gore-Clinton Commission recently recommended a tax exemption for electronic commerce, but the Europeans objected and have threatened to block U.S. Web sites in response.

William Watson asked about Ireland's plan to reduce their corporate income tax rate to 12%. Would the EU object? If we tried a similar approach, would Washington object?

Jack Mintz replied that past EU complaints had focused on selective Irish tax cuts for particular sectors such as International Finance Centres and manufacturing. However, Ireland is now moving to a general corporate rate of 12%. This approach will not be objectionable to the EU. Canada taxes some business sectors very highly relative to taxes in the United States. Many Canadians have an anti-big-business populist streak, especially when it comes to taxation, and believe that large corporations should be taxed heavily. But we are only hurting ourselves with such a policy. There would be major gains if we put in place a policy environment attractive for businesses to locate in Canada. Governments should move to establish an efficient set of policies to support production that will generate the revenues needed to support social policy.

Thomas Courchene closed the discussion by commenting that it will be interesting to observe the evolution of Ireland's place in the EU. Ireland still gets a lot of EU development grants as a "have-not" country, but now that the Irish are becoming relatively rich, they should be weaned off their grants. Will they be?

The Canadian Financial Sector in the Information Age

John F. Chant

Introduction

The "banks are dead" movement is alive and well in the world of finance (see, e.g., Miller, 1998; Berger *et al.*, 1995; Boyd and Gertler, 1994; and James and Houston, 1996). Fact and counterfact have fueled the debate. And the meaning of the debate shifts from participant to participant and from time to time. At times the significance of the issue may also be lost. What does it matter if banks are dead? How will it affect those who currently use their services? What public policy response is needed? Does it matter if they live, but their form and activities are totally transformed? Do the changes sweeping the financial sector give Canadian policy more or less room to manoeuvre?

It is hazardous to make predictions about the future of banking and the financial sector. The financial world is littered with failed past attempts. The "cashless" society so heralded in the 1970s has now emerged as the "less-cash society" and even then not greatly so. Despite the apparent hazards of the enterprise, this paper will be built around some possible directions for the financial sector's future. As the paper argues, the financial sector is a part of the economy that will be among the most profoundly affected by the rapid pace of change in information technology.

The benefits of such an exercise go beyond better understanding of the forces that may change the place of the banks as the most prominent feature of the financial system. It is also important from the perspective of public policy. The financial sector is one of the most regulated parts of the economy and financial institutions themselves are the object of the major part of that regulation. This regulation has been designed primarily for the purpose of offsetting the imbalance of information between suppliers of financial services and their customers. Regulations governing financial institutions are based on their existing structure, organization and the ways in which they perform their business. Changes to these from any source may require a rethinking of the present approach and the apparatus through which it operates. Changes resulting from developments in information technology are especially important because the management and communication of information are at the core of the business of financial institutions.

The regulatory needs and potential may be much different in the information age than they are at present; even though the speculations of the paper may prove to be misguided. Reactive policy change may not be adequate and take too long to deal with the problems. Some anticipation may be needed to assure that suitable solutions are at hand if and when problems present themselves.

Information and the Financial Sector

Implicit in the title of the paper is the suggestion that the current and emerging information age will make a difference to, or even transform, the financial sector. To some degree, the title of the paper is misleading, but only in terms of its understatement. The impact of information technology on the financial sector is nothing new. Information is and always has been vital to the financial sector. The very origins of banks are themselves a product of information technology. The business of money keeping was transformed into banking when for the first time a customer of a money changer accepted a bookkeeping promise for future payment of a fixed value instead of the return of exactly the same coins as deposited. Ever since, information has been, and remains, the stock in trade of banking and other financial services. True to the spirit of its title, the paper will try to suggest ways in which financial institutions may change as a result of current and foreseeable changes in information technology.

The management of information is vital for all of the core activities identified with financial institutions: deposit-taking, payment making and lending.[1] Deposit taking, at its heart, consists of record keeping of customers' balances. Payments services entail, on the one hand, the exchange of information among the payer, recipient and their financial institutions and, on the other, evaluation of information about counterparties in clearing and settlement. Lending requires collecting and assessing of information about the condition and prospects of potential borrowers and the monitoring of their performance once they have been given credit.

The information revolution has affected and will continue to affect the Canadian and other financial systems in a myriad of ways. Who would have thought 20 years ago that sheer computing power would have turned the blackboard scribbling of academics into a trillion-dollar world market for derivatives? The information revolution allowed the millions of calculations needed to price a customized derivative to take place in seconds. Who would have imagined that these changes would also lead pensioners to be purchasing index-linked GICs complete with collars and floors? These and other changes are altering fundamentally the ways the financial industry operates and the way it relates to its customers.

The Organization of the Paper

It is beyond the scope of this paper, and even further beyond the imagination of its author, to deal with the many ways that advances in information technology will influence and reshape the entire financial system. The paper will focus information technology's impact on the role of financial institutions, often called financial intermediaries, in the overall financial system. This paper examines one of the major pressures on the banks in terms of their place in the financial system — the incredible pace of information technology — and its consequences.

The features of our financial institutions are easy to take for granted, given our everyday familiarity with them. A close look at financial institutions reveals that they are a curious amalgam of diverse activities that can be

---

[1] The terms "bank", "financial institution" and "financial intermediary" will be used interchangeably throughout this paper.

and are in most instances undertaken separately. Part one of the paper describes the structure and organization of these institutions.

Financial institutions exist in large measure because of their advantages for dealing with information that is both costly to assess and inherently incomplete. Many aspects of the form and structure of financial institutions have their roots in organizational solutions to overcome these information problems. Part two of the paper reviews the current state of economic theory with respect to financial institutions, what they do and their structure and organization.

Part three is more speculative. It deals with the ways in which changes in information technology may alter the current place of intermediaries in the financial system. In particular, it analyzes how these changes could affect the organization of these institutions, the types of business that they do, and the ways in which they carry on their business. In particular, it describes the simultaneous tugging on the financial system of centrifugal forces leading to fragmentation of some types of businesses into specialized institutions and centripetal forces leading to consolidation of institutions in other areas.

Part four assesses the implications of these changes for public policy with particular attention to the room to manoeuvre. Currently, the regulation governing financial institutions consists primarily of prudential regulation that is designed to protect the public against the failure of the institutions to which they entrust their funds. Increasingly, financial institutions are becoming subject to consumer regulation that governs their dealings with customers. The paper raises possible changes in the approaches to regulation that may be necessary in order to realize the public interest objectives of policy in the changed environment.

The Current Structure and Organization of Financial Institutions

This paper focuses on banks as the most prominent financial institutions in the Canadian and other market economies. Banks as institutions are easy to identify because they usually exist under specific legislation that sets them apart from other financial institutions. The activity of banking itself is less easily identifiable or defined than other economic activities such as steelmaking or wheat growing. The difficulties in determining the distinguishing characteristics of banking are manifest in the lack of a legal definition for banking in Canada, other than a specification of those institutions that are chartered under the Bank Act. Americans, in contrast, have defined banking as the taking of deposits and the making of loans. This is hardly a better solution for avoiding the problem. There are other institutions performing both these activities that are not banks and there are banks that do not do both or even one of these activities.[2] This paper follows the Canadian tradition and focuses on the institutions that fall under the Bank Act together with other institutions that resemble them quite closely. In Canada, these institutions include trust companies and credit unions.

Banks represent a curious amalgam of activities. In the language of economists, they are vertically and horizontally integrated enterprises.[3] Horizontally, banks have traditionally integrated the separate businesses of deposit taking, the provision of payment services and investment and lending activities. More recently, the list has grown to include the securities business, the origination and trading of derivatives, trust activities and many others. Financial institutions also integrate vertically the different processes or stages in the supply of the services they offer to their customers. These processes can be described as distribution and production. Distribution refers to the process of attracting customers and supplying them with financial services offered by the institution. Production refers to the undertaking of the other side of the contract to that taken by the customer.

Banks and other financial institutions traditionally have both distributed the products that they produce and also produced the products that they have distributed. Unlike auto manufacturers and clothing makers, banks distribute their products through their own branches. Unlike other consumer-oriented businesses such as grocery and department stores, the branch networks of banks have concentrated on distributing their own products. This degree of vertical integration appears substantially greater than almost any other sector in the economy.

The relation between the horizontal and vertical integration of banks in their traditional activities of deposit taking and lending is illustrated in

---

[2]One suggestion that has been made for the definition of banking, which reflects our current banking law, is that banks are those financial institutions that are permitted neither to sell insurance in their branches nor to lease automobiles.

[3]Horizontal integration refers to the degree to which different products or services are produced within the same enterprise. Vertical integration, in contrast, refers to the degree to which different stages or processes in the production of a good or service are integrated in the same enterprise.

Figure 1. The horizontal integration of activities is shown by movement across the figure from deposit taking to lending. Similarly, the vertical integration of process is shown by the vertical movement from distribution to production. The distribution phase of deposit taking consists of the deposit collection whereas the distribution phase of lending consists of loan origination. The production phases consist of investment of funds for deposit taking and funding for lending activities.

The horizontal integration inherent in financial institutions is well recognized. The vertical integration is less apparent and less well understood. Deposit taking, for example, may not appear to be a vertical integration of

Figure 1: Integration of Financial Activities in Banks

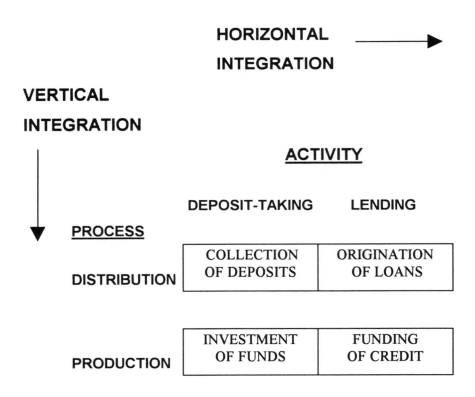

John F. Chant

activities. Yet, the degree of vertical integration can be illustrated by comparison with the banks' handling of mutual funds. Some banks now have started to distribute mutual funds that are the products of independent fund managers through their branches. In this case, there is a clear separation of distribution and production. In contrast, there is a vertical integration of the production and distribution when the bank sells its own mutual fund to a customer. Unlike the case for mutual funds, the distribution and production processes for deposits are virtually completely integrated.

Still, all the components of the amalgam can be and are performed separately. The vertical integration of the distribution and production of deposits can be undone through the use of brokers for dealing with depositors. Similarly, brokers or other agents could be used on the lending side. Horizontal integration could also be undone. The deposit-taking function can be performed separately from the lending side, and essentially is, by money-market mutual funds. Finance companies such as GE Capital and Newcourt perform the lending function without any participation in deposit taking. Finally, payments services, another activity associated with banks, could be separated from both the deposit-taking and the investment functions of intermediaries if they were offered through payments utilities. These could act on customers' instructions to transfer money from an account held by one customer to that of another customer, even when the accounts are held at different institutions.

The Genesis of the Structure of Intermediaries

In order to consider the impact of changing information technology on the place of financial institutions in the financial sector, it is important first to understand what that place is and why it is as it is. It may be surprising to non-economists that given the prominence of financial institutions in modern financial markets, economists have only recently directed attention to understanding the basis for their existence. To economists, it may be less surprising, given that economists have made great strides in the understanding of the nature of the firm only within this generation, leading to a Nobel prize for this contribution within the last ten years.

As already stated, financial institutions are an integral and prominent element of a modern financial system. Their place in the financial system raises many questions. Are financial institutions organized differently because they perform different functions than other parts of the financial system? How does the structure of financial institutions reflect the activities that they perform?

This section of the paper deals with three strands of analysis that can contribute towards an understanding of the functions and role of financial institutions. The first consists of description of the basic underlying functions that are performed by the financial system of an economy. Here, the paper follows the insights of the so-called functional view of the financial system. Next, attention will be directed to the forces that determine whether financial activities are undertaken through direct markets or through financial institutions such as banks. Finally, it describes the current organization of financial institutions and examines the role of information technology in shaping the form and specific organization of financial institutions. As will become apparent, these explanations relating to the structure and organization of financial institutions all strongly emphasize the role of information.

The Functions of the Financial System

The Global Financial System Project at the Harvard Business School has developed the functional view of the financial system as a guide to the understanding of changes underway in the financial system. Their approach, rather than taking existing institutions as a given, directs attention to the underlying functions of the financial system and seeks to explain the forms of organization that are used to satisfy these functions in different times and circumstances.[4]

Crane and Bodie identify the following six core needs that a financial system meets in a developed economy:

- methods of making payments in order to facilitate the exchange of goods and services;
- mechanisms for pooling resources to fund large-scale enterprises;
- ways to transfer economic resources over time and across distances, as in lending and investment;

---

[4]In addition, the same institutional form may serve quite different functions in different circumstances. The role of banks in the finance of industry differs substantially between Germany, on the one hand, and Canada and the United States, on the other.

- methods of managing risks, such a insuring, diversifying and hedging;
- price information, such as interest rates and securities prices, to help coordinate decentralized decision making in various sectors of the economy;
- ways to handle incentive problems that interfere with efficient business transactions. (Crane and Bodie, 1996, p. 110)

These functions meet basic needs common to all economies. The efficiency with which these functions are performed is vital to the efficiency of the economy and economic well-being of citizens.

The functions identified by Crane and Bodie are the building blocks of financial products and services. Different products and services perform these functions in different combinations and to different degrees. Savings deposits, for example, provide their holders with a method for carrying out payments; they allow the resources of many investors to be pooled into a larger mass of funds, they facilitate the transferring of economic resources over time and space, and they provide their holders with risk management through providing them with a fixed-value claim. This fixed-value claim is issued against the financial institution's portfolio of assets even though its value may vary over time.

Money market mutual funds also perform some, but not all, of the same functions. They do not in Canada, at least, provide a method of making payments. Like savings deposits, they facilitate the transfer of resources over time and space and allow the pooling of resources of many investors. Like savings deposits, they limit the risk faced by their holders by providing a fixed-value claim. They do this through holding a portfolio of fixed value assets rather than providing a fixed-value claim against a portfolio of variable priced assets.

The main contribution of the functional approach lies not in just identifying the functions, but in offering insights with respect to changes in the financial sector. The set of functions to be performed by the financial sector is common to all economies, though the importance of each may differ depending on the economy's needs. Yet, despite this similarity in the needs for the functions to be performed, the way in which they are performed can differ greatly over time and across places.

Crane and Bodie maintain that the main differences among financial sectors lie in the ways in which the functions are performed. The central point of their work for the present purpose is their observation: "as functions are performed more efficiently, institutions adapt to the changes. *Institu-*

tional form follows function (pp. 110-111). Differences in function do not explain the observed differences between institutions and structures in financial systems. This depends on factors such as traditional practice, regulations and the level of technology. The same function can be performed in many ways. It is the advantage of particular forms, given the state of technology and regulation, that determines how these functions are performed at any time and place.

The Choice Between Direct Markets and Financial Intermediaries

The most notable feature of the Canadian, and other market-based financial systems, is the prominent position of financial institutions, or intermediaries. A fundamental issue in the understanding of the workings of the financial system is the presence of financial institutions performing these economic functions. As an undergraduate money and banking text put it:

> Perhaps the most distinctive feature of financial markets is the presence of a group of institutions called financial intermediaries — institutions like banks, credit unions, and trust companies. These institutions are simultaneously engaged on both sides of the market. They borrow and they lend.... The first question is this: why do they exist? Much borrowing and lending occurs in financial markets between ultimate borrowers and lenders, without the benefit of financial intermediaries in this sense ... Financial intermediation absorbs scarce resources, and in that sense is costly. *Why do not all borrowers and lenders bypass intermediaries and deal directly?* (Shearer *et al.*, 1995, p. 263, emphasis added)

The theory of financial institutions has advanced considerably over the past decade. Emphasis has now shifted from explanations that emphasize the transfer and management of risk to explanations that emphasize monitoring and supervision of credit. The major contribution by Douglas Diamond characterized financial institutions as being "delegated monitors" (Diamond, 1984). This term describes the way in which financial institutions supervise their portfolios of loans and other assets on behalf of their depositors.

The theory of delegated monitoring explains well why lending is carried on collectively on behalf of many ultimate suppliers of credit. Ultimate lenders acting individually would duplicate each other's efforts in assessing the prospects and credit-worthiness of the borrowers, assembling and negotiating the contract that governs the loan, and monitoring and supervising the borrower after the loan has been made to assure its repayment. The collective use of a financial institution avoids the problem of duplication of effort with respect to the lending activity. They serve as agents on behalf of their customers by monitoring portfolios of loans.

Delegated monitoring by itself does not explain why some lending and borrowing takes place through the use of direct markets and some through the use of financial institutions. These differences reflect differences in the availability of information about the borrower. As Merton suggests, investors are best able to bypass intermediaries and lend through direct markets "when products have standardized terms, can serve a large number of customers, and are well-enough 'understood' for transactors to be comfortable in assessing their prices" (Merton, 1993, p. 22). The enterprises that borrow through direct markets are those that have the ability to generate credible information about their performance and prospects. In contrast, he suggests "banks are specialists in making loans that are difficult to assess without detailed and proprietary information about the borrower" (ibid., p. 13).

Even if it were feasible for an enterprise to make credible information about its activities publicly available, it may choose not to do so. Merton suggests another reason for borrowers to prefer using an intermediary:

> for competitive reasons borrowers are reluctant to reveal to the general public the information which would be necessary for direct placement of the debt. By being discreet with information provided by its borrowers and by developing a reputation for making profitable loans with its investors, banks help solve this asymmetric information problem. (ibid., p. 12)

Thus, the use of an intermediary for obtaining finance may still be preferred by enterprises that could provide the information needed for raising funds on direct markets.

Rajan added to this explanation of financial intermediaries stressing the role of contract incompleteness. Such incompleteness can arise from a number of sources. External incompleteness occurs when it is too costly to use the legal system to verify and enforce the outcome. Intrinsic incompleteness arises because it may be "very hard for the lender and borrower to contract on eventualities because they are too hard to describe and visualize in requisite detail" (Rajan, 1998, p. 533). Rajan also suggests that contracts may be left incomplete deliberately where worst outcomes may be avoided by not writing them out in all possible detail and are left incomplete.

Rajan suggests that the use of financial intermediaries may be an efficient means for dealing with incomplete contracts. The use of direct markets depends on the ability of the parties on each side of the transaction to be assured that the terms of the transaction can be fulfilled. This can be assured only if the contract is complete over all contingencies. In any circumstance not provided for in the contract, a borrower through direct markets would have to negotiate and bargain with numerous suppliers of funds. In contrast, borrowing from an intermediary reduces the dimensions of the bargaining by it confining to just the borrower and the intermediary.

To sum up, both Merton's and Rajan's approaches support the same conclusions. Those enterprises whose businesses are well understood and which can make public credible information about their performance and prospects will be most able to turn to public markets to obtain their funding. Financial intermediaries provide an effective alternative for other enterprises. The advantage of the financial institution lies in the avoidance of duplication of efforts in assessment, monitoring and supervision; their ability to preserve the value of proprietary information; and their efficiency in dealing with the costs of incomplete contracting.

The Structure of Financial Institutions

Explaining the choice between the use of markets and institutions helps to understand the reasons for the existence of financial institutions. It does not, however, explain their structure and form in terms of the different types of activities that are combined within these institutions. Moreover, critical for present purposes, it does not explain the role of information in determining this form.

Horizontal Integration of Lending and Deposit Taking. A number of explanations suggest that the horizontal integration deposit taking with "delegated monitoring" improves the efficiency of the arrangements between the suppliers of funds and the agents who manage the portfolio of loans. Among the factors that contribute to this increased efficiency are:

- the fixed value of deposits,
- the liquidity of many deposits, and
- the holding of deposits by borrowers to make transactions.

Diamond's explanation for the existence of financial institutions itself suggests that there will be benefits from the combination of delegated monitoring with deposit taking in financial intermediaries. These benefits arise because the fixed-value deposit provides the suppliers of funds with an efficient way of monitoring the performance of the intermediary as their agent in supervising its holding of loans. With a contract tied closely to the success of the loans, customers would need to monitor the value of the portfolio carefully in order to assure that they receive payments in accord with the agreed-upon formula. In contrast, with a fixed-value contract, customers need only monitor to the degree needed to assure that they will receive the promised payment. This monitoring can be effectively limited to the degree that financial institutions hold capital to provide its depositors with a margin of safety.

The liquidity of deposit contracts also allows the suppliers of funds to react to the performance of financial intermediaries. Unlike other debt, many deposits are liquid in the sense that they can be withdrawn on demand or short notice. As a result, any financial intermediary must be continually aware and sensitive to the possibility of withdrawal of funds in performing its role as agent. This liquidity helps to align the incentives of the agent closer to the interests of the supplier of funds.

Finally, the combination of lending and deposit taking offers a benefit with respect to monitoring and assessing potential lenders. As deposit-takers, financial institutions will hold the transactions accounts of potential and current borrowers. Holding these accounts allows institutions to gain credible information cheaply about the performance and condition of their borrowers that would be more difficult to collect if lending and deposit taking were conducted separately. This information can be used to assess the credit-worthiness of the borrower at the time of application and also to monitor the borrower's condition once the loan has been made.

Vertical Integration. While much attention has been directed to explaining the peculiar horizontal integration embodied in financial institutions, economic theory has provided less guidance regarding the vertically integrated structure of financial institutions. At a very basic level, the explanation lies with Coase's explanation of the limits to the firm. These limits are set where the advantages of internal decision making balance the costs of using the external market. Putting this wisdom to use in this particular case requires determining the advantages of vertical integration for the main activities of banking.

Vertical Integration and Deposit Taking. On the deposit side, the branch served as the key distribution point for financial institutions for their products and services. Alternatives to branches would include the use of agents for distributing the institution's products in much the same way as food manufacturers use grocery stores or automobile producers use dealers.

The advantages of branches include the ability to project an institution's reputation and possible savings in information costs. The branch provided a basis by which institutions could communicate their reputations to potential customers. Benjamin Klein, for example, argued that banks could create confidence by committing their resources to substantial and impressive buildings which would be unsuitable or difficult to convert to other uses.[5] If the bank exited from banking, these assets would be severely reduced in value. This form of "specific capital" signaled that a bank's owners are committed to the business of banking. Branch offices thus were a form of information that symbolized the strength of their institution and contributed to the confidence that customers needed to place their funds with it (Klein, 1974).

The use of branches would also have an efficiency advantage if the transfer of information were cheaper within an organization than outside. In the absence of branches, customers would have to communicate with head offices through an external means of communication. With a branch, customers need only communicate locally and the communication with the head office takes place internally. There are a number of possible sources of efficiency from the use of internal communications within an institution. The number of facilities required for any volume of communications may be less because of the ability to manage the information flow to avoid peak-load problems. Possibly more important are the differences in costs arising from the different volumes in the flow of information. In absence of a branch, customers would have to communicate with the bank with respect to every transaction they wish to undertake with the bank. Instead, the branch itself would be able to reduce the communications by reporting in some instances on only the net results of transactions with customers. A branch, for example, would need to report only the net changes in its deposits and cash

---

[5] It seems fairly general that churches and bank buildings were among the most substantial building in most cities as evidenced by their high proportion among the older buildings surviving in any city. Far less common are grocery, hardware and dry good stores where customers could determine the quality of the product more easily and were less dependent on the continuation of the business.

position to head office, a much lower volume of information than its total transactions with customers.

Vertical Integration and Lending. Credit assessment and lending in many communities removed from central management created substantial information problems for lending institutions. The branch provided a means by which banks could gain the information needed for them to carry on the business of lending on the local level. It was not the only alternative. They could have used local agents to channel loans to them, or they could have bought loans from local brokers who originated them.

Sound lending practices require much information about the quality of borrower before making loans, and on the borrower's performance afterward. Much of this information must be qualitative and reflect subjective judgements. What is the character of the borrower? Is the business plan sound? Can the borrower realize it? What is the value of the security? Do danger signals require remedial action? Will further credit turn the business around or will it be more good money wasted?

The centre needed to have confidence in the information coming to it from its local lending operations. The use of the branch allowed banks to internalize the information process. Such internalization allowed banks to develop procedures and systems to standardize information vital to its activities. The careerism of banking provided a means of assuring a common experience and training for its employees. Through this common experience, employees would be more likely to transmit similar information under the same circumstances. In addition, senior supervisors responsible for credit policy would have shared the experience of their subordinates and could bring it to bear in judging the information that they receive.

The use of external agents would raise questions of moral hazard if the agent served for others or held loans for itself. On what basis would the agent allocate loan sales among different holders? In using agents, banks faced the problem of avoiding being assigned "lemons".

The vertical integration of distribution and production of loans inherent in the branch banking system thus appears to reflect the information technology of the time. The integration made possible the use of internal processes for gaining and managing information that may have avoided the problems with the dependability of information gained through external agents.

Integration: Summary

To sum up, this review suggests that information needs and the technology for meeting them are very much at the front and centre in any explanation of the organization and structure of financial institutions. The horizontal integration of deposit-taking activities provides a number of ways for satisfying the needs of depositors seeking agents to whom they can delegate the responsibility for supervising lending activities and to the financial institutions themselves seeking to minimize their costs of monitoring the prospects and condition of their borrowers.

Similarly, the vertical integration of distribution for both lending and deposit taking reflects the state of information technology. Branches provide a means of communication for both financial institutions and their customers. From a narrow perspective, branches provide economies in communication, reducing the needs for individual customers to communicate to the operating centres of the institutions. Branches consolidate information internally at the local level, reducing the amount of information to be communicated to the centre. Less obviously, branches by their very presence communicate a "brand" and possibly indicate its reputation to potential customers. Branches also provide information to support programs of bank lending by allowing bank-customer relationships to be built at a local level. These relationships provide qualitative assessments that have served as a building block for much of the commercial lending of financial institutions. Given the importance of information to all dimensions of the intermediation process, the particular forms and organization of intermediation appear to reflect the state of information technology.

Possible Impacts of Information Technology

Elements of the present structure and organization of financial intermediaries go right back to the first deposit-takers in Italy in the fourteenth century. The form of the Canadian branch banking system is little changed from that established before Confederation. It has persisted despite substantial changes in information technology — the development of telegraph, telephone, and computer networks and progression from hand to machine to computer-based bookkeeping.

Given the durability of the present form of intermediation in the face of past change, there may be grounds for doubting any significant response to the current and foreseeable changes in information technology. Still, the magnitude of the change in information technology and its consequences for costs appear to swamp any thing that has gone before. McKinsey & Company describe the scale of change in their study for the Task Force on the Future of the Canadian Financial Services Sector:

> In 1982, microprocessors with a computing power of one million instructions per second (i.e. one MIP) cost almost $1,000. Today, one MIP costs about $1.30; within a decade, we estimate it will cost about $0.001. (McKinsey & Company, 1998, p. 24)

To most, the scale of such changes is difficult, if not impossible to imagine. Morley Winograd put this change in perspective in a recent speech, explaining that had this same progress taken place in the automotive industry, "a luxury car would cost about $2, would travel at the speed of sound and would consume only a thimbleful of gas every 1,000 kilometres" (Winograd, 1996, pp. 1-2, cited in Task Force, 1998b). Not as well recognized, but just as significant have been the advances to date and the potential advances in communications technology. Negroponte explains that compared to the typical modem of 9,600 bits per second, existing copper telephone wires have the capacity to carry up to six million bits per second with appropriate modems. The capacity of fibre is even greater:

> Recent research results indicate that we are close to being able to deliver 1,000 billion bits per second. This means a fibre the size of a human hair can deliver every issue ever made of the *Wall Street Journal* in less than one second. (Negroponte, 1995, pp. 22-23)

The increased ability to communicate and process information has also been reinforced by increased availability of information. As Rajan points out, rating agencies such as Moodys and S&P, data gatherers such as Lexis/Nexis and Datastream and disseminators such as Reuters and Bloomberg all produce and sell information through communications lines (Rajan, 1998, p. 538).

Impact on Horizontal Integration

Already advances in information availability and technology are starting to change practices in the business credit market in ways that may weaken the horizontal integration of deposit taking and lending. Credit scoring is a statistical technique through which quantitative information is used to make lending decisions. It relies on comparing the characteristics of a credit applicant with similar data accumulated over time for other borrowers to predict the borrower's probability of default. Asset-based lending also relies less on the qualities of the borrower and more of the qualities of the asset being financed. Asset-based lenders develop links with vendors of capital equipment and invest their efforts in credit risks more on the basis of the assets financed than on the characteristics of the borrower.

Both techniques seem likely to reduce the benefits to financial institutions from the integration of deposit taking and lending. These techniques both are substitutes for the types of quantitative and qualitative information that traditionally has been gained, in part, through borrowers holding their transactions balances with banks.

Credit scoring and asset-based lending also facilitate the development of markets in securitized loans. Securitization takes place when the lender that originates a loan sells it either separately or as part of a package to other investors. Litan and Rauch described the process of securitization:

> Securitization is accomplished by commercial and investment banks that package many different loans into large bundles of assets held in trust. They then issue securities representing indivisible interests in the trust. The investors who buy these securities receive, on a proportionate basis and minus a small transaction fee, the interest paid by the borrowers whose loans make up the trust. (Litan and Rauch, 1997)

Securitization of bank loans has expanded very rapidly in the United States. The amount of loans sold by U.S. banks grew more than ten-fold from $26 billion in the third quarter of 1983 to over $290 billion in the third quarter of 1989, before declining somewhat in the 1990s. Significantly, the majority of loans shifted from being investment grade to non-investment grade (Rajan, 1998, p. 540).

Rajan attributes this growth of securitization to a number of factors:

> Greater information availability about firms has reduced the asymmetric information about borrowers, greater computational power has reduced

the cost of slicing and dicing up loans into uniform saleable pieces, and loans sales have been structured so that the originator retains a stake. (ibid., p. 540)

He also sees the increased use of securitization reinforcing the conditions for further growth:

increased volume can improve liquidity. Buyers do not inspect what they buy very closely. Instead, they trust sellers. The reason they can do so is that the greater integration of markets has increased the frequency of transactions any single player undertakes. Reputation not only becomes easier to build, but also more important to maintain as banks fund loans through their placing power rather than their balance sheets. (ibid., p. 540)

Securitization reduces the benefits from the link between deposit taking and business lending. Securitization has been facilitated by the greater availability of information about the borrowers, made possible in part through credit scoring. This greater availability of information makes it possible for lenders other than financial institutions to participate as originators of loans. In addition, securitization allows these specialized lenders to provide business credit through financing provided by the continual turnover of their portfolio.

Impact on Vertical Integration

The same information advances affecting the horizontal integration structure of financial institutions will also influence the advantages of vertical integration. Indeed, many of these changes just reflect the other side of changes taking place in the horizontal integration.

The reductions in computing costs will also affect the role and the strengths of the branch as distribution centres. Most notably, the development of credit scoring and securitization weakens the link between distribution and production on the lending side. Credit scoring reduces the need for the qualitative information about borrowers that was provided by branches: the assessment of character and the borrower's performance that come from the branch's, and its manager's, place in the community, the face-to-face meetings with the borrower, and the ability to monitor a borrower's total business with the institution.[6] A movement towards credit scoring may diminish the role of the branch in the credit process, leading to greater centralization of credit administration.

Just as significant, by reducing these benefits from the branch system, credit scoring may place vertically integrated financial institutions on a closer footing to other lenders. Credit scoring could facilitate credit granting by lenders who do not have the relationship with borrowers made possible through the branch network. In addition, credit scoring could make it easier for specialized lenders to demonstrate the quality of their loans when they sell them as part of securitized packages.

Less apparent are possible changes in the distribution on the deposit side of the business. The great reductions in communication costs are diminishing the cost advantage of communications within an organization relative to those outside. The role of the branch as a distribution centre is diminishing. Changes in the costs of communication will, for example, alter the benefits from the bundling of messages which previously took place at the branch level. With communications at 10 cents per message unit, consolidating 1,000 messages at the branch saved $100 in communications costs. If changing technology reduces the costs of messages to 0.1 cent, the saving from bundling messages through the branch drops to $1 per 1,000 messages. Such a change will clearly affect the advantages of using branches for distribution. Institutions will find it more efficient to deal with customers directly through telephone banking, the intranet and Internet, bypassing the branch.

While these pressures will alter the distribution of activities between the periphery and the centre within financial institutions, they may also weaken the customer's identification with the institution at the same time. Communications with the central distribution centres of financial institutions will be little different than communications with financial institutions which do not have branch distribution networks or, perhaps more significantly, with third-party distributors that are not themselves financial service suppliers.

Banks and other institutions may also emphasize and extend further their own activities as distributors. In doing so, they may offer their customers products of other producers of financial services in addition to their own. Some trends in this direction are already apparent. Some banks now offer

---

[6]A consumer lender supposedly claims to have found that the single most important piece of information for assessing the credit-worthiness of personal borrowers is their postal code.

mutual funds from independent suppliers in addition to their own in-house funds. The ultimate direction for distribution will depend in large measure on several factors:

- the regulatory response to the changes,
- acceptance by consumers, and
- the ability of distributors to gain access to the payments system.

Regulatory Response. The movement of Internet, software or communications companies into distribution of financial services might appear to conflict with the traditional separation of financial and commercial activities which has shaped the financial regulation of many industrialized countries. Established financial institutions may challenge these inroads into their traditional activities, arguing that commercial enterprises can enter financial activities while financial institutions cannot enter the same commercial activities. Such an argument, however, misses the point of the separation. The concern with the combination of financial and commercial interests in the same enterprise reflects concerns with production activities. Separation of commercial and financial activity is to prevent the diversion of a financial institution's funds to the other interests of its owners. Such a diversion, however, would take place at the production stage in the making of loans, and not at the distribution stage.

Acceptance by Consumers. The decline of the importance of branches as a distribution channel will increase the significance of branding or reputation in the competition for consumers. Major institutions will be better able than smaller institutions to compete against third-party distributors. The third-party distributors themselves will have to invest substantially in their brands in order to establish their credibility with consumers. The consequences for the success of the third parties will be substantial. If third parties make significant inroads into distribution, financial institutions will be reduced to being producers of financial services distributed by others.

The branch in a reconstituted form may turn out to be a defence for large financial institutions which distinguishes them from their new competitors. Adding new functions such as insurance to the activities of the branch and increasing the role of the branch as an advice centre may allow existing institutions to differentiate themselves from specialized distributors in the minds of consumers. In a world where banking takes place primarily through electronic channels, whether telephone or Internet, third-party distributors will be on more even ground.

The competitive position of smaller financial institutions will be very much affected by the struggle among distributors. At present, deposit insurance strengthens their credibility with consumers and facilitates their competition with larger institutions. They will be disadvantaged in dealing directly with customers to the extent that large financial institutions and third-party distributors compete with each other through their investment in brands. On the other hand, the emergence of third-party distributors would reduce any brand advantages of large relative to small financial institutions. The distributors themselves must establish their brand in order to compete for clientele. Within the choices offered by the distributors, smaller institutions would be able to compete because price, not brand, would likely be a determining factor influencing the consumer's choices.

Payment Services. Integrated financial institutions at present have the advantage over third-party processors because transfers among different types of services and products can take place within the institutions. In contrast, such switches through a third-party distributor would require a transfer between the institutions that offer their services through the distributor. An individual transferring funds from a savings deposit to a mutual fund, for example, would need to transfer the funds received from the savings institution to the mutual fund supplier in order to make the transaction. Third-party distributors could enter the payments system as processors that arrange transfers among the institutions for which they distribute. Alternatively, these distributors could establish electronic links among their suppliers to allow such transfers to take place. These links would in effect be limited-purpose payments systems.

Overall Impact on Integration

The outcome of the reduced need for integration seems unclear in terms of the form and structure of the arrangements by consumers and businesses to gain access to financial services. The outcome will depend in large measure on who can control the gateway to financial services. It is possible that the gateway will be controlled by financial institutions with the electronic channels replacing the branch as the customer's point of access to the financial institution. Within this framework, financial institutions could continue to join distributors/suppliers for most financial services as they are now, or increasingly become distributors of other people's products. Another possibility is that specialized gateways, perhaps associated with communications companies such as BC Tel or software suppliers such as Intuit would provide customers with their main access to financial services. In this case, the gateway will act as an agent bringing together customers with suppliers of financial services.

Public Policy Implications of Changing Structure and Organization

Changing information technology has implications for financial market policy in both the short and long run. In the short run, current policies can facilitate or hamper the adjustments that institutions must make in order to remain competitive. The first part of this section will discuss these short-run issues with particular reference to the recent applications to merge made by major Canadian banks together with the minister's rejection of the applications. In the longer run, regulation must be adapted to any possible transformation of the structure of the financial sector so that its public interest objectives can be maintained. These longer run issues are discussed in the latter part of this section.

Bank Mergers: Dead-end or Delay?

McKinsey & Company, in its study for the Task Force on the Future of the Canadian Financial Services Sector, stressed that the technology spending undertaken by major international banks recently has dwarfed that of the large Canadian banks. Many argue that recent advances in information technology have raised the efficient scale of investment for integrated financial institutions such as the Canadian banks to levels that would be difficult to support at their current size. The proposed mergers can be seen as a response by the banks to gain the needed scale to support this level of expenditure.

At the time the mergers were announced, the Canadian approach to mergers was governed by the unwritten, but widely understood, "big-shall-not-buy-big" rule. Through the rule, the government had made it clear that mergers among the largest institutions in the Canadian financial sector would not be approved. The rule short-circuited competition and prudential concerns and provided a blanket proscription against such mergers.

The Task Force on the Future of the Canadian Financial Services Sector was not asked to comment on specific merger proposals, but did address the big-shall-not-buy-big rule, recommending its removal. Instead of the rule, the task force suggested procedures through which such merger proposals, though based on business decisions, should be judged like other major mergers on the basis of their impact on competition and, because of the nature of their business, on the basis of prudential concerns.

The minister of finance rejected both applications for mergers after receiving the views of the Director of Investigation and Research of the Competition Bureau and the Superintendent of Financial Institutions. The Director had expressed concerns about the competitive effects on the mergers with respect to branch banking services to individuals and businesses, to credit cards and to securities activities. The Superintendent, though satisfied with the likely state of the merged bank, claimed that a traditional method for dealing with a weak bank would be foreclosed by the merger. Specifically, a rescue by another large Canadian bank would no longer be feasible because of the size of the merged entities and a lack of appropriate acquirers. Any rescue would require a relaxing of current ownership restrictions in order to permit a takeover by a large international bank.[7]

In his statement, the minister suggested that his refusal to approve the merger is more a delay rather than a dead-end for mergers among major banks. He declared that "Whereas the merger proponents wanted the mergers to be allowed in order to change the status quo, we believe the status quo must be changed before any merger can be considered" (Martin, 1998). Among the measures that could alter the status quo, the minister pointed to legislation which would allow insurance companies to demutualize and would permit foreign banks to establish branches in Canada. He also referred to the implementation of recommendations put forward by the financial services task force and the House and Senate committees.

Nevertheless, the fact remains that the minister's refusal may turn out to be a dead-end to bank mergers in Canada. Despite the useful contribution that all these measures could make, it is difficult to forecast a significant

---

[7]The key restriction is the 10% limit to the ownership of a Schedule I bank by a single interest. This rule effectively prevents a foreign-owned bank from controlling a Schedule I bank.

shift in the status quo with respect to either the Superintendent's or the Director's concerns within the next three to five years, or even in a longer horizon.

None of the measures address the Superintendent's concern that the mergers foreclose important options for dealing with troubled banks. Any merger among major banks, by their very size, means that the takeover by another Canadian bank no longer remains an option for rescue of the resulting bank if it runs into difficulties.

The competitive concerns of the Director are unlikely to be eliminated by the legislative measures. The demutualization of insurance companies together with possible mergers among them may create stronger institutions that could extend the range of their activities further into personal financial services. Nevertheless, they would still lack the branch networks that continue to provide the point of contact with consumers and they would also remain small relative to their banking competitors. The foreign branching proposals restrict these branches from accepting deposits below $150,000 and, as a result, would not improve competition in branch services for individuals. Without the ability to supply banking services to individuals, foreign branches are likely to be concentrated in major centres and to have only a limited impact on businesses throughout the rest of the country.

The task force's recommendations should increase competition in the markets for personal and business financial services. Among these were proposals for broader participation in the payments system so as to include life insurers, mutual funds and investment dealers, and for the creation of cooperative banks to strengthen the competitive position of credit unions and caisses populaires. While all these measures have some potential to improve the financial services options available to individuals and businesses, none address in a significant way the Director's specific concerns about branching services to individuals and businesses, credit card services and securities activities.

The passage of time may be one way out of the status quo with respect to the Director's concerns. More foreign, most likely U.S., securities firms may follow the example of Merrill Lynch in entering into the Canadian market. Still, the opportunities to acquire significant Canadian players are few and *de novo* entry into the retail business will be difficult.

Technology may offer a possible solution to the concerns about competition in branch services through providing alternative channels for serving customers. Relying on technology to alter the status quo carries a possible danger of removing room to manoeuvre with respect to the future of the Canadian financial services industry. Now our banks compare favourably with foreign banks with respect to their credit ratings and have used this strength to be among the most active international banks relative to their size. Waiting for technology to change the status quo may also hamper the Canadian banks' ability to meet the challenges of new competitors for their domestic business. By the time the status quo has changed sufficiently to allow the restraints on possible mergers to be removed, the business advantages to be gained from the mergers could be lost.

Heeding this potential danger does not require accepting the view that new technologies will require a larger efficient scale. Some bankers argue that new technologies are quite divisible and can be readily adopted by smaller institutions. Nevertheless, the business of public policy should not be to judge the merits of alternative business strategies. Rather, it should provide a framework for protecting the public interest. The public interest entails, in addition to questions of competition and solvency, a framework of support for industries where Canada can maintain a comparative advantage. Management, not government, is best placed to determine the prospects of their industry.

The prognosis of a dead-end seems unavoidable if approval of mergers depends on the prior elimination of the Superintendent's and Director's concerns. Elimination of the Superintendent's concern appears unlikely under any circumstances given the size of possible merging banks. Despite the fast pace of technology and the prospect of policy changes, the competition issues, as identified by the Director, also seem unlikely to abate in the near future.

Canadian policymakers face a stark choice. They can hold out on the competition and prudential fronts, possibly at the expense of causing Canadian institutions to lag behind in the technology race and lose out in international markets and even in their ability to serve Canadians domestically.

An alternative approach based on recognition of the competition concerns and strategies to deal with them could avoid both dead-end and delay.[8] The minister of finance could declare that he would approve mergers among major banks if they can meet the Director's concerns about competition. These concerns about the securities business and credit cards could likely be met by the sale of the operating units of one of the merging parties.

---

[8] The Superintendent's concerns appear to create a permanent stumbling block for mergers among large Canadian institutions.

John F. Chant

The concerns about branching operations would be more difficult to meet. They would require divestiture of substantial numbers of branches in the case of mergers among major institutions. Still, such an alternative has the considerable advantage of leaving the decision with respect to the mergers as a business decision, albeit one subject to constraints. Banks exploring the possibilities of mergers would be able to tradeoff the benefits against the costs of concessions needed to put it on-side and pursue the possibility of merger if warranted. Without at least this room to manoeuvre, Canadians may find themselves increasingly marginalized both in their activities abroad and in their ability to serve Canadians. While the preservation of competitors should not be the objective of a policy, preventing Canadian banks from serving the needs of Canadians in the most effective way may be to the detriment of both.

The Impact of Technology on Regulation

Currently the financial sector is one of the most heavily regulated sectors in almost every economy. While regulation has the stated purpose of protecting the customers of financial institutions, the bulk of it takes the form of *prudential* regulation designed to reduce the possibility of the failure of institutions to honour their customers' claims and to reduce the impact of failure when it takes place. Until recently, less emphasis has been placed on *consumer interest* regulation which governs the terms of transactions between institutions and their customers. Consumer regulation relies on disclosure requirements with respect to the terms of transactions and, to a lesser degree, restrictions on the types and terms of transactions that can be undertaken.

The regulations governing financial institutions and their transactions with customers have been based on the present configuration of financial institutions. While the overall impact of changed information technology is difficult to predict, it is useful to consider whether the possible changes could create a need for change in the regulatory approach.

The earlier discussion suggests that changing information and communication technology will likely decrease the advantages from the present organization and structure of financial institutions. The discussion of the possible need for regulatory reform will be directed towards the consequences of a reduced degree of horizontal and vertical integration in the supply of financial services. In particular, attention will be focused on two changes: the separation of loan origination from loan financing, and the separation of distribution and production with respect to deposits and similar products. Technology also allows institutions to offer financial services to Canadians without a physical presence in Canada. The policy approach taken to this issue by the task force is also described.

Separation of Distribution and Production: Savings Products

The separation of distribution and production for deposits and similar products adds an additional layer between the customer and the institution with which its deals. With vertically integrated institutions, the customer chooses to place its funds on the basis of the reputation of competing institutions and the terms that they offer. The separation of distribution from production could alter the choices for the consumer.

The changed role of the distributor raises different information needs for the consumer. In dealing with the distributor, the consumer will gain information about and access to the products of a range of suppliers. In order to understand the basis on which they are making their choices, the consumer will need disclosure on a number of issues. The customers may wish to know about the producers and their relationship to them. Are their products covered by deposit insurance or similar forms of customer protection? What legal regime governs their relationship with the producer? They may also wish to know the arrangements between the distributor and the producer. What are their respective responsibilities to the customer? Is the distributor just a passive information agent bringing the customer and the supplier together or does the distributor bear greater responsibility? What are the terms of arrangements between the distributors and the producers, especially with respect to incentives?

These are the same types of consumer interest issues dealt with today by regulations governing intermediaries of the securities firms in the distribution of securities. This is not surprising. The undoing of the vertical integration between distribution and production effectively changes the role of financial institutions. By becoming distributors together with third-party distributors such as communications companies or software providers, they have shifted from being a principal to being an agent.

John F. Chant

Separation of Lending and Deposit Taking

The separation on a horizontal basis raises different questions from the vertical separation. The separation of financial institutions will show up in different ways. Such a separation would take place if the lending and investment functions of financial institutions were split from the deposit-taking function through securitization. For example, a deposit-taking institution might choose to exit from direct lending through mortgages and business loans and, instead, rely on loan originators to supply it with investment outlets. Some U.S. major banks such as Wells Fargo have already ceased originating mortgages. Similarly, hedge funds represent a similar separation of funding from investment activities.

The undoing of horizontal integration raises issues for prudential regulation. While it is the taking of public money from customers that should determine whether an institution should be subject to prudential regulation, the regulation itself focuses on the assets held by the institutions. The uncoupling of the deposit-taking function from that of lending and investment complicates this task. Securitization results in institutions holding claims originated and managed by other parties.

This separation of financial intermediation into smaller components raises similar issues as those raised by OSFI with respect to the holding company form of organization. OSFI has argued that it should be able to regulate the holding company that owns a bank or other regulated financial institution and to obtain information about the state of its unregulated subsidiaries. OSFI based its argument on a perception of interdependence among the entities through their common ownership in practice and also in the eyes of the public.

The separation of financial institutions creates a similar interdependence, though for different reasons. The concern arises not from a concern with common ownership, but because the stability of regulated financial institutions depends on the soundness of the claims they hold which have been generated by the credit decisions of others and which are monitored and supervised by others.[9]

---

[9]An entertaining account of the perils of relying on credit decisions made by others is provided by Mark Singer, *Funny Money,* which documents the role of Penn Square Bank as a loan conduit to many large U.S. banks in the 1970s and early 1980s.

An issue also arises with respect to so-called concentration regulations that are intended to prevent regulated financial institutions from being overly exposed to specific risks. These requirements limit the proportion of an institution's capital that can be advanced to an entity or exposed to a specific risk.

Investment through instruments such as hedge funds may subvert the purpose of concentration requirements. Even though an investment in a hedge fund and the risks that it poses may by itself leave a regulated financial institution below its concentration thresholds, the overall pattern of exposures through investment in hedge funds may not. The recent episode of Long Term Capital Management showed that the ultimate investors in the hedge funds may not be aware of, or to be stronger, were unable to determine the risks that were undertaken by the fund in which they had invested. To the extent that different hedge funds take similar risks, investment in different funds would not provide the same spreading of risks as independent investments.

The separation of the present integration of deposit taking, on the one hand, and lending and investment, on the other, may necessitate a change in the approach to prudential regulation. With the integration, the institution itself can be the focus of regulation. Its soundness and stability depends on the quality of the portfolio of loans and investments that it originates and manages. The separation of activities leaves the regulators of these institutions one further step removed from knowing the current quality of these assets. Regulators will be less able to draw lines neatly around regulated institutions and direct their attentions. They may instead need to be concerned with the affairs of originators and managers of investments and loans on whom the regulated institutions depend.

Entry without a Physical Presence

The use of electronic media for distribution raises a further issue that is different from those considered so far. Any concern with regulation, whether prudential or consumer interest, may be irrelevant to the degree that distributors, whether financial institutions or third-party distributors, fall outside its coverage through offering their services to Canadians from outside the country. In addition, the customers of such institutions may find that they are subject to the laws of the institution's home country (see Rowe, 1998, pp. 165-182 cited in Task Force, 1998c, p. 74).

The task force considered this issue on the Future of the Canadian Financial Services Sector. In approaching the issue, the task force started with three objectives:

- There should be no restriction on Canadians' abilities to choose from the widest possible selection of financial services and products.
- To the greatest extent practicable, information should be easily available about providers so that Canadians can make informed choices.
- Any regulatory regime must be workable and not discourage entry into Canada (Task Force, 1998a, pp. 188-190).

The task force also recognized that lending money and soliciting money through deposits raised distinctly different concerns.

The present Canadian approach to foreign banks fails to deal with providers who have no physical presence in Canada. Foreign banks are prohibited from conducting any banking business in Canada except through having a physical presence in the country. In addition, there are no criteria for establishing whether a foreign entity is undertaking banking business in Canada when it undertakes transactions with Canadian residents.[10]

The task force proposed a regime consisting of the following three elements:

- identification of the potential providers and the regulatory authority assigned for dealing with them;
- separate treatment for those that wish to lend money to Canadians and those that wish to take money from them; and
- development of appropriate measures to deal with each category of provider. (Task Force, 1998a, p. 189)

---

[10]This ambiguity creates uncertainties as to what a foreign bank can or cannot do. Wells Fargo, for example, committed itself to a number of conditions to resolve the uncertainty by assuring that it was not conducting banking business in Canada. Among the provisions were commitments to mail letters and statements from the United States, that its call centre would be located outside Canada, and that payments of interest would be mailed by borrowers to a post office box outside Canada (and then trucked back to Canada for clearing with the correspondent bank). See Task Force (1998c, p. 77).

A limited definition of "banking business" was proposed by the task force which would include any provision of financial services from outside of Canada that uses mass solicitations and target marketing to gain business from Canadians. This definition was intended to resolve the uncertainty for foreign suppliers by making clear the types of business that they could undertake in Canada and the conditions for undertaking them.

On the basis of this definition, foreign banks could obtain regulatory permission to carry on lending to Canadians. The conditions to do so include complying with the market conduct applicable to banks in Canada, disclosing that the institution is not regulated in Canada and providing a dispute-resolution mechanism in Canada. An institution accepting these conditions could gain certification from the OSFI and be allowed to develop a business plan that could include certain activities such as call centres within Canada.

The task force recognized that taking money from Canadians raises far more serious issues that lending to them. As a consequence, it argued that the current situation where these activities can be undertaken only through either a regulated subsidiary or branch should remain in place.[11] At the same time, it encouraged efforts at the international level to develop a common approach based on mutual recognition of home-country jurisdiction.

Still, as the task force recognized, any measures to deal with entrants without a physical presence are limited, given the means of communication such as the Internet. In these circumstances, consumers can only be protected by giving them as much information as possible so as to make informed choices. The task force recommended that OSFI make efforts to give greater exposure to its circulated list of regulated institutions operating in Canada and its "Warning Circular" listing entities that might possibly be operating in Canada illegally.

Conclusion

This paper has dealt more with the convergence part of the conference theme and less with its global dimension. Its thesis in addressing the impact of the

---

[11]These measures would do nothing to prevent Canadians from placing their funds abroad with foreign institutions. The "bank business" provision would only be triggered if an entity actively solicited business from Canadians through mass solicitations or target marketing.

John F. Chant

information revolution on the financial sector was that the structure and organization of the financial sector are very much the product of existing technologies for communication, processing and analysis of information. This is true for both core activities of financial institutions: deposit taking and credit granting. The continuing transformation of information technology appears to have the potential to alter the landscape of the financial sector substantially.

The financial sector will be subject to both diverging and converging pressures. At the production level, information advances seem likely to erode the advantages of combining financial activities within the same institution and shift production away from integrated financial institutions towards more specialized suppliers. At the same time, this breakup of formerly integrated activities would necessarily change the current vertical integration of the distribution and production processes within the same institution. The outcome here seems less clear. The separation of production and distribution may open distribution to new entrants such as software developers and communications firms.

Much of the current financial regulation is implicitly based on an understood integration of activities within financial institutions. As with the convergence discussed in other papers, this reconfiguration of financial activities — the divergence in production and the convergence in distribution — will require a rethinking of both the prudential and consumer regulation governing the financial sector.

Canadian institutions must be given the freedom to adapt to the changes in ways that allow them to serve Canadians and develop their international strengths. It is not clear whether the recent rejection of the mergers of major banks was a delay or a dead-end. Even delay could be costly given the rapid pace of technology. A dead-end would almost certainly be detrimental to both Canadian banks and their customers.

References

Berger, A., A. Kashap and J. Scalise (1995), "The Transformation of the U.S. Banking Industry: What a Long Strange Trip It Has Been", *Brookings Papers on Economic Activity* 2, 55-217.

Boyd, J. and M. Gertler (1994), "Are Banks Dead? Or Are the Reports Greatly Exaggerated?" *Federal Reserve Bank of Minneapolis Quarterly Review* (Summer).

Chant, J. (1987), *Regulation of Financial Institutions — Functional Analysis*, Technical Report No. 45 (Ottawa: Bank of Canada).

_____ (1992), "The New Theory of Financial Intermediation", in K. Dowd and M. Lewis (eds.), *Current Issues in Monetary and Financial Economics* (London: Macmillan), 42-65.

Crane, D.B. and Z. Bodie (1996), "Form Follows Function: The Transformation of Banking", *Harvard Business Review* (March-April), 109 -117.

Diamond, D. (1984), "Financial Intermediation and Delegated Monitoring", *Review of Economic Studies*, 393-414.

Freedman, C. and C. Goodlet (1997), "The Financial Services Sector: Past Changes and Future Prospects", a background document for the Ditchley Canada Conference, October 3-5.

Franke, G. (1998), "Transformation of Banks and Bank Services", *Journal of Institutional and Theoretical Economics*, 109-133.

James, C. and J. Houston (1996), "Evolution or Extinction: Where are Banks Headed?" *Bank of America Journal of Applied Corporate Finance* (Summer).

Klein, B. (1974), "The Competitive Supply of Money", *Journal of Money, Credit and Banking* (November), 423-453.

Litan, R.E. and J. Rauch (1997), *American Finance for the 21st Century* (Washington, DC: United States Department of the Treasury).

Martin, P. (1998), "Statement by the Honourable Paul Martin, Minister of Finance, on the Bank Merger Proposals", December 14.

McKinsey & Company (1998), "The Changing Landscape for Canadian Financial Services: New Forces, New Competitors, New Choices", research paper prepared for the Task Force on the Future of the Canadian Financial Services Sector.

Merton, R. (1993), "Operation and Regulation in Financial Intermediation: A Functional Perspective", Working Paper No. 93-020 (Cambridge, MA: Division of Research, Harvard Business School).

Miller, G. (1998), "On the Obsolescence of Commercial Banking", *Journal of Institutional and Theoretical Economics*, 60-73.

Negroponte, N. (1995), *Being Digital* (London: Hodder & Stoughton).

Rajan, R.G. (1998), "The Past and Future of Commercial Banking Viewed through an Incomplete Contract Lens", *Journal of Money, Credit and Banking* 30(3), 524-550.

Rowe, H. (1998), "Electronic Commerce and Consumers", *International Business Lawyer* 26(4), 165-182.

Shearer, R., J. Chant and D. Bond (1995), *The Economics of the Canadian Financial System: Theory, Policy & Institutions,* 3d ed. (Toronto: Prentice Hall).

Task Force on the Future of the Canadian Financial Services Sector (1998a), *Change, Challenge and Opportunity: Report of the Task Force* (Ottawa: Supply and Services Canada).

John F. Chant

_____ (1998b), "Competition, Competitiveness and the Public Interest", Background Paper No. 1 (Ottawa: Supply and Services Canada).

_____ (1998c), "Improving the Regulatory Framework", Background Paper No. 5 (Ottawa: Supply and Services Canada).

Winograd, M. (1996), "A Social Contract for the Information Age: Future Presidential Campaign" (Los Angeles).

Canadian Financial Regulation in the Information Age

Edwin H. Neave

Introduction

Canada's financial system continues to evolve, and in some areas the pace of change even continues to increase. Today's financial system is vastly different from that of ten years ago, and in another ten years still more changes will have occurred. Keeping up with the changes requires us periodically to rethink the bases of financial legislation. The principal areas in which rethinking is needed are those of prudential supervision and consumer protection, but this paper is mainly concerned with the former. It argues that one of the neglected contemporary issues in regulatory revision concerns the role of information production, both by institutions themselves and by regulators. The issue of whether greater transparency would improve system operations and supervision is not raised in the McKay task force report, and this paper argues that additional benefits could be realized by complementing the McKay approach.

Although the rest of the paper is concerned with prudential issues, for the sake of perspective it may also be useful to comment on the task force's

A version of this paper also appears in *Policy Options* 20, No. 2, March 1999, 35-39.

approach to protecting consumer interests. Consumer interests should certainly be defended, but on my reading, the McKay report goes beyond a defence to advance, at least by implication, the view that financial institutions are instruments of public policy. The recently released Ianno report adopts a similar stance. The rationales of both the task force and Ianno may rest on the belief that financial companies are coddled by governments, that as a result they earn substantial monopoly or oligopoly rents, and that in exchange for the rents, institutions should fulfill social responsibilities. Whether or not this view is defensible should be debated, not assumed as it has been in most of the public commentary. To me, debate on the future of Canada's financial system ought to examine whether it is indeed in the country's best interests to employ the financial system as a social policy instrument. The question of whether we can afford to do so becomes particularly compelling in a world of integrated financial markets. However, as yet these issues have not publicly been explored.

Are Banks Dead or Dying?

Let us now turn to issues of prudential regulation. There is a currently popular argument that today's banks are dead, or at least dying. If this argument were correct, the financial-system evolution might mean we would eventually have no intermediaries to regulate. For example, the Harvard functional approach to financial-system analysis argues that institutions are dynamically complementary (see, e.g., Merton and Bodie, 1995), which means that banks may have carried out certain transactions yesterday, but that markets will perform those functions tomorrow. The greater use by corporations of market debt, the invention of credit derivatives, consumers turning to mutual funds, and securitization are all offered as evidence favouring the dynamic complementarities interpretation. Although this view leaves room for banks to invent new business which will later migrate to markets, it does not establish that banks perform functions which are permanently capable of adding value to financial transactions. By inference, the banks, if not yet dead, may indeed be dying.

Dynamic complementarity describes a good deal of market evolution, particularly in the more highly developed economies such as that of the United States or the United Kingdom. However, the Harvard functional approach does not recognize that the financial system also exhibits static complementarity. That is, banks and other lenders have advantages over markets in assessing the quality of some kinds of loan applications, and not just because the economics of their operations are different. Rather, the screening and monitoring functions performed by financial institutions are genuinely different from those performed by market agents (see Neave, 1997). On this view, both bank-like and market-like functions will continue to be needed in the future, even though either may be modified by advances in financial technology.

To advance the argument in a bit more detail, consider in turn securitization and the invention of credit derivatives. The growth of securitization neither argues for the death of banking nor for the irrelevance of static complementarity. Securitization simply shifts the function of originally providing funding, and in so doing separates bank-like screening and monitoring functions from money raising. In particular, securitization does not modify the need to manage moral hazard: write-offs can increase with increasing securitization unless the original screening and monitoring continue to be performed.

A similar argument can be made with respect to credit derivatives. Banks that sell off default risks may have diminished incentives to govern their loans as carefully as before, and in the absence of governance changes this too could mean increased loan write-offs. That is, credit derivatives can be used to shift risk, but the risks themselves can also change — unless the original bank-like screening and monitoring continue to be performed.

Information Production and Banking Supervision

If banks are neither dead nor moribund, the question of how to supervise them most effectively gains in importance. I believe that more information about portfolio quality could improve the performance of financial institutions themselves, the ability of regulators to supervise, and the ability of investors to assess the institutions. The efficient allocation of financial resources requires widely distributed, reliable and timely information. It has long been recognized that efficiency in trading and pricing stocks, including the stocks of intermediaries, depends critically on a widely distributed information base and on good information processing. Yet it is only recently that research has begun to show how widely stock markets vary with respect to the quality of the information base on which trading takes place (Yu, 1997; Bhattacharya, 1998).

As with market transactions, the allocative efficiency of intermediary operations depends critically on a widely distributed information base and on good information processing. However, the public availability of asset quality information varies widely. Moreover, much of the relevant asset information produced by intermediaries is intended for their own use, and is therefore not widely distributed. As a result, it is often difficult for either investors or regulators to obtain pertinent asset quality information. In recognition of this difficulty, Steven Ross (1989) distinguishes between institutions whose asset portfolio quality is difficult to determine, or opaque, and institutions whose asset quality is transparent.

The McKay Task Force and Information Production

Measures to reduce institutional opacity could both improve the efficiency of the resource-allocation process and enhance our capability for prudential regulation. While providing more and better information is not a panacea, it could play both proactive and retroactive roles in managing financial difficulties, including the periodic recurrence of financial crises. If one accepts this view, one is led to conclude that regulatory revision should address itself more aggressively to information production and dissemination than has been done in the past.

No new forms of information production are discussed in the task force report. Nor does the task force discuss how informational problems can contribute to institutional difficulties. Perhaps the task force accepts the standard argument offered by many regulators, which holds that producing too much information can make it difficult for the regulators to negotiate with troubled institutions. While this argument has some virtues, I believe its benefits are heavily outweighed by the benefits to a policy of greater openness. The advantages to greater openness have both proactive and retroactive aspects that can best be appreciated by considering the anatomy of financial difficulty.

Anatomy of Financial Difficulty

Financial difficulty can stem from either liquidity or solvency problems. Of course, it can be practically difficult to distinguish between liquidity and solvency problems, but that should not prevent us from exploring the

Edwin H. Neave

differences conceptually. Liquidity problems arise when entities (financial institutions, countries, or non-financial companies like real-estate developers) that hold mainly illiquid assets face unanticipated short-term cash outflows. Examples include the recent difficulties of Long Term Capital Management, Olympia and York during the 1980s, runs on banks prior to the advent of deposit insurance, and many others. Merton Miller recently observed that there is no lesson to be learned from the difficulties of Long Term Capital Management. I think Miller is observing there is no *new* lesson to be learned. There is certainly an old lesson worthy of restating: information dissemination can provide a valuable check on overly optimistic position taking and excessive use of leverage — at least so long as investors heed the information.

There are at least three ways of dealing with possible liquidity problems. First, institutions can be required to hold so much capital that a liquidity crisis will almost never arise. Clearly, managers would resist this kind of solution because of its potential for reducing their return on equity. Second, as exemplified by the provision of deposit insurance, supervisory authorities can modify the incentives for depositors and other short-term investors to withdraw funds from a troubled institution. Creditors will not rush to draw out funds if they can be reasonably confident that any prospective losses will not be increased by delays in withdrawing funds. (Bankruptcy law has a role to play here also, but that is outside the scope of the present discussion.) Third, as and when a liquidity crisis does arise it may be possible to obtain emergency liquidity from other financiers. The third solution is especially likely if creditors or investors come to believe their own interests will best be served by providing additional funds, but its benefits have to be balanced against the moral hazard of encouraging institutions to take their own management responsibilities too lightly.

A solvency crisis arises when an intermediary (or investors in the intermediary's shares) finds that the value of intermediary assets is less than that of its liabilities. Solvency crises frequently follow fads in lending or investing. Such fads arise in many contexts, including the 1970s and 1980s sovereign loan mania, and the 1980s real-estate lending in both North America and Japan.

Lending or investing fads are almost always fuelled by over-optimistic forecasts. One peculiar feature of these forecasts is that while they have almost invariably been proven wrong in the past, in each new fad the managers who stand to profit essentially argue "this time is different". As Merton Miller's comments imply, financiers do not seem to draw obvious lessons from history. Space does not permit us here to advance theories of why learning does not take place. Suffice it to say that solvency crises stem from over-optimistic forecasts of asset value, and that the forecasts are usually affected by short-term profitability considerations. Moreover, and as is well known, incentives to lend or invest recklessly can be fuelled by the prospect of generous bailout policies.

Information as a Partial Remedy

The best insurance against a liquidity crisis is to disseminate timely information about asset quality. If asset quality is decreasing, the possibility of its endangering the risk-taking institution should be publicized well before real problems start to arise. Emerging liquidity difficulties can usually be overcome relatively easily, so long as the underlying entity is demonstrably solvent. However, credible information regarding asset values is needed to demonstrate soundness. Regular, consistent and early public reporting of asset quality information seem to me a much more effective way of demonstrating soundness than does the practice of making emergency statements after the crisis has arisen. Some regulators argue that if they do not release information about impending difficulty, the looming problem can be dealt with quietly, without any need to disturb more than an informed few. But if the regulators were to release more information about institutions' condition on a regular basis, interested parties would not be taken by surprise to the same extent as they now can be. Rather, interested parties could judge for themselves what a series of reports meant. The impact of their judgements might mean that institutions would be less likely to get into trouble in the first place.

Solvency crises cannot be overcome as easily as liquidity crises, because the asset value needed to redeem liabilities simply does not exist. Indeed, to manage solvency crises effectively, it becomes necessary to manage the incentives that contribute to solvency problems. The main defence against overly optimistic managers is probably to bring contrarian thinking to bear on them. However, a policy that relies on critical thinking must by implication rely on the availability of credible asset valuations, which can then be used to support the thinking.

Regular, consistent and early reporting of asset quality information seem to me a much more effective way of demonstrating soundness than does our current practice. (I see current practice as making use of emergency

Edwin H. Neave

statements, and of finding emergency financing, when a solvency crisis appears to be imminent.) A second advantage to a proactive approach is that it could be used to help show problem institutions how they are likely to face difficulties if they persist in making weak loans. In addition, the proactive approach could help make it clear to riskier institutions that they would have little prospect of being bailed out if they persisted in taking undue risks. That is, information release should provide at least some incentive for institutions to work on reducing portfolio risk. Bailouts are generally criticized for contributing to moral hazard, but the proactive approach to developing information might actually reduce moral hazard. Even if the public opprobrium attendant on information release is insufficient to discourage risk-loving management, information release might still be of value. The release could make it easier for regulators to defend any "cease and desist" actions they might have to take in such circumstances. Third, proactive management of potentially emerging solvency crises offers dynamic advantages discussed, for example, in publications of the C. D. Howe Research Institute (Neave, 1997; Neave and Milne, 1998).

The idea of information release is, of course, not new. One suggestion along these lines is that banks may be able to supervise each other's portfolio quality. The mutual supervision suggestion has much in common with the idea that institutions might from time to time sell off representative parts of their asset portfolios to permit better outside evaluations of asset quality. A difficulty with the peer review suggestion is that in the past some institutions have been demonstrably deficient in their policing activities. For examples, recall again the problems of Long Term Capital Management and of Olympia and York. In both cases there were lending banks that did not ask for relevant financial information. In the Long Term Capital Management situation some banks apparently did ask, were refused and invested anyway. The prospect of large profits can blind even conservative bankers to the risks they might be taking. The contrarian thinking of regulators is needed to offset this over-optimism, and regulatory judgements need to be published in a timely fashion to be effective. That is why the release of authoritative and credible asset quality information is so important.

Small Institutions

The McKay task force recommends, and in my judgement correctly, that Canada attempt to encourage the growth of more small financial institutions.

If more small institutions were to spring up, they might enhance financial-system competitiveness while simultaneously offering new ways of doing business. On the other hand, experience suggests that small, closely held institutions encounter solvency difficulties relatively often. In the past, many regulators have preferred to negotiate with troubled institutions, without publicly revealing their concern. Their views appear to be that a policy of information revelation could affect negatively their ability to negotiate with troubled institutions. To me the benefits to be gained by timely and regular release of pertinent information regarding asset quality are greater than the benefits identified by the regulatory argument. On the other hand, a policy of publicizing changes in asset quality as they evolve should help investors to assess which institutions might be troubled, and possibly to correct a deteriorating situation before too much damage has been done.

References

Bhattacharya, U. (1998), "When an Event is not an Event: The Strange Case of Mexico", Working Paper (Bloomington, IN: Indiana University).

Merton, R.C. and Z. Bodie (1995), "A Conceptual Framework for Analyzing the Financial Environment", in Crane, D.B. *et al.* (eds.), *The Global Financial System: A Functional Perspective* (Cambridge, MA: Harvard Business School).

Neave, E.H. (1997), *Canadian Financial Regulation: A System in Transition* (Toronto: C.D. Howe Institute).

Neave, E.H. and F. Milne (1998), *Revising Canada's Financial Regulation: Analyses and Recommendations* (Toronto: C.D. Howe Institute).

Ross, S.A. (1989), "Institutional Markets, Financial Marketing, and Financial Innovation", *Journal of Finance* 44(3), 541-556.

Yu, W.W. (1997), "Essays on Capital Markets", unpublished PhD dissertation (Edmonton: University of Alberta).

Summary of Discussion

Louis Pauly commented that ministers and regulators shrink from shutting down a badly-managed financial institution because of the spectre of setting off the systemic banking problems of the 1930s. Ministers have always liked having the option of merging a weak financial institution with a strong institution. Is there any economic rationale for this preference? Also, is it better to have a couple of large institutions with national portfolios diversified within those institutions or is it better to have a national portfolio diversified across a number of institutions?

Ted Neave stressed the need to separate economics from politics. More information would improve both sets of incentives. The more the public knows about what is going on, the greater the pressure on politicians to act in the public interest. Public access to information on financial institutions is the key to effective regulation, not the number and size of institutions.

David Slater accepted the principle of better public information generating better outcomes. But he wondered whether information could be transmitted effectively to the public. One problem is that some financial reporters are as prone as some crime reporters to stir up trouble and excitement that may not be warranted by the facts.

Ted Neave did not minimize the difficulties. The regulators would have to be responsible for a credible information base. At the moment, the Canada Deposit Insurance Corporation (CDIC) and the Office of the Superintendent of Financial Institutions (OFSI) are reluctant to be involved in releasing more information because of their concern that it would then be more difficult to deal with financial institutions in a collegial manner. However, if credible information were out there, financial reporters could take different positions and report the assessments of financial analysts taking different positions. People could then make up their own minds about the credit-worthiness of financial institutions.

John Chant mentioned a recent proposal requiring all financial institutions to have part of their unsecured debt held by other financial institutions so that people in the business would effectively do the rating.

Peter Kirkham cautioned that borrowers would have privacy concerns about banks releasing information on their loan portfolio. Information would always be clouded by gray areas, in particular the difficulty of assessing loan portfolios. Even within a financial institution, there is debate over the extent to which their loans are potentially delinquent.

Ted Neave warned that the best can become the enemy of the good. His proposed scheme would work most of the time, but would not be perfect. A successful scheme would have to be devised jointly by industry and regulatory representatives, so that it could withstand those occasions when the regulatory scheme itself is blamed for the difficulties of financial institutions. He was arguing for greater disclosure before the Long Term Capital Management crisis. He was pleased to see press discussion about the need for bankers to exercise more due diligence and for investment funds to report more information.

Thomas Courchene recalled his prediction that we will still need banking services in the twenty-first century, but we may not need banks. Securities firms, not banks, are the type of financial institution likely to be at the centre of finance in the future. We are one regulatory step from moving everything away from banks. If securities firms were allowed to issue plastic cards that could be used in retail stores, many people might move all their deposits to securities firms. That being the case, we have to look at bank mergers differently. Canadians are worried about competition declining if five or six Canadian banks merge into two entities, but we might end up with 40 institutions competing to provide banking services before we know what is happening. What is important is to make sure that Canadian-based institutions can push into North America. But if the federal government concerns itself with branch closures, the bulk of our banking services will end up being provided by U.S.-based institutions.

Tom Phelps added that the cost of information technology is one of the problems lurking behind the scenes. The cost of new systems for items such as Internet transactions is often so large that the banks are forced to consider joint ventures. Mergers can perhaps be thought of as a natural extension of these trends.

Summary of Discussion

Ted Neave corroborated this impression. U.S. credit card specialists will still have lower unit costs than Canadian banks' credit card operations even if the mergers take place. Parts of the financial industry have impressive scale economies. Part of the argument for the mergers is that mergers are needed to capture scale economies. For some types of operations, our banks may have to cut deals with U.S. companies to capture these scale economies.

Peter Kirkham picked up on Chant's references in his paper to banks' vertical and horizontal integration. Banks organize themselves around customer segments — large corporations, medium-size companies, small businesses, individuals and governments. Each customer segment receives five service components: medium of exchange, store of value, unit of account, risk management and financing. Banks' overriding advantage is in the unit of account activity. People choose a financial institution to reduce their own accounting activity. The mergers are being driven by pressures that the banks are facing in the financing component of their large corporate customer segment. Corporations are getting larger and their financing needs are greater. As Canadian corporations move operations to the United States and list on the New York Stock Exchange, they have more liquidity and a lower cost of capital. Are we going to allow Canadian corporations to move their financing south or are we going to try to retain this business with Canadian institutions?

Ted Neave identified several issues with respect to bank mergers. First, how do you introduce the reality of the international economy to backbench Members of Parliament (MPs) who will play a role in the government's decision. Branches will close whether mergers proceed or not. Banks are fighting for business in international markets where size counts. A large percentage of financial service income now comes from abroad. How do we continue to serve the public on main street and convince the public that you can still receive banking services after the disappearance of branches? International competition facing banks is real and will become more pressing. But the merger debate is often framed as: "Why can't the 1950s continue forever?"

An unidentified participant defended MPs. They do not ignore the global economy. But they view the banks' policy argument in favour of the merger as simplistic. The banks' argument can be boiled down to: "We need to compete in the world market and we need to be big to do that." MPs hear from their constituents about problems with the current level of service from banks. The conundrum for MPs is that the banks are perceived to be doing a lousy job serving domestic customers and they do not see a connection between world competitiveness and domestic service gains. The banks have not articulated a convincing argument for the mergers.

Ted Neave agreed that the banks have not presented a convincing case. They should adopt a policy of openness, identify the competition and the cost pressures that they are facing and be frank about branch closings. Canadians should hear the business case for the mergers. The editorial in *The Globe and Mail* of November 6 posed debate over the bank mergers in stark terms. Perhaps the banks will now feel compelled to respond.

Peter Kirkham reiterated that large business financing activity will move outside Canada in the absence of the mergers. If the banks lose large business activity, they will lose the ability to spread costs and compete in other business activities. The federal government has already selected Citigroup to handle its credit card business. Banks will lose profitability, which will ultimately affect their ability to meet the minimum capitalization ratios set by the Bank of International Settlements. This could lead to a contraction of the Canadian banking system if the banks have trouble finding new capital investment. Canadian banks currently earn 60 to 70 basis points per dollar of assets and U.S. banks typically earn 100 to 160 basis points. Canadians would not invest in Canadian banks without the rule restricting foreign holdings to 20% of pension and Registered Retirement Savings Plan investments.

Richard Harris reported the striking home bias in investment portfolios in all countries, despite evidence of globalization in other aspects of capital markets. Canadians display one of the biggest home biases, because the 20% rule effectively captures our savings. The interests of savers have been forgotten. Removing the 20% limit and allowing portfolio diversification would generate one of the single largest welfare gains from any policy change that we can think of. Nevertheless, he doubted that the federal government would follow this advice.

David Baar asked for comments on whether Canada should adopt U.S.-style rules requiring community investments by the banks. There have been some suggestions that the banks would accept such rules in return for approval of the mergers

John Chant noted that the MacKay task force recommended that the banks provide more information on their community investment activities. However, the U.S. rules reflect particular circumstances in the United States, which has a more extensive regulatory and reporting framework. The first step in Canada would be to generate the reporting of the information and we can then think about moving on to setting rules.

Ted Neave saw room in Canada for community reinvestment banks like the Grameen Development Bank in Bangladesh. However, he was not sure that our chartered banks would be the best institutions to run such operations. Credit unions might be more suited to this task, but we have not seen them move into this field.

Room to Manoeuvre:
Rapporteur's Remarks

Jack M. Mintz

This conference has provided a rather full agenda for considering the implications of globalization on policy convergence. The ideas are based on a set of wide-ranging and well-thought-out papers, written by eminent economists, political scientists, lawyers and other specialists. The task of a rapporteur for this conference is no easy one. Since I have a limited perspective, it is likely that I will not fully synthesize the many interesting points brought out in the papers. But, I will try to provide an overall perspective about globalization and policy convergence with these remarks.

To begin, it would be useful to consider the title for this conference as a way of bringing together the many insights expressed. The topic — Room to Manoeuvre: Globalization and Policy Convergence — is in itself thought provoking. What do we mean by globalization and why is it important today? What is policy convergence and should we even care about it? Is room available for autonomous decision making by sovereign governments? How should governments respond to globalization? Below, I will order my remarks in response to each of these questions.

What is Globalization?

Globalization is a well-used term but it often implies different things to different people. Globalization may be defined in economic terms — as Robert Wolfe did — or in cultural terms — as Louis Pauly did. This will be further elaborated on below.

Economic Globalization

Wolfe's economic definition of globalization was related to trade. To paraphrase his definition, trade arises from the condition that the domestic price of a product is more than the import price plus transactions costs of importing the good. If the converse holds, then imported products cannot compete with domestic products. Local products, however, could be exported to foreign countries, but the transactions costs may be sufficiently large to prevent their export to foreign markets. Thus, with high transactions costs, no trade may arise. The imported product does not come into the country nor can the product be exported to international markets. However, if transactions costs — those associated with communication and transportation — decline due to technological change, trade can increase and economies can become more integrated. Thus, the process of globalization arises from technological change that facilitates much lower transactions costs and results in increased trade.

This useful conceptualization of globalization is related to not just tangible goods like agriculture and manufactured products but also intangible products such as financial services and research and development. Trade can also be related to the mobility of factors of production such as capital and labour services across national boundaries. The sense that we have regarding the process of globalization is that the decline in transactions costs due to technological change have increased world trade and made countries more interdependent.

However, as pointed out by William Watson, the concept of trade in goods and capital is not new. There have been periods of substantial trade in products and capital (foreign direct investment) in the late 1800s and early 1900s, almost as much in relation to gross domestic product (GDP) as today. Canada has always been an open economy — as suggested by Innis' staple theory of growth through resource exports — and one could argue that globalization is therefore not a new reality.

Although it is useful to remember historical trends in trade and capital flows, I would suggest that a more important change had been with respect to the structure of trade, rather than just the quantity of trade. As pointed out in the report of the Technical Committee on Business Taxation (1998), services — often viewed as non-tradeable commodities — have become much more subject to international competition. Even industries like business services, utilities, communications and transportation now have a significant component of their output traded directly or indirectly with other countries.

Further, there has been a tremendous increase in cross-border financial transactions. As pointed out by the Organization for Economic Cooperation and Development (OECD), such transactions have risen from less than 5% of GDP in 1980 to over 150% in the 1990s. In just a span of 15 years there has been more than a thirty-fold increase in cross-border financial transactions. As financial services comprise almost 20% of GDP today, this sharp increase in cross-border financial transactions has significant impacts on the economy.

Globalization has also resulted in other important changes to the Canadian economy. Canada has moved from the historical position of importing capital to a new position as a capital exporter whereby capital outflows are more than capital inflows. The stock of assets held by Canadian businesses in foreign countries is now close to the stock of assets held by foreign businesses in Canada. Further, skilled labour is becoming increasingly mobile — outflows of Canadian professionals have almost doubled since the inception of the Canada-U.S. Free Trade Agreement in 1989.

It would seem to me that it is critical to understand how globalization affects the structure of trade in products and factors rather than just the quantity of trade. The new trends — international competition for service sectors, growth of outbound investment and greater trade in skilled labour — are the critical issues to be considered by Canadian governments as they develop their policies in face of globalization. It is not just a matter of increased trade but a change in the structure of trade that is becoming important.

One further point is worth stating about globalization that I felt was not sufficiently discussed in the papers. Much of the economic focus on globalization was related to trade, as if countries operated independently of each other except for selling and buying commodities in international markets. However, another by-product of globalization has been the increased amount of intra-firm trade, which involves no transactions through markets, but cross-border trade within the multinational enterprise. I raise this issue since there is a vast difference, when considering government policy, between a world with countries that have independent production processes and another world whereby countries are linked through multinational entities with worldwide production processes. For example, when a government provides industrial support for multinationals, this will affect not only the multinational's operations within the country but throughout the world. Policies become even more interdependent amongst countries since incentives in one country might improve the overall competitiveness of the multinational to the benefit of operations in other countries.

A good example of the implications of multinational intra-firm trade is related to the growth of financial centres for multinational companies in European countries like Belgium, Luxembourg, Netherlands and Ireland. As a result of favourable tax regimes, headquarter financing operations have been located in certain countries to provide financial services to subsidiaries located in other parts of the world. Recently, the European countries have engaged in substantial tax competition to lure these financial centres of multinationals — France, Denmark and Spain recently introduced provisions to attract such companies in reaction to Belgian and Irish incentives. Along with the headquarters might come increased research and development expenditure and other complementary activities. For governments, the role of foreign direct investment by multinationals becomes important for the development of the economy since multinationals facilitate the transfer of technology among countries.

Cultural Globalization

As an economist, this is dangerous territory for me to tread, but I shall do so nonetheless. It is important that one should recognize that globalization can be defined in cultural rather than economic terms. William Watson, in his address, referred to the idea of "one global culture" whereby different cultural identities would mesh together into a single one — a notion he dismissed. I think his argument is right. I have been persuaded by Samuel Huntington's book (1997) on the "clash of civilizations" that cultures are increasingly being defined globally but are not integrating into one common culture. Huntington argues that civilizations — for example, African, Chinese, Indian, Islamic, Japanese, Latin American and Western — are being globalized in the sense that a cultural group in one country (e.g., Saudi Arabia) strongly identifies with a similar cultural group in another (e.g.,

Bosnia). Just as technological change in communication and transportation has encouraged greater economic integration, so has technology — including the mass media — encouraged greater cultural integration at the global level. However, Huntington did not argue that cultures at the international level would converge. Instead, each culture or civilization would maintain its own identity and compete at the international level. This process is really no different than what has occurred in the past for specific countries with heterogeneous peoples, like Russia, Canada and the United States, but the current political institutions have not yet developed to cope with these trends.

Cultural globalization thus raises an interesting contrast to economic globalization. Economic forces may force business and labour institutions to define themselves at the international or, as we are now witnessing in Europe, regional level. Cultural forces result in a closer identification of populations to specific religions or nationalities. The nation state does not necessarily serve as a good vehicle for such cultural identification if it does not encompass a specific and unique culture. Global cultures may create new forms of political alliances amongst individuals that are not consistent with the current political institutions. Thus, it is not surprising that one response is for a decentralization of political power to local, more homogeneous-populated governments existing along-side international or regional economic entities.

The multinational enterprise is an example of an economic entity reflecting economic globalization. But, does the multinational also reflect culture globalization? Louis Pauly explores the interesting concept that multinational enterprises may keep their national identities as determined by their home base. Thus, a U.S. multinational in Canada would behave differently than one based in another country like the United Kingdom or Sweden. For example, national identity may determine where research and development or charitable support takes place.

Although I think that Pauly's argument has some legitimacy, there are constraints to firms that pursue activities in the interest of their national identity. Competition forces businesses to choose what would be profitable rather than satisfy some other objective. If, for example, a multinational decides to purchase high-cost domestic goods and services rather than inputs that are more competitively priced abroad, it may lose its international market share to local and foreign competitors. Of course, this is the critical political issue involved with globalization — multinationals may not necessarily do what is best for a home country as opposed to satisfying their owners with more income.

Moreover, one needs to make room in theories as to why corporations might change national identities. Ericsson in Sweden is moving its headquarters to London. Is Ericsson Swedish or British? Moore Corporation, headquartered in Canada, is about 80% owned by U.S. residents. Is Moore Canadian or American?

Even if we identify that a multinational has control and ownership from a particular country, what is the national identity of the country itself? At the conference, Pierre-Paul Proulx made the interesting comment that some national identities are stronger than others, when defining a specific culture. If that is the case, is Quebec Inc. linked more to its home base — Quebec — compared to Canada Inc. being linked to Canada?

I think the paradigm, that a multinational is identified with a specific nationality, will be eventually replaced by a new one that recognizes that many multinationals are not easily identified with a single country even in terms of ownership and control. Certainly, we are beginning to see the growth of mega-mergers at the international level such as between German and American firms. What is the national identity of the multinational? One of the popular courses in business schools today is related to the theory of organizations faced with cross-cultural investments since employees of different cultures may have to work together within the same firm.

Policy Convergence

Much of the debate in the past two days centred on the desirability of policy convergence in face of globalization rather than what we mean by the term "globalization". Is policy convergence a result of globalization? Is convergence a good or bad thing for a country?

The conference discussed a number of important policies affected by globalization: monetary (Courchene), fiscal/tax (Olewiler), financial (Chant), culture (Waverman) and regulation (Wolfe). One could add on a long list of other policy issues related to globalization and convergence such as social and environmental policies. Prior to discussing some of the issues raised, it would be useful to first outline what we mean by "policy" and "convergence".

What Policies?

Policy refers to specific decisions by governments reflecting the desires of their electorates. Clearly, one should therefore define policy at the "national" level — Canada — and the provincial/local levels. As Robin Boadway commented in his remarks, it is important to keep in mind that globalization can have quite different impacts for provincial/local governments compared to the national government. In fact, can we say that provincial government policies tend to converge among themselves in a federal state compared to policies at the international level. I am aware of no empirical work to suggest that there is more policy convergence between, for example, Michigan and California compared to Alberta and Texas.

For a federal state like Canada, it is important to keep in mind that policy convergence might mean quite different things to federal and provincial/local governments. In particular, there are two factors to keep in mind with respect to these differences.

First, each level of government has had its own expenditure and taxing powers and the forces of globalization can have different kinds of impacts on each type of power. For example, globalization affects the provincial education powers in a limited way through competition with the international market for academics and students. However, financial regulation at the federal (banking) and provincial level (security markets and credit unions) is substantially directly affected by globalization. Similarly, the taxation of capital income — a primarily federal source of revenue — is clearly more affected by globalization than property taxes — a local government source of revenue — in part because property taxes tend to be shifted onto land values and are less important to international competition for resources.

Second, there is no reason to expect, especially in a geographically dispersed country like Canada, that globalization will have similar impacts on each region, as discussed by both Thomas Courchene and Richard Harris in their review of the case for a common currency with the United States. There are economic similarities between U.S. regions adjacent to Canadian regions (e.g., Northwest United States and Western Canada or Ontario and mid-east and eastern U.S. states) but not between Canada and the United States as a whole. International competition in the forest industry, for example, might be important to the west coast of North America, but less so for other regions. Thus, there is no reason to expect that the electorate and the government in each region of Canada would necessarily respond in the same way to globalization. This makes it much more difficult for the federal government to develop policies in reaction to globalization since some of the issues will be regionally based.

Thus, when we discuss convergence of policies, do we mean national or provincial policies? Further, does one expect more or less policy convergence by federal or provincial governments with policies of foreign governments? I have no real answers to these questions since it is not obvious to me, given the current allocation of expenditure and taxing powers in Canada, that provincial policy convergence is any more likely than federal convergence with policies of other countries.

Meaning and Measure of Convergence

Even if we sort out what policies we expect to converge, it would be useful to understand what we mean by convergence. Here, we have some quite important differences in interpretation among the papers.

- Some view convergence to mean that the choice made by a sovereign government results in "uniform" policies that are virtually identical.
- Another measure of convergence is that policies become harmonized in that they are similar but not identical.
- A third notion of convergence is that the policies are coordinated to avoid situations of harm that one government might cause on another government or its electorate (this was termed by Wolfe as the "rhythm" method).

It matters a great deal as to how we define convergence if we are to determine whether governments are being constrained by globalization. For example, consider the case of taxation. If we were to measure policies in terms of uniformity, then we would want to determine whether tax rates and bases are identical. On the other hand, harmonization might mean that tax structures are similar (such as tax/GDP ratios for specific taxes) but only for those policies for which harmonization is important for the free flow of goods, services, labour and capital across national boundaries. Coordination would be measured according to whether governments choose policies that minimize spillovers (rates of tax need not be the same or even similar as long as the structure of the tax system avoids conflict).

Outside the Olewiler paper on taxation, few tried to measure convergence explicitly. But even in the one case, it is unclear that the measures, movements in tax/GDP ratios, were appropriate to determine convergence. Tax/GDP ratios are simply the amount of tax paid divided by GDP — they fail to measure the degree to which taxes might affect production internationally. Instead, production decisions and factor movements are affected by taxation at the margin. Therefore, a better measure of convergence would be to look at those aspects of the tax system that might cause something to move from one country to another. For example, effective marginal tax rates — the amount of tax paid by the use of the last unit in production — should incorporate all relevant taxes on capital (corporate, sales taxes on capital inputs, etc.) and labour (personal income, payroll and consumption taxes) that would affect mobility. Even with this calculation, one would still want to consider how benefits from public sector activities that vary across countries might affect mobility. Further, the sensitivity of some tax bases is related to some specific aspect of the tax system. For example, if one were interested in knowing how corporate income might shift between countries, the effective statutory tax rate on such income is most relevant.

Does Convergence Matter?

Even if one was to agree on what we mean by convergence and can measure it, should we even care about it? Harry Arthurs in his TINA paper stresses the problem faced by a small country like Canada that must converge with its largest trading partner, the United States, if such convergence were desirable. Arthurs identifies the most salient and difficult issue faced by Canada with its unique position in world markets and regionally oriented political structure. Convergence for Canada could mean moving to the U.S. standard not to some standard reflecting Canadian and U.S. preferences. There may be an economic gain to such convergence but there may equally be resistance to convergence if it threatens Canadian culture, assuming such culture can be defined easily for our federal state.

A clear example of such tensions with convergence arises with the debate over a common currency or fixed exchange rate with the United States, as discussed by Courchene and Harris in their session. There are strong economic arguments for a common currency or fixed exchange rate. Canadian and U.S. bilateral trade and factor movements add up to over one trillion U.S. dollars per year. To avoid uncertainties with the fluctuation of currency values that increase the transaction costs of such trade, a fixed exchange rate would help avoid these costs. There are also important economic arguments against a common currency or fixed exchange rate — a resource-based economy like Canada can better absorb specific shocks with flexible exchange rates, thereby lessening economic fluctuations related to inflation or unemployment. Indeed, historically, Canada has fixed its exchange rate, but the policy was abandoned when it became too difficult to maintain the same value of the currency without major devaluation (remember the "Diefenbuck"?). Nonetheless, Courchene and Harris make the persuasive point that perhaps the economic benefits of a common currency are now dominating the economic costs, given increased economic integration with the United States in the past two decades. At present, the economic case for a common currency or fixed exchange rate with the United States is therefore strengthening, not weakening.

However, even if there is an economic case for a common currency or fixed exchange rate, is there a political case? Unlike the European Union's recent monetary integration and development of its new currency, the Euro, a common currency with the United States would likely involve the adoption of the U.S. dollar or Canada fixing its exchange rate with the United States. Canada would therefore move to the U.S. standard, not Canada and the United States to some common standard. Perhaps, moving closer to the United States with respect to monetary policy would be economically sensible but it does raise issues of political sovereignty and the citizenry's identification with the Canadian federal government.

The issue of monetary policy convergence illustrates the common debate that will be continuously encountered by Canadians as we enter the twenty-first century. Whether it is tax, financial, regulatory or trade policies, the convergence issue will first have to be debated in terms of economic benefits and costs and then in terms of other political criteria. In some cases, convergence will not matter in the sense that there is no economic case for it. In other cases, convergence will be economically desirable but not necessarily politically desirable. Regardless, however, we should expect more pressure over time to conform our policies to those of the United States.

Manoeuvrability

Related to the question of the desirability of convergence is the issue as to whether countries are able to choose independent policies. In other words, do governments have room to manoeuvre? The implication of this question is important. Would governments prefer a different course of action if globalization could be ignored?

One view expressed at the conference by both William Watson and Nancy Olewiler was that governments certainly have room to manoeuvre and there is little evidence to demonstrate the contrary. For example, governments have chosen quite different tax structures and there is little evidence that such structures are converging.

An opposing view is that globalization reduces the scope for national independent decision making. The strongest case provided in support of this argument was made by Harry Arthurs. He suggested that the international institutionalization of economic relationships such as through North American Free Trade Agreement (NAFTA) and the World Trade Organization has put national policies into a straight jacket. Such international agreements often involve constraints imposed on governments that were not necessarily understood at the time that the agreement was concluded. In part, this reflects the reality that it is virtually impossible to anticipate all the impacts of an agreement given the uncertainties faced by the negotiating parties. Once the agreement is made, countries limit their scope to manoeuvre.

A more moderate position as to whether there is room for manoeuvrability is taken by most of the papers. One particular view given is that there may be some constraints on the use of instruments but the objectives of governments need not change. As Leonard Waverman, John Chant and Edwin Neave argued in their remarks, governments might have to adjust their instruments to achieve desired ends, but the objectives need not change. For example, as Waverman points out, the convergence of technologies makes it more difficult for governments to regulate Canadian broadcasting requirements since individuals can access certain technologies without restrictions. However, if the government chooses to subsidize Canadian content, then cultural objectives can be pursued, either more or less effectively.

Even if international agreements impose some constraints on a government's manoeuvrability in certain dimensions, it could improve it with respect to others. For example, economists have pointed out that it is increasingly more difficult to tax capital income since individuals and businesses may be able to shift their income to low-tax jurisdictions and avoid the Canadian tax. If this is the fact that one must face, there are two possible responses. The first is for a government to give up entirely its taxation of capital income in favour of other forms of taxes (consumption and payroll). This would be a situation in which governments would have less room to manoeuvre. The second course of action is for governments to enter into an international agreement to enforce the taxation of capital income. Although this might limit countries in developing their capital income tax as they see fit, such cooperative action can provide more flexibility to choose a desired tax structure that includes the taxation of capital income.

Policy Responses

Overall, the general impression given by the papers is that globalization does impose some limits on the room for governments to manoeuvre although there is little evidence given to suggest that policy convergence is a necessary outcome of globalization. It seems that there was a fair amount of agreement that globalization has been changing the Canadian economy. This includes the growth of service sectors that have become more open to international competition, closer economic integration with the United States, increased capital exports from Canada but diminished reliance on foreign investment in Canada.

In the face of globalization, how should Canadian federal and provincial governments respond? There seems to be several strategies suggested at the conference although no paper tried to bring them together. In the last part of my remarks, I would like to suggest a number of strategies, some much better than others (for further elaboration, see Mintz, 1998).

• *Impede economic integration.* One set of policies that could be followed by governments in the face of globalization is to "close" the economy by reducing the mobility of goods, services and factors into and out of the country. Policies in pursuit of a closed economy include tariffs, currency controls, a Tobin tax on foreign currency transactions and foreign investment controls. These policies have been suggested by a number of special interest groups, but they are unlikely to succeed in the long run. There are significant gains from the process of globalization since countries can specialize in the production of goods and services in which they have a comparative advantage, as well as enjoy the benefits from the transfer of technology through trade and capital flows. Trying to close the economy may impede economic growth and productivity in the long run since the country isolates itself from the benefits of international trade and innovation.

- *Make governments smaller.* At times, many liberal and left-wing analysts mistrust globalization as a process since they believe that the ultimate consequence is to have a smaller government, much to the satisfaction of the neo-conservative agenda. There are two particular concerns:

    (i) The mobility of capital and skilled labour may raise the cost of taxation sufficiently high such that governments will be forced to reduce their size, and

    (ii) Competition amongst government will cause a "race to the bottom" whereby taxes and regulations (e.g., environmental) will be ineffective.

It should not be concluded, however, that globalization necessarily results in small governments. As pointed out in the literature, globalization may open up opportunities for governments to tax certain goods and services if the tax is primarily borne by non-residents (e.g., Prince Edward Island property tax on foreign-owned property). Instead of increasing the cost of raising taxes, globalization can result in a lower cost of taxation through tax exportation. As William Watson and Nancy Olewiler discussed, there is little evidence that globalization is causing tax/GDP ratios to decline. Indeed, the opposite is true — tax/GDP ratios for OECD countries have grown in the past two decades.

- *Government intervention to promote national interests.* Rather than stop globalization or react passively, governments could pursue policies that satisfy national aims and objectives, but are compatible with the growing economic integration in the world economy. Such policies, including industrial and cultural policies, could be achievable even if there are constraints imposed by trade and investment agreements. For example, few agreements have limited all the powers of governments over taxation and regulations that may be used to promote particular objectives. This response simply means that globalization imposes certain constraints on instruments but governments can manoeuvre around these constraints with new types of policies. Whether these policies are wise in the first place is a separate issue for discussion.

- *Coordination with other governments.* Another response to globalization is for governments to coordinate their policies in the interest of achieving political objectives that are common to them. For example, if governments wish to protect their revenue base or encourage better environmental practices, they can enter into multilateral or bilateral agreements with other governments interested in the same objectives. Such coordination at the international level can create greater opportunities for policy initiatives than would otherwise be available. Globalization may be feared as a process that limits the possibility of such multilateral actions but I take the opposite view that globalization will often force governments to undertake actions that they would otherwise not do. For example, the growth of intra-firm cross-border trade is making it more difficult for governments to operate independent corporate income taxes since it is more difficult to determine where income is earned according to the arm's length principle. Rather than abandon the corporate tax field, governments will prefer to continue to tax businesses by "globalizing" the corporate tax, which has been happening in recent years through transfer pricing agreements and bilateral treaties.

- *Creating the Canadian advantage.* Instead of being defensive and viewing globalization as a process that inhibits opportunities for governments to manoeuvre, one can embrace globalization as creating new opportunities for Canadians that should be promoted by governments. Gains from international trade, the transfer of technology, global rationalization of businesses and increased worldwide competition can provide significant economic gains without necessarily reducing the power of governments which is feared by so many. Some countries have strategically chosen a set of policies that could take advantage of new opportunities for economic growth. For example, Ireland, which now has a per capita income above the United Kingdom, has followed two types of policies to encourage economic growth. Some policies have been to improve the education system to create a larger pool of skilled workers for industry. However, these policies were destined to fail if skilled workers left for Britain because of insufficient job opportunities in Ireland. Thus, a critical set of policies was designed to encourage the location of businesses in Ireland as a stepping stone to the rest of the European Union — of which Ireland was a member. These policies included major business tax and regulatory reform that attracted many multinationals to Ireland. Some policies, such as tax holidays for manufacturing, were challenged by other European countries to be unfair trading practices. However, these policies are now being changed in favour of new ones that will not be challenged under European Union directives. The point is that Canada, a small country under the North

American Free Trade Agreement, can embrace globalization by creating the "Canadian economic advantage" in the North American market, just like Ireland in the European market.

Concluding Remarks

This conference provides a stimulating set of papers on a topic that will be of ongoing interest to researchers in the coming years. The paper-givers and discussants, as well as the conference organizer, Thomas Courchene, deserve much credit for outlining a number of fascinating issues for analysts and policymakers to consider as they continue to come to grips with the fast changing practices of businesses at the international level. In these remarks, I hope that I have conveyed the impression that globalization is not something to stop, fear or ignore. Instead, Canadians can harness the forces of globalization to their advantage by choosing policies of advantage to them. Perhaps we have less room to manoeuvre in terms of maintaining our old ways and ideas — but we can achieve a great deal as a federation by developing new, innovative policies which are consistent with the dramatic changes that are now occurring in the Canadian economy.

References

Huntington, S.P. (1997), *The Clash of Civilizations: Remaking of World Order* (New York: Touchstone Books).

Mintz, J. (1998), "Is National Tax Policy Viable in the Face of Globalization?", Working Paper (Toronto: Institute of International Business, University of Toronto).

Technical Committee on Business Taxation (TCBT) (1998), *Report* (Ottawa: Department of Finance).

Contributors

Authors

H.W. Arthurs	Osgoode Hall Law School, York University
Louis W. Pauly	Centre for International Studies, University of Toronto
Leonard Waverman	Centre for International Studies, University of Toronto and London Business School
Robert Wolfe	School of Policy Studies, Queen's University
William Watson	Department of Economics, McGill University and IRPP
Thomas J. Courchene	John Deutsch Institute, Queen's University
Nancy Olewiler	Department of Economics, Simon Fraser University
John F. Chant	Department of Economics, Simon Fraser University
Jack M. Mintz	J. L. Rotman School of Management, University of Toronto

Commentators

Daniel Schwanen	C.D. Howe Institute, Toronto
Maureen Appel Molot	The Norman Paterson School of International Affairs, Carleton University
Dale Orr	WEFA Canada Inc., Ottawa
Klaus Stegemann	Department of Economics, Queen's University
Richard G. Harris	Department of Economics, Simon Fraser University and Canadian Institute for Advanced Research
Robin Boadway	Department of Economics, Queen's University
Edwin H. Neave	School of Business, Queen's University

The Bell Canada Papers on Economic and Public Policy, Volume 1
Productivity, Growth and Canada's International Competitiveness

Contents

The Bell Canada Papers on Economic and Public Policy, Volume 2
Stabilization, Growth and Distribution: Linkages in the Knowledge Era

Contents

The Bell Canada Papers on Economic and Public Policy, Volume 3
Technology, Information and Public Policy

Contents

The Bell Canada Papers on Economic and Public Policy,
Volume 4
Policy Frameworks for a Knowledge Economy

Contents

The Bell Canada Papers on Economic and Public Policy,
Volume 5
**The Nation State in a Global/Information Era:
Policy Challenges**

Contents

Queen's Policy Studies
Recent Publications

The Queen's Policy Studies Series is dedicated to the exploration of major policy issues that confront governments in Canada and other western nations. McGill-Queen's University Press is the exclusive world representative and distributor of books in the series.

School of Policy Studies

The Communications Revolution at Work: The Social, Economic and Political Impacts of Technological Change, Robert Boyce (ed.), 1999 Paper ISBN 0-88911-805-1 Cloth 0-88911-807-8

Diplomatic Missions: The Ambassador in Canadian Foreign Policy, Robert Wolfe (ed.), 1998
Paper ISBN 0-88911-801-9 Cloth ISBN 0-88911-803-5

Issues in Defence Management, Douglas L. Bland (ed.), 1998
Paper ISBN 0-88911-809-4 Cloth ISBN 0-88911-811-6

Canada's National Defence, vol. 2, *Defence Organization*, Douglas L. Bland (ed.), 1998
Paper ISBN 0-88911-797-7 Cloth ISBN 0-88911-799-3

Canada's National Defence, vol. 1, *Defence Policy*, Douglas L. Bland (ed.), 1997
Paper ISBN 0-88911-792-6 Cloth ISBN 0-88911-790-X

Lone-Parent Incomes and Social-Policy Outcomes: Canada in International Perspective, Terrance Hunsley, 1997 Paper ISBN 0-88911-751-9 Cloth ISBN 0-88911-757-8

Institute of Intergovernmental Relations

Canada: The State of the Federation 1997, vol. 12, *Non-Constitutional Renewal*, Harvey Lazar (ed.), 1998 Paper ISBN 0-88911-765-9 Cloth ISBN 0-88911-767-5

Canadian Constitutional Dilemmas Revisited, Denis Magnusson (ed.), 1997
Paper ISBN 0-88911-593-1 Cloth ISBN 0-88911-595-8

Canada: The State of the Federation 1996, Patrick C. Fafard and Douglas M. Brown (eds.), 1997
Paper ISBN 0-88911-587-7 Cloth ISBN 0-88911-597-4

Comparing Federal Systems in the 1990s, Ronald Watts, 1997
Paper ISBN 0-88911-589-3 Cloth ISBN 0-88911-763-2

John Deutsch Institute for the Study of Economic Policy

Women and Work, Richard P. Chaykowski and Lisa M. Powell (eds.), 1999
Paper ISBN 0-88911-808-6 Cloth ISBN 0-88911-806-X

Equalization: Its Contribution to Canada's Economic and Fiscal Progress, Robin W. Boadway and Paul A.R. Hobson (eds.), Policy Forum Series no. 36, 1998
Paper ISBN 0-88911-780-2 Cloth ISBN 0-88911-804-3

Fiscal Targets and Economic Growth, Thomas J. Courchene and Thomas A. Wilson (eds.), Roundtable Series no. 12, 1998 Paper ISBN 0-88911-778-0 Cloth ISBN 0-88911-776-4

The 1997 Federal Budget: Retrospect and Prospect, Thomas J. Courchene and Thomas A. Wilson (eds.), Policy Forum Series no. 35, 1997 Paper ISBN 0-88911-774-8 Cloth ISBN 0-88911-772-1

The Nation State in a Global/Information Era: Policy Challenges, Thomas J. Courchene (ed.), Bell Canada Papers no. 5, 1997 Paper ISBN 0-88911-770-5 Cloth ISBN 0-88911-766-7

Available from:
McGill-Queen's University Press
Tel: 1-800-387-0141 (ON and QC excluding Northwestern ON)
        1-800-387-0172 (all other provinces and Northwestern ON)
E-mail: customer.service@ccmailgw.genpub.com